AA

Big Easy Read BRITAIN

2023

C000162604

Scale 1:160,000
or 2.52 miles to 1 inch

18th edition June 2022 © AA Media Limited 2022
Original edition printed 1991.

All cartography in this atlas edited, designed and produced by the Mapping Services Department of AA Media Limited (A05812).

This atlas contains Ordnance Survey data © Crown copyright and database right 2022. Contains public sector information licensed under the Open Government Licence v3.0. Distances and journey times contains data available from openstreetmap.org © under the Open Database License found at opendatacommons.org

Published by AA Media Limited, whose registered office is Grove House, Lutyens Close, Basingstoke, Hampshire RG24 8AG, UK. Registered number 06112600

ISBN: 978 0 7495 8293 7 (spiral bound)
ISBN: 978 0 7495 8292 0 (paperback)

A CIP catalogue record for this book is available from The British Library.

Acknowledgements: AA Media Limited would like to thank the following for information used in the creation of this atlas:
Cadw, English Heritage, Forestry Commission, Historic Scotland, National Trust and National Trust for Scotland, RSPB, The Wildlife Trust, Scottish Natural Heritage, Natural England, The Countryside Council for Wales. Award winning beaches from 'Blue Flag' and 'Keep Scotland Beautiful' (summer 2021 data): for latest information visit www.blueflag.org and www.keepscotlandbeautiful.org. Road signs are © Crown Copyright 2022. Reproduced under the terms of the Open Government Licence.
Printed by Elcograf S.p.A, Italy

Contents

Map pages	**inside front cover**
Route planning	**II–XII**
Route planner	II–V
Caravan and camping sites in Britain	VI–VII
Traffic signs and road markings	VIII–IX
Ferries and port plans	X–XII
Motorways	**XIII–XVI**
Restricted junctions	XIII
M25 London Orbital motorway	XIV
M6 Toll motorway	XV
Smart motorways	XVI
Atlas symbols	**1**
Road maps 1:160,000 scale	**2–152**
Channel Islands 1:113,000 scale	12–13
Isle of Man 1:200,000 scale	102
Orkney and Shetland Islands 1:605,000 scale	147
Western Isles 1:528,000 scale	152

Ferry ports

Aberdeen Harbour..........XII	Harwich International	Liverpool Docks..............XII	Port of Tyne....................XII
Calais X	Port XII	Newhaven Harbour XI	Portsmouth Harbour........X
Channel Tunnel...............XI	Heysham Harbour XII	Pembroke Dock XII	Southampton, Port of......X
Dover, Port of XI	Holyhead Harbour XII	Plymouth, Port of X	
Fishguard Harbour.........XII	Hull, Port of XII	Poole, Port of X	

Town plans

Aberdeen....................133	Durham 154	London........................156	St Andrews..................125
Aberystwyth 48	Edinburgh...................154	Manchester 156	Salisbury.....................157
Bath 153	Exeter............................9	Middlesbrough 93	Scarborough 93
Birmingham................153	Glasgow 155	Milton Keynes..............156	Sheffield 157
Blackpool 82	Great Yarmouth 71	Newcastle upon	Shrewsbury 157
Bradford 153	Harrogate 155	Tyne.......................101	Southampton 158
Bristol 153	Inverness....................155	Newquay........................3	Southend-on-Sea.........35
Cambridge 153	Ipswich.........................47	Norwich.......................156	Stratford-upon-Avon....158
Canterbury 153	Kingston upon Hull.....155	Nottingham 156	Sunderland..................101
Cardiff........................154	Leeds 155	Oxford 157	Swansea 26
Chester 154	Leicester.....................155	Peterborough 157	Swindon 158
Coventry 154	Lincoln........................156	Plymouth 4	Wolverhampton 158
Derby 154	Liverpool 74	Portsmouth 157	Worcester...................158
Dundee 125	Llandudno 73	Ramsgate.....................35	York............................158

Tourist sites with satnav friendly postcodes	**159**
London district map	**160–161**
Index to place names	**162–192**
County, administrative area map	162
Place name index	162–192
Distances and journey times	**inside back cover**

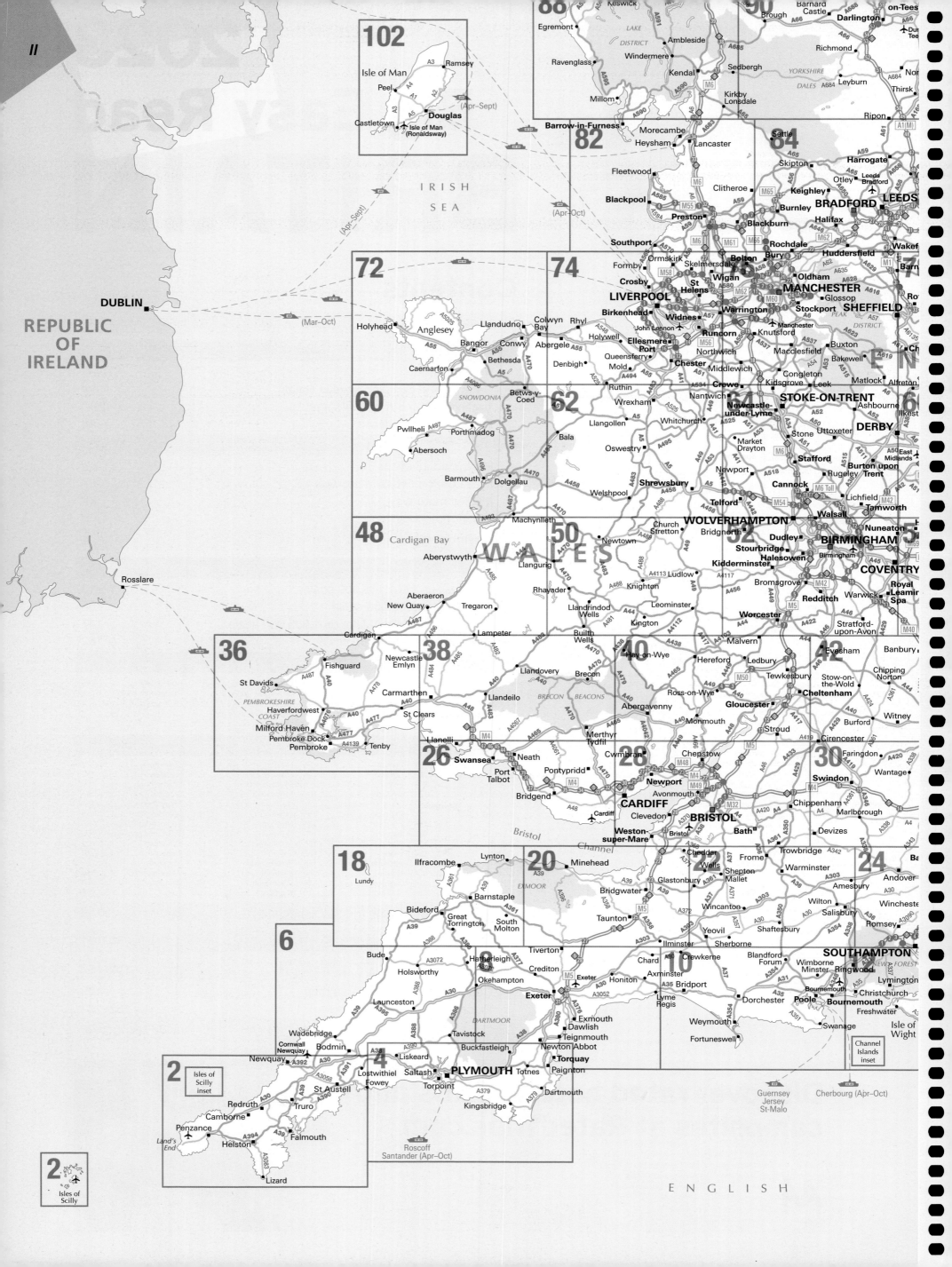

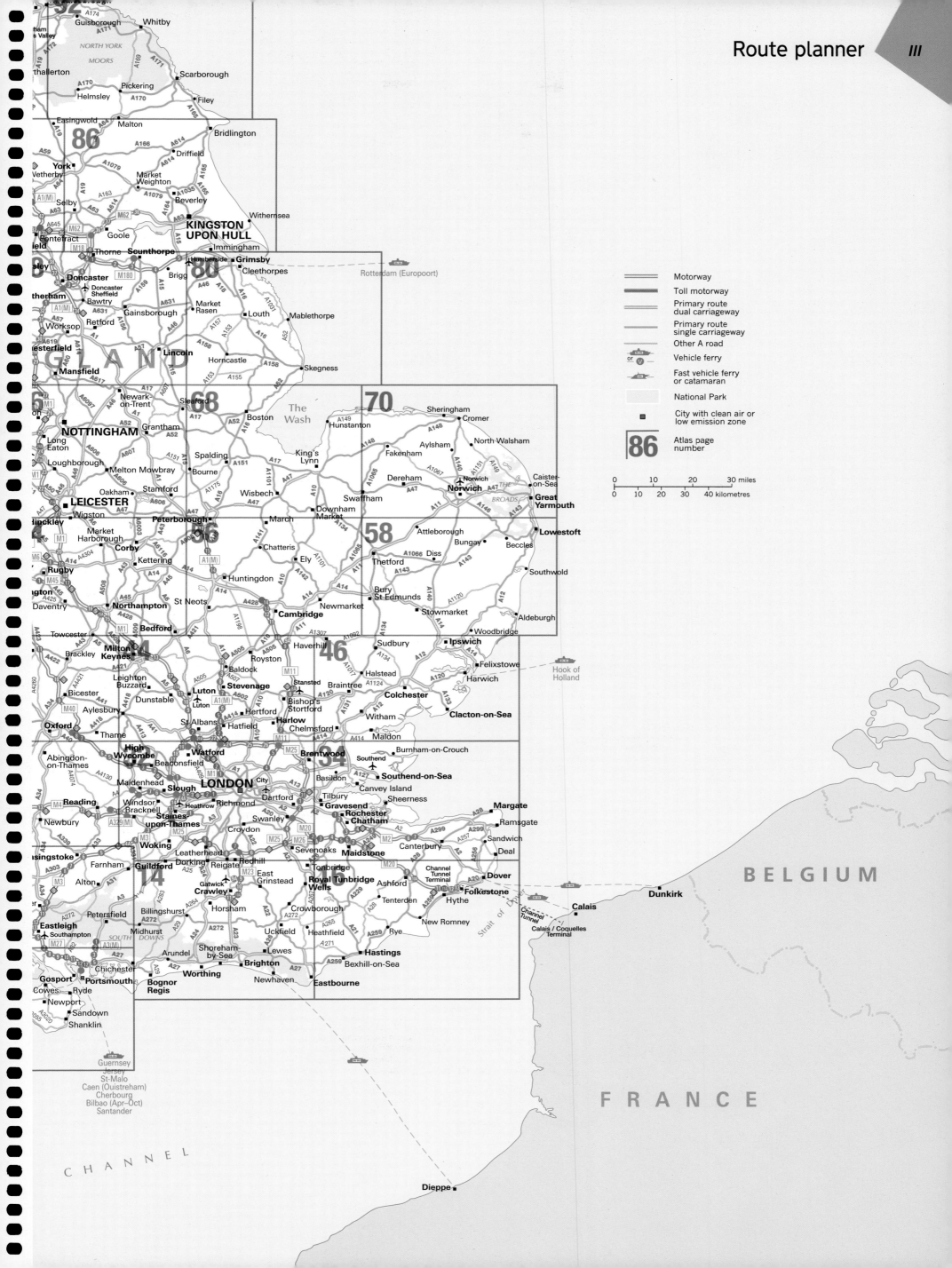

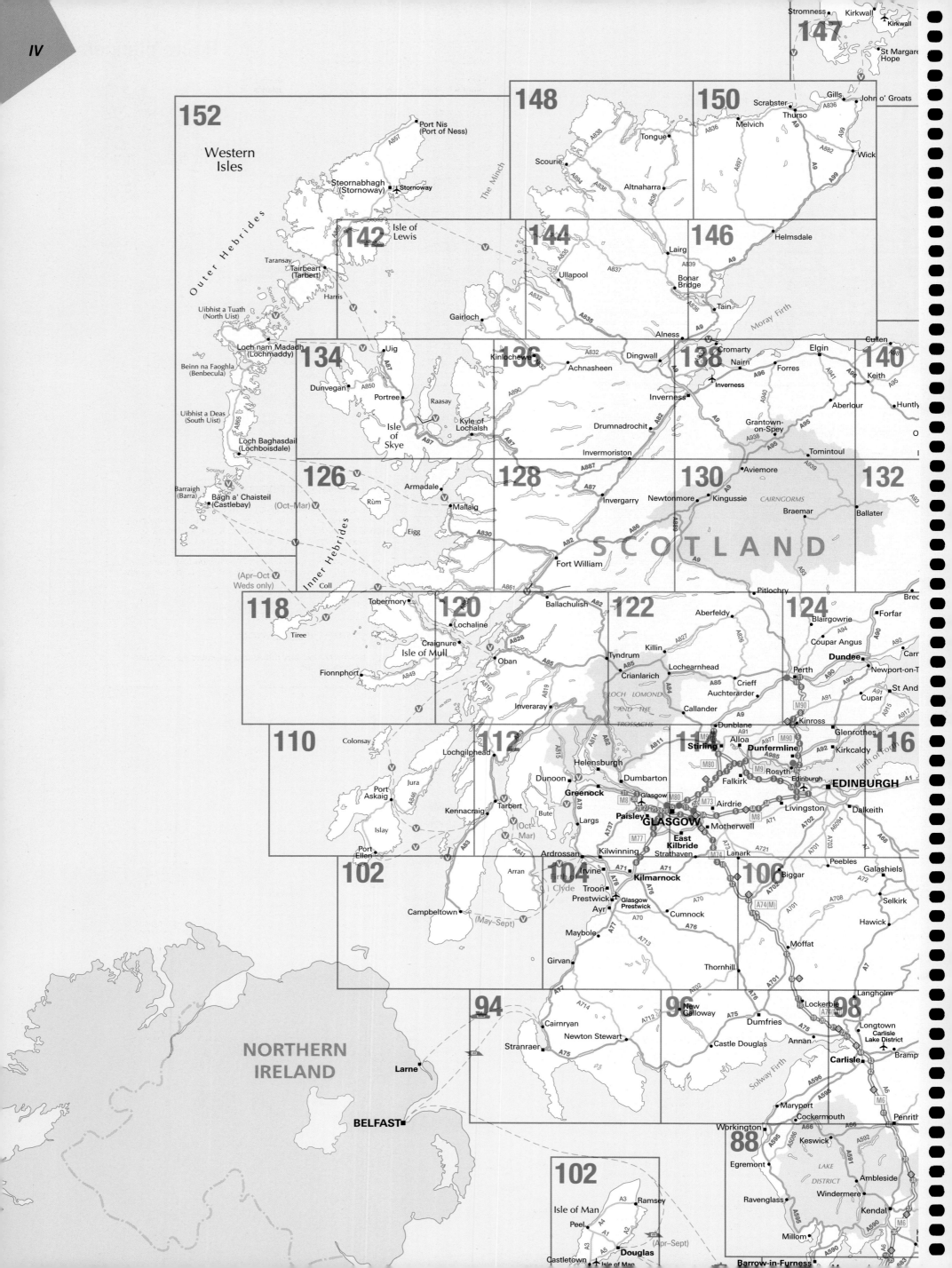

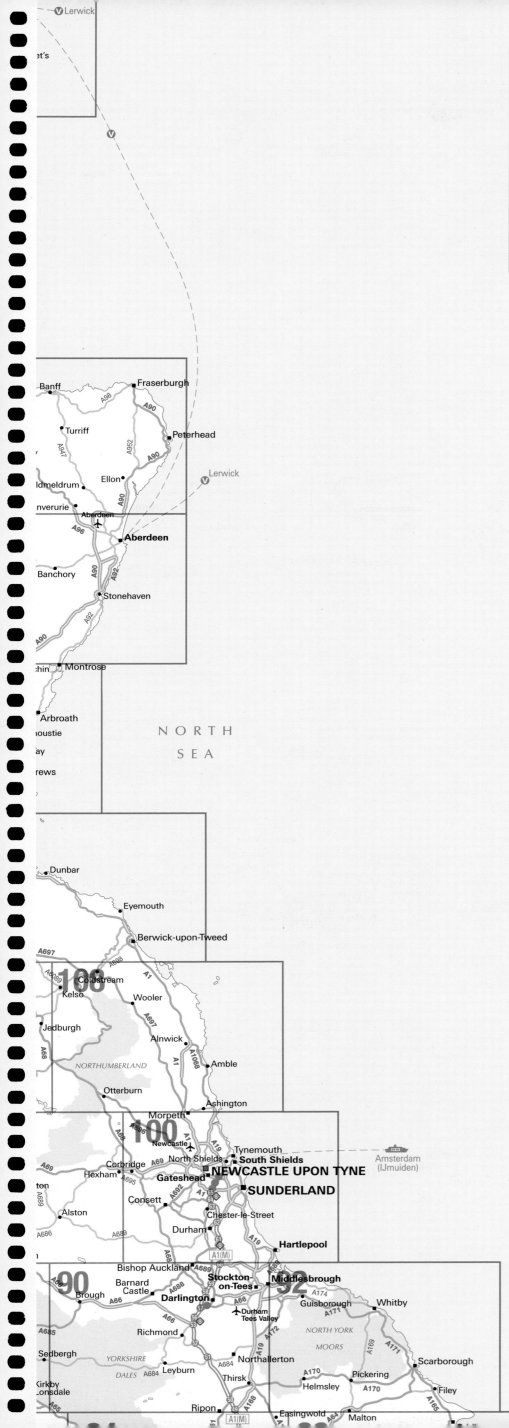

147
Orkney
Islands

147
Shetland
Islands

EMERGENCY DIVERSION ROUTES

In an emergency it may be necessary to close a section of motorway or other main road to traffic, so a temporary sign may advise drivers to follow a diversion route. To help drivers navigate the route, black symbols on yellow patches may be permanently displayed on existing direction signs, including motorway signs. Symbols may also be used on separate signs with yellow backgrounds.

FERRY INFORMATION

Information on ferry routes and operators can be found on pages *X–XII*.

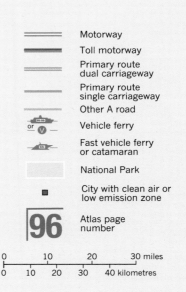

	Motorway
	Toll motorway
	Primary route dual carriageway
	Primary route single carriageway
	Other A road
or ⓥ	Vehicle ferry
	Fast vehicle ferry or catamaran
	National Park
▪	City with clean air or low emission zone
96	Atlas page number

```
0      10      20      30 miles
0   10  20  30   40 kilometres
```

Caravan and camping sites in Britain

These pages list the top 300 AA-inspected Caravan and Camping (C & C) sites in the Pennant rating scheme. **Five Pennant Premier sites are shown in green,** Four Pennant sites are shown in blue.
Listings include addresses, telephone numbers and websites together with page and grid references to locate the sites in the atlas. The total number of touring pitches is also included for each site, together with the type of pitch available.
The following abbreviations are used: **C = Caravan CV = Campervan T = Tent**
To discover more AA-rated caravan and camping sites not included on these pages please visit **RatedTrips.com**

ENGLAND

Alders Caravan Park
Home Farm, Alne, York
YO61 1RY
Tel: 01347 838722 85 P2
alderscaravanpark.co.uk
Total Pitches: 91 (C, CV & T)

Andrewshayes Holiday Park
Dalwood, Axminster
EX13 7DY
Tel: 01404 831225 9 N5
andrewshayes.co.uk
Total Pitches: 230 (C, CV & T)

Atlantic Bays Holiday Park
Padstow, Cornwall
PL28 8PY
Tel: 01841 520855 6 C10
atlanticbaysholidaypark.co.uk
Total Pitches: 241 (C, CV & T)

Ayr Holiday Park
St Ives, Cornwall
TR26 1EJ
Tel: 01736 795855 2 E6
ayrholidaypark.co.uk
Total Pitches: 40 (C, CV & T)

Back of Beyond Touring Park
234 Ringwood Road, St Leonards, Dorset
BH24 2SB
Tel: 01202 876968 11 Q4
backofbeyondtouringpark.co.uk
Total Pitches: 83 (C, CV & T)

Bagwell Farm Touring Park
Knights in the Bottom, Chickerell, Weymouth
DT3 4EA
Tel: 01305 782575 10 G8
bagwellfarm.co.uk
Total Pitches: 320 (C, CV & T)

Bardsea Leisure Park
Priory Road, Ulverston
LA12 9QE
Tel: 01229 584712 89 J11
bardsealeisure.co.uk
Total Pitches: 171 (C & CV)

Bath Chew Valley Caravan Park
Ham Lane, Bishop Sutton
BS39 5TZ
Tel: 01275 332127 29 J10
bathchewvalley.co.uk
Total Pitches: 45 (C, CV & T)

Bay View Farm C & C Park
Croyde, Devon
EX33 1PN
Tel: 01271 890501 19 J6
bayviewfarm.co.uk
Total Pitches: 75 (C, CV & T)

Bay View Holiday Park
Bolton le Sands, Carnforth
LA5 9TN
Tel: 01524 732854 83 L1
holgates.co.uk
Total Pitches: 202 (C, CV & T)

Beacon Cottage Farm Touring Park
Beacon Drive, St Agnes
TR5 0NU
Tel: 01872 552347 2 H4
beaconcottagefarmholidays.co.uk
Total Pitches: 70 (C, CV & T)

Beaconsfield Farm Caravan Park
Battlefield, Shrewsbury
SY4 4AA
Tel: 01939 210370 63 N8
beaconsfieldholidaypark.co.uk
Total Pitches: 95 (C & CV)

Beech Croft Farm C & C Park
Beech Croft, Blackwell in the Peak, Buxton
SK17 9TQ
Tel: 01298 85330 77 L9
beechcroftfarm.co.uk
Total Pitches: 30 (C, CV & T)

Bellingham C & C Club Site
Brown Rigg, Bellingham
NE48 2JY
Tel: 01434 220175 99 N2
campingandcaravanningclub.co.uk/bellingham
Total Pitches: 68 (C, CV & T)

Beverley Park C & C Park
Goodrington Road, Paignton
TQ4 7JE
Tel: 01803 843887 5 Q5
beverley-holidays.co.uk
Total Pitches: 149 (C, CV & T)

Blue Rose Caravan & Country Park
Star Carr Lane, Brandesburton
YO25 8RU
Tel: 01964 543366 87 L6
bluerosepark.com
Total Pitches: 114 (C & CV)

Briarfields Motel & Touring Park
Gloucester Road, Cheltenham
GL51 0SX
Tel: 01242 235324 41 P7
briarfields.net
Total Pitches: 72 (C, CV & T)

Broadhembury C & C Park
Steeds Lane, Kingsnorth, Ashford
TN26 1NQ
Tel: 01233 620859 16 H3
broadhembury.co.uk
Total Pitches: 120 (C, CV & T)

Brook Lodge Farm C & C Park
Cowslip Green, Redhill, Bristol, Somerset
BS40 5RB
Tel: 01934 862311 28 G10
brooklodgefarm.com
Total Pitches: 129 (C, CV & T)

Burnham-on-Sea Holiday Village
Marine Drive, Burnham-on-Sea
TA8 1LA
Tel: 01278 783391 21 M4
haven.com/burnhamonsea
Total Pitches: 781 (C, CV & T)

Burrowhayes Farm C & C Site & Riding Stables
West Luccombe, Porlock, Minehead
TA24 8HT
Tel: 01643 862463 20 D4
burrowhayes.co.uk
Total Pitches: 139 (C, CV & T)

Burton Constable Holiday Park & Arboretum
Old Lodges, Sproatley, Hull
HU11 4LJ
Tel: 01964 562508 87 M8
burtonconstableholidaypark.co.uk
Total Pitches: 500 (C, CV & T)

Caister-on-Sea Holiday Park
Ormesby Road, Caister-on-Sea, Great Yarmouth
NR30 5NH
Tel: 01493 728931 71 Q9
haven.com/caister
Total Pitches: 949 (C & CV)

Caistor Lakes Leisure Park
99a Brigg Road, Caistor
LN7 6RX
Tel: 01472 859626 80 B3
caistorlakes.co.uk
Total Pitches: 36 (C & CV)

Cakes & Ale
Abbey Lane, Theberton, Leiston
IP16 4TE
Tel: 01728 831655 59 N8
cakesandale.co.uk
Total Pitches: 255 (C, CV & T)

Calloose C & C Park
Leedstown, Hayle
TR27 5ET
Tel: 01736 850431 2 F7
calloose.co.uk
Total Pitches: 134 (C, CV & T)

Camping Caradon Touring Park
Trelawne, Looe
PL13 2NA
Tel: 01503 272388 4 C6
campingcaradon.co.uk
Total Pitches: 75 (C, CV & T)

Capesthorne Hall
Congleton Road, Siddington, Macclesfield
SK11 9JY
Tel: 01625 861221 76 F9
capesthorne.com/caravan-park
Total Pitches: 50 (C & CV)

Carlyon Bay C & C Park
Bethesda, Cypress Avenue, Carlyon Bay
PL25 3RE
Tel: 01726 812735 3 P4
carlyonbay.net
Total Pitches: 180 (C, CV & T)

Carnevas Holiday Park
Carnevas Farm, St Merryn, Cornwall
PL28 8PN
Tel: 01841 520230 6 B10
carnevasholidaypark.com
Total Pitches: 209 (C, CV & T)

Cartref C & C
Cartref, Ford Heath, Shrewsbury, Shropshire
SY5 9GD
Tel: 01743 821688 63 L10
cartrefcaravansite.co.uk
Total Pitches: 44 (C, CV & T)

Carvynick Holiday Park
Summercourt, Newquay
TR8 5AF
Tel: 01872 510716 3 L3
carvynick.co.uk
Total Pitches: 47 (C, CV & T)

Castlerigg Hall C & C Park
Castlerigg Hall, Keswick
CA12 4TE
Tel: 017687 74499 89 J2
castlerigg.co.uk
Total Pitches: 105 (C, CV & T)

Cheddar Mendip Heights C & C Club Site
Townsend, Priddy, Wells
BA5 3BP
Tel: 01749 870241 22 C3
campingandcaravanningclub.co.uk/cheddar
Total Pitches: 92 (C, CV & T)

Chy Carne Holiday Park
Kuggar, Ruan Minor, Helston, Cornwall
TR12 7LX
Tel: 01326 290200 2 H11
chycarne.co.uk
Total Pitches: 60 (C, CV & T)

Clippesby Hall
Hall Lane, Clippesby, Great Yarmouth
NR29 3BL
Tel: 01493 367800 71 N9
clippesbyhall.com
Total Pitches: 120 (C, CV & T)

Cofton Holidays
Starcross, Dawlish
EX6 8RP
Tel: 01626 890111 8 H8
coftonholidays.co.uk
Total Pitches: 532 (C, CV & T)

Concierge Camping
Ratham Estate, Ratham Lane, West Ashling, Chichester
PO18 8DL
Tel: 01243 573118 13 P3
conciergecamping.co.uk
Total Pitches: 27 (C & CV)

Coombe Touring Park
Race Plain, Netherhampton, Salisbury
SP2 8PN
Tel: 01722 328451 23 N7
coombecaravanpark.co.uk
Total Pitches: 56 (C, CV & T)

Cornish Farm Touring Park
Shoreditch, Taunton
TA3 7BS
Tel: 01823 327746 21 K9
cornishfarm.com
Total Pitches: 48 (C, CV & T)

Cosawes Park
Perranarworthal, Truro
TR3 7QS
Tel: 01872 863724 3 J7
cosawes.co.uk
Total Pitches: 59 (C, CV & T)

Cote Ghyll C & C Park
Osmotherley, Northallerton
DL6 3AH
Tel: 01609 883425 91 Q7
coteghyll.com
Total Pitches: 95 (C, CV & T)

Country View Holiday Park
Sand Road, Sand Bay, Weston-super-Mare
BS22 9UJ
Tel: 01934 627595 28 D9
cvhp.co.uk
Total Pitches: 255 (C, CV & T)

Crealy Theme Park & Resort
Sidmouth Road, Clyst St Mary, Exeter
EX5 1DR
Tel: 01395 234888 9 J6
crealy.co.uk
Total Pitches: 127 (C, CV & T)

Crows Nest Caravan Park
Gristhorpe, Filey
YO14 9PS
Tel: 01723 582206 93 M10
crowsnestcaravanpark.com
Total Pitches: 263 (C, CV & T)

Deepdale Backpackers & Camping
Deepdale Farm, Burnham Deepdale
PE31 8DD
Tel: 01485 210256 69 Q3
deepdalebackpackers.co.uk
Total Pitches: 80 (CV & T)

Dibles Park
Dibles Road, Warsash, Southampton, Hampshire
SO31 9SA
Tel: 01489 575232 12 H3
diblespark.co.uk
Total Pitches: 57 (C, CV & T)

Dornafield
Dornafield Farm, Two Mile Oak, Newton Abbot
TQ12 6DD
Tel: 01803 812732 5 P3
dornafield.com
Total Pitches: 135 (C, CV & T)

East Fleet Farm Touring Park
Chickerell, Weymouth
DT3 4DW
Tel: 01305 785768 10 G9
eastfleet.co.uk
Total Pitches: 400 (C, CV & T)

Eastham Hall Holiday Park
Saltcotes Road, Lytham St Annes, Lancashire
FY8 4LS
Tel: 01253 737907 83 J9
easthamhall.co.uk
Total Pitches: 274 (C & CV)

Eden Valley Holiday Park
Lanlivery, Nr Lostwithiel
PL30 5BU
Tel: 01208 872277 3 Q3
edenvalleyholidaypark.co.uk
Total Pitches: 94 (C, CV & T)

Exe Valley Caravan Site
Mill House, Bridgetown, Dulverton
TA22 9JR
Tel: 01643 851432 20 E7
exevalleycamping.co.uk
Total Pitches: 48 (C, CV & T)

Eye Kettleby Lakes
Eye Kettleby, Melton Mowbray
LE14 2TN
Tel: 01664 565900 67 J9
eyekettlebylakes.com
Total Pitches: 130 (C, CV & T)

Fen Farm Caravan Site
Moore Lane, East Mersea, Mersea Island, Colchester, Essex
CO5 8FE
Tel: 01206 383275 47 J9
fenfarm.co.uk
Total Pitches: 180 (C, CV & T)

Fernwood Caravan Park
Lyneal, Ellesmere, Shropshire
SY12 0QF
Tel: 01948 710221 63 M5
fernwoodpark.co.uk
Total Pitches: 225 (C & CV)

Fields End Water Caravan Park & Fishery
Benwick Road, Doddington, March
PE15 0TY
Tel: 01354 740199 56 G2
fieldsendwater.co.uk
Total Pitches: 90 (C, CV & T)

Flower of May Holiday Park
Lebberston Cliff, Filey, Scarborough
YO11 3NU
Tel: 01723 584311 93 M10
flowerofmay.com
Total Pitches: 503 (C, CV & T)

Forest Glade Holiday Park
Near Kentisbeare, Cullompton, Devon
EX15 2DT
Tel: 01404 841381 9 L3
forest-glade.co.uk
Total Pitches: 124 (C, CV & T)

Freshwater Beach Holiday Park
Burton Bradstock, Bridport
DT6 4PT
Tel: 01308 897317 10 D7
freshwaterbeach.co.uk
Total Pitches: 750 (C, CV & T)

Glenfield Caravan Park
Blackmoor Lane, Bardsey, Leeds
LS17 9DZ
Tel: 01937 574657 85 M7
glenfieldcaravanpark.co.uk
Total Pitches: 31 (C, CV & T)

Globe Vale Holiday Park
Radnor, Redruth
TR16 4BH
Tel: 01209 891183 2 H5
globevale.co.uk
Total Pitches: 195 (C, CV & T)

Glororum Caravan Park
Glororum Farm, Bamburgh
NE69 7AW
Tel: 01670 860256 109 K3
northumbrianleisure.co.uk
Total Pitches: 213 (C & CV)

Golden Cap Holiday Park
Seatown, Chideock, Bridport
DT6 6JX
Tel: 01308 422139 10 C6
wdlh.co.uk
Total Pitches: 345 (C, CV & T)

Golden Coast Holiday Park
Station Road, Woolacombe
EX34 7HW
Tel: 01271 872302 19 J5
woolacombe.com
Total Pitches: 431 (C, CV & T)

Golden Sands Holiday Park
Quebec Road, Mablethorpe
LN12 1QJ
Tel: 01507 477871 81 J6
haven.com/goldensands
Total Pitches: 1672 (C, CV & T)

Golden Square C & C Park
Oswaldkirk, Helmsley
YO62 5YQ
Tel: 01439 788269 92 C10
goldensquarecaravanpark.com
Total Pitches: 150 (C, CV & T)

Golden Valley C & C Park
Coach Road, Ripley, Derbyshire
DE55 4ES
Tel: 01773 513881 66 C2
goldenvalleycaravanpark.co.uk
Total Pitches: 47 (C, CV & T)

Goosewood Holiday Park
Sutton-on-the-Forest, York
YO61 1ET
Tel: 01347 810829 86 B3
flowerofmay.com
Total Pitches: 145 (C & CV)

Greenacre Place Touring Caravan Park
Bristol Road, Edithmead, Highbridge
TA9 4HA
Tel: 01278 785227 21 M4
greenacreplace.com
Total Pitches: 10 (C & CV)

Green Acres Caravan Park
High Knells, Houghton, Carlisle
CA6 4JW
Tel: 01228 675418 98 E6
caravanpark-cumbria.com
Total Pitches: 35 (C, CV & T)

Greenhill Farm C & C Park
Greenhill Farm, New Road, Landford, Salisbury
SP5 2AZ
Tel: 01794 324117 24 D9
greenhillfarm.co.uk
Total Pitches: 160 (C, CV & T)

Greenhills Holiday Park
Crowhill Lane, Bakewell, Derbyshire
DE45 1PX
Tel: 01629 813052 77 M10
greenhillsholidaypark.co.uk
Total Pitches: 245 (C, CV & T)

Grouse Hill Caravan Park
Flask Bungalow Farm, Fylingdales, Robin Hood's Bay
YO22 4QH
Tel: 01947 880543 93 J7
grousehill.co.uk
Total Pitches: 192 (C, CV & T)

Gunvenna Holiday Park
St Minver, Wadebridge
PL27 6QN
Tel: 01208 862405 6 D9
gunvenna.com
Total Pitches: 131 (C, CV & T)

Haggerston Castle Holiday Park
Beal, Berwick-upon-Tweed
TD15 2PA
Tel: 01289 381333 108 G1
haven.com/haggerstoncastle
Total Pitches: 1340 (C & CV)

Harbury Fields
Harbury Fields Farm, Harbury, Nr Leamington Spa
CV33 9JN
Tel: 01926 612457 54 B8
harburyfields.co.uk
Total Pitches: 59 (C & CV)

Harford Bridge Holiday Park
Peter Tavy, Tavistock
PL19 9LS
Tel: 01822 810349 7 P9
harfordbridge.co.uk
Total Pitches: 198 (C, CV & T)

Haw Wood Farm Caravan Park
Hinton, Saxmundham
IP17 3QT
Tel: 01502 359550 59 N6
hawwoodfarm.co.uk
Total Pitches: 115 (C, CV & T)

Heathfield Farm Camping
Heathfield Road, Freshwater, Isle of Wight
PO40 9SH
Tel: 01983 407822 12 E7
heathfieldcamping.co.uk
Total Pitches: 75 (C, CV & T)

Heathland Beach Holiday Park
London Road, Kessingland
NR33 7PJ
Tel: 01502 740337 59 Q3
heathlandbeach.co.uk
Total Pitches: 263 (C, CV & T)

Hedley Wood C & C Park
Bridgerule, Holsworthy, Devon
EX22 7ED
Tel: 01288 381404 7 K4
hedleywood.co.uk
Total Pitches: 138 (C, CV & T)

Hendra Holiday Park
Newquay
TR8 4NY
Tel: 01637 875778 3 K2
hendra-holidays.com
Total Pitches: 865 (C, CV & T)

Herding Hill Farm Touring & Camping Site
Shield Hill, Haltwhistle, Northumberland
NE49 9NW
Tel: 01434 320175 99 K5
herdinghillfarm.co.uk
Total Pitches: 22 (C, CV & T)

Highfield Farm Touring Park
Long Road, Comberton, Cambridge
CB23 7DG
Tel: 01223 262308 56 H9
highfieldfarmtouringpark.co.uk
Total Pitches: 120 (C, CV & T)

Highlands End Holiday Park
Eype, Bridport, Dorset
DT6 6AR
Tel: 01308 422139 10 C6
wdlh.co.uk
Total Pitches: 357 (C, CV & T)

Hill of Oaks & Blakeholme
Windermere
LA12 8NR
Tel: 015395 31578 89 K9
hillofoaks.co.uk
Total Pitches: 263 (C & CV)

Hillside Caravan Park
Canvas Farm, Moor Road, Knayton, Thirsk
YO7 4BR
Tel: 01845 537349 91 Q9
hillsidecaravanpark.co.uk
Total Pitches: 52 (C & CV)

Holiday Resort Unity
Coast Road, Brean Sands, Brean
TA8 2RB
Tel: 01278 751235 21 L3
hru.co.uk
Total Pitches: 1114 (C, CV & T)

Hollins Farm C & C
Far Arnside, Carnforth
LA5 0SL
Tel: 01524 701767 89 M11
holgates.co.uk
Total Pitches: 14 (C, CV & T)

Hylton Caravan Park
Eden Street, Silloth
CA7 4AY
Tel: 016973 32666 97 M7
stanwix.com
Total Pitches: 303 (C, CV & T)

Island Lodge C & C Site
Stumpy Post Cross, Kingsbridge
TQ7 4BL
Tel: 01548 852956 5 M7
islandlodgesite.co.uk
Total Pitches: 30 (C, CV & T)

Isle of Avalon Touring Caravan Park
Godney Road, Glastonbury
BA6 9AF
Tel: 01458 833618 22 C5
avaloncaravanpark.co.uk
Total Pitches: 120 (C, CV & T)

Jasmine Caravan Park
Cross Lane, Snainton, Scarborough
YO13 9BE
Tel: 01723 859240 93 J10
jasminepark.co.uk
Total Pitches: 84 (C, CV & T)

Kennford International Holiday Park
Kennford, Exeter
EX6 7YN
Tel: 01392 833046 8 G7
kennfordinternational.co.uk
Total Pitches: 87 (C, CV & T)

Killiwerris Touring Park
Penstraze, Chacewater, Truro, Cornwall
TR4 8PF
Tel: 01872 561356 3 J5
killiwerris.co.uk
Total Pitches: 17 (C & CV)

King's Lynn C & C Park
New Road, North Runcton, King's Lynn
PE33 0RA
Tel: 01553 840004 69 M9
kl-cc.co.uk
Total Pitches: 170 (C, CV & T)

Kloofs Caravan Park
Sandhurst Lane, Bexhill
TN39 4RG
Tel: 01424 842839 16 C9
kloofs.com
Total Pitches: 125 (C, CV & T)

Kneps Farm Holiday Caravan Park
River Road, Stanah, Thornton-Cleveleys, Blackpool
FY5 5LR
Tel: 01253 823632 83 J6
knepsfarm.co.uk
Total Pitches: 86 (C & CV)

Knight Stainforth Hall Caravan & Campsite
Stainforth, Settle
BD24 0DP
Tel: 01729 822200 84 B2
knightstainforth.co.uk
Total Pitches: 160 (C, CV & T)

Ladycross Plantation Caravan Park
Egton, Whitby
YO21 1UA
Tel: 01947 895502 92 G5
ladycrossplantation.co.uk
Total Pitches: 130 (C & CV)

Lady's Mile Holiday Park
Dawlish, Devon
EX7 0LX
Tel: 01626 863411 8 H9
ladysmile.co.uk
Total Pitches: 692 (C, CV & T)

Lakeland Leisure Park
Moor Lane, Flookburgh
LA11 7LT
Tel: 01539 558556 89 K12
haven.com/lakeland
Total Pitches: 977 (C, CV & T)

Lamb Cottage Caravan Park
Dalefords Lane, Whitegate, Northwich
CW8 2BN
Tel: 01606 882302 75 Q10
lambcottage.co.uk
Total Pitches: 71 (C & CV)

Langstone Manor C & C Park
Moortown, Tavistock
PL19 9JZ
Tel: 01822 613371 7 P10
langstonemanor.co.uk
Total Pitches: 83 (C, CV & T)

Lanyon Holiday Park
Loscombe Lane, Four Lanes, Redruth
TR16 6LP
Tel: 01209 313474 2 H7
lanyonholidaypark.co.uk
Total Pitches: 74 (C, CV & T)

Lickpenny Caravan Site
Lickpenny Lane, Tansley, Matlock
DE4 5GF
Tel: 01629 583040 77 Q11
lickpennycaravanpark.co.uk
Total Pitches: 80 (C & CV)

Lime Tree Park
Dukes Drive, Buxton
SK17 9RP
Tel: 01298 22988 77 K9
limetreeparkbuxton.com
Total Pitches: 149 (C, CV & T)

Lincoln Farm Park Oxfordshire
High Street, Standlake
OX29 7RH
Tel: 01865 300239 43 J11
lincolnfarmpark.co.uk
Total Pitches: 90 (C, CV & T)

Littlesea Holiday Park
Lynch Lane, Weymouth
DT4 9DT
Tel: 01305 774414 10 G9
haven.com/littlesea
Total Pitches: 861 (C, CV & T)

Little Trevothan C & C Park
Trevothan, Coverack, Helston, Cornwall
TR12 6SD
Tel: 01326 280260 3 J11
littletrevothan.co.uk
Total Pitches: 108 (C, CV & T)

Long Acres Touring Park
Station Road, Old Leake, Boston
PE22 9RF
Tel: 01205 871555 68 G2
long-acres.co.uk
Total Pitches: 40 (C, CV & T)

Long Hazel Park
High Street, Sparkford, Yeovil, Somerset
BA22 7JH
Tel: 01963 440002 22 E8
longhazelpark.co.uk
Total Pitches: 50 (C, CV & T)

Longnor Wood Holiday Park
Newtown, Longnor, Nr Buxton
SK17 0NG
Tel: 01298 83648 77 K11
longnorwood.co.uk
Total Pitches: 68 (C, CV & T)

Manor Wood Country Caravan Park
Manor Wood, Coddington, Chester
CH3 9EN
Tel: 01829 782990 63 M1
cheshire-caravan-sites.co.uk
Total Pitches: 66 (C, CV & T)

Marton Mere Holiday Village
Mythop Road, Blackpool
FY4 4XN
Tel: 01253 767544 82 H8
haven.com/martonmere
Total Pitches: 782 (C & CV)

Mayfield Park
Cheltenham Road, Cirencester
GL7 7BH
Tel: 01285 831301 42 B10
mayfieldpark.co.uk
Total Pitches: 105 (C, CV & T)

Meadow Lakes Holiday Park
Hewas Water, St Austell, Cornwall
PL26 7JG
Tel: 01726 882540 3 N5
meadow-lakes.co.uk
Total Pitches: 232 (C, CV & T)

Meadowbank Holidays
Stour Way, Christchurch
BH23 2PQ
Tel: 01202 483597 12 B6
meadowbank-holidays.co.uk
Total Pitches: 221 (C & CV)

Middlewood Farm Holiday Park
Middlewood Lane, Fylingthorpe, Robin Hood's Bay, Whitby
YO22 4UF
Tel: 01947 880414 93 J6
middlewoodfarm.com
Total Pitches: 144 (C, CV & T)

Mill Farm C & C Park
Fiddington, Bridgwater, Somerset
TA5 1JQ
Tel: 01278 732286 21 K5
millfarm.biz
Total Pitches: 275 (C, CV & T)

Mill Park Touring C & C Park
Mill Lane, Berrynarbor, Ilfracombe, Devon
EX34 9SH
Tel: 01271 882647 19 L4
millpark.com
Total Pitches: 160 (C, CV & T)

Minnows Touring Park
Holbrook Lane, Sampford Peverell
EX16 7EN
Tel: 01884 821770 20 G10
minnowstouringpark.co.uk
Total Pitches: 60 (C, CV & T)

Monkey Tree Holiday Park
Hendra Croft, Scotland Road, Newquay
TR8 5QR
Tel: 01872 572032 3 K4
monkeytreeholidaypark.co.uk
Total Pitches: 700 (C, CV & T)

Moon & Sixpence
Newbourn Road, Waldringfield, Woodbridge
IP12 4PP
Tel: 01473 736650 47 N3
moonandsixpence.co.uk
Total Pitches: 275 (C & CV)

Moss Wood Caravan Park
Crimbles Lane, Cockerham
LA2 0ES
Tel: 01524 791041 83 L5
mosswood.co.uk
Total Pitches: 168 (C & CV)

Naburn Lock Caravan Park
Naburn
YO19 4RU
Tel: 01904 728697 86 B6
naburnlock.co.uk
Total Pitches: 115 (C, CV & T)

New Lodge Farm C & C Site
New Lodge Farm, Bulwick, Corby
NN17 3DU
Tel: 01780 450493 55 N2
newlodgefarm.com
Total Pitches: 72 (C, CV & T)

Newberry Valley Park
Woodlands, Combe Martin
EX34 0AT
Tel: 01271 882334 19 L4
newberryvalleypark.co.uk
Total Pitches: 112 (C, CV & T)

Newlands Holidays
Charmouth, Bridport
DT6 6RB
Tel: 01297 560259 10 B6
newlandsholidays.co.uk
Total Pitches: 330 (C, CV & T)

Ninham Country Holidays
Ninham, Shanklin, Isle of Wight
PO37 7PL
Tel: 01983 864243 13 J8
ninham-holidays.co.uk
Total Pitches: 135 (C, CV & T)

North Morte Farm C & C Park
North Morte Road, Mortehoe, Woolacombe
EX34 7EG
Tel: 01271 870381 19 J4
northmortefarm.co.uk
Total Pitches: 253 (C, CV & T)

Northam Farm Caravan & Touring Park
Brean, Burnham-on-Sea
TA8 2SE
Tel: 01278 751244 21 M2
northamfarm.co.uk
Total Pitches: 350 (C, CV & T)

Oakdown Country Holiday Park
Gatedown Lane, Weston, Sidmouth
EX10 0PT
Tel: 01297 680387 9 M7
oakdown.co.uk
Total Pitches: 170 (C, CV & T)

Old Hall Caravan Park
Capernwray, Carnforth
LA6 1AD
Tel: 01524 733276 83 M1
oldhallcaravanpark.co.uk
Total Pitches: 298 (C & CV)

Old Oaks Touring & Glamping
Wick Farm, Wick, Glastonbury
BA6 8JS
Tel: 01458 831437 22 C5
theoldoaks.co.uk
Total Pitches: 100 (C, CV & T)

Orchard Farm Holiday Village
Stonegate, Hunmanby, Filey, North Yorkshire
YO14 0PU
Tel: 01723 891582 93 M11
orchardfarmholidayvillage.co.uk
Total Pitches: 137 (C, CV & T)

Orchard Park
Frampton Lane, Hubbert's Bridge, Boston, Lincolnshire
PE20 3QU
Tel: 01205 290328 68 E4
orchardpark.co.uk
Total Pitches: 251 (C, CV & T)

Ord House Country Park
East Ord, Berwick-upon-Tweed
TD15 2NS
Tel: 01289 305288 117 L11
maguirescountryparks.co.uk
Total Pitches: 344 (C, CV & T)

Otterington Park
Station Farm, South Otterington, Northallerton, North Yorkshire
DL7 9JB
Tel: 01609 780656 91 P9
otteringtonpark.com
Total Pitches: 67 (C, CV & T)

Oxon Hall Touring Park
Welshpool Road, Shrewsbury
SY3 5FB
Tel: 01743 340868 63 M9
morris-leisure.co.uk
Total Pitches: 165 (C, CV & T)

Park Cliffe C & C Estate
Birks Road, Tower Wood, Windermere
LA23 3PG
Tel: 015395 31344 89 L8
parkcliffe.co.uk
Total Pitches: 126 (C, CV & T)

Parkers Farm Holiday Park
Higher Mead Farm, Ashburton, Devon
TQ13 7LJ
Tel: 01364 654869 8 E10
parkersfarmholidays.co.uk
Total Pitches: 118 (C, CV & T)

Park Foot C & C Park
Howtown Road, Pooley Bridge
CA10 2NA
Tel: 017684 86309 89 M2
parkfootullswater.co.uk
Total Pitches: 454 (C, CV & T)

Parkland C & C Site
Sorley Green Cross, Kingsbridge
TQ7 4AF
Tel: 01548 852723 5 M7
parklandsite.co.uk
Total Pitches: 50 (C, CV & T)

Pebble Bank Caravan Park
Camp Road, Wyke Regis, Weymouth
DT4 9HF
Tel: 01305 774844 10 G9
pebblebank.co.uk
Total Pitches: 120 (C, CV & T)

Perran Sands Holiday Park
Perranporth, Truro
TR6 0AQ
Tel: 01872 573551 3 J3
haven.com/perransands
Total Pitches: 1012 (C, CV & T)

Petwood Caravan Park
Off Stixwould Road, Woodhall Spa
LN10 6QH
Tel: 01526 354799 80 D11
petwoodcaravanpark.com
Total Pitches: 98 (C, CV & T)

Plough Lane Touring Caravan Site
Plough Lane, Chippenham, Wiltshire
SN15 5PS
Tel: 01249 750146 29 Q7
ploughlane.co.uk
Total Pitches: 52 (C & CV)

Polladras Holiday Park
Carleen, Breage, Helston
TR13 9NX
Tel: 01736 762220 2 F8
polladrasholidaypark.co.uk
Total Pitches: 42 (C, CV & T)

Polmanter Touring Park
Halsetown, St Ives
TR26 3LX
Tel: 01736 795640 2 E7
polmanter.com
Total Pitches: 294 (C, CV & T)

Porthtowan Tourist Park
Mile Hill, Porthtowan, Truro
TR4 8TY
Tel: 01209 890256 2 H5
porthtowantouristpark.co.uk
Total Pitches: 80 (C, CV & T)

Primrose Valley Holiday Park
Filey
YO14 9RF
Tel: 01723 513771 93 M11
haven.com/primrosevalley
Total Pitches: 1549 (C & CV)

Ranch Caravan Park
Station Road, Honeybourne,
Evesham
WR11 7PR
Tel: 01386 830744 42 C3
ranch.co.uk
Total Pitches: 338 (C & CV)

Ripley Caravan Park
Knaresborough Road, Ripley,
Harrogate
HG3 3AU
Tel: 01423 770050 85 L3
ripleycaravanpark.com
Total Pitches: 135 (C, CV & T)

River Dart Country Park
Holne Park, Ashburton
TQ13 7NP
Tel: 01364 652511 5 M3
riverdart.co.uk
Total Pitches: 170 (C, CV & T)

River Valley Holiday Park
London Apprentice, St Austell
PL26 7AP
Tel: 01726 73533 3 N4
rivervalleyholidaypark.co.uk
Total Pitches: 85 (C, CV & T)

Riverside C & C Park
Marsh Lane, North Molton Road,
South Molton
EX36 3HQ
Tel: 01769 579269 19 P8
exmoorriverside.co.uk
Total Pitches: 61 (C, CV & T)

Riverside Caravan Park
High Bentham, Lancaster
LA2 7FJ
Tel: 015242 61272 83 P1
riversidecaravanpark.co.uk
Total Pitches: 267 (C & CV)

Riverside Meadows Country
Caravan Park
Ure Bank Top, Ripon
HG4 1JD
Tel: 01765 602964 91 N12
flowerofmay.com
Total Pitches: 349 (C)

Robin Hood C & C Park
Green Dyke Lane, Slingsby
YO62 4AP
Tel: 01653 628391 92 E11
robinhoodcaravanpark.co.uk
Total Pitches: 66 (C, CV & T)

Rose Farm Touring & Camping Park
Stepshort, Belton, Nr Great Yarmouth
NR31 9JS
Tel: 01493 738292 71 P11
rosefarmtouringpark.com
Total Pitches: 147 (C, CV & T)

Rosedale Abbey Caravan Park
Rosedale Abbey, Pickering
YO18 8SA
Tel: 01751 417272 92 E7
rosedaleabbeycaravanpark.co.uk
Total Pitches: 141 (C, CV & T)

Rudding Holiday Park
Follifoot, Harrogate
HG3 1JH
Tel: 01423 870439 85 L4
ruddingholidaypark.co.uk
Total Pitches: 143 (C, CV & T)

Run Cottage Touring Park
Alderton Road, Hollesley, Woodbridge
IP12 3RQ
Tel: 01394 411309 47 P3
runcottage.co.uk
Total Pitches: 47 (C, CV & T)

Rutland C & C
Park Lane, Greetham, Oakham
LE15 7FN
Tel: 01572 813520 67 M9
rutlandcaravanandcamping.co.uk
Total Pitches: 130 (C, CV & T)

St Helens in the Park
Wykeham, Scarborough
YO13 9QD
Tel: 01723 862771 93 K10
sthelenscaravanpark.co.uk
Total Pitches: 260 (C, CV & T)

St Ives Bay Holiday Park
73 Loggans Road, Upton Towans, Hayle
TR27 5BH
Tel: 01736 752274 2 F6
stivesbay.co.uk
Total Pitches: 507 (C, CV & T)

Salcombe Regis C & C Park
Salcombe Regis, Sidmouth
EX10 0JH
Tel: 01395 514303 9 M7
salcombe-regis.co.uk
Total Pitches: 110 (C, CV & T)

Sand le Mere Holiday Village
Southfield Lane, Tunstall
HU12 0JF
Tel: 01964 670403 87 P9
sand-le-mere.co.uk
Total Pitches: 89 (C & CV)

Searles Leisure Resort
South Beach Road, Hunstanton
PE36 5BB
Tel: 01485 534211 69 M4
searles.co.uk
Total Pitches: 413 (C, CV & T)

Seaview Holiday Park
Preston, Weymouth
DT3 6DZ
Tel: 01305 832271 10 H8
haven.com/parks/dorset/seaview
Total Pitches: 347 (C, CV & T)

Severn Gorge Park
Bridgnorth Road, Tweedale, Telford
TF7 4JB
Tel: 01952 684789 64 D11
severngorgepark.co.uk
Total Pitches: 132 (C & CV)

Shamba Holidays
East Moors Lane, St Leonards,
Ringwood
BH24 2SB
Tel: 01202 873302 11 Q4
shambaholidays.co.uk
Total Pitches: 150 (C, CV & T)

Shrubbery Touring Park
Rousdon, Lyme Regis
DT7 3XW
Tel: 01297 442227 9 P6
shrubberypark.co.uk
Total Pitches: 122 (C, CV & T)

Silverdale Caravan Park
Middlebarrow Plain, Cove Road,
Silverdale, Nr Carnforth
LA5 0SH
Tel: 01524 701508 89 M11
holgates.co.uk
Total Pitches: 427 (C, CV & T)

Skelwith Fold Caravan Park
Ambleside, Cumbria
LA22 0HX
Tel: 015394 32277 89 K6
skelwith.com
Total Pitches: 470 (C & CV)

Skirlington Leisure Park
Driffield, Skipsea
YO25 8SY
Tel: 01262 468213 87 M5
skirlington.com
Total Pitches: 930 (C & CV)

Sleningford Watermill
Caravan Camping Park
North Stainley, Ripon
HG4 3HQ
Tel: 01765 635201 91 M11
sleningfordwatermill.co.uk
Total Pitches: 150 (C, CV & T)

Somers Wood Caravan Park
Somers Road, Meriden
CV7 7PL
Tel: 01676 522978 53 N4
somerswood.co.uk
Total Pitches: 48 (C & CV)

Southfork Caravan Park
Parrett Works, Martock,
Somerset
TA12 6AE
Tel: 01935 825661 21 P9
southforkcaravans.co.uk
Total Pitches: 30 (C, CV & T)

South Lea Caravan Park
The Balk, Pocklington, York,
North Yorkshire
YO42 2NX
Tel: 01759 303467 86 E6
south-lea.co.uk
Total Pitches: 97 (C, CV & T)

South Lytchett Manor C & C Park
Dorchester Road,
Lytchett Minster, Poole
BH16 6JB
Tel: 01202 622577 11 M6
southlytchettmanor.co.uk
Total Pitches: 154 (C, CV & T)

South Meadows Caravan Park
South Road, Belford
NE70 7DP
Tel: 01668 213326 109 J3
southmeadows.co.uk
Total Pitches: 273 (C, CV & T)

Stanmore Hall Touring Park
Stourbridge Road, Bridgnorth
WV15 6DT
Tel: 01746 761761 52 D2
morris-leisure.co.uk
Total Pitches: 129 (C, CV & T)

Stanwix Park Holiday Centre
Greenrow, Silloth
CA7 4HH
Tel: 016973 32666 97 M7
stanwix.com
Total Pitches: 337 (C, CV & T)

Stroud Hill Park
Fen Road, Pidley, St Ives
PE28 3DE
Tel: 01487 741333 56 G5
stroudhillpark.co.uk
Total Pitches: 60 (C, CV & T)

Summers Ponds Fishery & Campsite
Chapel Road, Barns Green, Horsham
RH13 0PR
Tel: 01403 732539 14 G5
summersponds.co.uk
Total Pitches: 90 (C, CV & T)

Swiss Farm Touring & Camping
Marlow Road, Henley-on-Thames
RG9 2HY
Tel: 01491 573419 31 Q6
swissfarmhenley.co.uk
Total Pitches: 148 (C, CV & T)

Tanner Farm Touring C & C Park
Tanner Farm, Goudhurst Road,
Marden
TN12 9ND
Tel: 01622 832399 16 C3
tannerfarmpark.co.uk
Total Pitches: 122 (C, CV & T)

Tehidy Holiday Park
Harris Mill, Illogan, Portreath
TR16 4JQ
Tel: 01209 216489 2 H6
tehidy.co.uk
Total Pitches: 52 (C, CV & T)

Tencreek Holiday Park
Polperro Road, Looe
PL13 2JR
Tel: 01503 262447 4 C6
dolphinholidays.co.uk
Total Pitches: 355 (C, CV & T)

Teversal C & C Club Site
Silverhill Lane, Teversal
NG17 3JJ
Tel: 01623 551838 78 D11
campingandcaravanningclub.co.uk/teversal
Total Pitches: 136 (C, CV & T)

The Inside Park
Down House Estate,
Blandford Forum, Dorset
DT11 9AD
Tel: 01258 453719 11 L4
theinsidepark.co.uk
Total Pitches: 125 (C, CV & T)

The Laurels Holiday Park
Padstow Road, Whitecross,
Wadebridge
PL27 7JQ
Tel: 01208 813341 6 D10
thelaurelsholidaypark.co.uk
Total Pitches: 30 (C, CV & T)

The Old Brick Kilns
Little Barney Lane, Barney,
Fakenham
NR21 0NL
Tel: 01328 878305 70 E5
old-brick-kilns.co.uk
Total Pitches: 65 (C, CV & T)

The Orchards Holiday Caravan Park
Main Road, Newbridge, Yarmouth,
Isle of Wight
PO41 0TS
Tel: 01983 531331 12 G7
orchards-holiday-park.co.uk
Total Pitches: 225 (C, CV & T)

The Quiet Site
Ullswater, Watermillock
CA11 0LS
Tel: 07768 727016 89 L2
thequietsite.co.uk
Total Pitches: 151 (C, CV & T)

Thornton's Holt Camping Park
Stragglethorpe Road, Stragglethorpe,
Radcliffe on Trent
NG12 2JZ
Tel: 0115 933 2125 66 G5
thorntons-holt.co.uk
Total Pitches: 155 (C, CV & T)

Thornwick Bay Holiday Village
North Marine Road, Flamborough
YO15 1AU
Tel: 01262 850569 93 P12
haven.com/parks/yorkshire/thornwick-bay
Total Pitches: 225 (C, CV & T)

Thorpe Park Holiday Centre
Cleethorpes
DN35 0PW
Tel: 01472 813395 80 F2
haven.com/thorpepark
Total Pitches: 1491 (C, CV & T)

Treago Farm Caravan Site
Crantock, Newquay
TR8 5QS
Tel: 01637 830277 3 J2
treagofarm.co.uk
Total Pitches: 100 (C, CV & T)

Treloy Touring Park
Newquay
TR8 4JN
Tel: 01637 872063 3 L2
treloy.co.uk
Total Pitches: 223 (C, CV & T)

Trencreek Holiday Park
Hillcrest, Higher Trencreek, Newquay
TR8 4NS
Tel: 01637 874210 3 K2
trencreekholidaypark.co.uk
Total Pitches: 200 (C, CV & T)

Trethem Mill Touring Park
St Just-in-Roseland,
Nr St Mawes, Truro
TR2 5JF
Tel: 01872 580504 3 L7
trethem.com
Total Pitches: 84 (C, CV & T)

Trevalgan Touring Park
Trevalgan, St Ives
TR26 3BJ
Tel: 01736 791892 2 D6
trevalgantouringpark.co.uk
Total Pitches: 135 (C, CV & T)

Trevarrian Holiday Park
Mawgan Porth, Newquay, Cornwall
TR8 4AQ
Tel: 01637 860381 6 B11
trevarrian.co.uk
Total Pitches: 185 (C, CV & T)

Trevarth Holiday Park
Blackwater, Truro
TR4 8HR
Tel: 01872 560266 3 J5
trevarth.co.uk
Total Pitches: 50 (C, CV & T)

Trevedra Farm C & C Site
Sennen, Penzance
TR19 7BE
Tel: 01736 871818 2 B9
trevedrafarm.co.uk
Total Pitches: 100 (C, CV & T)

Trevella Park
Crantock, Newquay
TR8 5EW
Tel: 01637 830308 3 K3
trevella.co.uk
Total Pitches: 290 (C, CV & T)

Trevornick
Holywell Bay, Newquay
TR8 5PW
Tel: 01637 830531 3 J3
trevornick.co.uk
Total Pitches: 600 (C, CV & T)

Trewan Hall
St Columb Major, Cornwall
TR9 6DB
Tel: 01637 880261 3 M2
trewan-hall.co.uk
Total Pitches: 200 (C, CV & T)

Tudor C & C
Shepherds Patch, Slimbridge, Gloucester
GL2 7BP
Tel: 01453 890483 41 L11
tudorcaravanpark.com
Total Pitches: 75 (C, CV & T)

Twitchen House Holiday Park
Mortehoe Station Road, Mortehoe,
Woolacombe
EX34 7ES
Tel: 01271 872302 19 J4
woolacombe.com
Total Pitches: 569 (C, CV & T)

Two Mills Touring Park
Yarmouth Road, North Walsham
NR28 9NA
Tel: 01692 405829 71 K6
twomills.co.uk
Total Pitches: 81 (C, CV & T)

Ulwell Cottage Caravan Park
Ulwell Cottage, Ulwell, Swanage
BH19 3DG
Tel: 01929 422823 11 N8
ulwellcottagepark.co.uk
Total Pitches: 219 (C, CV & T)

Upper Lynstone Caravan Park
Lynstone, Bude
EX23 0LP
Tel: 01288 352017 7 J4
upperlynstone.co.uk
Total Pitches: 106 (C, CV & T)

Vale of Pickering Caravan Park
Carr House Farm, Allerston, Pickering
YO18 7PQ
Tel: 01723 859280 92 H10
valeofpickering.co.uk
Total Pitches: 120 (C, CV & T)

Waldegraves Holiday Park
Mersea Island, Colchester
CO5 8SE
Tel: 01206 382898 47 J9
waldegraves.co.uk
Total Pitches: 126 (C, CV & T)

Waleswood C &C Park
Delves Lane, Waleswood, Wales Bar,
Wales, South Yorkshire
S26 5RN
Tel: 07825 125328 78 D7
waleswood.co.uk
Total Pitches: 163 (C, CV & T)

Warcombe Farm C & C Park
Station Road, Mortehoe, Woolacombe
EX34 7EJ
Tel: 01271 870690 19 J4
warcombefarm.co.uk
Total Pitches: 250 (C, CV & T)

Wareham Forest Tourist Park
North Trigon, Wareham
BH20 7NZ
Tel: 01929 551393 11 L6
warehamforest.co.uk
Total Pitches: 200 (C, CV & T)

Waren C & C Park
Waren Mill, Bamburgh
NE70 7EE
Tel: 01668 214366 109 J3
meadowhead.co.uk/parks/waren
Total Pitches: 458 (C, CV & T)

Warren Farm Holiday Centre
Brean Sands, Brean, Burnham-on-Sea
TA8 2RP
Tel: 01278 751227 28 D11
warrenfarm.co.uk
Total Pitches: 975 (C, CV & T)

Waterfoot Caravan Park
Pooley Bridge, Penrith,
Cumbria
CA11 0JF
Tel: 017684 86302 89 M2
waterfootpark.co.uk
Total Pitches: 184 (C, CV & T)

Watergate Bay Touring Park
Watergate Bay, Tregurrian
TR8 4AD
Tel: 01637 860387 6 B11
watergatebaytouringpark.co.uk
Total Pitches: 173 (C, CV & T)

Waterrow Touring Park
Wiveliscombe, Taunton
TA4 2AZ
Tel: 01984 623464 20 G8
waterrowpark.co.uk
Total Pitches: 42 (C, CV & T)

Wayfarers C & C Park
Relubbus Lane, St Hilary, Penzance
TR20 9EF
Tel: 01736 763326 2 E8
wayfarerspark.co.uk
Total Pitches: 35 (C, CV & T)

Wayside Holiday Park
Wrelton, Pickering,
North Yorkshire
YO18 8PG
Tel: 01751 472608 92 F9
waysideparks.co.uk
Total Pitches: 152 (C & CV)

Wells Touring Park
Haybridge, Wells
BA5 1AJ
Tel: 01749 676869 22 C4
wellstouringpark.co.uk
Total Pitches: 56 (C & CV)

Westbrook Park
Little Hereford, Herefordshire
SY8 4AU
Tel: 01584 711280 51 P7
westbrookpark.co.uk
Total Pitches: 59 (C, CV & T)

Wheathill Touring Park
Wheathill, Bridgnorth
WV16 6QT
Tel: 01584 823456 51 Q4
wheathillpark.co.uk
Total Pitches: 50 (C & CV)

Whitefield Forest Touring Park
Brading Road, Ryde,
Isle of Wight
PO33 1QL
Tel: 01983 617069 13 K7
whitefieldforest.co.uk
Total Pitches: 90 (C, CV & T)

Whitehill Country Park
Stoke Road, Paignton, Devon
TQ4 7PF
Tel: 01803 782338 5 P5
whitehill-park.co.uk
Total Pitches: 325 (C, CV & T)

Whitemead Caravan Park
East Burton Road, Wool
BH20 6HG
Tel: 01929 462241 11 K7
whitemeadcaravanpark.co.uk
Total Pitches: 105 (C, CV & T)

Willowbank Holiday Home
& Touring Park
Coastal Road, Ainsdale,
Southport
PR8 3ST
Tel: 01704 571566 75 K2
willowbankcp.co.uk
Total Pitches: 315 (C & CV)

Willow Valley Holiday Park
Bush, Bude, Cornwall
EX23 9LB
Tel: 01288 353104 7 J3
willowvalley.co.uk
Total Pitches: 44 (C, CV & T)

Wilson House Holiday Park
Lancaster Road, Out Rawcliffe,
Preston, Lancashire
PR3 6BN
Tel: 07807 560685 83 K6
whhp.co.uk
Total Pitches: 40 (C & CV)

Wolds View Touring Park
115 Brigg Road, Caistor
LN7 6RX
Tel: 01472 851099 80 B3
woldsviewtouringpark.co.uk
Total Pitches: 60 (C, CV & T)

Wooda Farm Holiday Park
Poughill, Bude
EX23 9HJ
Tel: 01288 352069 7 J3
wooda.co.uk
Total Pitches: 255 (C, CV & T)

Woodclose Caravan Park
High Casterton, Kirkby Lonsdale
LA6 2SE
Tel: 01524 271597 89 Q11
woodclosepark.com
Total Pitches: 117 (C & CV)

Woodhall Country Park
Stixwold Road, Woodhall Spa
LN10 6UJ
Tel: 01526 353710 80 D10
woodhallcountrypark.co.uk
Total Pitches: 120 (C, CV & T)

Woodland Springs Adult Touring Park
Venton, Drewsteignton
EX6 6PG
Tel: 01647 231648 8 D6
woodlandsprings.co.uk
Total Pitches: 93 (C, CV & T)

Woodlands Grove C & C Park
Blackawton, Dartmouth
TQ9 7DQ
Tel: 01803 712598 5 N6
woodlandsgrove.com
Total Pitches: 350 (C, CV & T)

Woodovis Park
Gulworthy, Tavistock
PL19 8NY
Tel: 01822 832968 7 N10
woodovis.com
Total Pitches: 89 (C, CV & T)

Yeatheridge Farm Caravan Park
East Worlington, Crediton,
Devon
EX17 4TN
Tel: 01884 860330 8 E3
yeatheridge.co.uk
Total Pitches: 122 (C, CV & T)

York Caravan Park
Stockton Lane, York,
North Yorkshire
YO32 9UB
Tel: 01904 424222 86 B4
yorkcaravanpark.com
Total Pitches: 55 (C & CV)

York Meadows Caravan Park
York Road, Sheriff Hutton, York,
North Yorkshire
YO60 6QP
Tel: 01347 878508 86 B2
yorkmeadowscaravanpark.com
Total Pitches: 60 (C, CV & T)

SCOTLAND

Auchenlarie Holiday Park
Gatehouse of Fleet
DG7 2EX
Tel: 01556 506200 95 P8
swalwellholidaygroup.co.uk
Total Pitches: 451 (C, CV & T)

Banff Links Caravan Park
Inverboyndie, Banff, Aberdeenshire
AB45 2JJ
Tel: 01261 812228 140 G3
banfflinkscaravanpark.co.uk
Total Pitches: 93 (C, CV & T)

Beecraigs C & C Site
Beecraigs Country Park,
The Visitor Centre, Linlithgow
EH49 6PL
Tel: 01506 284516 115 J6
westlothian.gov.uk/stay-at-beecraigs
Total Pitches: 38 (C, CV & T)

Belhaven Bay C & C Park
Belhaven Bay, Dunbar, East Lothian
EH42 1TS
Tel: 01368 865956 116 F5
meadowhead.co.uk
Total Pitches: 119 (C, CV & T)

Blair Castle Caravan Park
Blair Atholl, Pitlochry
PH18 5SR
Tel: 01796 481263 130 F11
blaircastlecaravanpark.co.uk
Total Pitches: 338 (C, CV & T)

Brighouse Bay Holiday Park
Brighouse Bay, Borgue, Kirkcudbright
DG6 4TS
Tel: 01557 870267 96 D9
gillespie-leisure.co.uk
Total Pitches: 418 (C, CV & T)

Cairnsmill Holiday Park
Largo Road, St Andrews
KY16 8NN
Tel: 01334 473604 125 K10
cairnsmill.co.uk
Total Pitches: 256 (C, CV & T)

Craig Tara Holiday Park
Ayr
KA7 4LB
Tel: 0800 975 7579 104 E6
haven.com/craigtara
Total Pitches: 1144 (C & CV)

Craigtoun Meadows Holiday Park
Mount Melville, St Andrews
KY16 8PQ
Tel: 01334 475959 125 J10
craigtounmeadows.co.uk
Total Pitches: 257 (C, CV & T)

Faskally Caravan Park
Pitlochry
PH16 5LA
Tel: 01796 472007 130 G12
faskally.co.uk
Total Pitches: 430 (C, CV & T)

Glenearly Caravan Park
Dalbeattie, Dumfries & Galloway
DG5 4NE
Tel: 01556 611393 96 G6
glenearlycaravanpark.co.uk
Total Pitches: 113 (C, CV & T)

Glen Nevis C & C Park
Glen Nevis, Fort William
PH33 6SX
Tel: 01397 702191 128 F10
glen-nevis.co.uk
Total Pitches: 415 (C, CV & T)

Hoddom Castle Caravan Park
Hoddom, Lockerbie
DG11 1AS
Tel: 01576 300251 97 N4
hoddomcastle.co.uk
Total Pitches: 265 (C, CV & T)

Huntly Castle Caravan Park
The Meadow, Huntly
AB54 4UJ
Tel: 01466 794999 140 E8
huntlycastle.co.uk
Total Pitches: 130 (C, CV & T)

Invercoe C & C Park
Ballachulish, Glencoe
PH49 4HP
Tel: 01855 811210 121 L1
invercoe.co.uk
Total Pitches: 66 (C, CV & T)

Linwater Caravan Park
West Clifton, East Calder
EH53 0HT
Tel: 0131 333 3326 115 K7
linwater.co.uk
Total Pitches: 64 (C, CV & T)

Milton of Fonab Caravan Park
Bridge Road, Pitlochry
PH16 5NA
Tel: 01796 472882 123 N1
fonab.co.uk
Total Pitches: 181 (C, CV & T)

Sands of Luce Holiday Park
Sands of Luce, Sandhead, Stranraer
DG9 9JN
Tel: 01776 830456 94 G8
sandsofluce.com
Total Pitches: 350 (C, CV & T)

Seal Shore Camping and Touring Site
Kildonan, Isle of Arran, North Ayrshire
KA27 8SE
Tel: 01770 820320 103 Q5
campingarran.com
Total Pitches: 47 (C, CV & T)

Seaward Holiday Park
Dhoon Bay, Kirkudbright
DG6 4TJ
Tel: 01557 870267 96 D8
gillespie-leisure.co.uk
Total Pitches: 84 (C, CV & T)

Seton Sands Holiday Village
Longniddry
EH32 0QF
Tel: 01875 813333 116 A6
haven.com/setonsands
Total Pitches: 640 (C & CV)

Shieling Holidays Mull
Craignure, Isle of Mull, Argyll & Bute
PA65 6AY
Tel: 01680 812496 120 D5
shielingholidays.co.uk
Total Pitches: 106 (C, CV & T)

Silver Sands Holiday Park
Covesea, West Beach, Lossiemouth
IV31 6SP
Tel: 01343 813262 147 M11
silver-sands.co.uk
Total Pitches: 340 (C, CV & T)

Skye C & C Club Site
Loch Greshornish, Borve, Arnisort,
Edinbane, Isle of Skye
IV51 9PS
Tel: 01470 582230 134 F5
campingandcaravanningclub.co.uk/skye
Total Pitches: 107 (C, CV & T)

Thurston Manor Leisure Park
Innerwick, Dunbar
EH42 1SA
Tel: 01368 840643 116 G6
thurstonmanor.co.uk
Total Pitches: 690 (C & CV)

Witches Craig C & C Park
Blairlogie, Stirling
FK9 5PX
Tel: 01786 474947 114 E2
witchescraig.co.uk
Total Pitches: 60 (C, CV & T)

WALES

Bron Derw Touring Caravan Park
Llanrwst
LL26 0YT
Tel: 01492 640494 73 N11
bronderw-wales.co.uk
Total Pitches: 48 (C & CV)

Bryn Gloch C & C Park
Betws Garmon, Caernarfon
LL54 7YY
Tel: 01286 650216 73 J12
campwales.co.uk
Total Pitches: 177 (C, CV & T)

Caerfai Bay Caravan & Tent Park
Caerfai Bay, St Davids, Haverfordwest
SA62 6QT
Tel: 01437 720274 36 E5
caerfaibay.co.uk
Total Pitches: 136 (C, CV & T)

Cenarth Falls Holiday Park
Cenarth, Newcastle Emlyn
SA38 9JS
Tel: 01239 710345 37 P2
cenarth-holipark.co.uk
Total Pitches: 119 (C, CV & T)

Daisy Bank Caravan Park
Snead, Montgomery
SY15 6EB
Tel: 01588 620471 51 K2
daisy-bank.co.uk
Total Pitches: 78 (C, CV & T)

Dinlle Caravan Park
Dinas Dinlle, Caernarfon
LL54 5TW
Tel: 01286 830324 72 G12
thornleyleisure.co.uk
Total Pitches: 349 (C, CV & T)

Eisteddfa
Eisteddfa Lodge, Pentrefelin, Criccieth
LL52 0PT
Tel: 01766 522696 61 J4
eisteddfapark.co.uk
Total Pitches: 116 (C, CV & T)

Fforest Fields C & C Park
Hundred House, Builth Wells
LD1 5RT
Tel: 01982 570406 50 F10
fforestfields.co.uk
Total Pitches: 122 (C, CV & T)

Fishguard Bay Resort
Garn Gelli, Fishguard
SA65 9ET
Tel: 01348 811415 37 J3
fishguardbay.com
Total Pitches: 102 (C, CV & T)

Greenacres Holiday Park
Black Rock Sands, Morfa Bychan,
Porthmadog
LL49 9YF
Tel: 01766 512781 61 J5
haven.com/greenacres
Total Pitches: 945 (C & CV)

Hafan y Môr Holiday Park
Pwllheli
LL53 6HJ
Tel: 01758 612112 60 G5
haven.com/hafanymor
Total Pitches: 875 (C & CV)

Hendre Mynach Touring C & C Park
Llanaber Road, Barmouth
LL42 1YR
Tel: 01341 280262 61 K8
hendremynach.co.uk
Total Pitches: 241 (C, CV & T)

Home Farm Caravan Park
Marian-glas, Isle of Anglesey
LL73 8PH
Tel: 01248 410614 72 H7
homefarm-anglesey.co.uk
Total Pitches: 186 (C, CV & T)

Islawrffordd Caravan Park
Talybont, Barmouth
LL43 2AQ
Tel: 01341 247269 61 K8
islawrffordd.co.uk
Total Pitches: 306 (C & CV)

Kiln Park Holiday Centre
Marsh Road, Tenby
SA70 8RB
Tel: 01834 844121 37 M10
haven.com/kilnpark
Total Pitches: 849 (C, CV & T)

Pencelli Castle C & C Park
Pencelli, Brecon
LD3 7LX
Tel: 01874 665451 39 P7
pencelli-castle.com
Total Pitches: 80 (C, CV & T)

Penisar Mynydd Caravan Park
Caerwys Road, Rhuallt, St Asaph
LL17 0TY
Tel: 01745 582227 74 F8
penisarmynydd.co.uk
Total Pitches: 71 (C, CV & T)

Plassey Holiday Park
The Plassey, Eyton, Wrexham
LL13 0SP
Tel: 01978 780277 63 K3
plassey.com
Total Pitches: 123 (C, CV & T)

Pont Kemys C & C Park
Chainbridge, Abergavenny
NP7 9DS
Tel: 01873 880688 40 D10
pontkemys.com
Total Pitches: 65 (C, CV & T)

Presthaven Sands Holiday Park
Gronant, Prestatyn
LL19 9TT
Tel: 01745 856471 74 F7
haven.com/presthavensands
Total Pitches: 1102 (C & CV)

Red Kite Touring Park
Van Road, Llanidloes
SY18 6NG
Tel: 01686 412122 50 C4
redkitetouringpark.co.uk
Total Pitches: 66 (C & CV)

Riverside Camping
Seiont Nurseries, Pont Rug, Caernarfon
LL55 2BB
Tel: 01286 678781 72 H11
riversidecamping.co.uk
Total Pitches: 73 (C, CV & T)

The Trotting Mare Caravan Park
Overton, Wrexham
LL13 0LE
Tel: 01978 711963 63 L4
thetrottingmare.co.uk
Total Pitches: 65 (C, CV & T)

Trawsdir Touring C & C Park
Llanaber, Barmouth
LL42 1RR
Tel: 01341 280999 61 K8
barmouthholidays.co.uk
Total Pitches: 80 (C, CV & T)

Tyddyn Isaf Caravan Park
Lligwy Bay, Dulas,
Isle of Anglesey
LL70 9PQ
Tel: 01248 410203 72 H6
tyddynisaf.co.uk
Total Pitches: 136 (C, CV & T)

White Tower Caravan Park
Llandwrog, Caernarfon
LL54 5UH
Tel: 01286 830649 72 G12
whitetowerpark.co.uk
Total Pitches: 52 (C, CV & T)

CHANNEL ISLANDS

La Bailloterie Camping
Bailloterie Lane, Vale, Guernsey
GY3 5HA
Tel: 01481 243636 12 c1
campinginguernsey.com
Total Pitches: 109 (C, CV & T)

Motoring information

M4	Motorway with number	3	Restricted primary route junctions	Narrow primary/other A/B road with passing places (Scotland)	Railway line, in tunnel
Toll / T4	Toll motorway with toll station	S	Primary route service area	Road under construction	Railway station, tram stop, level crossing
6	Motorway junction with and without number	BATH	Primary route destination	Road tunnel	Preserved or tourist railway
5	Restricted motorway junctions	A1123	Other A road single/ dual carriageway	Toll → Road toll, steep gradient (arrows point downhill)	Airport (major/minor)
Fleet S / R Todhills	Motorway service area, rest area	B2070	B road single/ dual carriageway	5 Distance in miles between symbols	Heliport
	Motorway and junction under construction		Minor road more than 4 metres wide, less than 4 metres wide	Vehicle ferry (all year, seasonal)	International freight terminal
A3	Primary route single/ dual carriageway		Roundabout	Fast vehicle ferry or catamaran	24-hour Accident & Emergency hospital
1	Primary route junction with and without number		Interchange/junction	Passenger ferry (all year, seasonal)	Crematorium

P·R	Park and Ride (at least 6 days per week)
	City, town, village or other built-up area
628 ▲	Height in metres
Lecht Summit 637	Mountain pass
	Snow gates (on main routes)
	National boundary
	County or administrative boundary
	City with clean air zone, low emission zone (visit *www.gov.uk/guidance/ driving-in-a-clean-air-zone*)

Touring information

To avoid disappointment, check opening times before visiting

	Scenic route		Industrial interest		RSPB site		Cave or cavern		National Trust site

i	Tourist Information Centre		Aqueduct or viaduct		National Nature Reserve (England, Scotland, Wales)		Windmill, monument or memorial
i	Tourist Information Centre (seasonal)		Vineyard		Local nature reserve		Beach (award winning)
V	Visitor or heritage centre		Brewery or distillery		Wildlife Trust reserve		Lighthouse
	Picnic site		Garden		Forest drive		Golf course
	Caravan site (AA inspected)		Arboretum		National trail		Football stadium
▲	Camping site (AA inspected)		Country park		Viewpoint		County cricket ground
▲	Caravan & camping site (AA inspected)		Showground		Waterfall		Rugby Union national stadium
	Abbey, cathedral or priory		Theme park		Hill-fort		International athletics stadium
	Ruined abbey, cathedral or priory		Farm or animal centre		Roman antiquity		Horse racing, show jumping
✗	Castle		Zoological or wildlife collection		Prehistoric monument		Motor-racing circuit
	Historic house or building		Bird collection	1066	Battle site with year		Air show venue
M	Museum or art gallery		Aquarium		Preserved or tourist railway		Ski slope (natural, artificial)

	National Trust for Scotland site
	English Heritage site
	Historic Scotland site
	Cadw (Welsh heritage) site
★	Other place of interest
☐	Boxed symbols indicate attractions within urban area
⊙	World Heritage Site (UNESCO)
	National Park and National Scenic Area (Scotland)
	Forest Park
	Sandy beach
	Heritage coast
	Major shopping centre

Town plans

2	Motorway and junction		Railway station		Toilet, with facilities for the less able	i	Tourist Information Centre
4	Primary road single/ dual carriageway and numbered junction		Tramway		Building of interest	V	Visitor or heritage centre
37	A road single/ dual carriageway and numbered junction	⊖	London Underground station		Ruined building		Post Office
	B road single/ dual carriageway	⊖	London Overground station		City wall		Public library
	Local road single/ dual carriageway	⊖	Rail interchange		Cliff lift		Shopping centre
	Other road single/dual carriageway, minor road	⊖	Docklands Light Railway (DLR) station		Escarpment		Shopmobility
→	One-way, gated/ closed road	○	Light rapid transit system station		River/canal, lake		Theatre or performing arts centre
	Restricted access road	/ H	Airport, heliport		Lock, weir		Cinema
	Pedestrian area	R	Railair terminal		Park/sports ground	M	Museum
- - - -	Footpath	P·R	Park and Ride (at least 6 days per week)		Cemetery	✗	Castle
- - - -	Road under construction	P P	Car park, with electric charging point		Woodland		Castle mound
	Road tunnel		Bus/coach station		Built-up area	•	Monument, memorial, statue
	Level crossing	H H	Hospital, 24-hour Accident & Emergency hospital		Beach		Viewpoint

†	Abbey, chapel, church
✡	Synagogue
☾	Mosque
	Golf course
	Racecourse
	Nature reserve
	Aquarium
⊙	World Heritage Site (UNESCO)
	English Heritage site
	Historic Scotland site
	Cadw (Welsh heritage) site
	National Trust site
	National Trust Scotland site

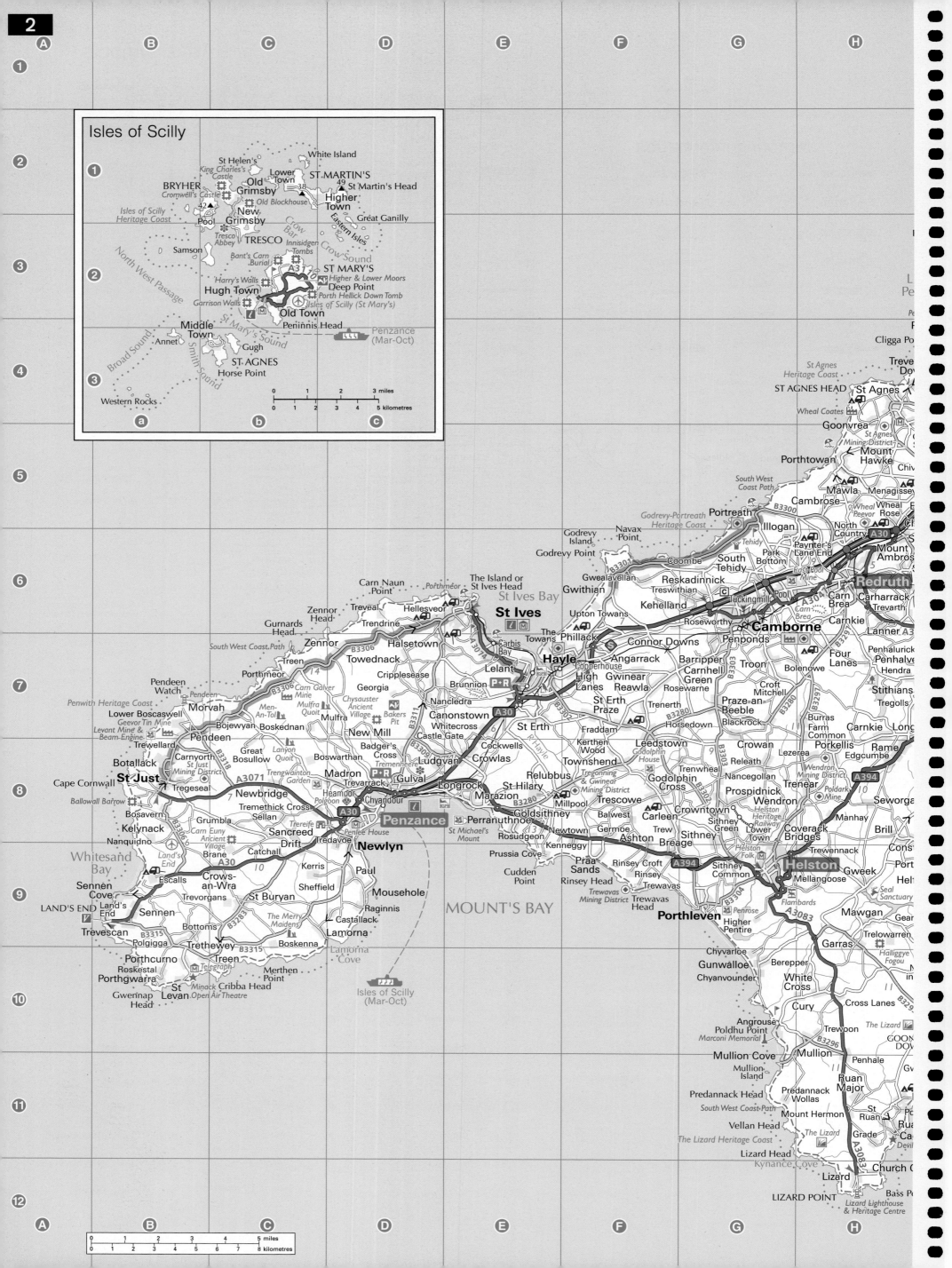

A B C D E F G H

1
2
3
4
5
6
7
8
9
10
11
12

Isles of Scilly

St Helen's
White Island
King Charles's Castle
Lower Town
ST. MARTIN'S
BRYHER
Old Grimsby
St Martin's Head
Cromwell's Castle
Old Blockhouse
Higher Town
New Grimsby
Great Ganilly
Isles of Scilly Heritage Coast
Pool
Eastern Isles
Samson
Tresco Abbey
TRESCO
Crow Bar
Bant's Carn Burial
Innisidgen Tombs
Crow Sound
North West Passage
'Harry's Walls
ST MARY'S
Higher & Lower Moors
Hugh Town
Deep Point
Porth Hellick Down Tomb
Garrison Walls
Isles of Scilly (St Mary's)
Old Town
Middle Town
Peninnis Head
Penzance (Mar-Oct)
Annet
St Mary's Sound
Gugh
Broad Sound
ST. AGNES
Smith Sound
Horse Point
Western Rocks

0   1   2   3 miles
0 1 2 3 4 5 kilometres

a   b   c

Carn Naun Point
Porthmeor
The Island or St Ives Head
St Ives Bay
St Agnes Heritage Coast
St Agnes
Zennor Head
Treveal
Hellesveor
St Ives
ST AGNES HEAD
Wheal Coates
Gurnards Head
Trendrine
Carbis Bay
The Towans
Goonvrea
Porthtowan
Mount Hawke
South West Coast Path
Zennor
Halsetown
Hayle
Phillack
St Agnes Mining District
Mawla
Menagissey
Towednack
Lelant
Copperhouse
Angarrack
Mount Rose
Cambrose
Wheal Peevor
Godrevy-Portreath Heritage Coast
Cripplesease
Brunnion
High Gwinear
Barripper
North Country
Mount Ambrose
Treen
Carn Galver Mine
Georgia
Nancledra
P+R
Lanes
Reawla
Carnhell Green
Redruth
Godrevy Island
Illogan
Porthmeor
Mulfra Quoit
Chysauster Ancient Village
Canonstown
Rosewarne
Reskadinnick
Treswithian
Park Bottom
Paynter's Lane End
Camborne
Godrevy Point
Men-An-Tol
Bakers Pit
Whitecross
St Erth
Praze
Trenerth
Penponds
Tuckingmill
Pendeen Watch
Mulfra
Castle Gate
St Erth
Fraddam
Leedstown
Horsedown
Praze-an-Beeble
Troon
Carnkie
Lanner
Penwith Heritage Coast
Pendeen
Bojewyan
Boskednan
New Mill
Cockwells
Kerthen Wood
Crowan
Releath
Stithians
Lower Boscaswell
Geevor Tin Mine
Morvah
Badger's Cross
Ludgvan
Crowlas
Townshend
Croft Mitchell
Releath
Nancegollan
Burras
Trewellard
Levant Mine & Beam Engine
Boswarthan
Tremenheere
Godolphin House
Praze-an-Beeble
Carnkie Farm Common
Pendeen
Great Bosullow
Lanyon Quoit
Trengwainton Garden
Madron
Relubbus
Tregonning & Gwinear Mining District
Godolphin Cross
Trenwheal
Nancegollan
Prospidnick
Trenear
Carnyorth
St Just Mining District
Heamoor
P+R
Gulval
Longrock
St-Hilary
Germoe
Trescowe
Crowntown
Wendron Mining District
Botallack
Chyandour
Marazion
Millpool
Balwest
Sithney Green
Wendron
Trenear
A394
St Just
Trevarrack
Penzance
Goldsithney
Newtown
Carleen
Poldark Mine
Cape Cornwall
Tregeseal
Newbridge
Tremethick Cross
Penlee House
Perranuthnoe
Rosudgeon
Ashton
Trew
Sithney
Lower Town
Helston Heritage Folk
Helston
Sewerga
Ballowall Barrow
Bosavern
Grumbla
Sellan
Trereife
St Michael's Mount
Kenneggy
Breage
Germoe
Coverack Bridges
Trewennack
Bosavern
Kelynack
Carn Euny Ancient Village
Sancreed
Chyandour
Prussia Cove
Rinsey Croft
Sithney Common
Mellangoose
Gweek
Nanquidno
Brane
Drift
Tredavoe
Newlyn
Cudden Point
Praa Sands
Rinsey
Helston
Brill
Whitesand Bay
Land's End
A30
Catchall
Kerris
Paul
Rinsey Head
Trewavas Mining District
Trewavas Head
A3083
Mawgan
Sennen Cove
Escalls
Crows-an-Wra
Sheffield
Mousehole
Porthleven
Higher Pentire
Trelowarren
Land's End
Sennen
Trevorgans
St Buryan
Raginnis
MOUNT'S BAY
Garras
LAND'S END
Bottoms
The Merry Maidens
Castallack
Lamorna
Chyvarloe
Halliggye Fogou
Trevescan
Polgigga
Trethewey
Treen
Boskenna
Lamorna Cove
Isles of Scilly (Mar-Oct)
Gunwalloe
Berepper
Porthcurno
Roskestal
Minack Open Air Theatre
Cribba Head
Merthen Point
Chyanvounder
White Cross
Porthgwarra
Telegraph
Angrouse
Poldhu Point
Marconi Memorial
Gwennap Head
St Levan
Mullion Cove
Trewoon
Cross Lanes
Cury
Mullion Island
Mullion
Penhale
Predannack Head
Ruan Major
Predannack Wollas
Mount Hermon
St Ruan
Vellan Head
South West Coast Path
Grade
The Lizard
Lizard Head
Kynance Cove
Church
The Lizard Heritage Coast
Lizard
Bass
LIZARD POINT
Lizard Lighthouse & Heritage Centre

A B C D E F G H

0   1   2   3   4   5 miles
0 1 2 3 4 5 6 7 8 kilometres

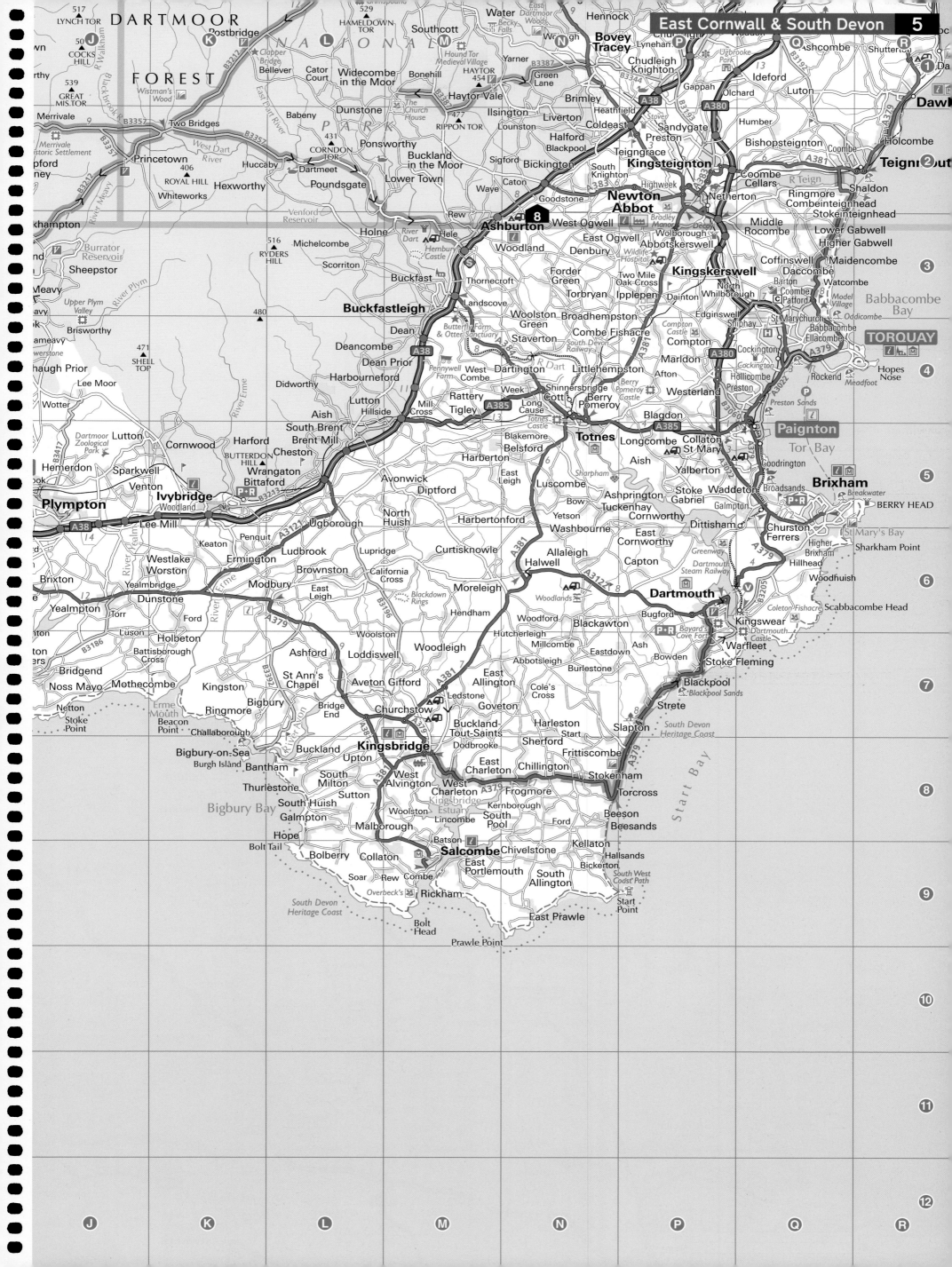

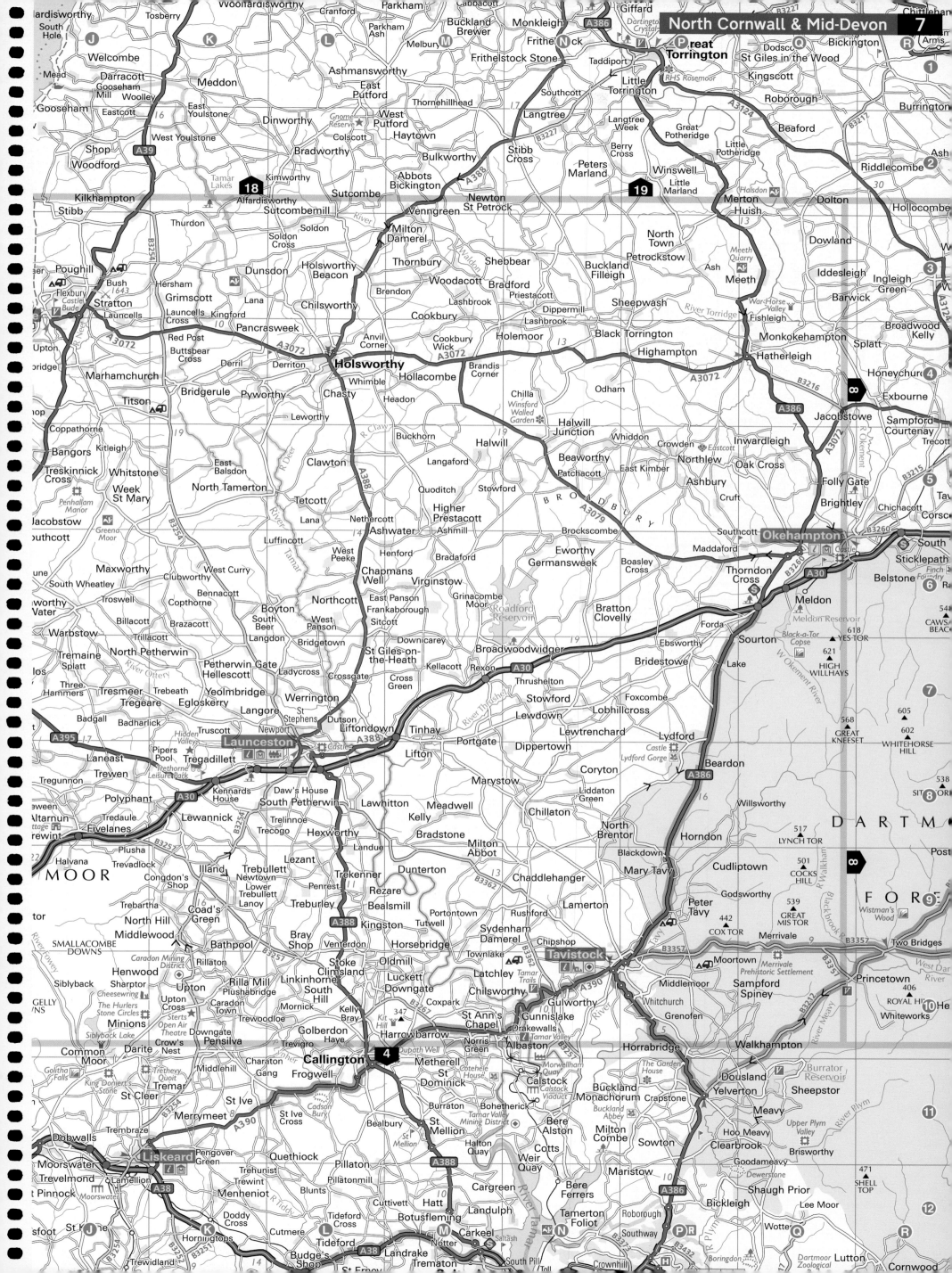

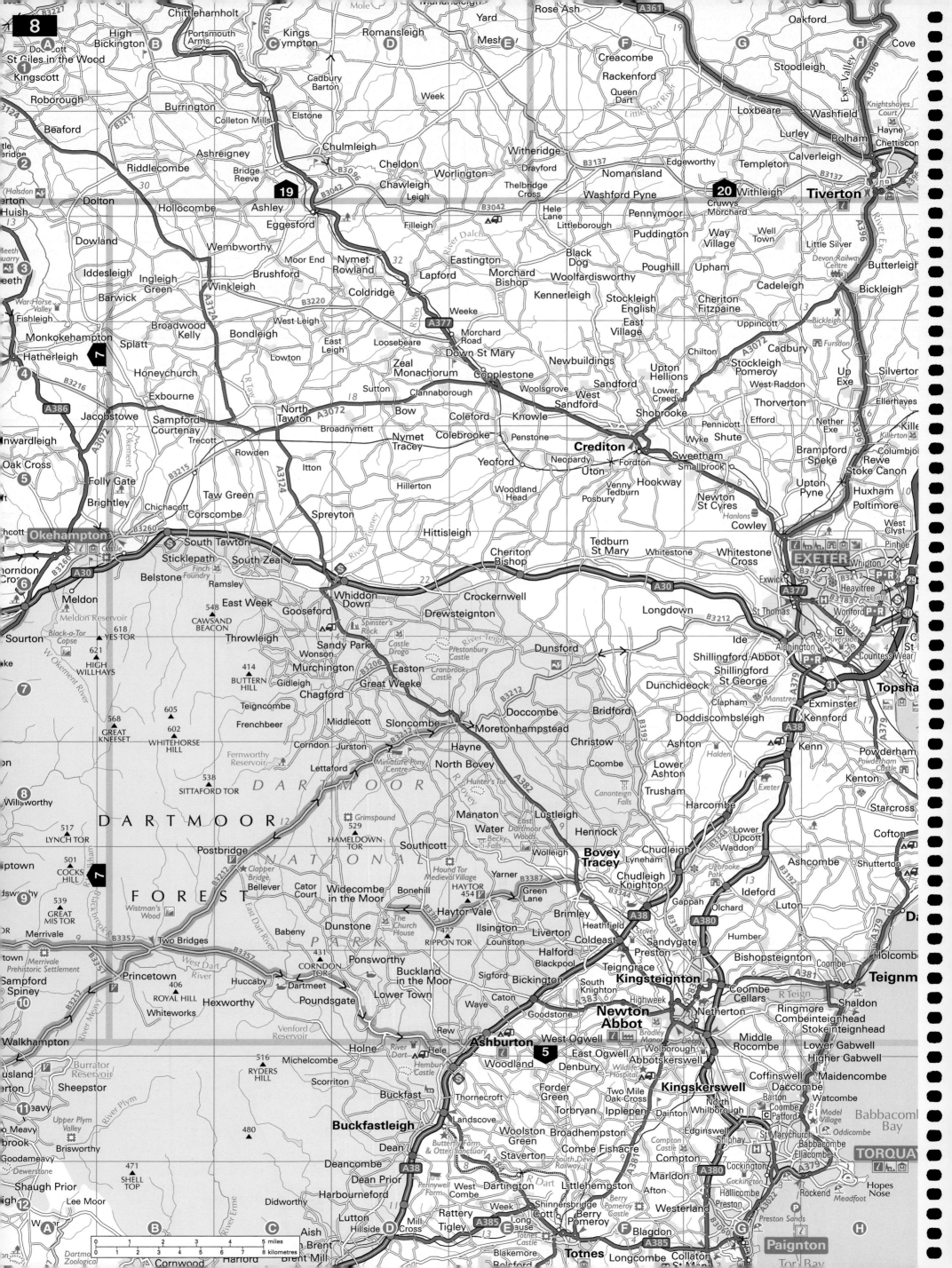

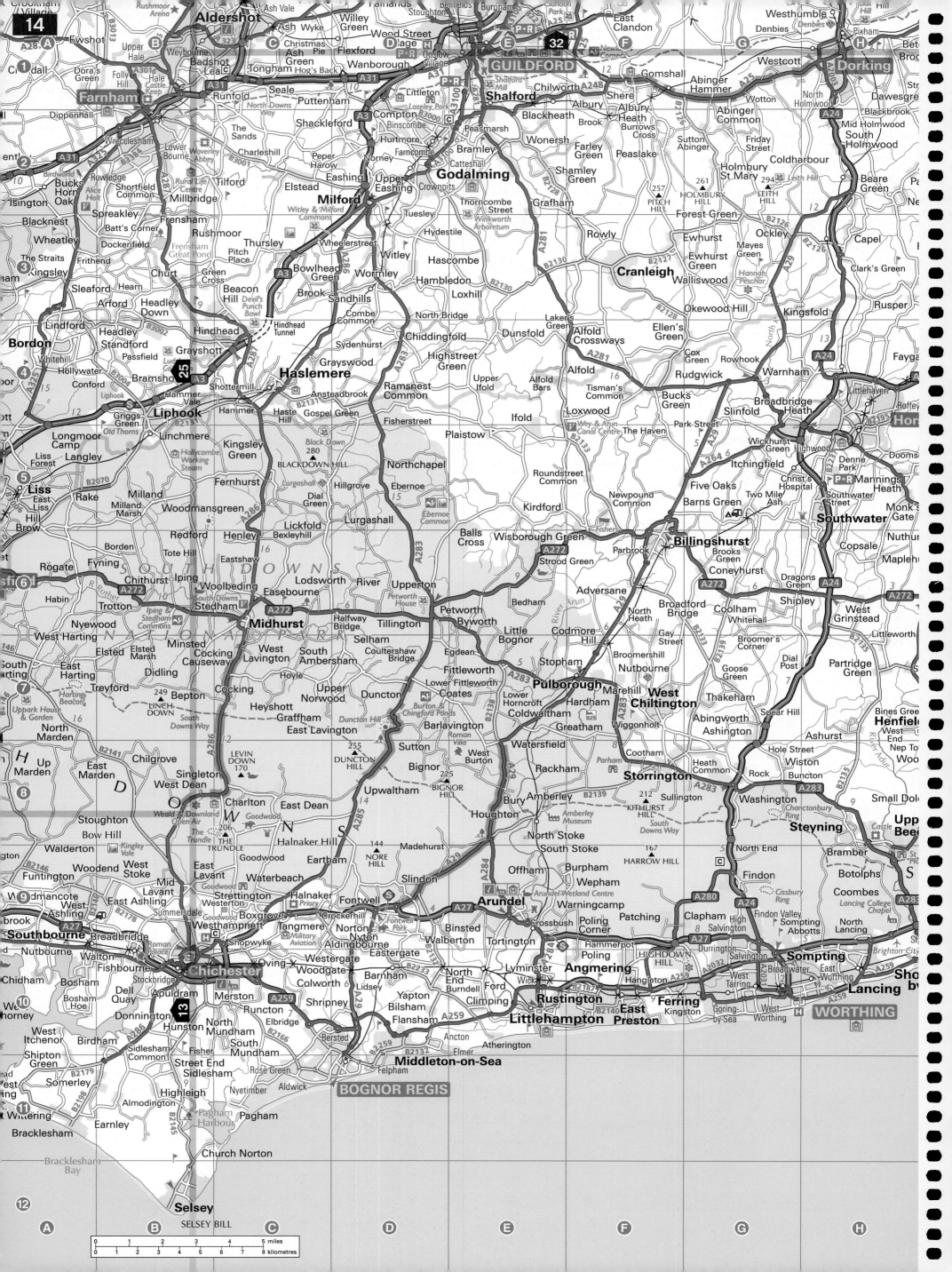

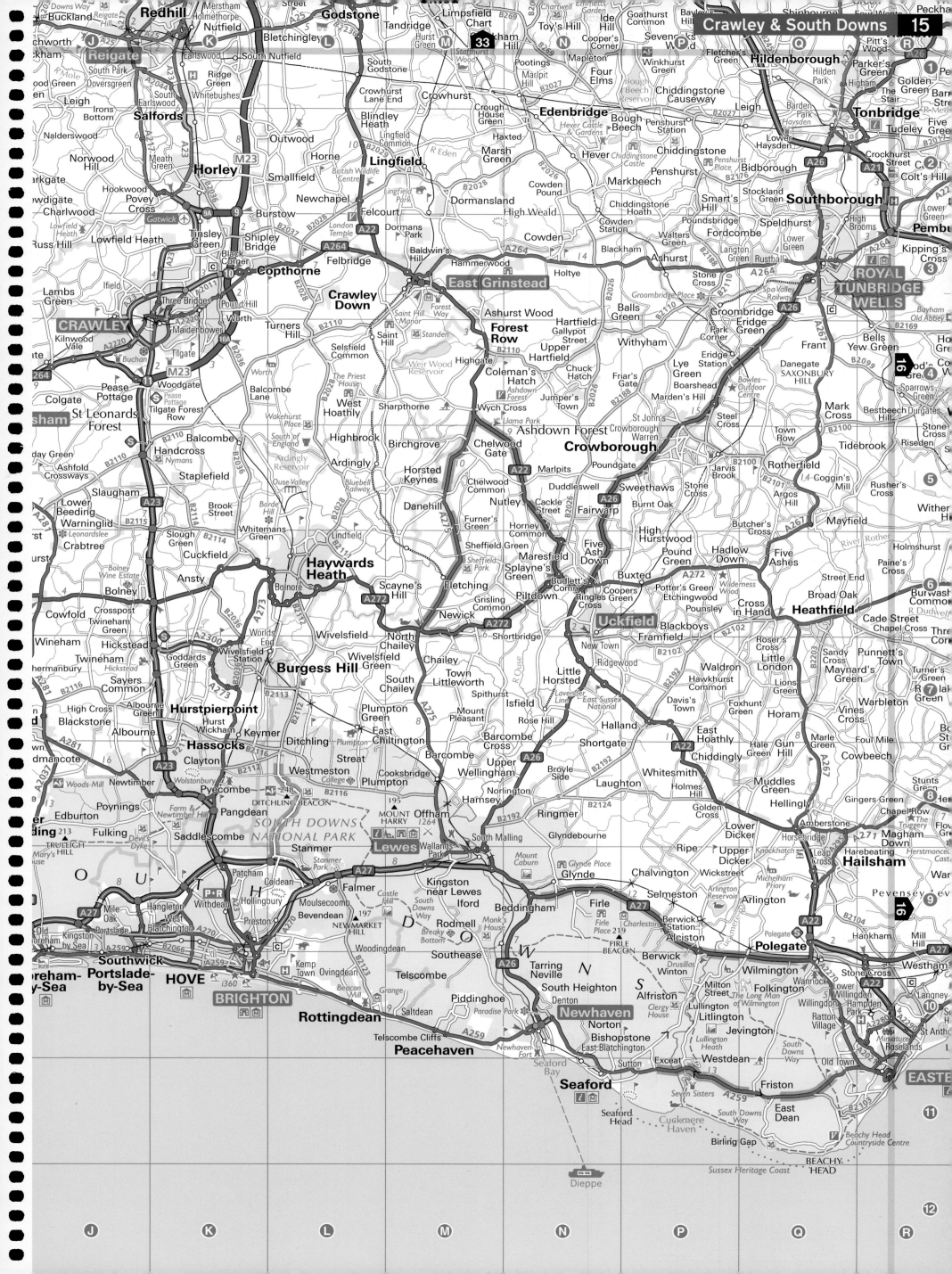

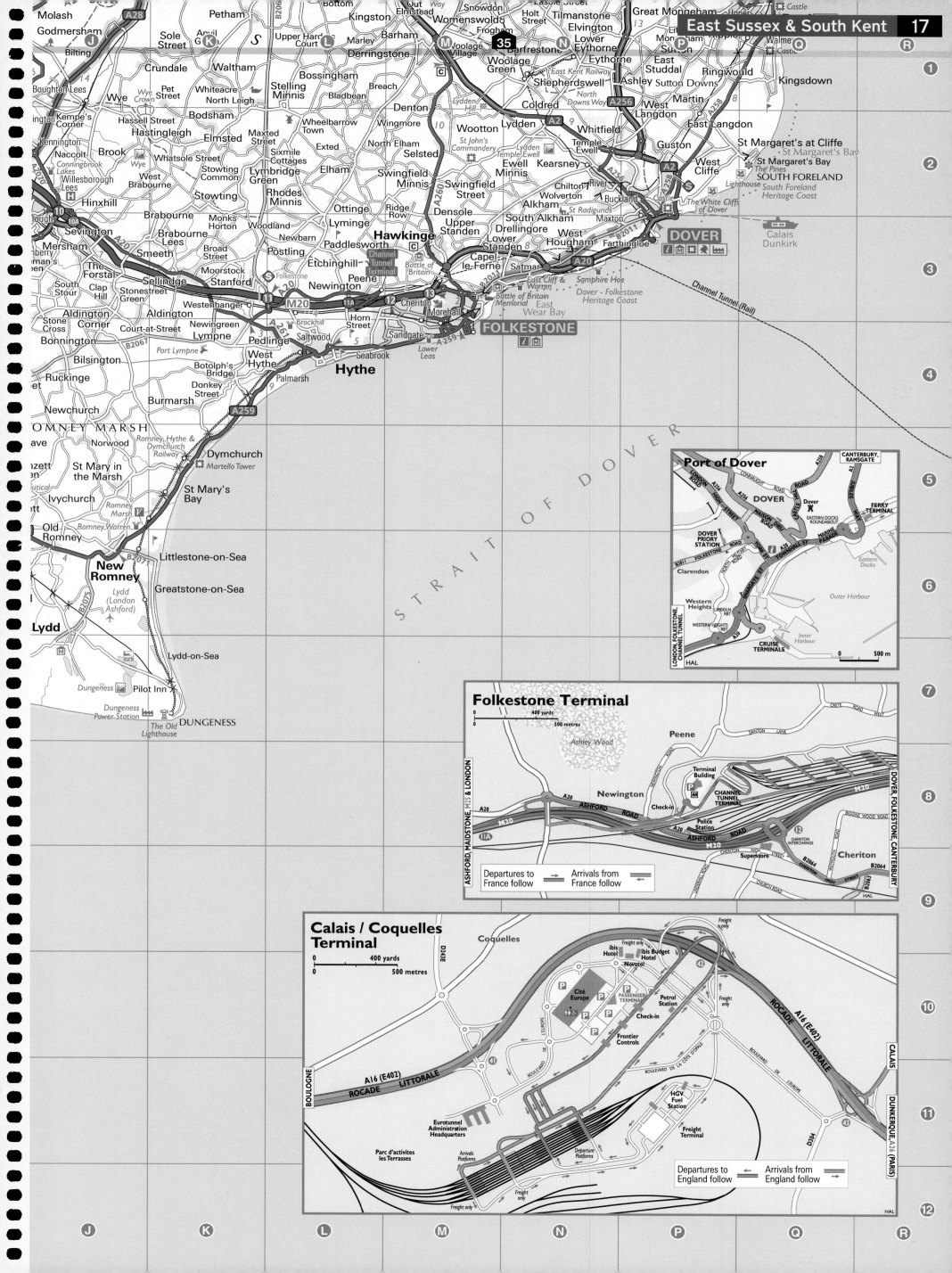

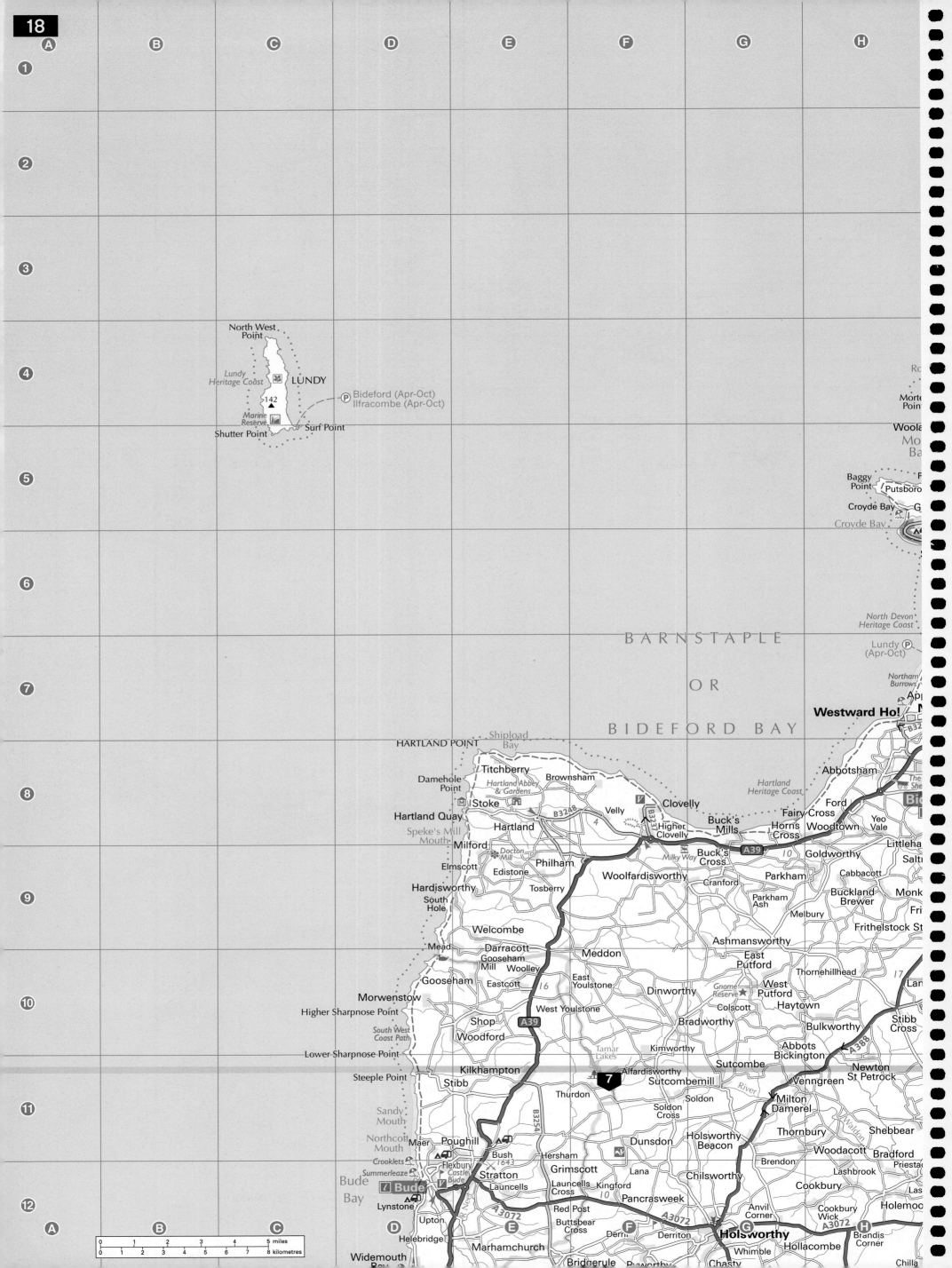

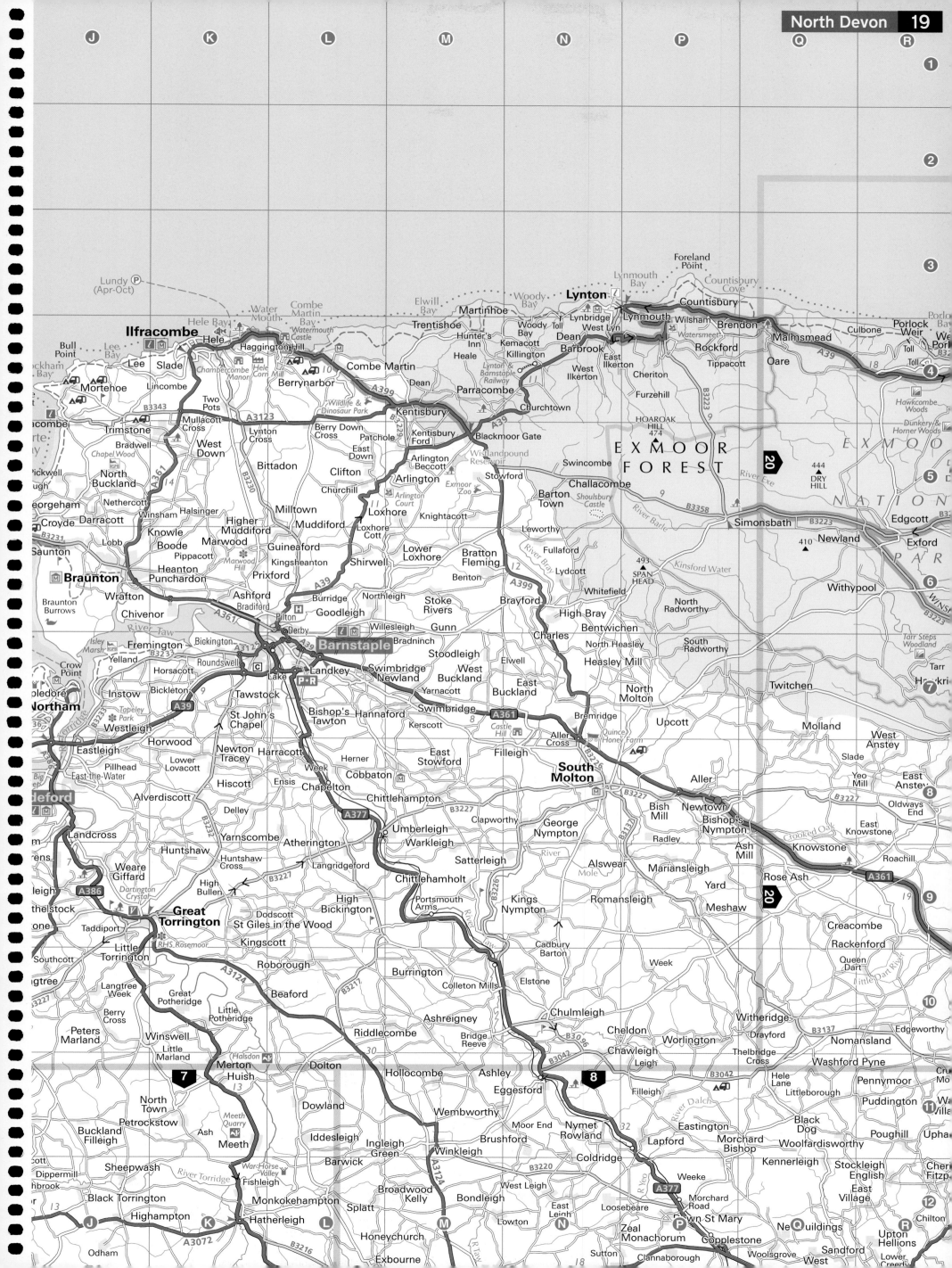

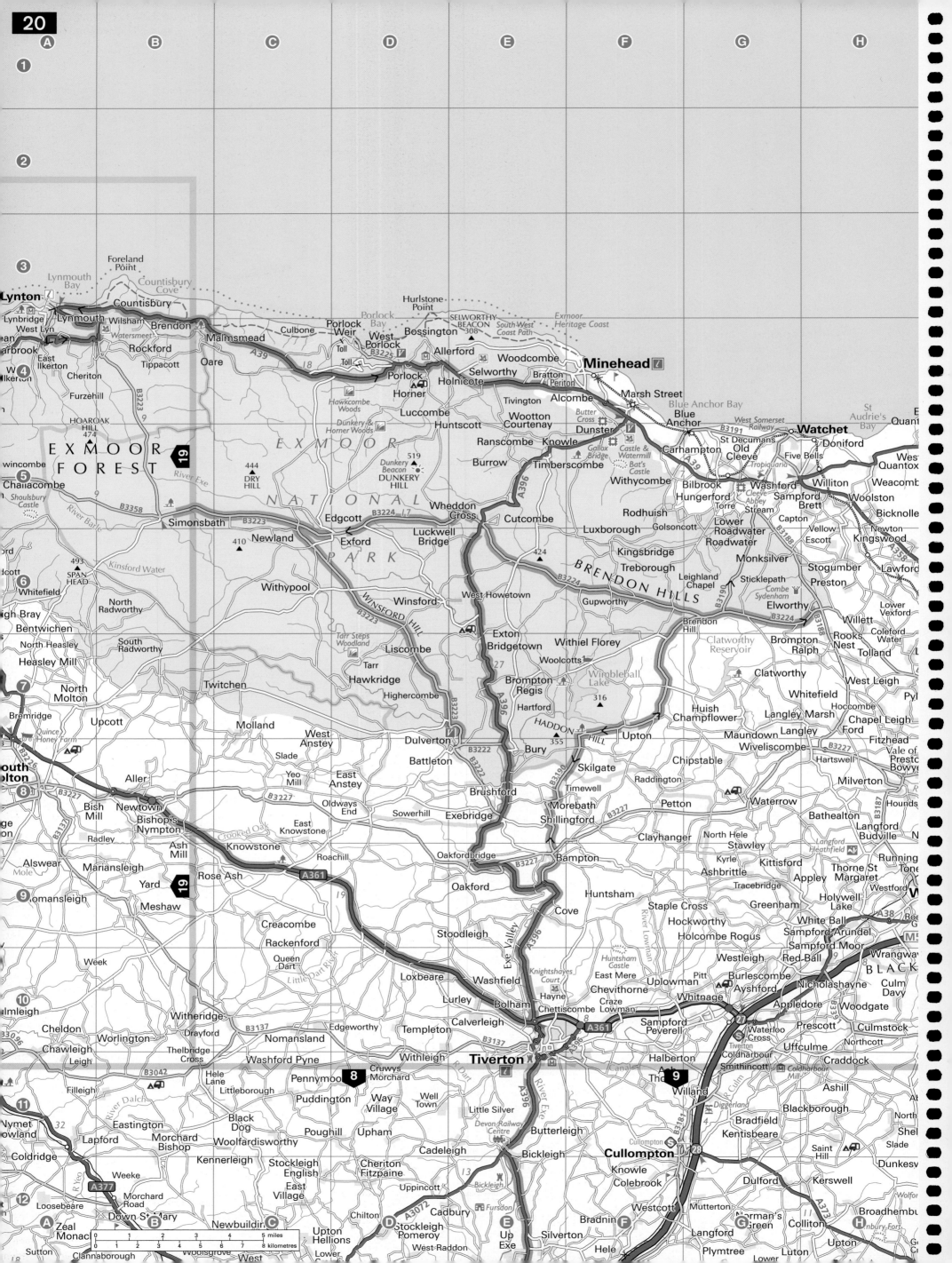

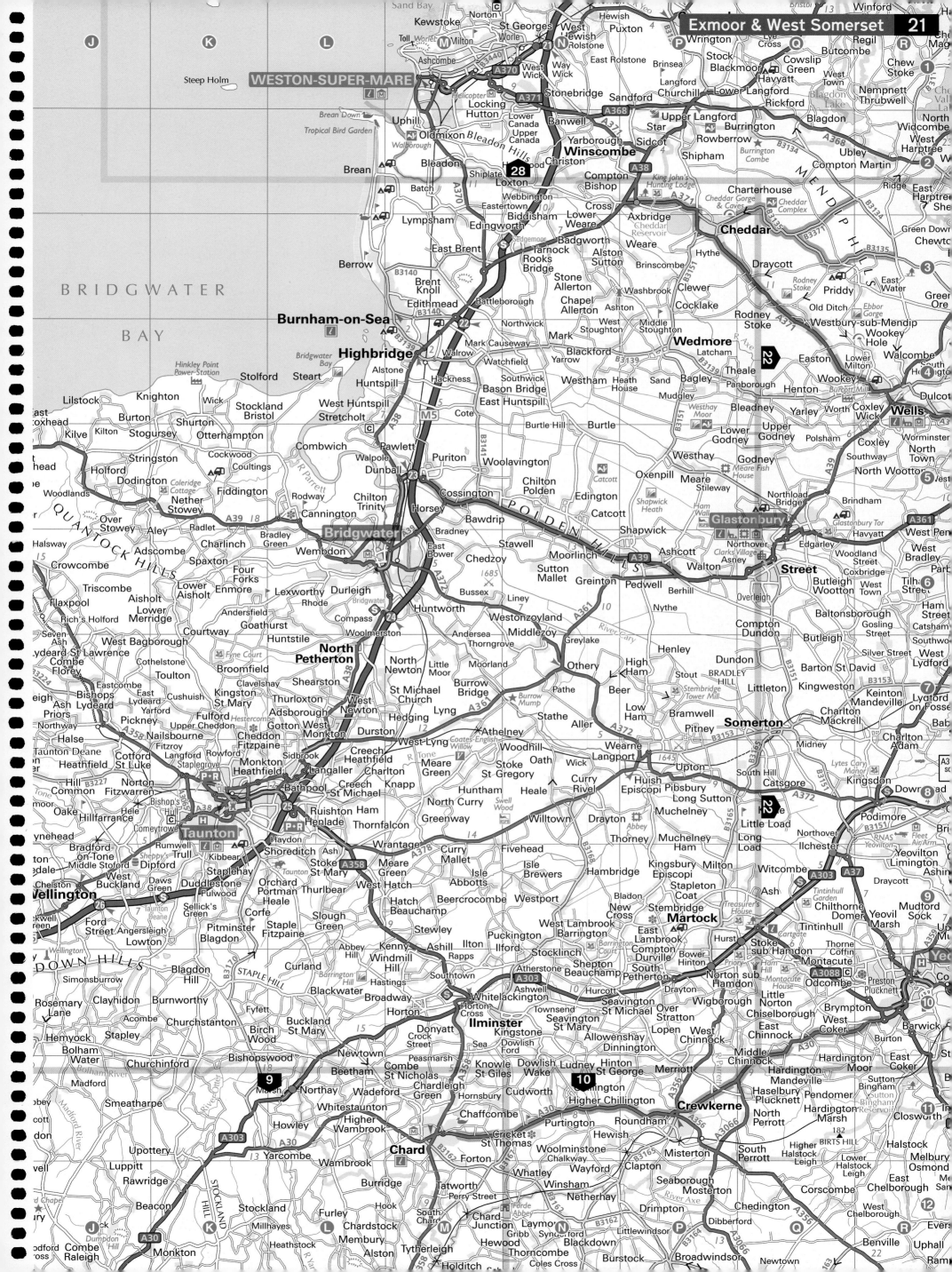

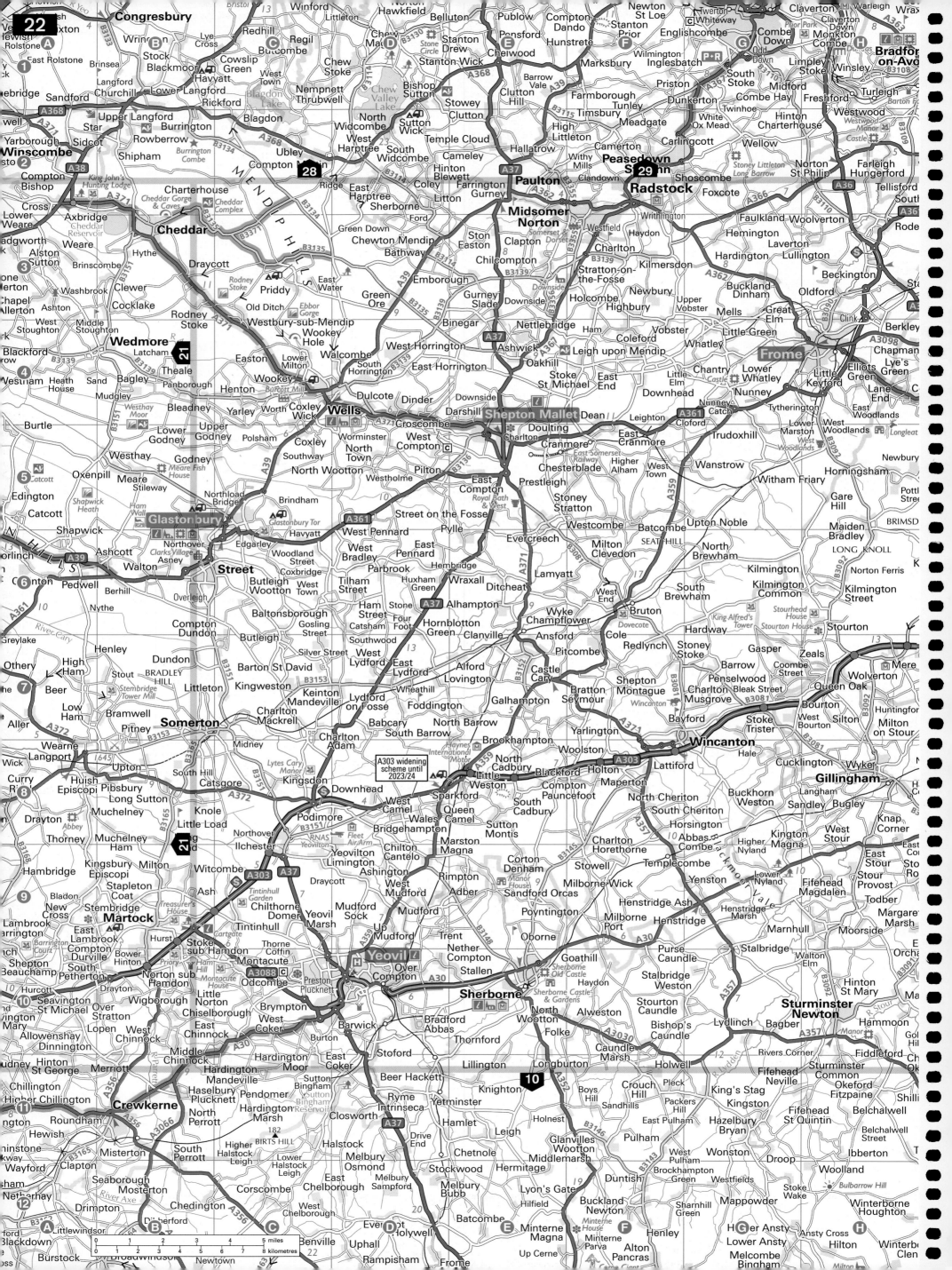

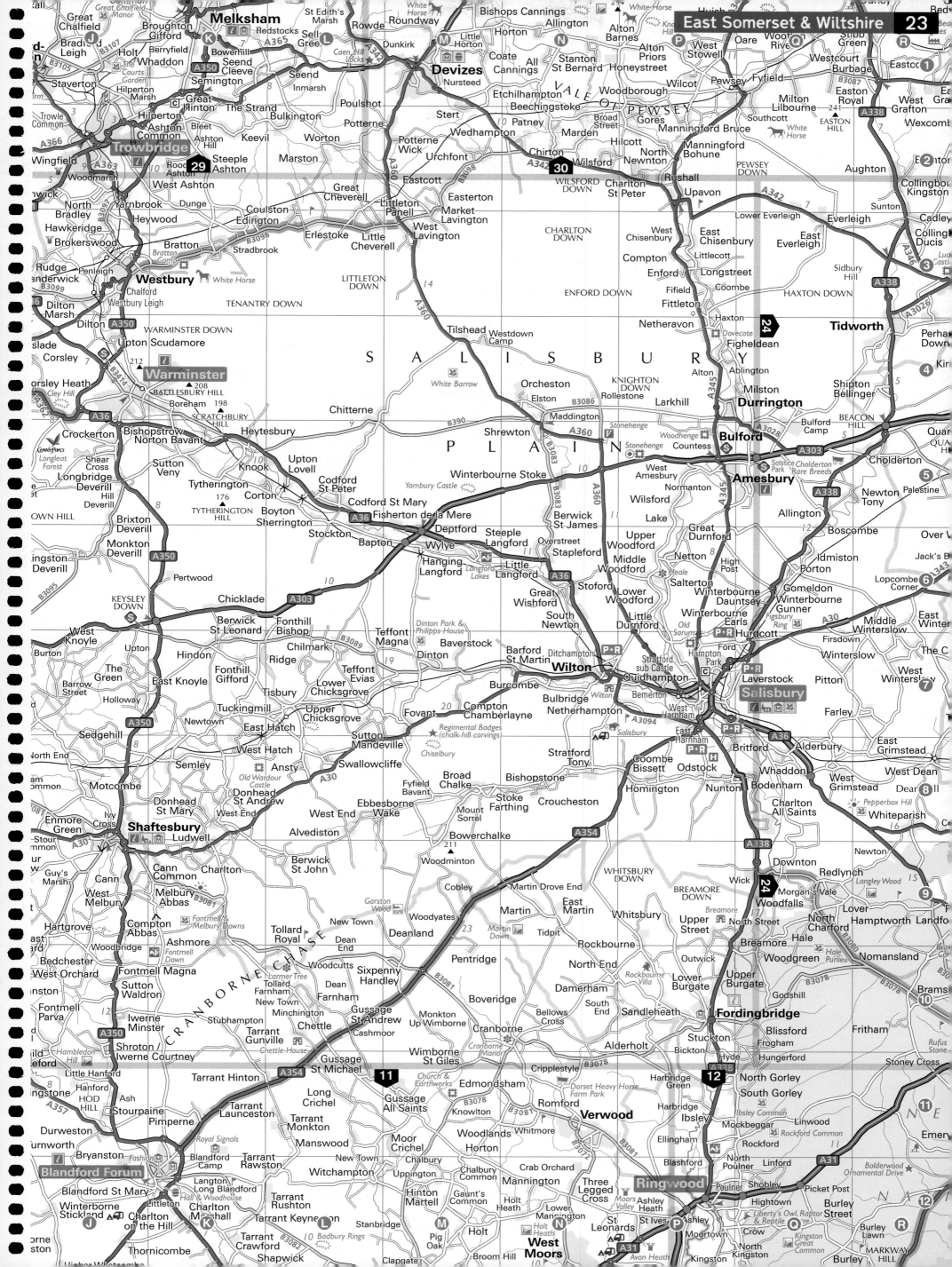

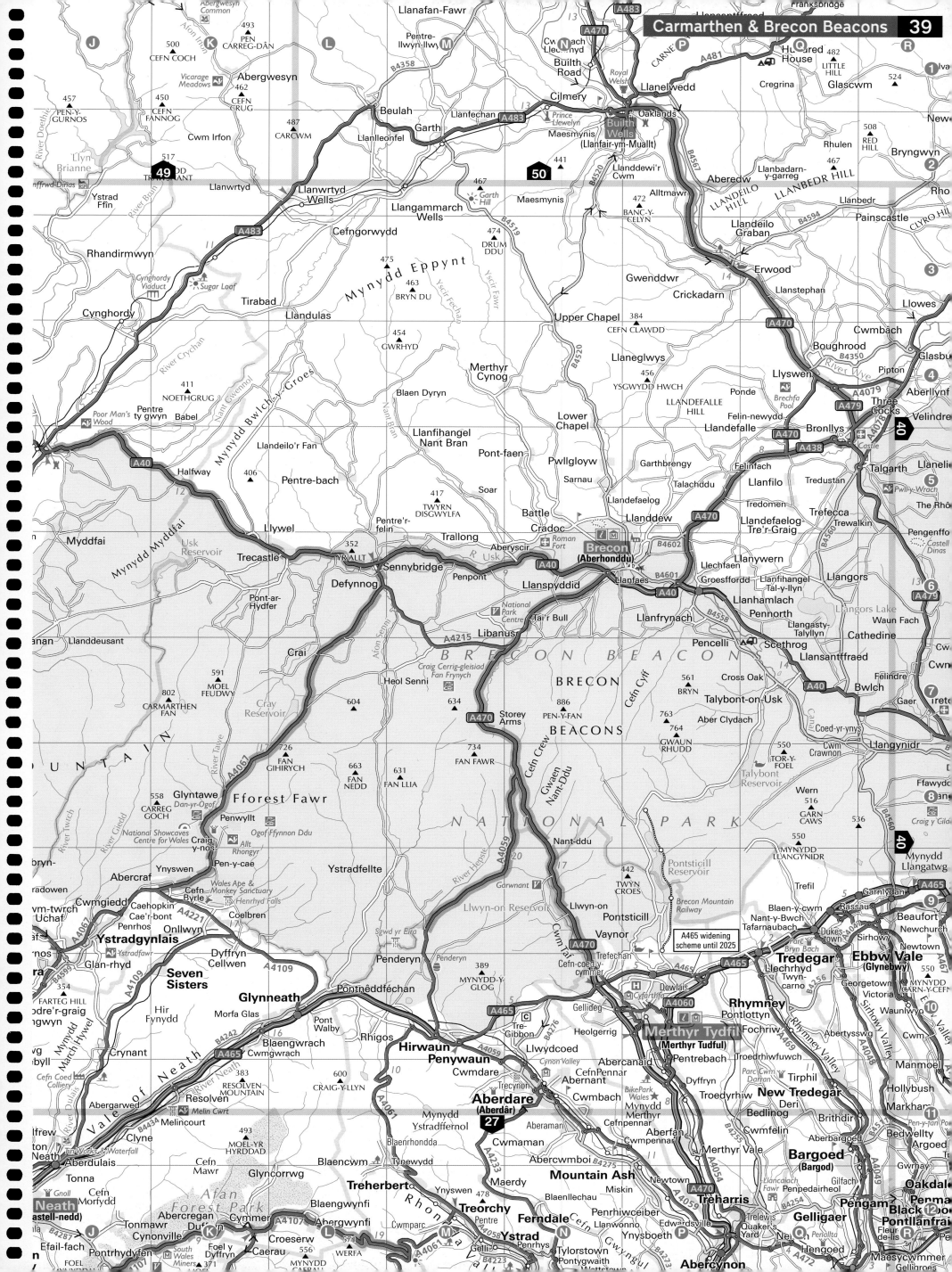

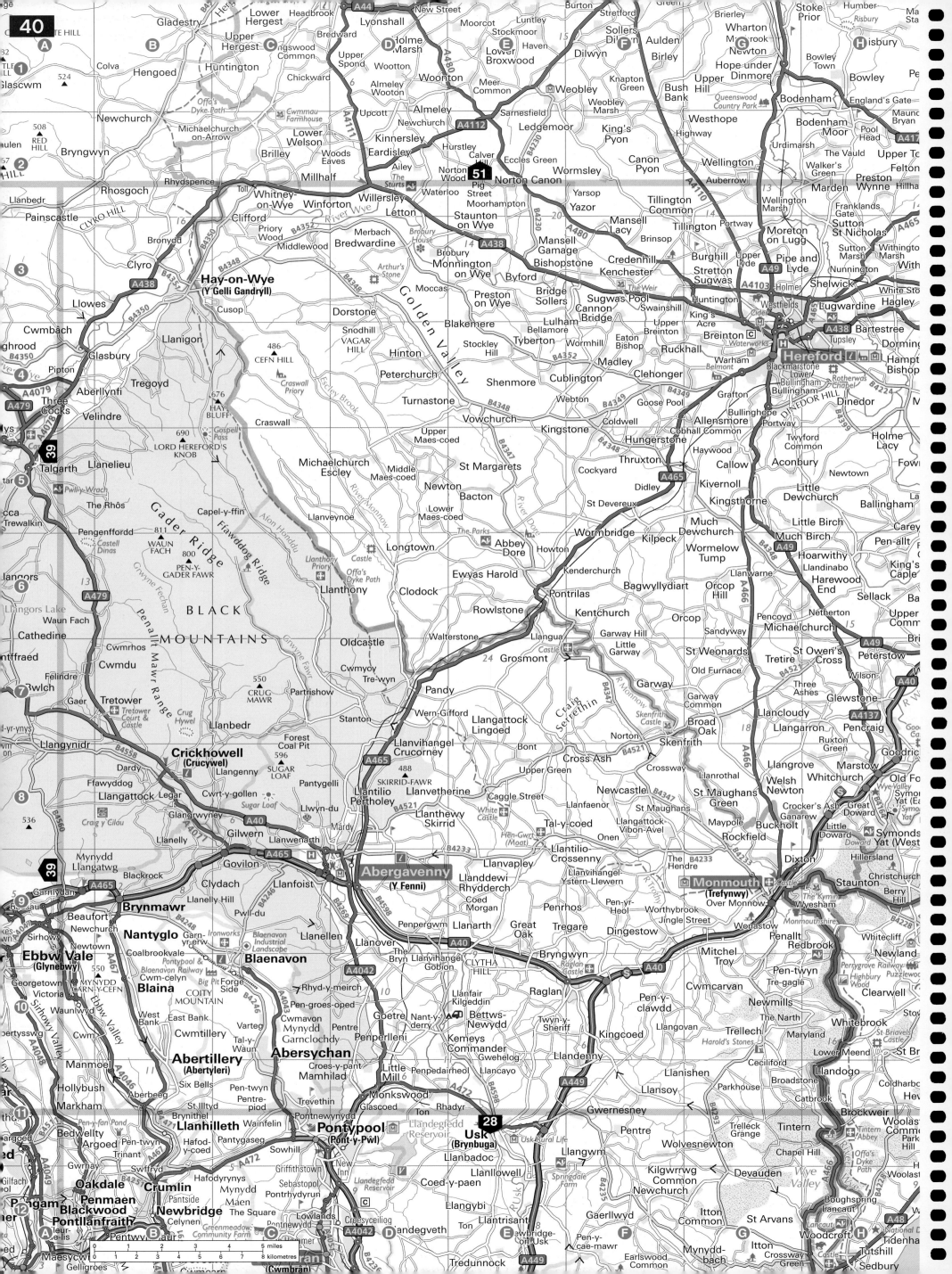

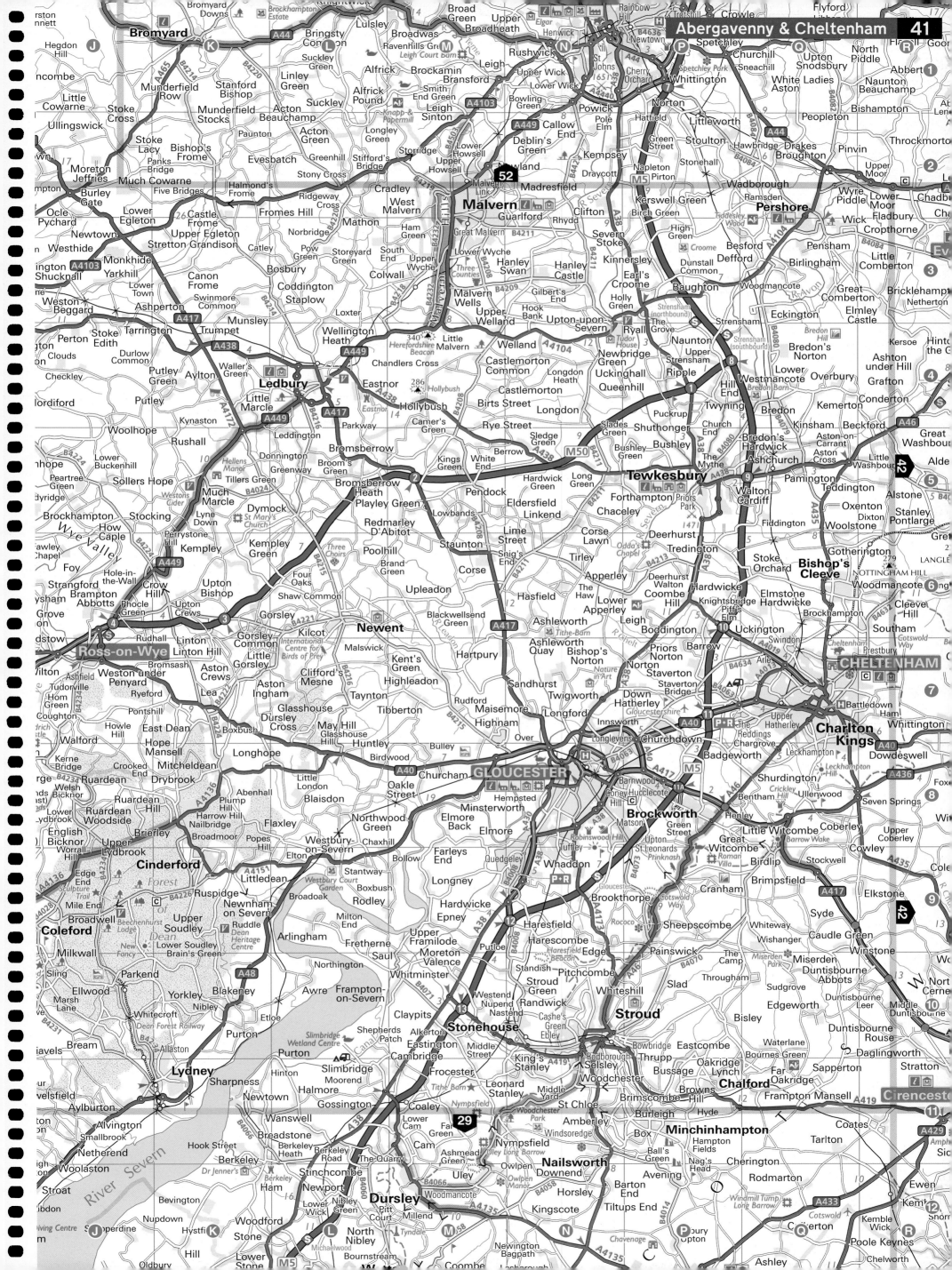

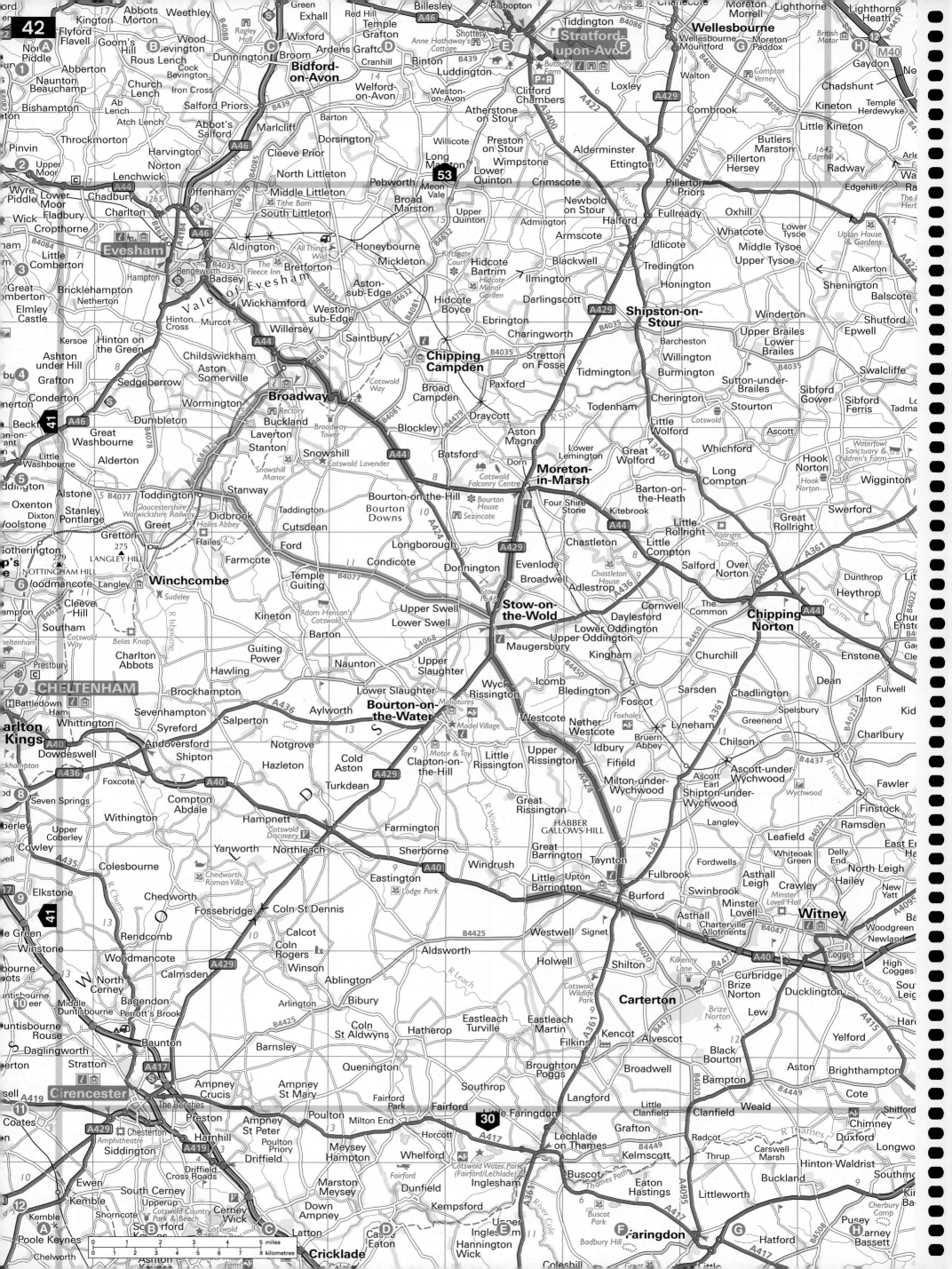

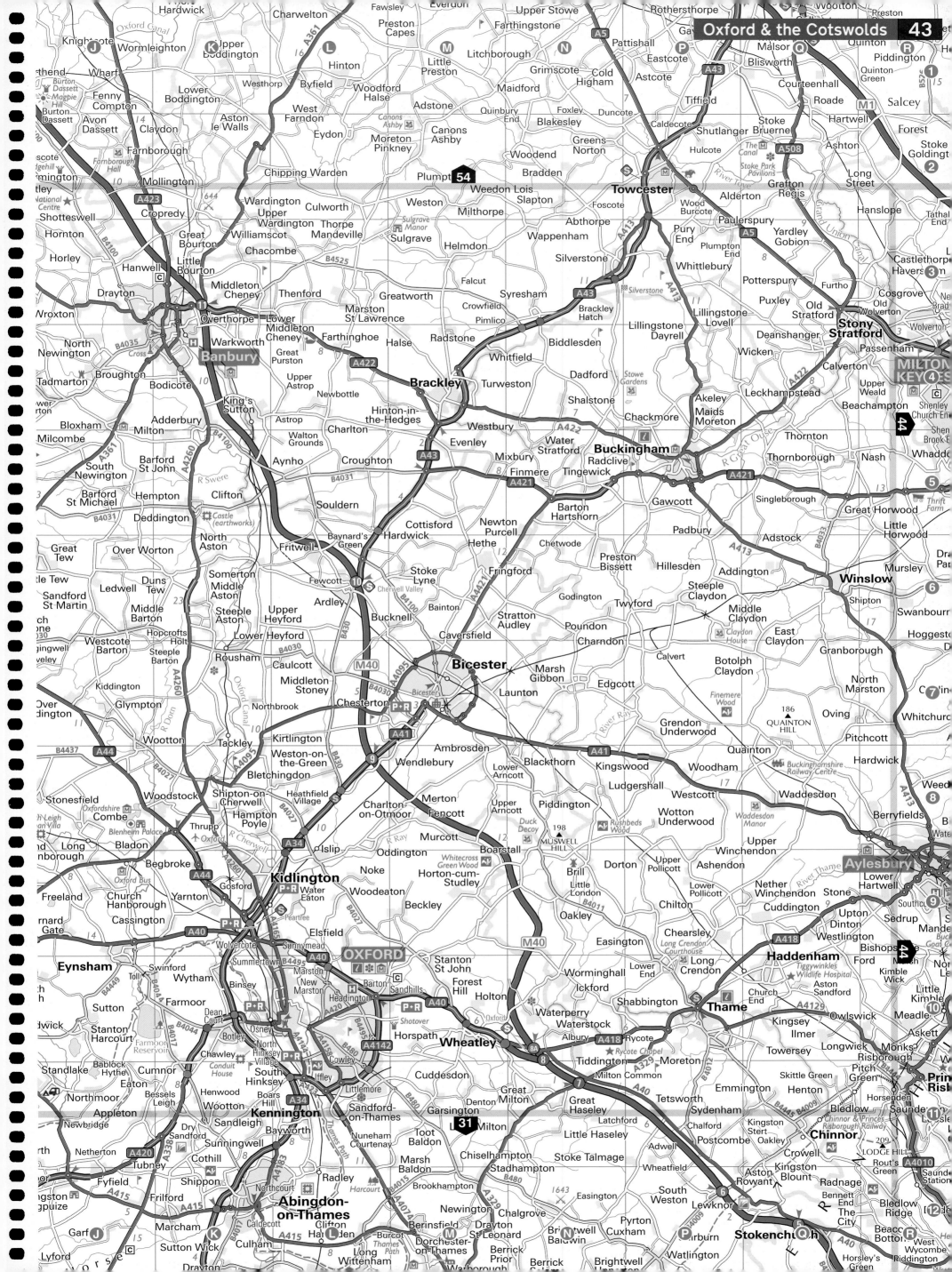

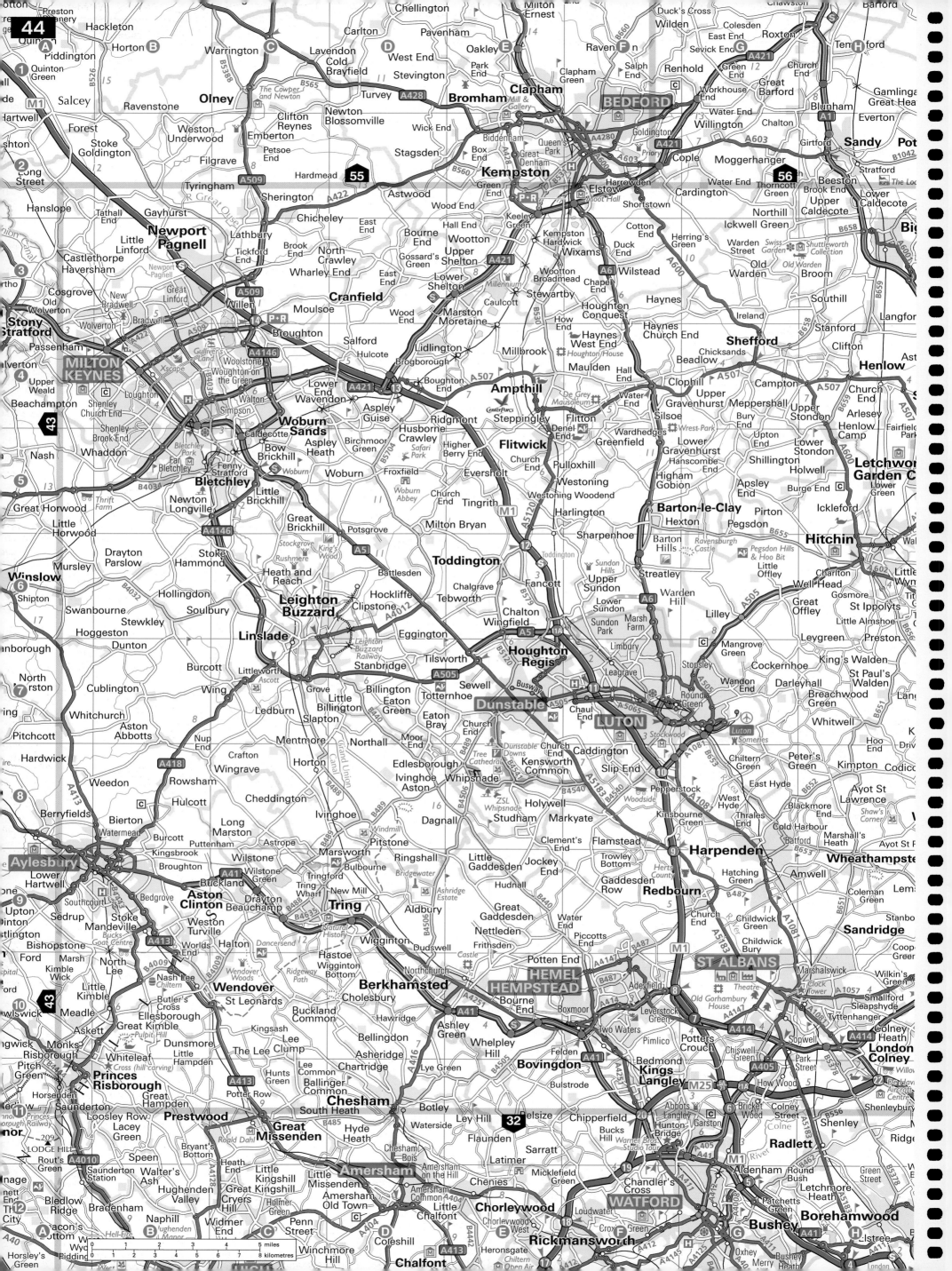

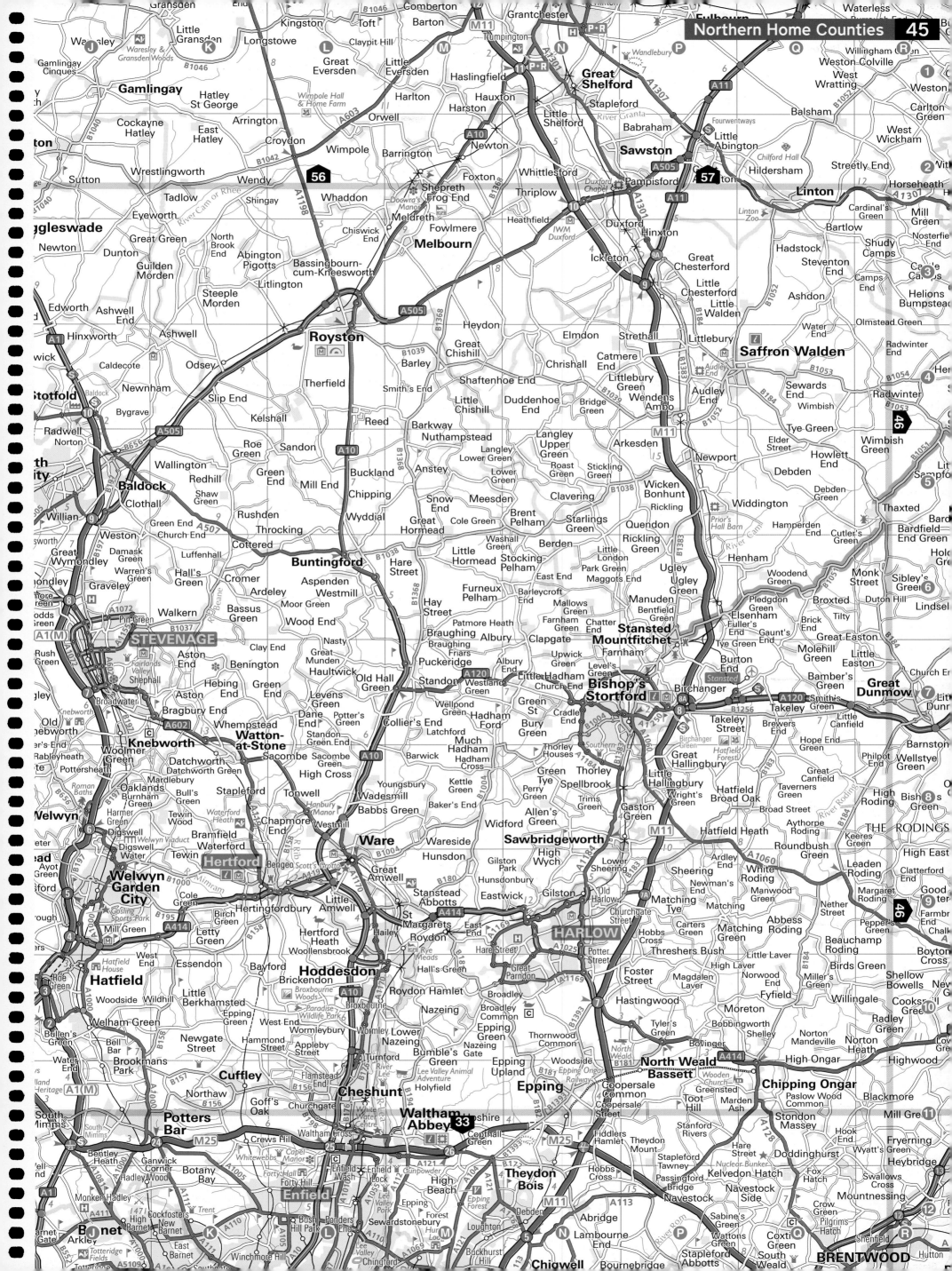

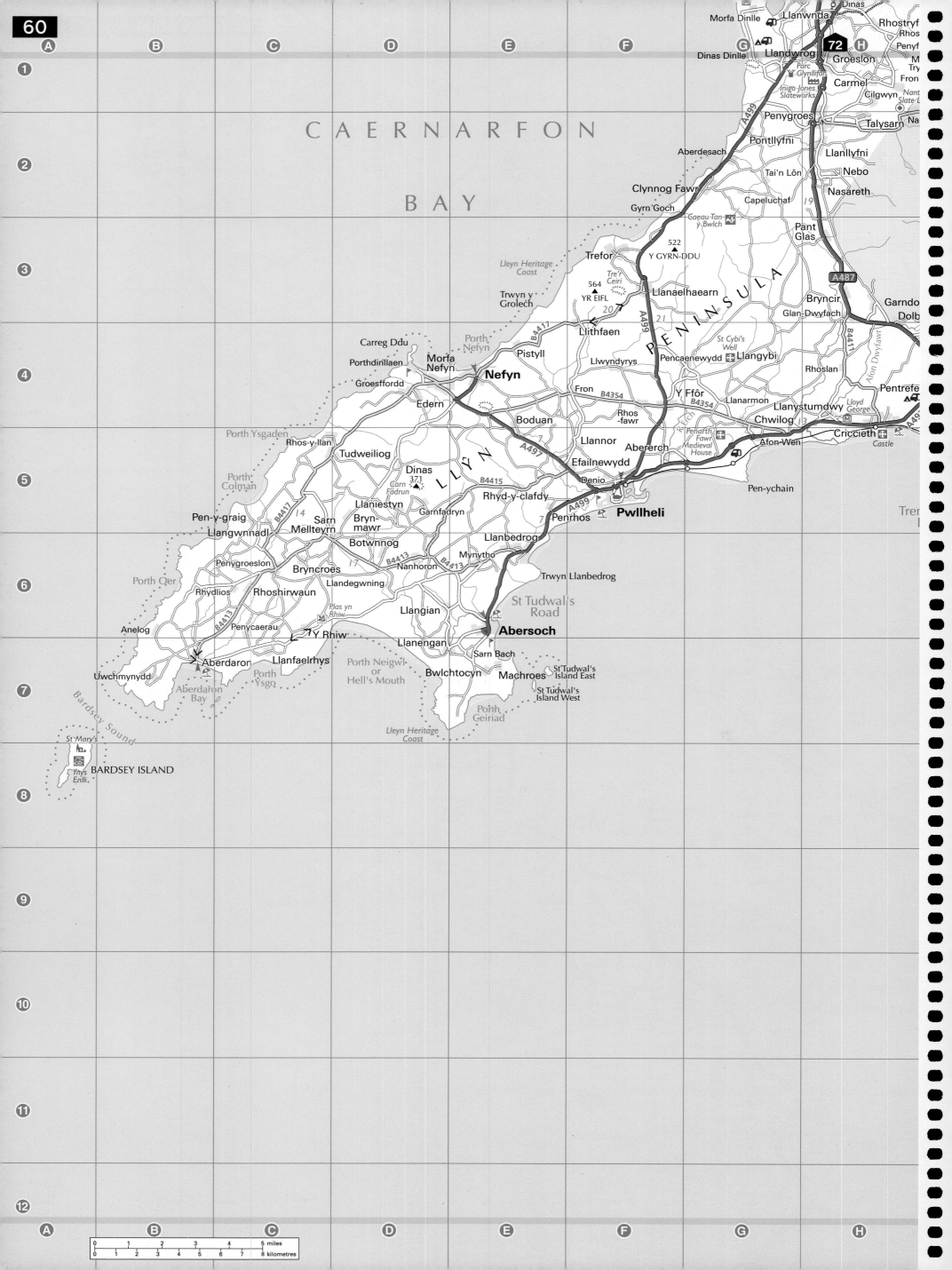

CAERNARFON

BAY

Llynndan
Morfa Dinlle
Rhostryf
Rhos
Penyf
Dinas Dinlle
Llandwrog
Groeslon
Parc
Glynllifon
Carmel
Cilgwyn
Nant
Inigo Jones
Slateworks
Penygroes
Pontllyfni
Talysarn
Aberdesach
Tai'n Lôn
Llanllyfni
Nebo
Clynnog Fawr
Capeluchaf
Pant Glas
Gyrn Goch
Gaeau-Tan-y-Bwlch
Nasareth
Trefor
522 Y GYRN-DDU
Lleyn Heritage Coast
Tre'r Ceiri
Llanaelhaearn
A487
Bryncir
Trwyn y Grolech
564 YR EIFL
PENINSULA
Glan-Dwyfach
Garndo
Dolb
Carreg Ddu
Llithfaen
St Cybi's Well
Llangybi
B4411
Porth Nefyn
Pistyll
Llwyndyrys
Pencaenewydd
Rhoslan
Porthdinllaen
Morfa Nefyn
Fron B4354
Y Ffôr
Aton Dwyfawr
Groesffordd
Nefyn
Boduan
Rhos-fawr
Llanarmon
Llanystumdwy
Lloyd George
Pentrefe
Edern
Chwilog
Porth Ysgaden
Llannor
Abererch
Penarth Fawr Medieval House
Criccieth
Castle
Rhos-y-llan
Tudweiliog
LLŶN
A497
Efailnewydd
Afon-Wen
Dinas 371
Carn Fadrun
B4415
Rhyd-y-clafdy
Denio
Pen-ychain
Tren
Llaniestyn
Garnfadryn
A499
Pwllheli
Pen-y-graig
Sarn Mellteyrn
Bryn-mawr
Penrhos
St Tudwal's Road
Llangwnnadl
Botwnnog
Llanbedrog
Penygroeslon
Bryncroes
Nanhoron
B4413
Mynytho
Trwyn Llanbedrog
Porth Qer
Llandegwning
Rhydlios
Rhoshirwaun
Llangian
Abersoch
Plas yn Rhiw
Sarn Bach
Anelog
Penycaerau
Y Rhiw
Llanengan
St Tudwal's Island East
Uwchmynydd
Aberdaron
Llanfaelrhys
Porth Neigwl or Hell's Mouth
Bwlchtocyn
Machroes
St Tudwal's Island West
Porth Ysgo
Aberdaron Bay
Porth Geiriad
Bardsey Sound
Lleyn Heritage Coast
St Mary's
Ynys Enlli
BARDSEY ISLAND

0 1 2 3 4 5 miles
0 1 2 3 4 5 6 7 8 kilometres

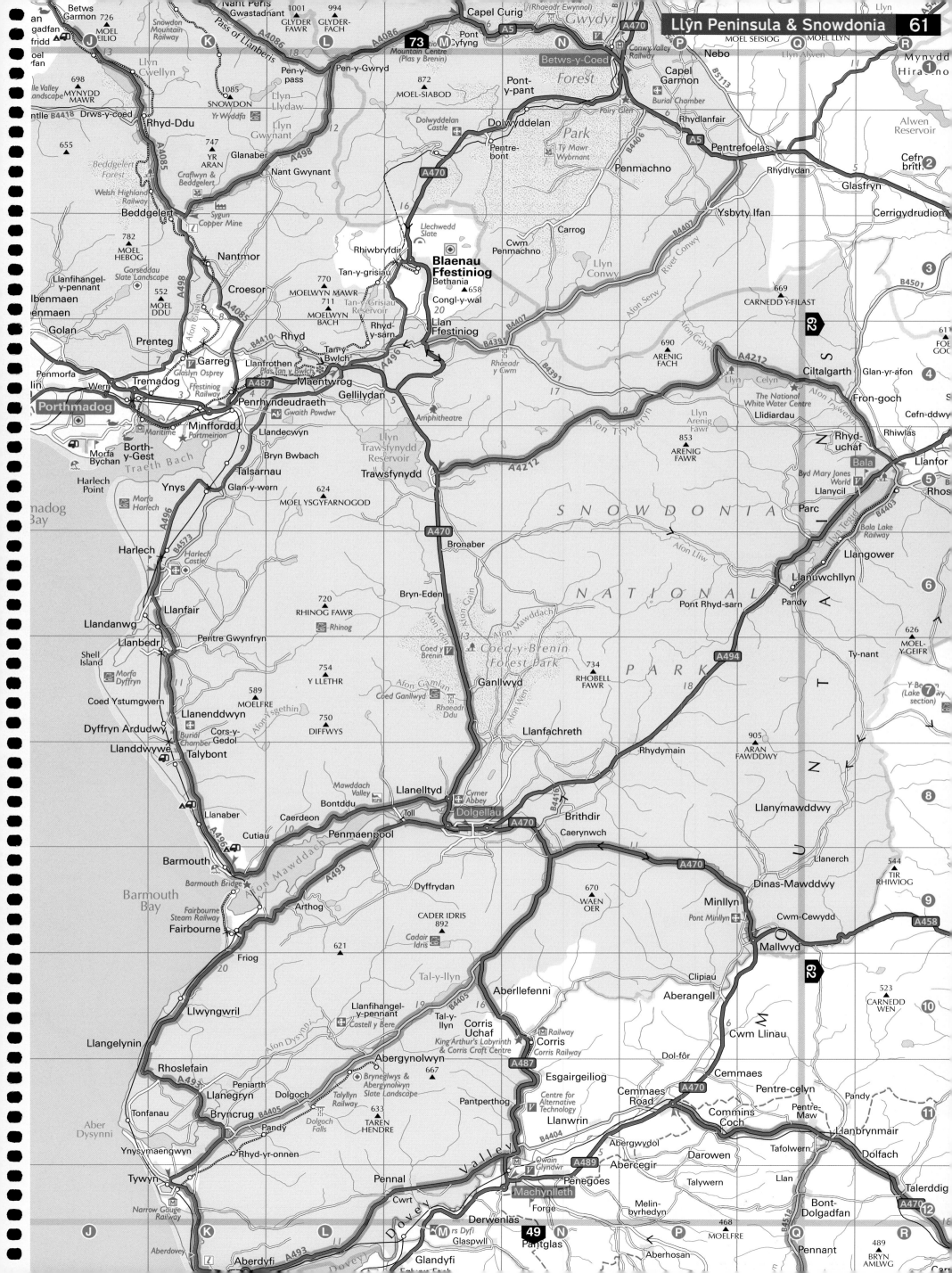

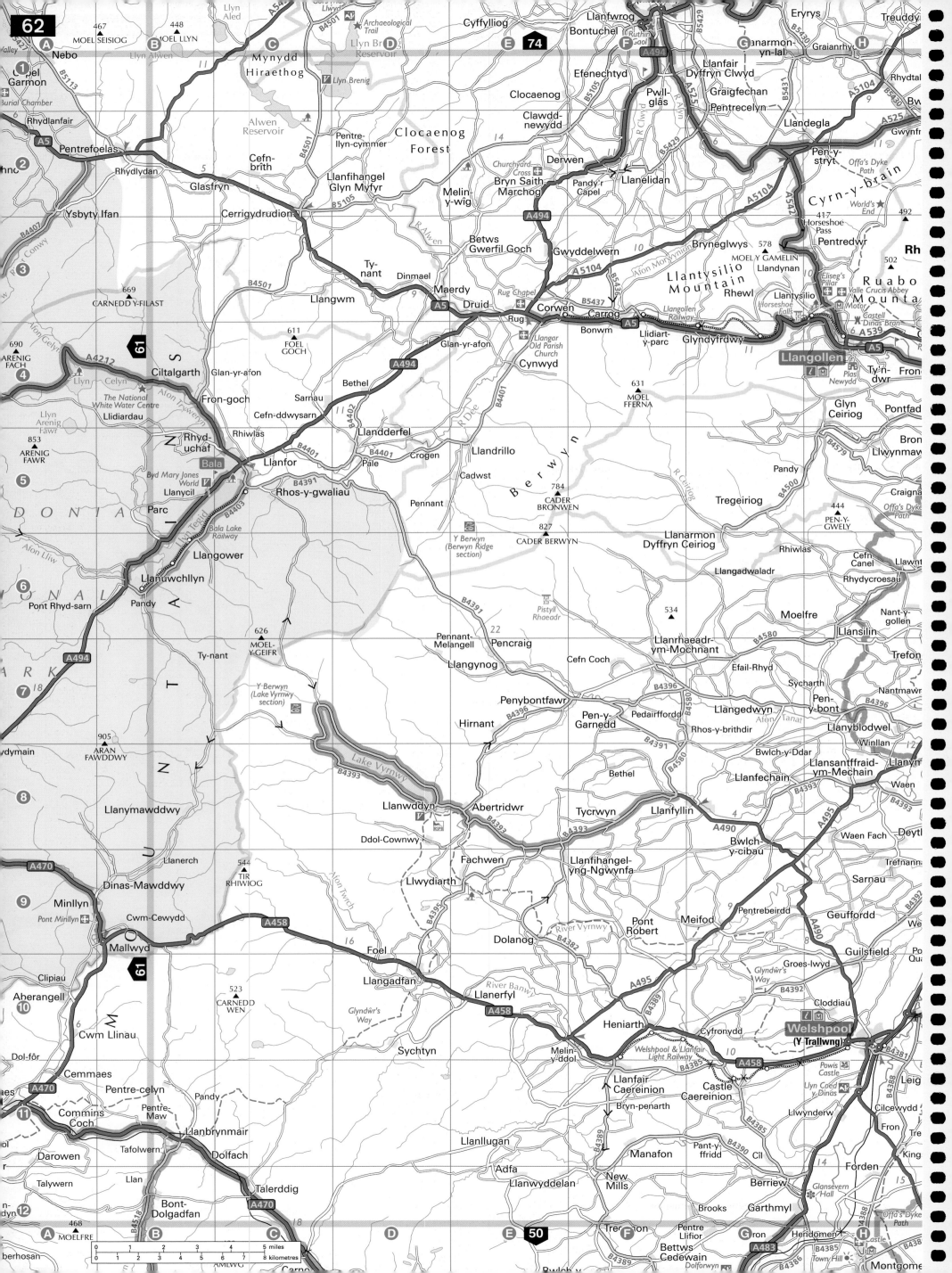

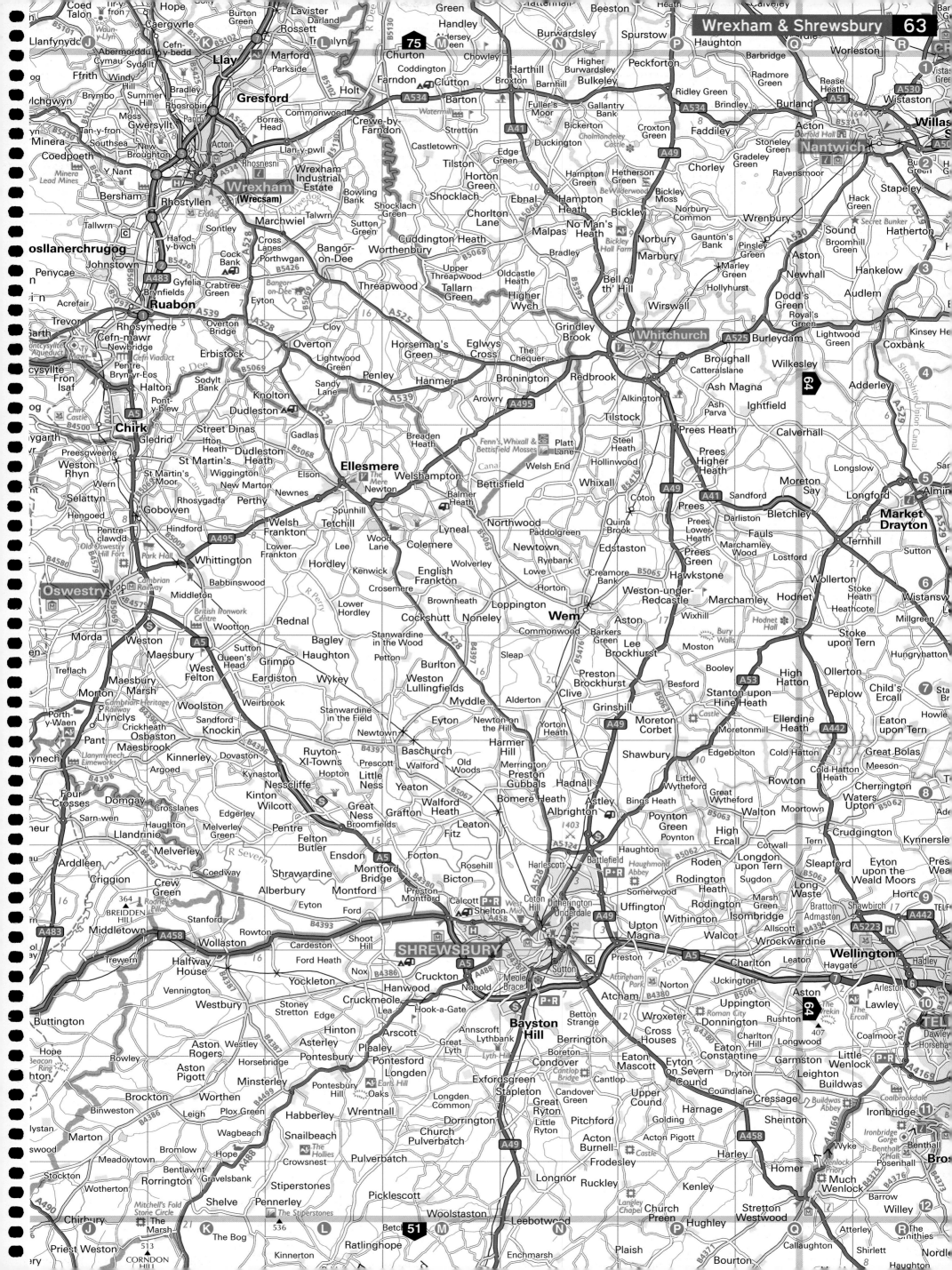

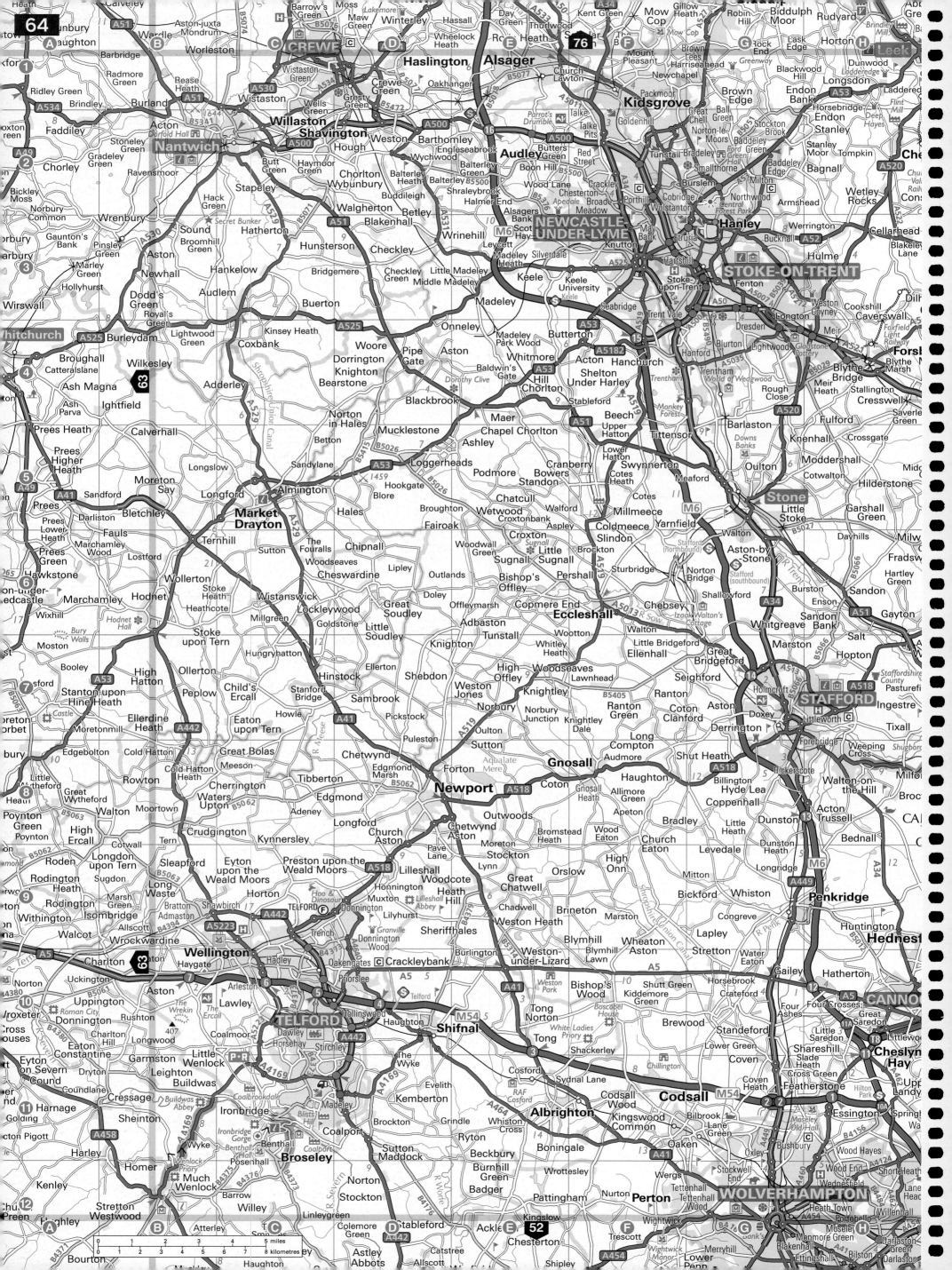

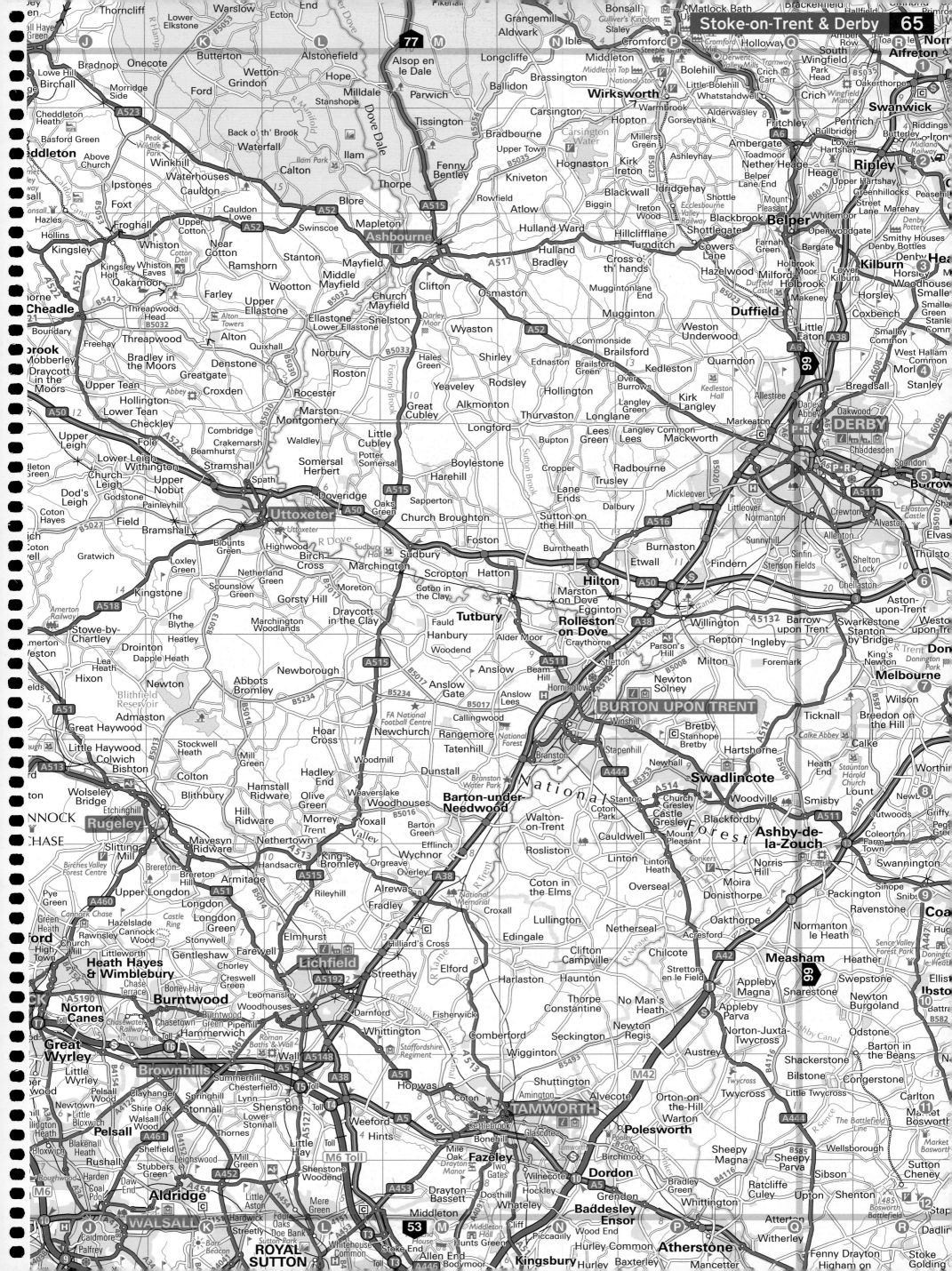

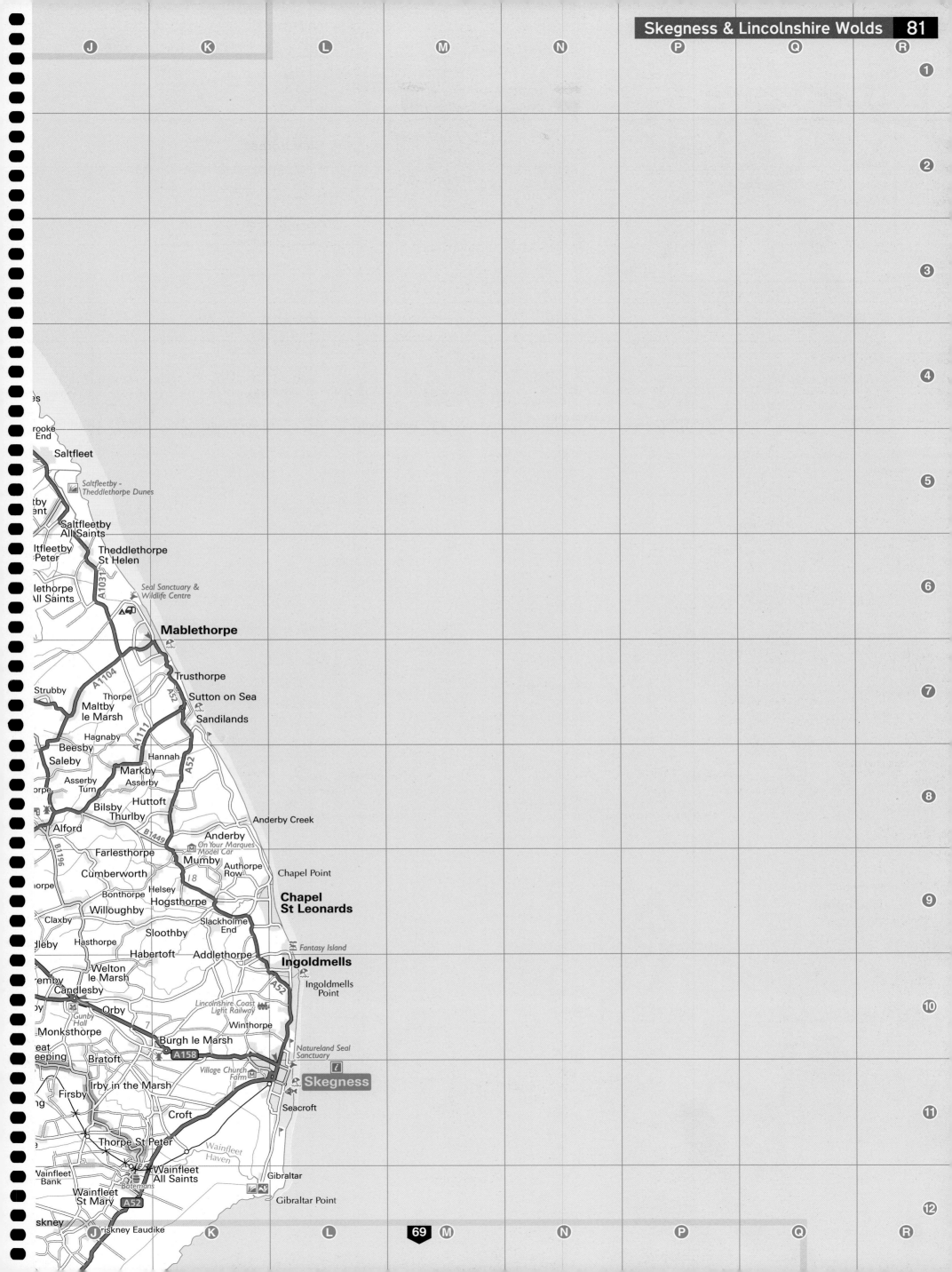

J   K   L   M   N   P   Q   R

1
2
3
4
5
6
7
8
9
10
11
12

Saltfleet

Saltfleetby -
Theddlethorpe Dunes

...es

...rooke
End

...by
...ent

Saltfleetby
All Saints

...tfleetby
...Peter

Theddlethorpe
St Helen

...lethorpe
...ll Saints

Seal Sanctuary &
Wildlife Centre

A1031

Mablethorpe

A1104

Trusthorpe

A52

Strubby

Thorpe

Sutton on Sea

Maltby
le Marsh

Sandilands

A111?

Hagnaby

Beesby

Hannah

Saleby

A52

Markby

Asserby

Asserby
Turn

...rpe

Huttoft

Bilsby

Anderby Creek

Thurlby

B1449

Alford

Anderby

On Your Marques
Model Car

Farlesthorpe

Mumby

B1196

Cumberworth

Authorpe
Row

Chapel Point

Helsey

18

...rpe

Bonthorpe

Hogsthorpe

**Chapel
St Leonards**

Willoughby

Claxby

Slackholme
End

...dleby

Hasthorpe

Sloothby

Fantasy Island

Habertoft

Addlethorpe

Ingoldmells

Welton
le Marsh

Ingoldmells
Point

...remby

Candlesby

Lincolnshire Coast
Light Railway

Orby

Gunby
Hall

Winthorpe

...by

7

...reat
...eeping

Monksthorpe

Burgh le Marsh

A158

Natureland Seal
Sanctuary

Bratoft

Village Church
Farm

Skegness

Firsby

...g

Irby in the Marsh

Seacroft

Croft

Thorpe St Peter

Wainfleet
Haven

Wainfleet
Bank

Wainfleet
All Saints

Gibraltar

Batemans

Wainfleet
St Mary

A52

Gibraltar Point

...skney

J   riskney Eaudike   K   L   **69** M   N   P   Q   R

A B C D 88 E 89 H

1
2
3
4
5
6
7
8
9
10
11
12

Heysham Harbour

0 500 m

MORECAMBE

Lower Heysham

HEYSHAM

Heysham Sands

Half Moon Bay

Higher Heysham

HEYSHAM PORT STATION
Freight Terminal

ISLE OF MAN FERRY TERMINAL

Nuclear Power Stations

LANCASTER

A683

A589

A683

A683

HAL

North Walney

Dalton-in-Furness

Urswick

Scales

Bow End

Bardsea

Baycliff

BARROW-IN-FURNESS

Furness Abbey

Bow Bridge

Newton

Staintor with Adgarley

Watermill

Aldingham

North Scale

Dendron

Gleaston

Vickerstown

Roose

Leece

Newbiggin

Walney

Biggar

Roosebeck

ISLE OF WALNEY

Roa Island

Rampside

Sheep Island

Piel Castle

Foulney Island

Piel Island

Hilpsford Point

South Walney

Piel Bar

A590

A5087

A5087

Douglas

Fleetwood

Rossall Point

Knott End

River Wyre

Burn Naze

Trunnah

Cleveleys

Thornton

Norcross

Little Bispham

Churchtown

Norbreck

Bispham

Carleton

Warbreck

North Shore

Hoohill

Normoss

BLACKPOOL

Great Marton

Model Village

South Shore

Common Edge

A587

A585

A588

A586

B5268

B5269

B5266

B5124

B5261

B5262

B5230

St Anne's

Royal Lytham & St Annes

Ansdell

Fairhaven

Lytham St Annes

SOUTHPORT

Pleasureland

P+R

British Lawnmower

The Royal Birkdale

Birkdale

Shir

Marsh

Blackpool

0 200 m

FLEETWOOD

BLACKPOOL NORTH STATION

LANCASTER

PROMENADE

Metropole Hotel

North Pier

Grundy Art Gallery

Jobcentre Plus

Superstore

Sports Barn

Council Offices

Sacred Heart

TALBOT ROAD

DICKSON ROAD

GEORGE STREET

ABINGDON STREET

CARON STREET

GRANVILLE ROAD

St John the Evangelist

CHURCH STREET

PRESTON, (M55)

Travelodge

Grand

Winter Gardens

Medical Centre

Salvation Army

St John's School

Meeting House

The Blackpool Tower & Ballroom

Houndshill

Council Offices

Spiritualist

Register Office

St John Ambulance

Tower Festival Headland

Kingdom Hall

Blackpool & Fylde College

ALBERT ROAD

CORONATION STREET

A5099

A583

Coral Island

Lifeboat Station

PROMENADE

Market

Police Station

County Court

Blackpool Magistrates' Court

Blackpool & Fylde College

Sea Life

Madame Tussauds

CENTRAL DRIVE

HORNBY ROAD

READS AVENUE

PALATINE ROAD

BLENHEIM AVENUE

Central Pier

Central Pier

CHAPEL STREET

YORK STREET

HAL

LYTHAM ST ANNES

PRESTON, (M55)

A B C D E F G H

0 1 2 3 4 5 miles
0 1 2 3 4 5 6 7 8 kilometres

Ainsdale-on-Sea

Ainsdale

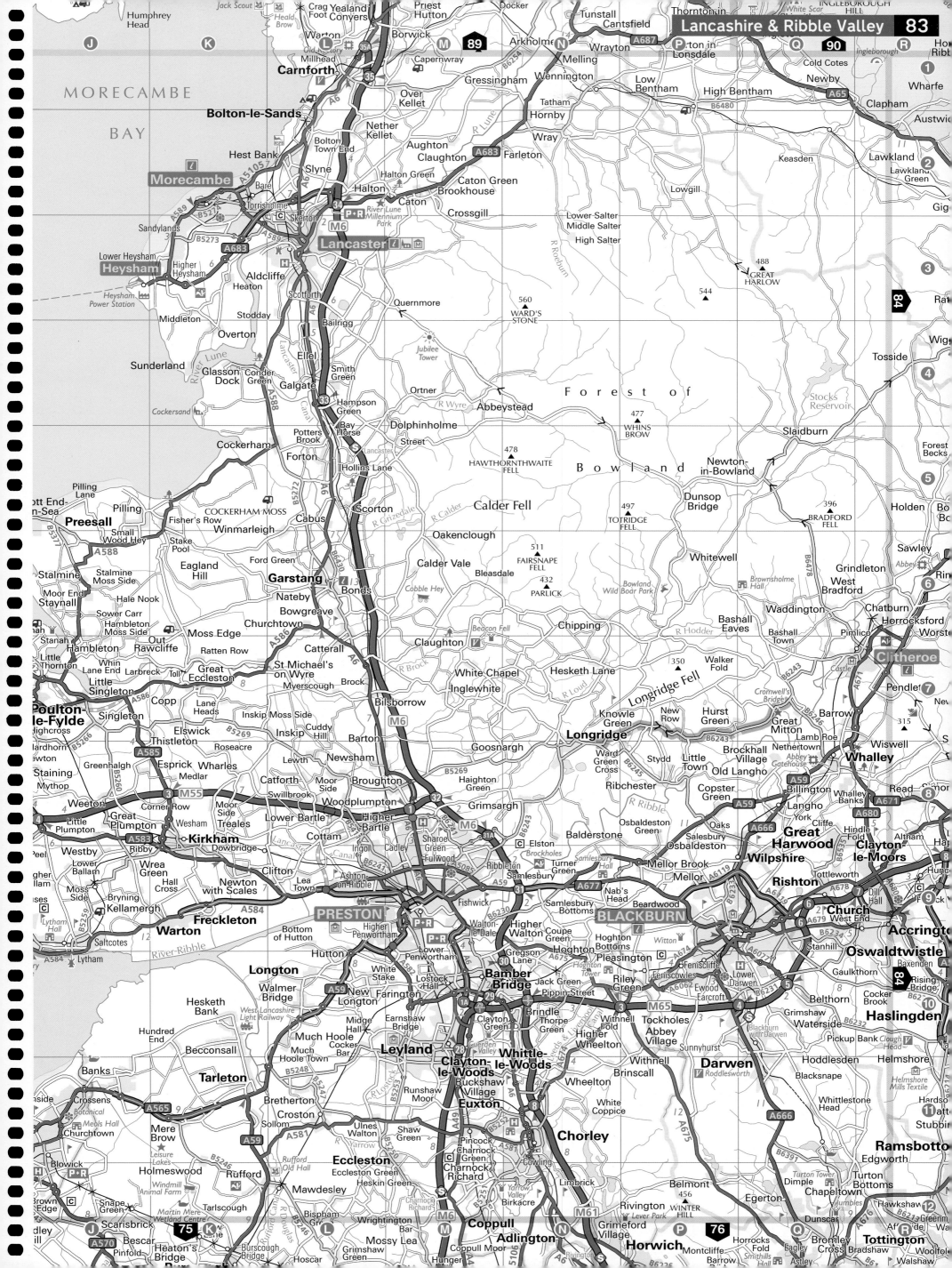

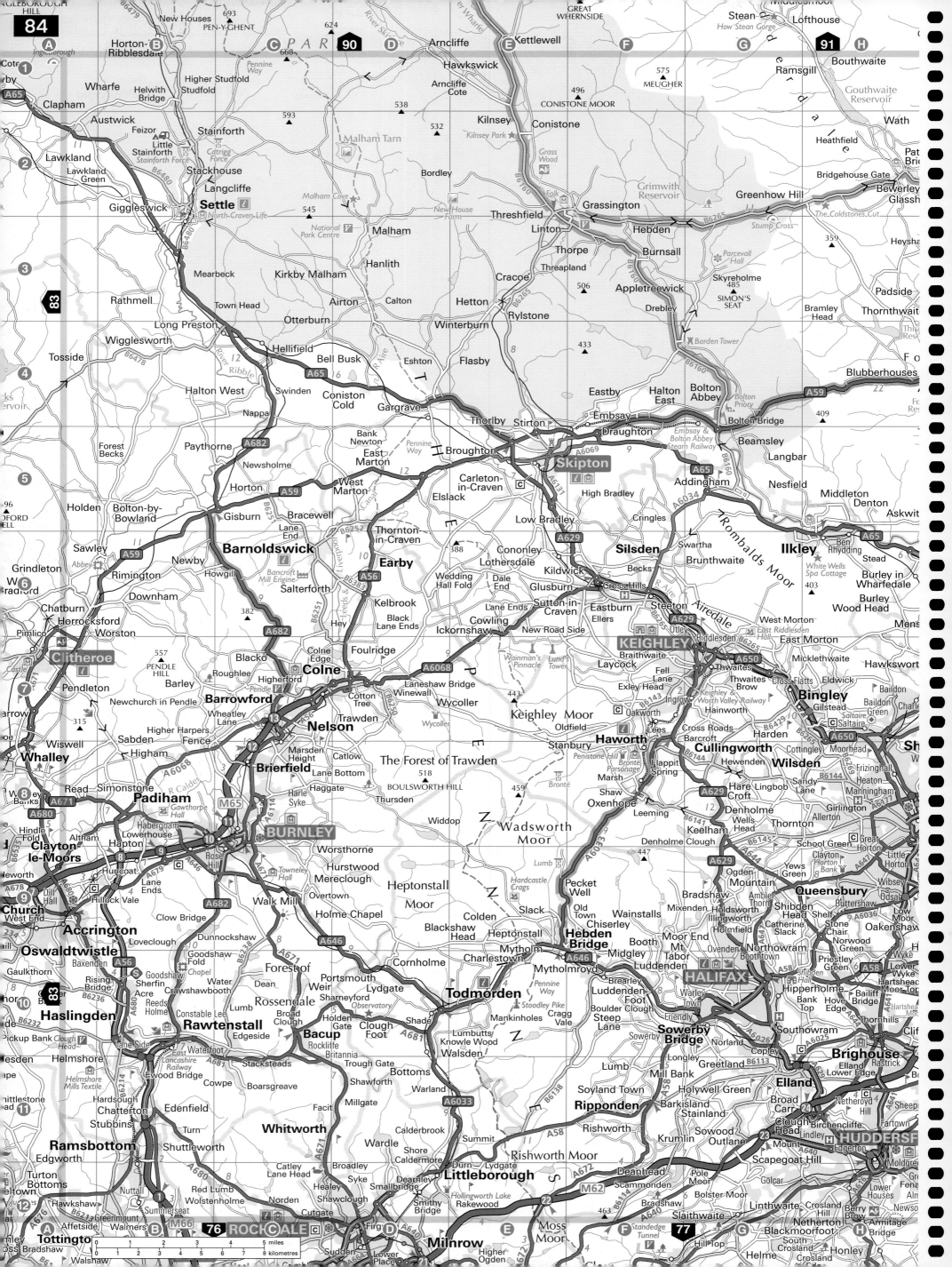

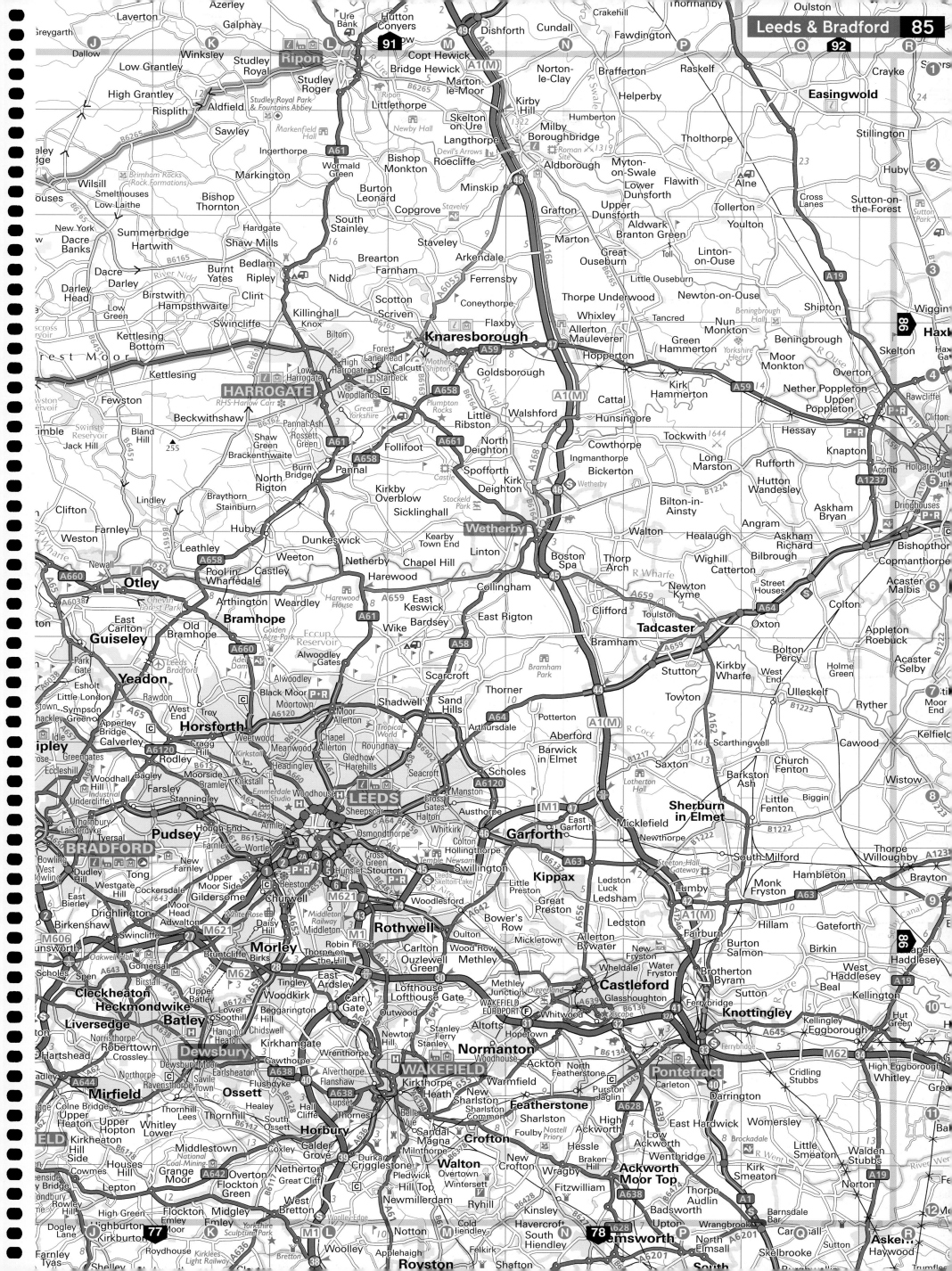

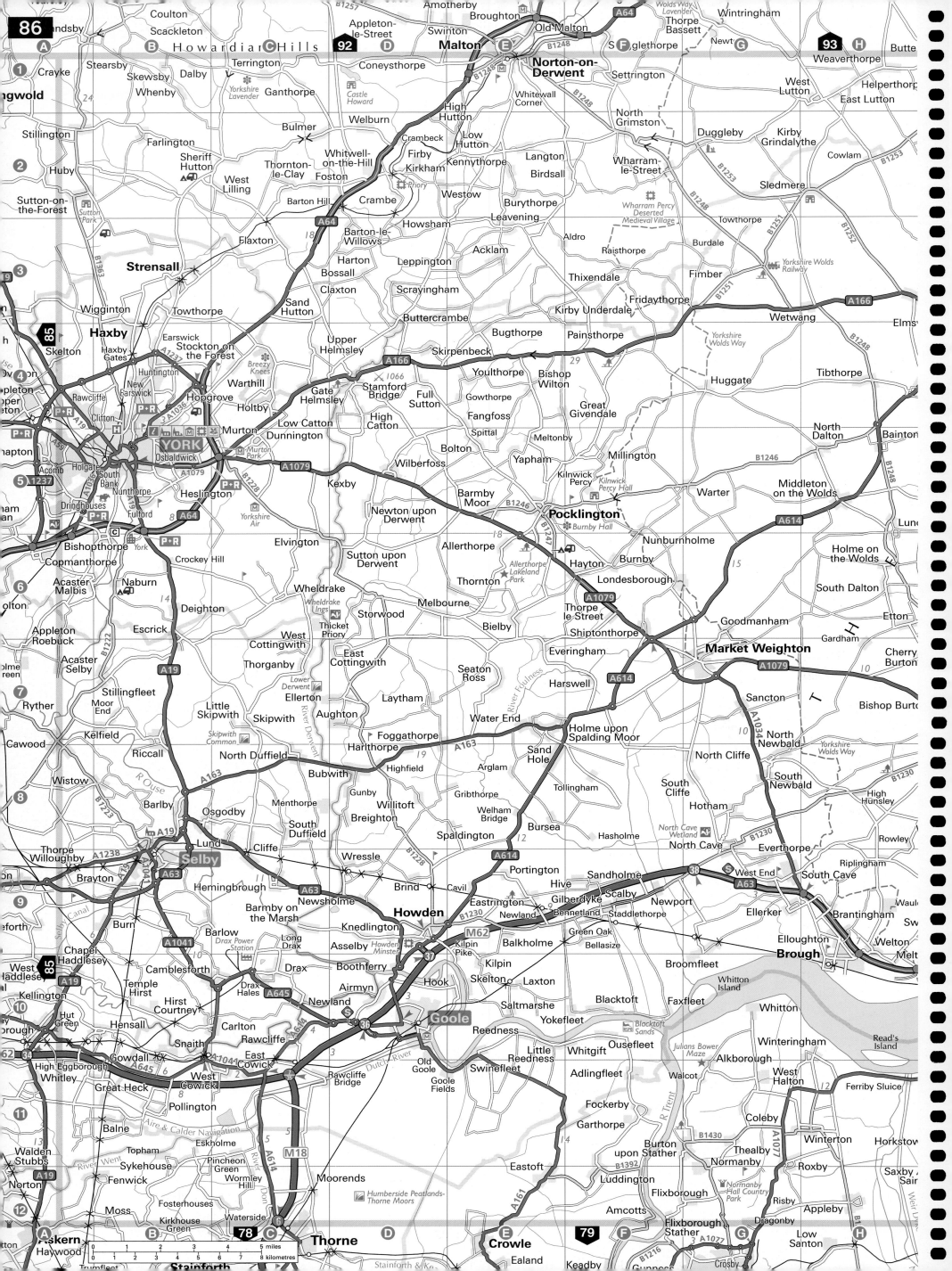

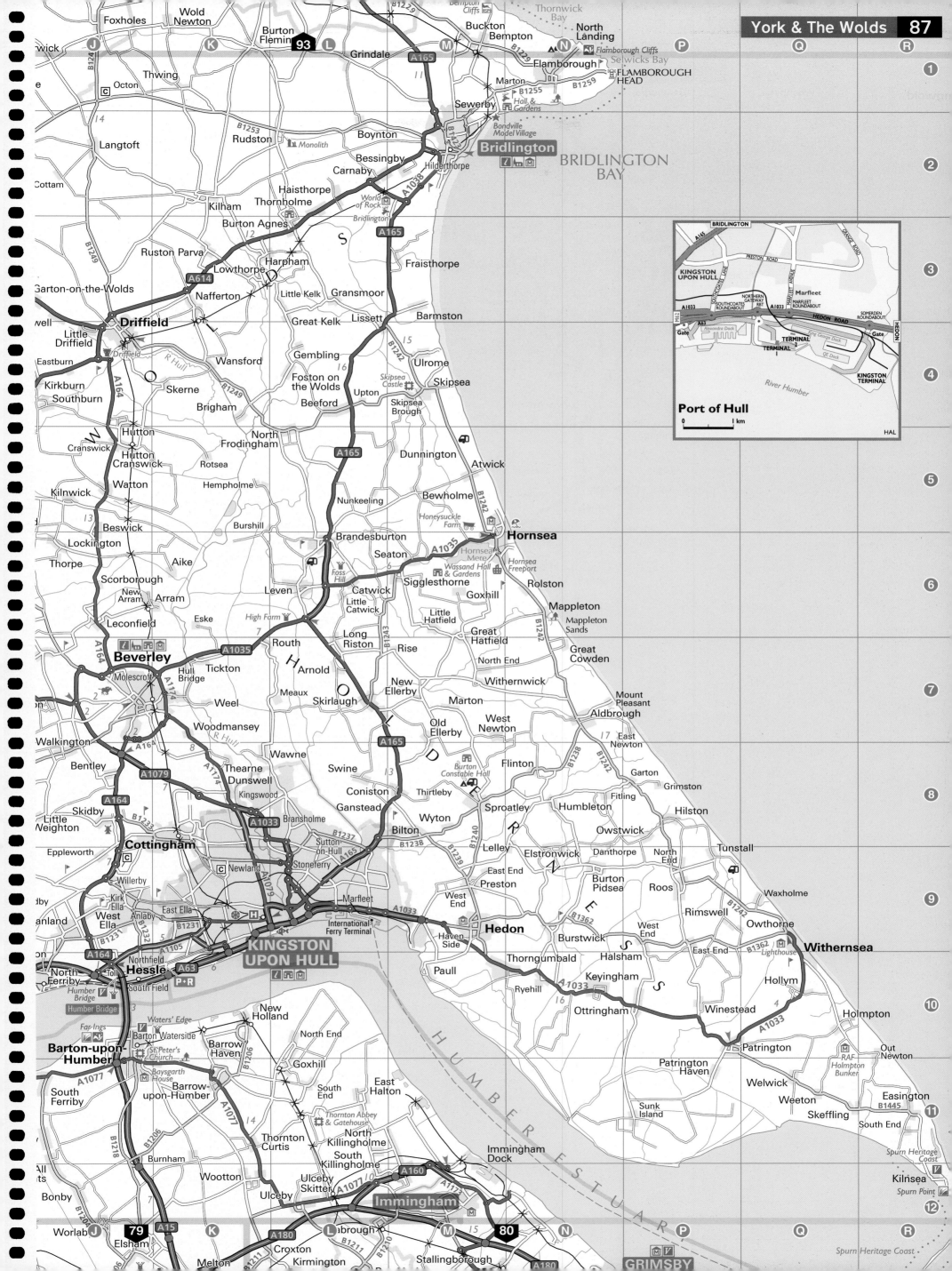

BRIDLINGTON

Port of Hull

0   1 km

HAL

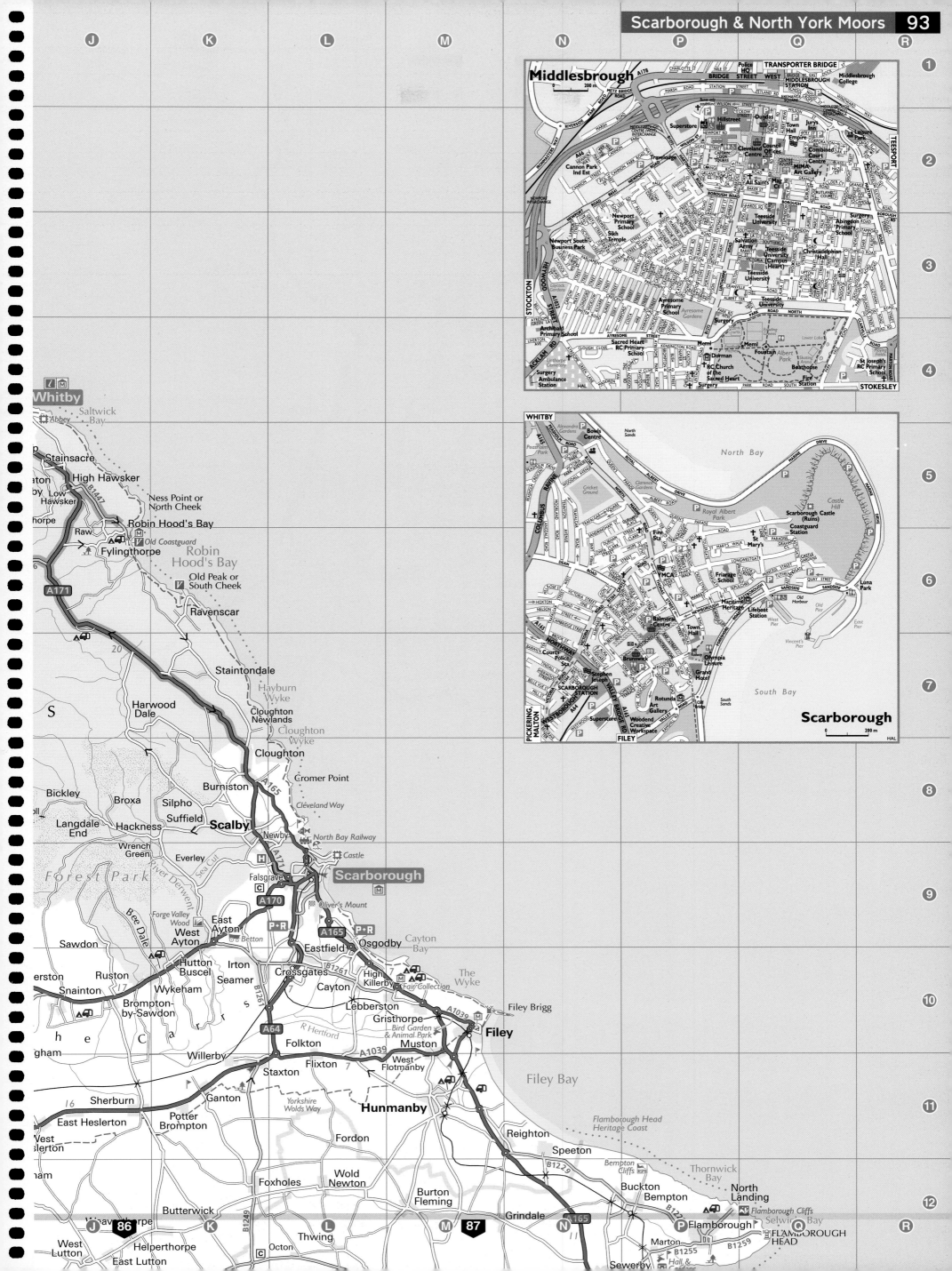

Middlesbrough

TRANSPORTER BRIDGE

Charlotte St · Police HQ
BRIDGE STREET WEST · Middlesbrough Station · Middlesbrough College

METZ BRIDGE ROAD · MARSH ROAD · STATION STREET · ZETLAND RD

RIVERSIDE PARK ROAD

Jurys · Leisure Park

MIDDLESBROUGH CENTRE (WEST) INTERCHANGE

Superstore · Hillstreet · Dundas · Town Hall · Empire · CORPORATION

STOCKTON

NEWPORT INTERCHANGE

Cannon Park Ind Est · Cleveland Centre · Combined Court Centre

MIMA Art Gallery

Travelodge · All Saints

BOROUGH ROAD · BOROUGH ROAD

Newport Primary School · Sikh Temple · Teesside University · Baker St · Surgery · Abingdon Primary School

Newport South Business Park · Salvation Army · Teesside University (Heart) · Christadelphian Hall

Victoria · Teesside University (Campus Heart) · GRANVILLE

Ayresome Primary School · Teesside University · Surgery

ALBERT TER · PARK ROAD NORTH

Archibald Primary School · AYRESOME STREET · Ayresome Gardens

Linthorpe Cemetery · CLOUGH CLOSE · KENSINGTON ROAD · Meml · Meml · Fountain · Albert Park · Boathouse

Sacred Heart RC Primary School · Dorman · Skating · St Joseph's RC Primary School

Surgery · Ambulance Station · RC Church of the Sacred Heart · Surgery · Fire Station

HAL · PARK ROAD SOUTH · STOKESLEY

200 m

WHITBY

Alexandra Gardens · Bowls Centre · North Sands

Peasholm Park · North Bay

Cricket Ground · MARINE DRIVE

Royal Albert Park · Castle Hill · Scarborough Castle (Ruins) · Coastguard Station

Fire Sta · St Mary's

YMCA · Friarage School

Maritime Heritage · Lifeboat Station · Luna Park

Nelson St · Balmoral Centre · Old Harbour

PICKERING, MALTON · Police Sta · St Stephen Joseph · SCARBOROUGH STATION · Town Hall · Grand Hotel · Old Pier · West Pier · East Pier · Vincent's Pier

Brunswick · Olympia Leisure · South Bay

Rotunda Art Gallery · Woodend Creative Workspace · Superstore · South Sands

FILEY

Scarborough

0   200 m   HAL

Whitby · Saltwick Bay · Abbey

Stainsacre · High Hawsker · Low Hawsker · B1447

Raw · Robin Hood's Bay · Ness Point or North Cheek

Fylingthorpe · Old Coastguard · Robin Hood's Bay

A171 · Old Peak or South Cheek

Ravenscar

20 · Staintondale

Hayburn Wyke

Harwood Dale · Cloughton Newlands

Cloughton Wyke

Cloughton

Cromer Point

S · Bickley · Broxa · Silpho · Burniston · A165 · Cleveland Way

Langdale End · Hackness · Suffield · Scalby · Newby · North Bay Railway

Wrench Green · Everley · Castle

Forest Park · River Derwent · Sea Cut · Falsgrave · Scarborough

A170 · Oliver's Mount

Bee Dale · Forge Valley Wood · East Ayton · P+R · A165 · P+R · Cayton Bay

West Ayton · Betton · Eastfield · Osgodby

Sawdon · Irton · Crossgates · The Wyke

Ruston · Wykeham · Seamer · Cayton · High Killerby · Fair Collection

Snainton · B1261 · Lebberston · A1039 · Filey Brigg

Brompton-by-Sawdon · Gristhorpe · Filey

A64 · R Hertford · Folkton · Bird Garden & Animal Park · Muston

Willerby · Flixton · A1039 · West Flotmanby · Filey Bay

Staxton · Ganton · Yorkshire Wolds Way · Hunmanby

Sherburn · Potter Brompton · Fordon · Reighton · Flamborough Head Heritage Coast

East Heslerton · Speeton · Bempton Cliffs

West Heslerton · Butterwick · Foxholes · Wold Newton · Burton Fleming · Grindale · B1229 · Thornwick Bay · North Landing

Vernaldthorpe · 86 · Thwing · 87 · Buckton · Bempton · Flamborough Cliffs · Selwick Bay

West Lutton · Helperthorpe · East Lutton · Octon · B1249 · Flamborough · FLAMBOROUGH HEAD

Marton · B1255 · B1259 · Sewerby · Hall & Gardens

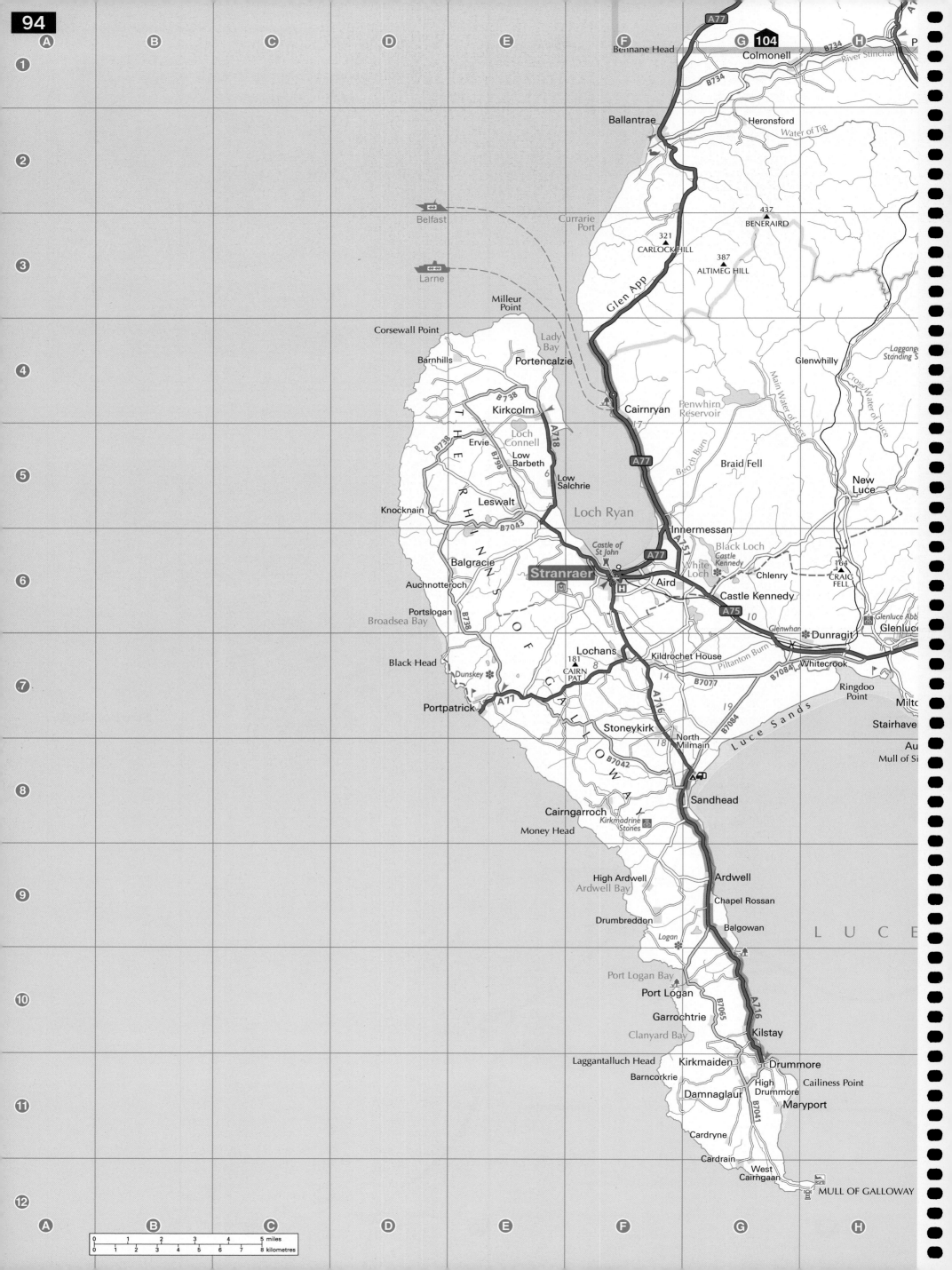

A　　B　　C　　D　　E　　F　　G　104　H

1

2

Bennane Head

Colmonell

River Stinchar

A77

B734

B734

Ballantrae

Heronsford

Water of Tig

3

Belfast

Currarie Port

Larne

BENERAIRD 437

321 CARLOCK HILL

387 ALTIMEG HILL

Glen App

Milleur Point

Lady Bay

Laggangarn Standing S

4

Corsewall Point

Barnhills

Portencalzie

Glenwhilly

Penwhirn Reservoir

Main Water of Luce

Cross Water of Luce

Cairnryan

B738

Kirkcolm

A718

Loch Connell

17

Ervie

Low Barbeth

Beoch Burn

Braid Fell

New Luce

5

B738

B908

Low Salchrie

A77

Knocknain

Leswalt

B7043

Loch Ryan

Innermessan

A751

Black Loch

Castle Kennedy

White Loch

Chlenry

164 CRAIG FELL

6

Balgracie

Castle of St John

A77

Stranraer

H

Aird

Castle Kennedy

A75

10

Glenwhan

Dunragit

Glenluce Abb

Glenluce

Auchnotteroch

Portslogan

B738

Broadsea Bay

Lochans

Kildrochet House

Piltanton Burn

B7084

Whitecrook

7

Black Head

Dunskey

181 CAIRN PAT

8

A716

14

B7077

Ringdoo Point

Milto

Portpatrick

A77

Stoneykirk

18

B7084

19

Luce Sands

Stairhave

8

B7042

North Milmain

Sandhead

Au Mull of Si

Cairngarroch

Kirkmadrine Stones

Money Head

9

High Ardwell

Ardwell Bay

Drumbreddon

Logan

Ardwell

Chapel Rossan

Balgowan

L U C E

10

Port Logan Bay

Port Logan

B7065

A716

Garrochtrie

Clanyard Bay

Kilstay

11

Laggantalluch Head

Barncorkrie

Kirkmaiden

Damnaglaur

High Drummore

B7041

Drummore

Cailiness Point

Maryport

Cardryne

Cardrain

12

West Cairngaan

MULL OF GALLOWAY

A　　B　　C　　D　　E　　F　　G　　H

0　1　2　3　4　5 miles
0　1　2　3　4　5　6　7　8 kilometres

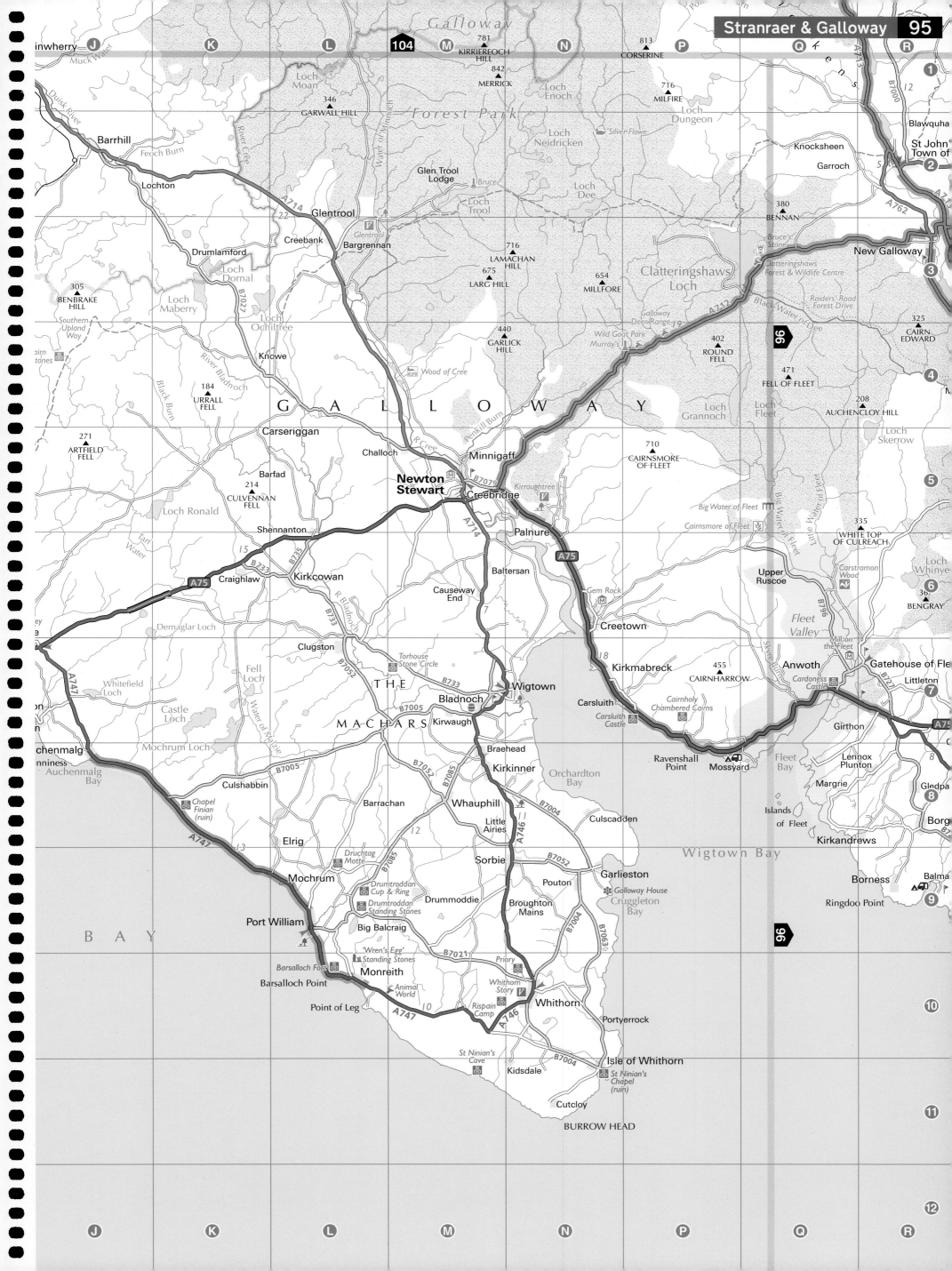

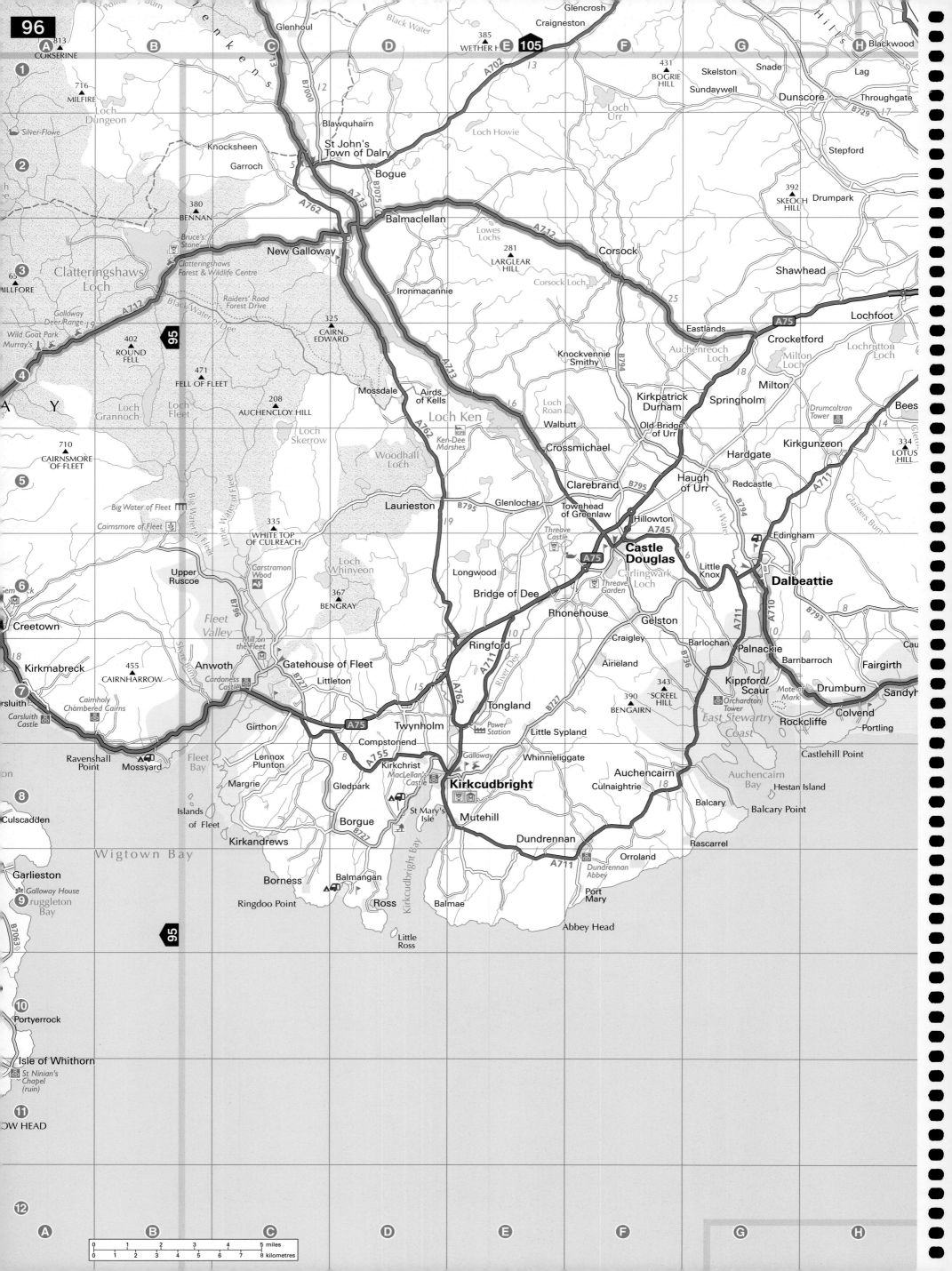

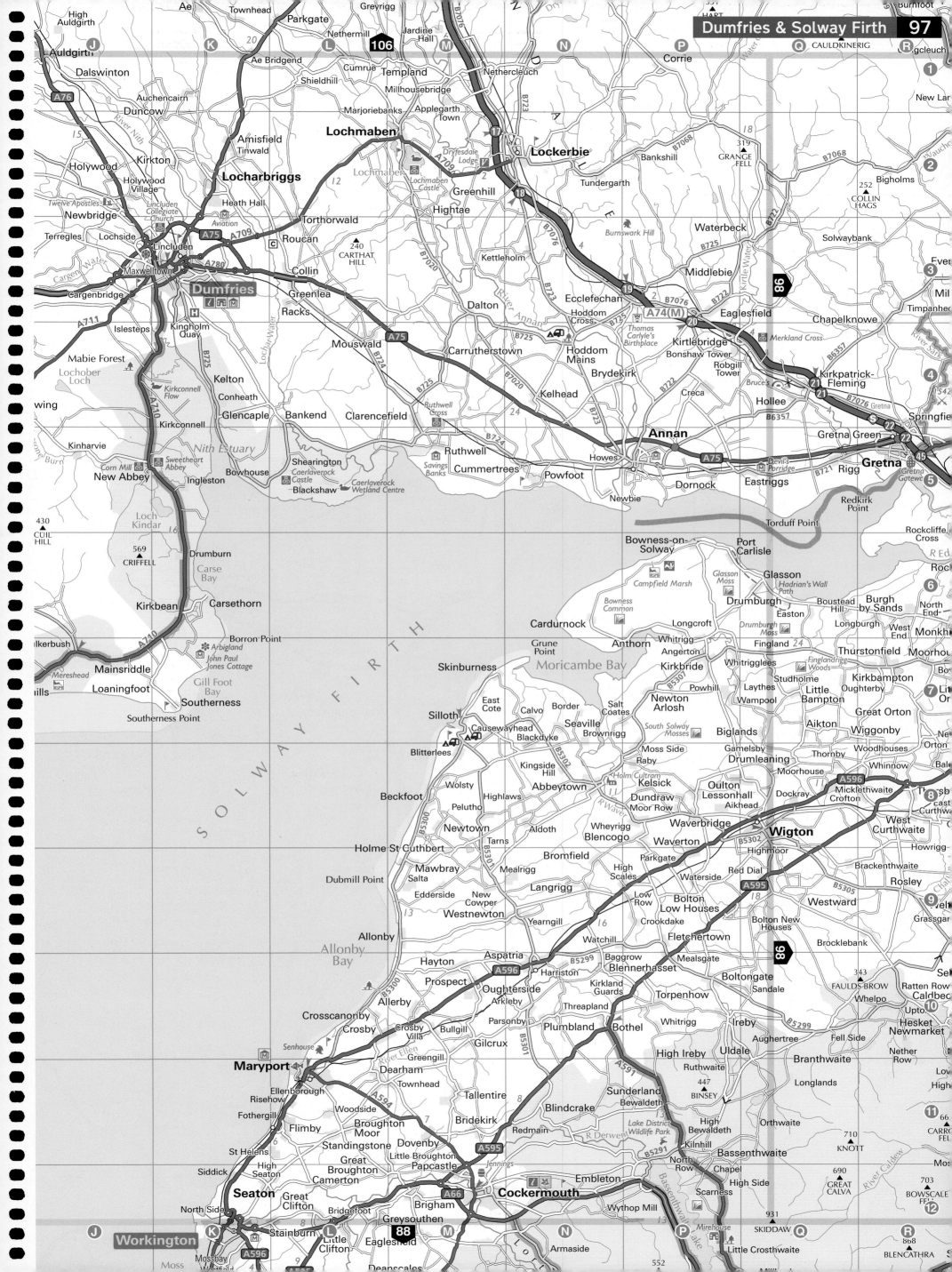

CAULDKINERIG
gcleuch

High Auldgirth
Townhead
Ae
Greyrigg
Parkgate
Nethermill
Jardine Hall
Nethercleuch
HART
Burnfoot

Auldgirth
Dalswinton
Ae Bridgend
Cumrue
Templand
Millhousebridge
Corrie

Duncow
Auchencairn
Shieldhill
Marjoriebanks
Applegarth Town
Bankshill
Netherhill
GRANGE FELL
Bigholms

New Lar

Kirkton
Amisfield
Tinwald
Lochmaben
Lockerbie
Tundergarth
COLLIN HAGS

Holywood
Holywood Village
Heath Hall
Torthorwald
Greenhill
Hightae
Waterbeck
Solwaybank

Newbridge
Aviation
Roucan
Kettleholm
Burnswark Hill
Middlebie
Chapelknowe

Terregles
Lochside
Lincluden Collegiate Church
Collin
Greenlea
Dalton
Ecclefechan
Eaglesfield
Timpanhec

Maxwelltown
Dumfries
Racks
Carrutherstown
Hoddom Cross
Thomas Carlyle's Birthplace
Kirtlebridge
Mil

Cargenbridge
Islesteps
Kingholm Quay
Mouswald
Hoddom Mains
Bonshaw Tower
Robgill Tower
Kirkpatrick-Fleming

New Abbey
Kelton
Conheath
Glencaple
Bankend
Clarencefield
Brydekirk
Creca
Hollee

Kirkconnell Flow
Kirkconnell
Ruthwell Cross
Kelhead
Bruce's
Springfie

Mabie Forest
Lochober Loch
Nith Estuary
Shearington
Caerlaverock Castle
Savings Banks
Ruthwell
Cummertrees
Annan
Gretna Green
Gretna

Sweetheart Abbey
Ingleston
Bowhouse
Blackshaw
Caerlaverock Wetland Centre
Powfoot
Howes
Dornock
Eastriggs
Rigg

CRIFFELL
Kirkbean
Carsethorn
Newbie
Redkirk Point
Gretna Gatewa

Loch Kindar
Carse Bay
Drumburn
Torduff Point

Mainsriddle
Borron Point
Arbigland
John Paul Jones Cottage
Bowness-on-Solway
Port Carlisle
Glasson
Rockcliffe Cross

Loaningfoot
Mereshead
Southerness
Gill Foot Bay
Campfield Marsh
Bowness Common
Drumburgh
Easton
Boustead Hill
Burgh by Sands

Southerness Point
Skinburness
Grune Point
Moricambe Bay
Cardurnock
Anthorn
Whitrigg
Angerton
Kirkbride
Powhill
Longburgh
North End
Monkhi

SOLWAY FIRTH
East Cote
Calvo
Border
Salt Coates
Newton Arlosh
Laythes
Wampool
Studholme
Little Bampton
Kirkbampton
Oughterby

Silloth
Seaville
Brownrigg
South Solway Mosses
Biglands
Great Orton

Causewayhead
Blackdyke
Moss Side
Raby
Gamelsby
Aikton
Wiggonby

Blitterlees
Kingside Hill
Drumleaning
Moorhouse
Thornby
Woodhouses
Whinnow
Orton

Beckfoot
Wolsty
Highlaws
Abbeytown
Holm Cultram
Kelsick
Oulton Lessonhall
Micklethwaite
Crofton

Pelutho
Newtown
Aldoth
Dundraw
Moor Row
Aikhead
Dockray
West Curthwaite

Holme St Cuthbert
Tarns
Wheyrigg
Blencogo
Waverbridge
Waverton
Wigton
Highmoor

Mawbray
Salta
Mealrigg
Bromfield
Parkgate
Red Dial
Brackenthwaite

Dubmill Point
Edderside
New Cowper
Langrigg
High Scales
Low Row
Bolton Low Houses
Westward
Rosley

Allonby
Westnewton
Yearngill
Crookdake
Fletchertown
Bolton New Houses
Grassgar

Allonby Bay
Hayton
Aspatria
Watchill
Brocklebank

Prospect
Harriston
Baggrow
Blennerhasset
Mealsgate
Boltongate
Sandale
FAULDS BROW
Whelpo
Ratten Row
Caldbeck

Crosscanonby
Crosby
Oughterside
Arkleby
Kirkland Guards
Threapland
Torpenhow
Whitrigg
Ireby
Aughertree
Fell Side
Hesket Newmarket

Maryport
Crosby Villa
Bullgill
Parsonby
Plumbland
Bothel
High Ireby
Uldale
Branthwaite

Senhouse
Gilcrux
Greengill
Sunderland
Bewaldeth
Ruthwaite
BINSEY
Longlands
Nether Row

Ellenborough
Risehow
Dearham
Townhead
Tallentire
Blindcrake
Lake District Wildlife Park
Sunderland
Orthwaite
CARR FEL

Flimby
Woodside
Bridekirk
Redmain
High Bewaldeth
Kilnhill
Bassenthwaite

St Helens
Broughton Moor
Dovenby
KNOTT
Chapel
High Side
GREAT CALVA
BOWSCALE FEL

Siddick
Standingstone
Little Broughton
Papcastle
Jennings
North Row
Scarness

Seaton
Great Clifton
Great Broughton
Camerton
Brigham
Embleton
Mirehouse
SKIDDAW
BLENCATHRA

Workington
North Side
Bridgefoot
Greysouthen
Cockermouth
Wythop Mill
High Crosthwaite

Mossbay
Stainburn
Little Clifton
Eaglesfield
Deanscales
Armaside
Little Crosthwaite

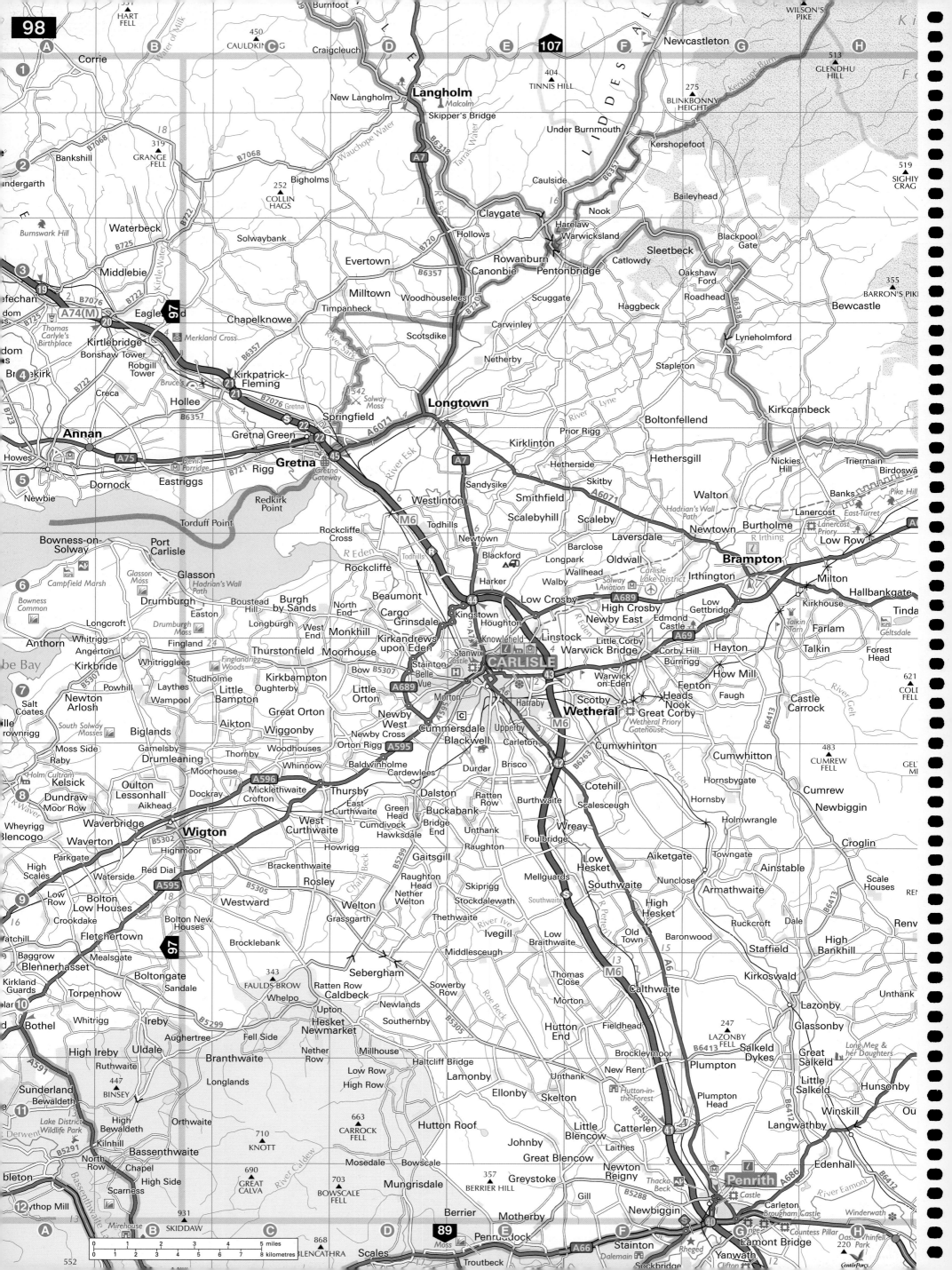

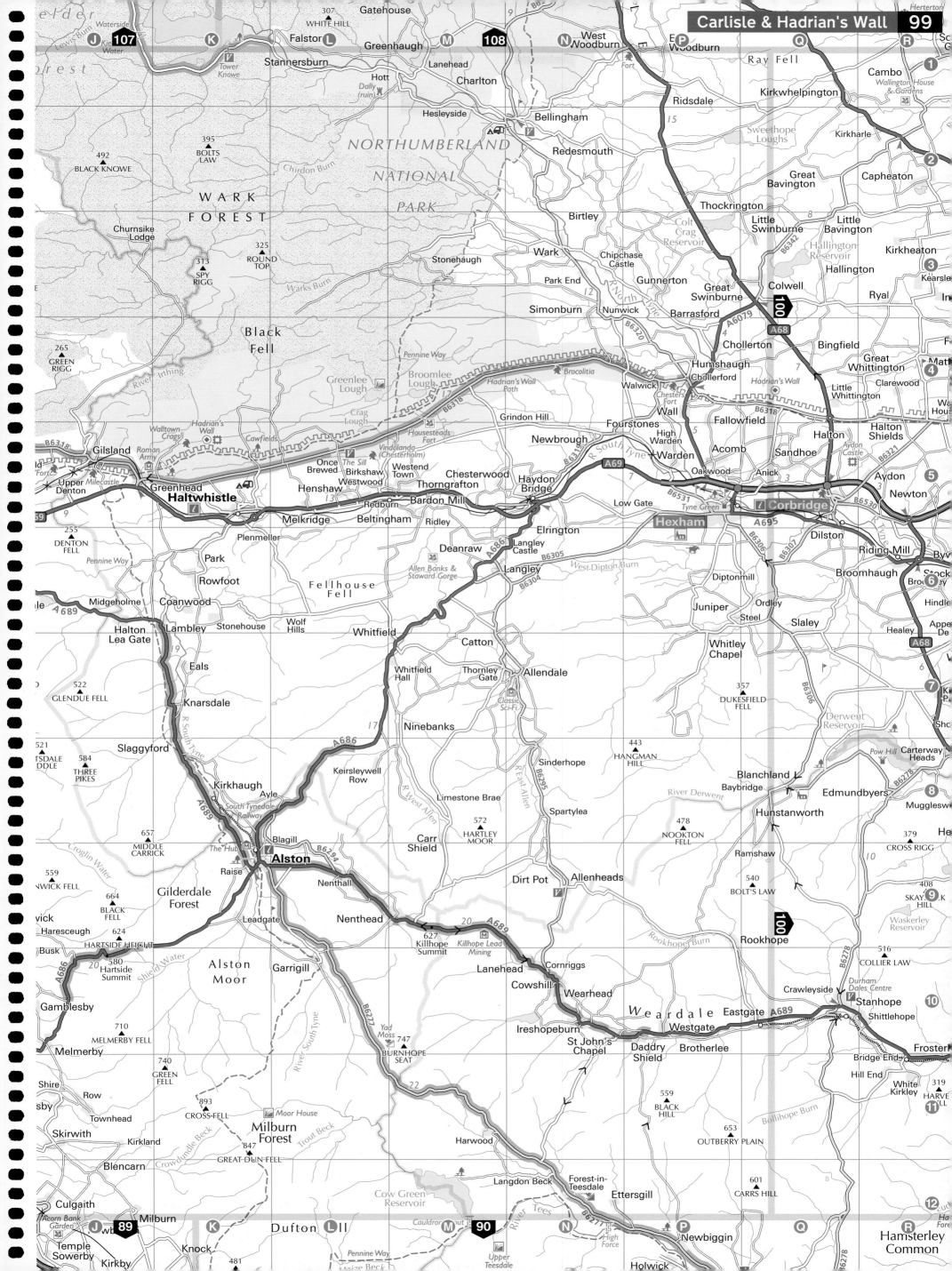

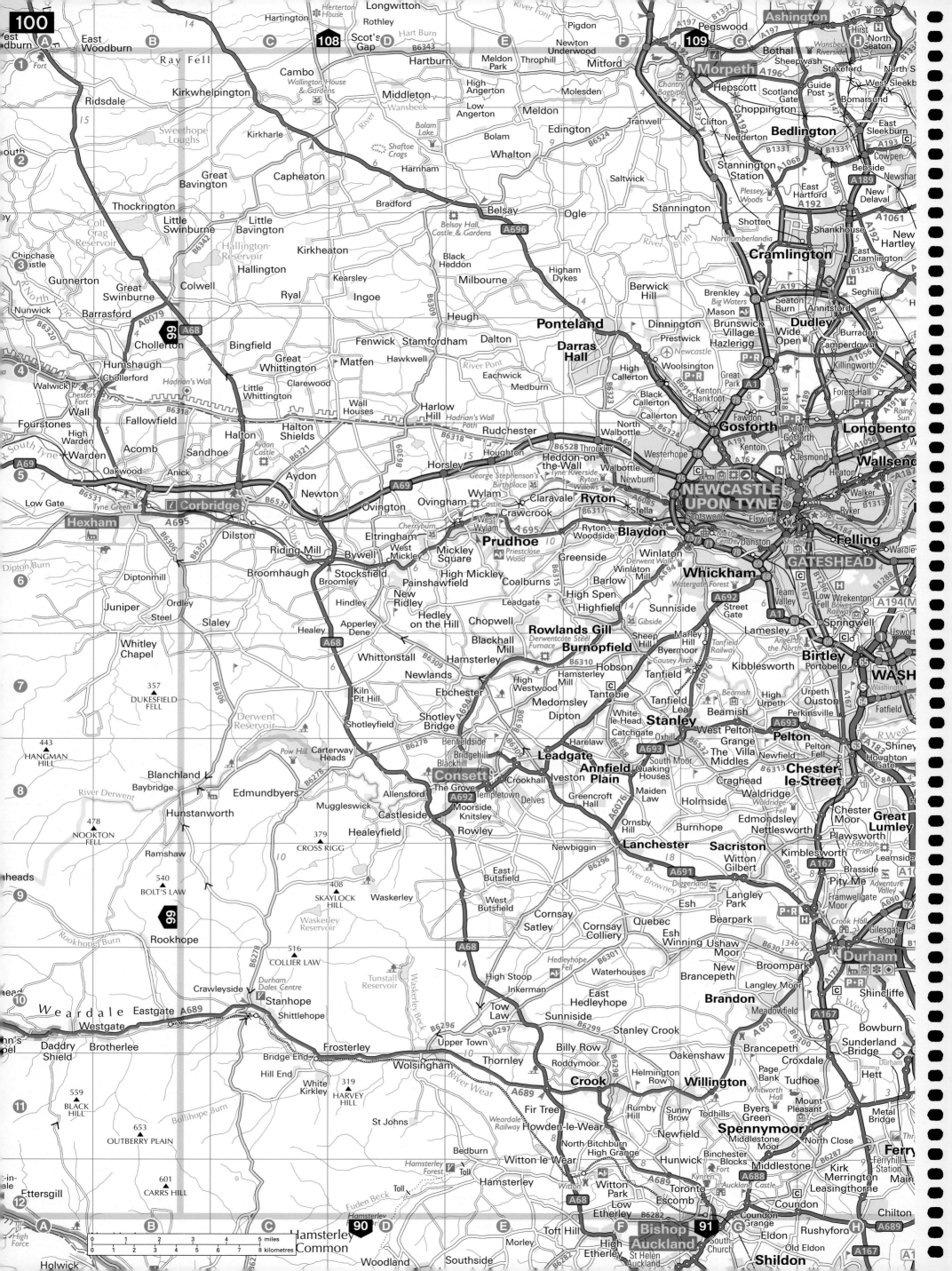

Isle of Man

0 1 2 3 4 5 miles
0 1 2 3 4 5 6 7 8 kilometres

Manx Heritage site

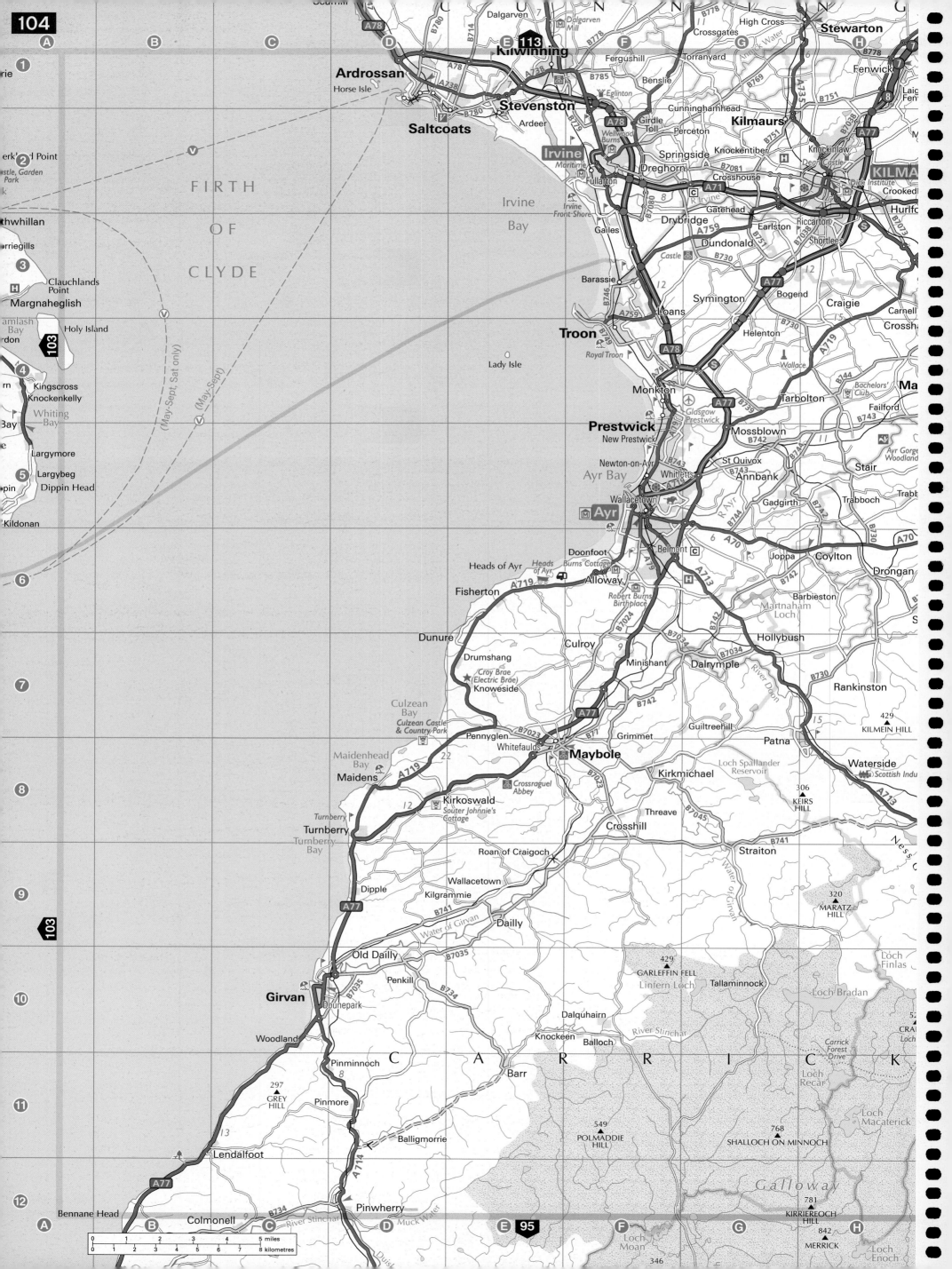

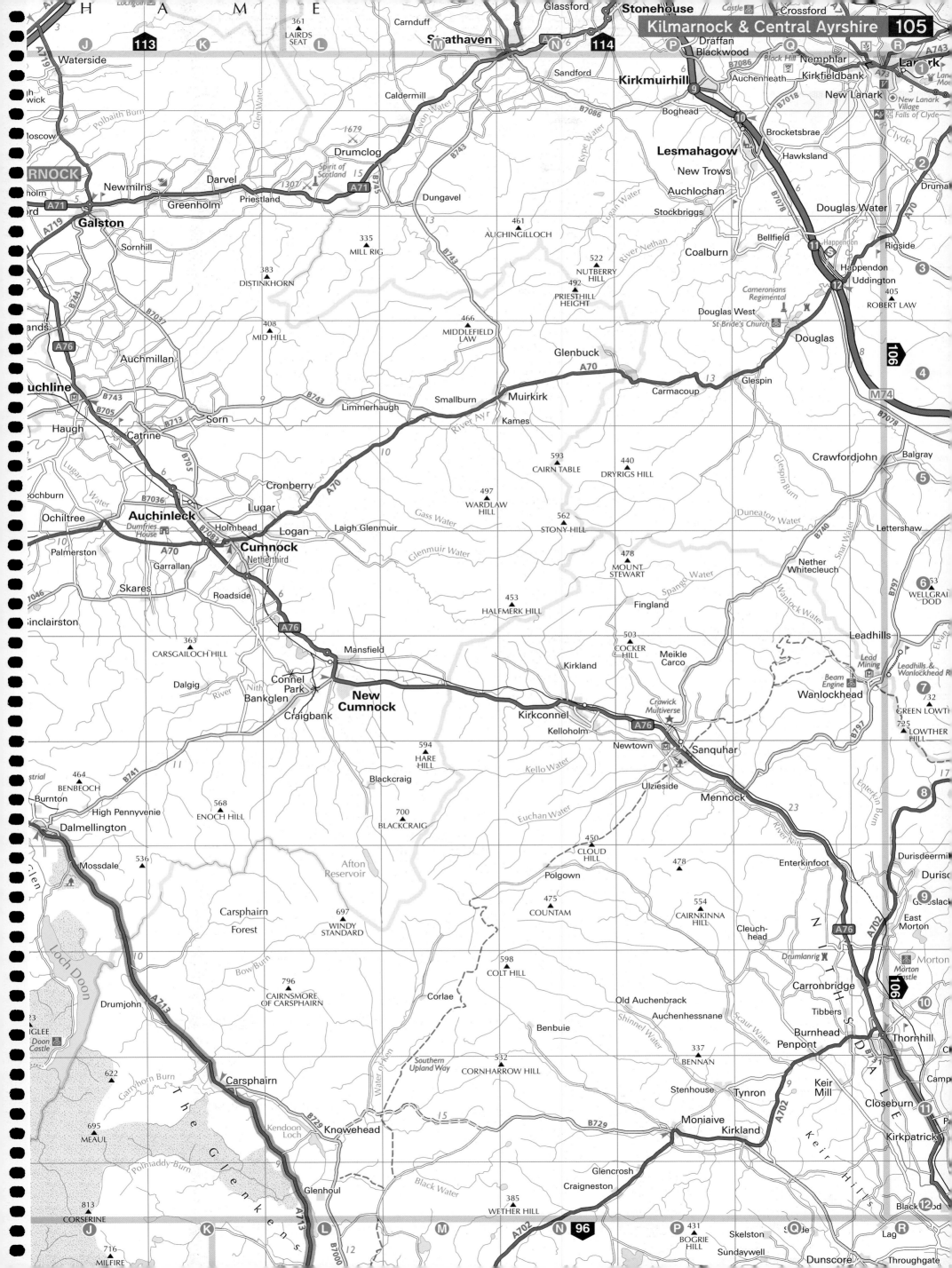

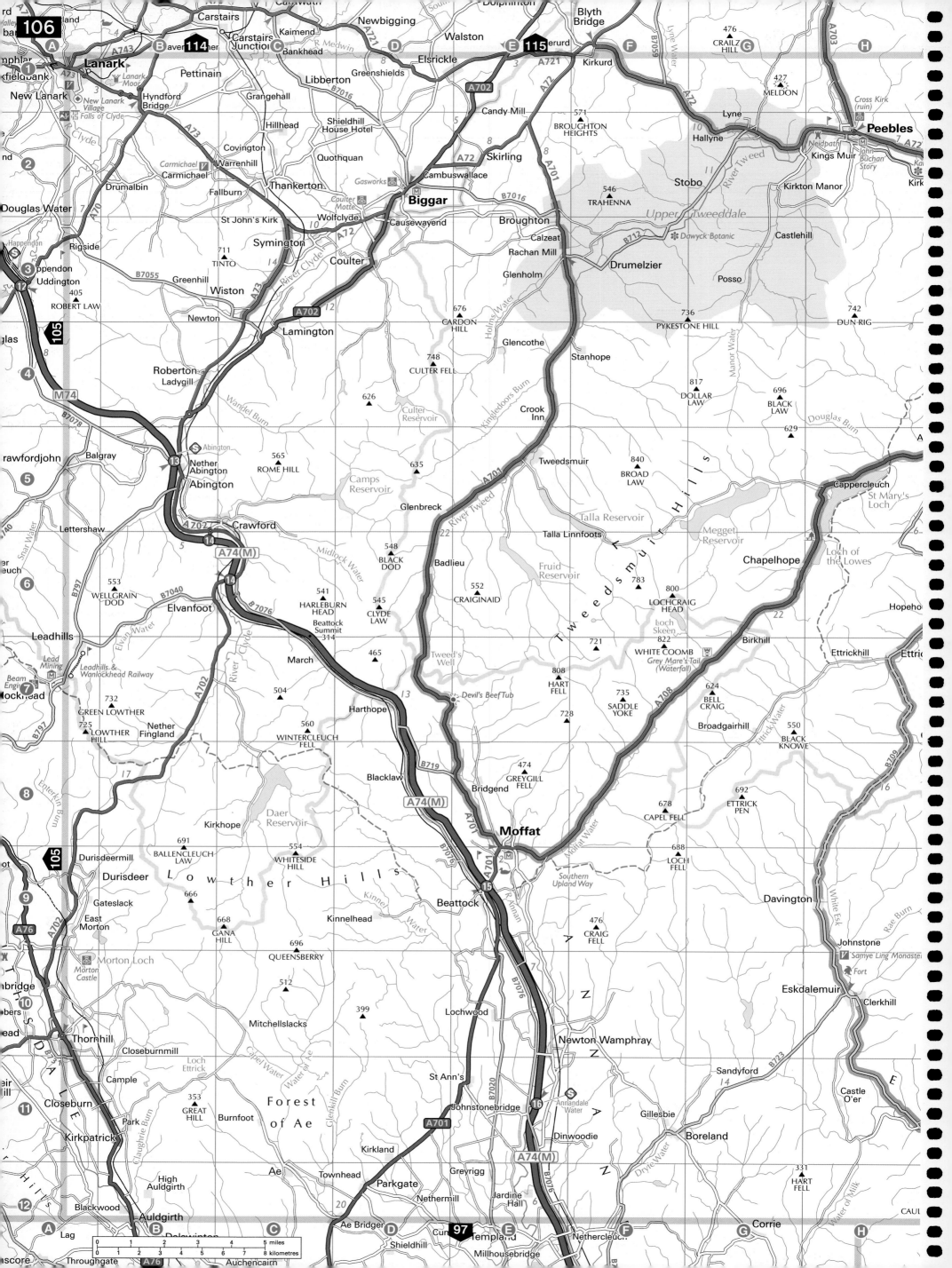

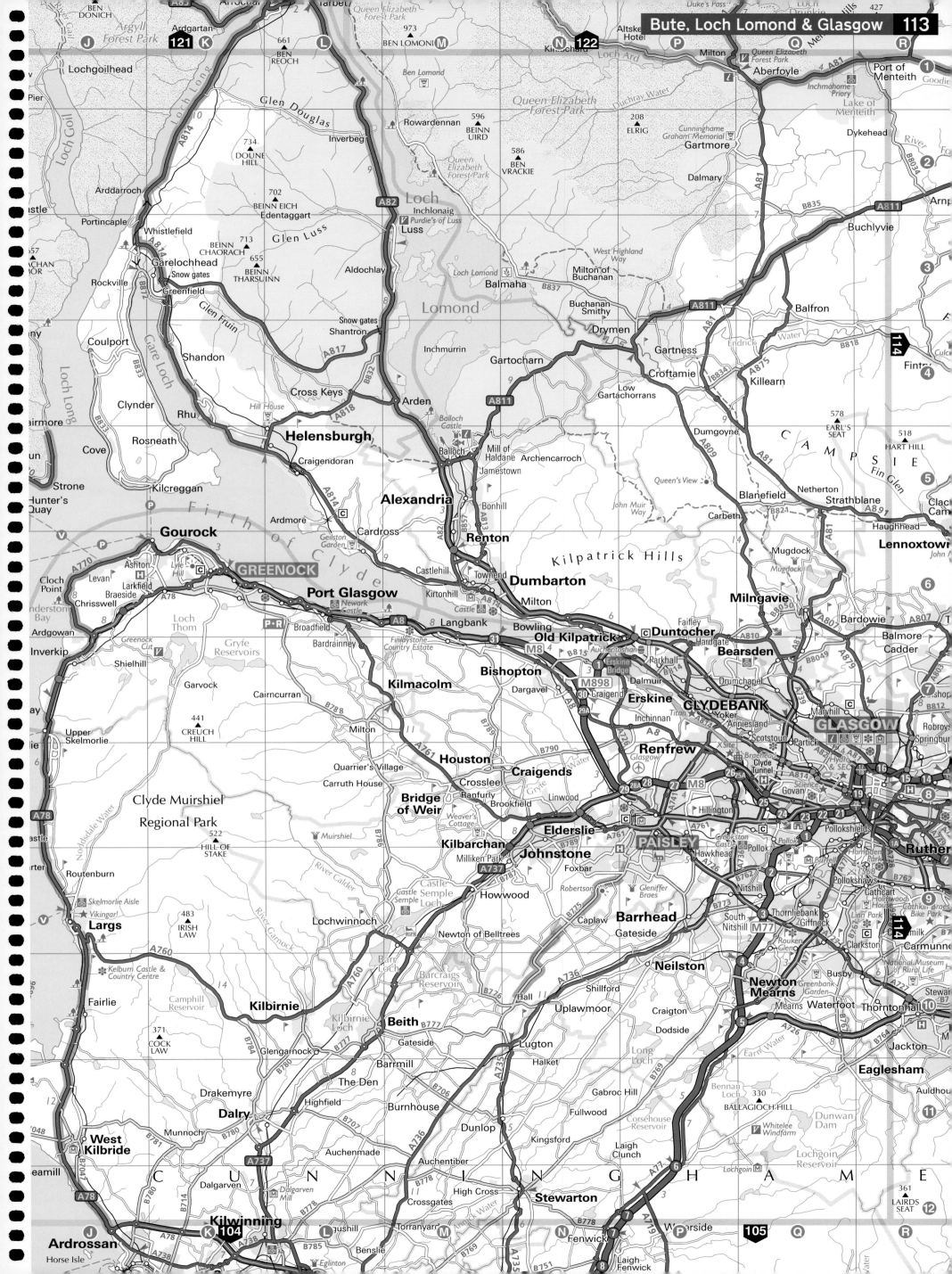

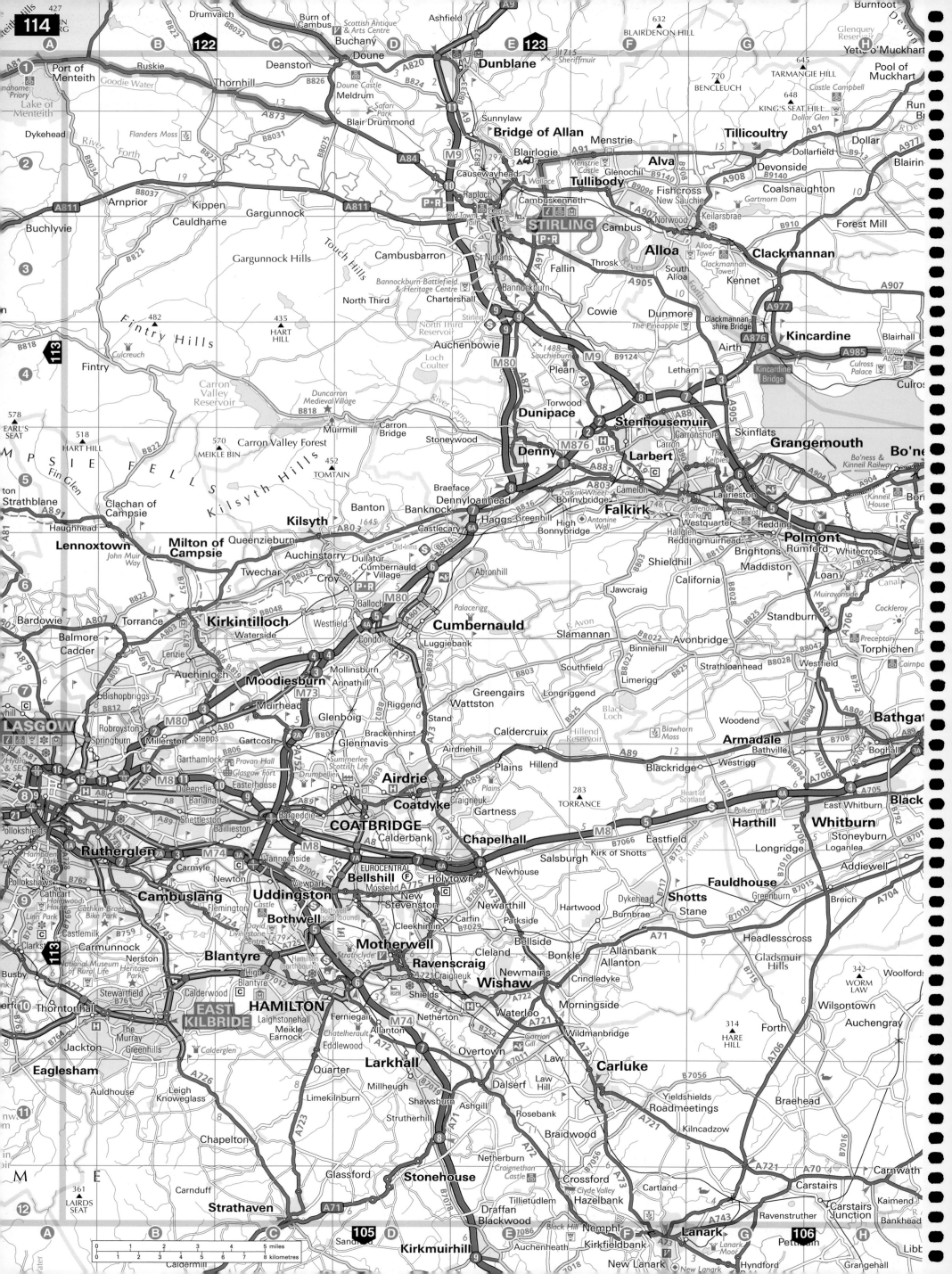

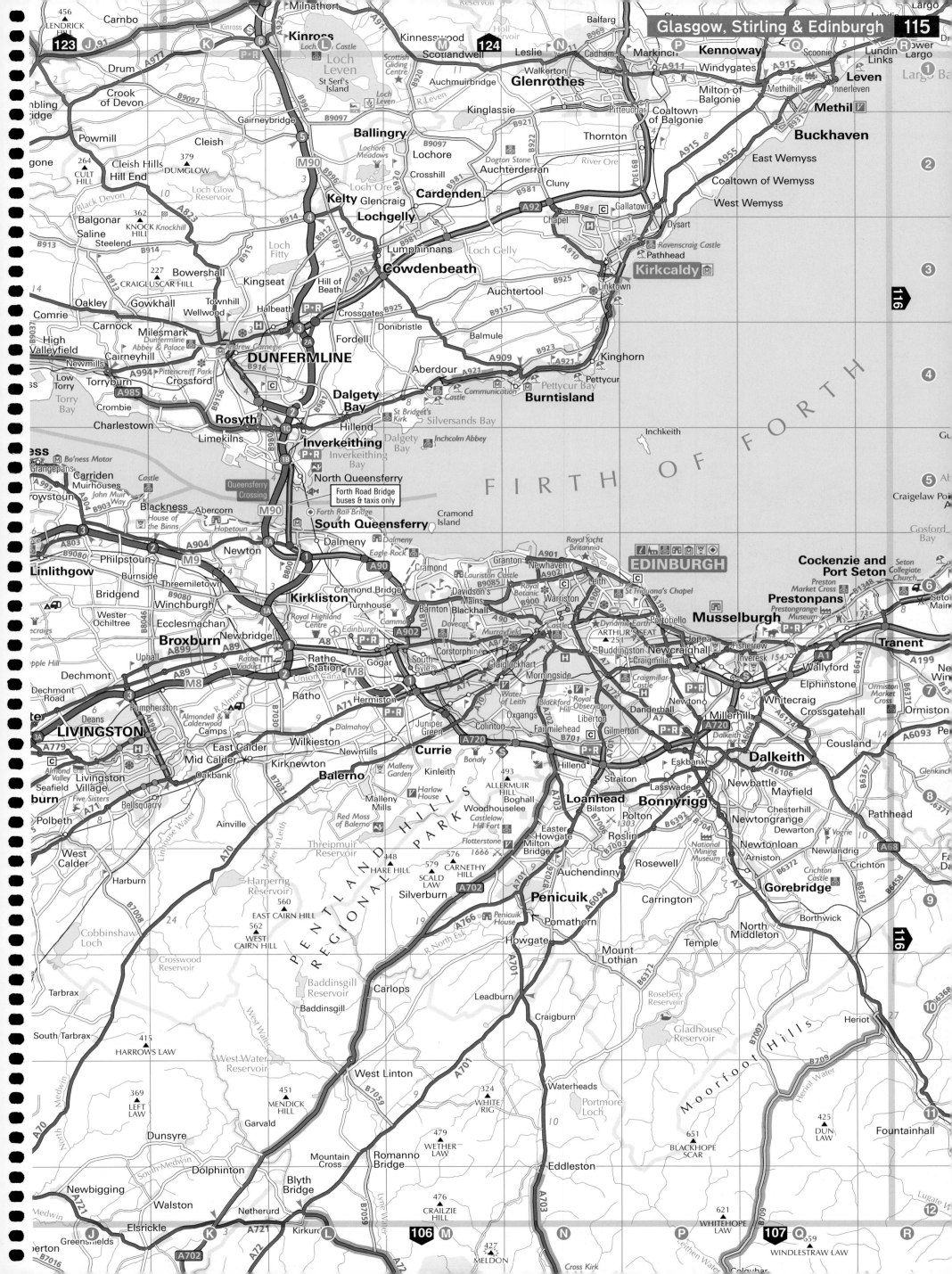

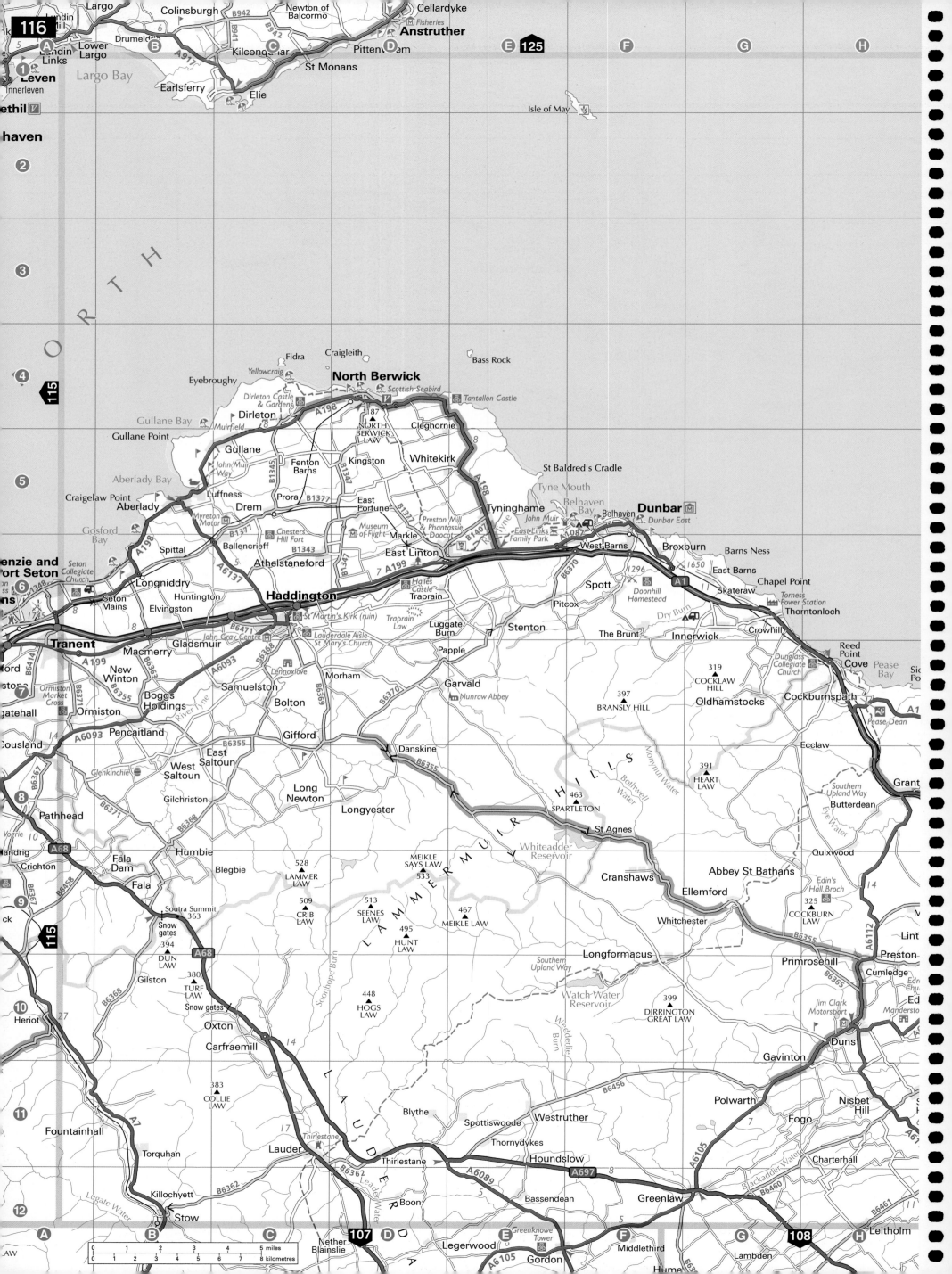

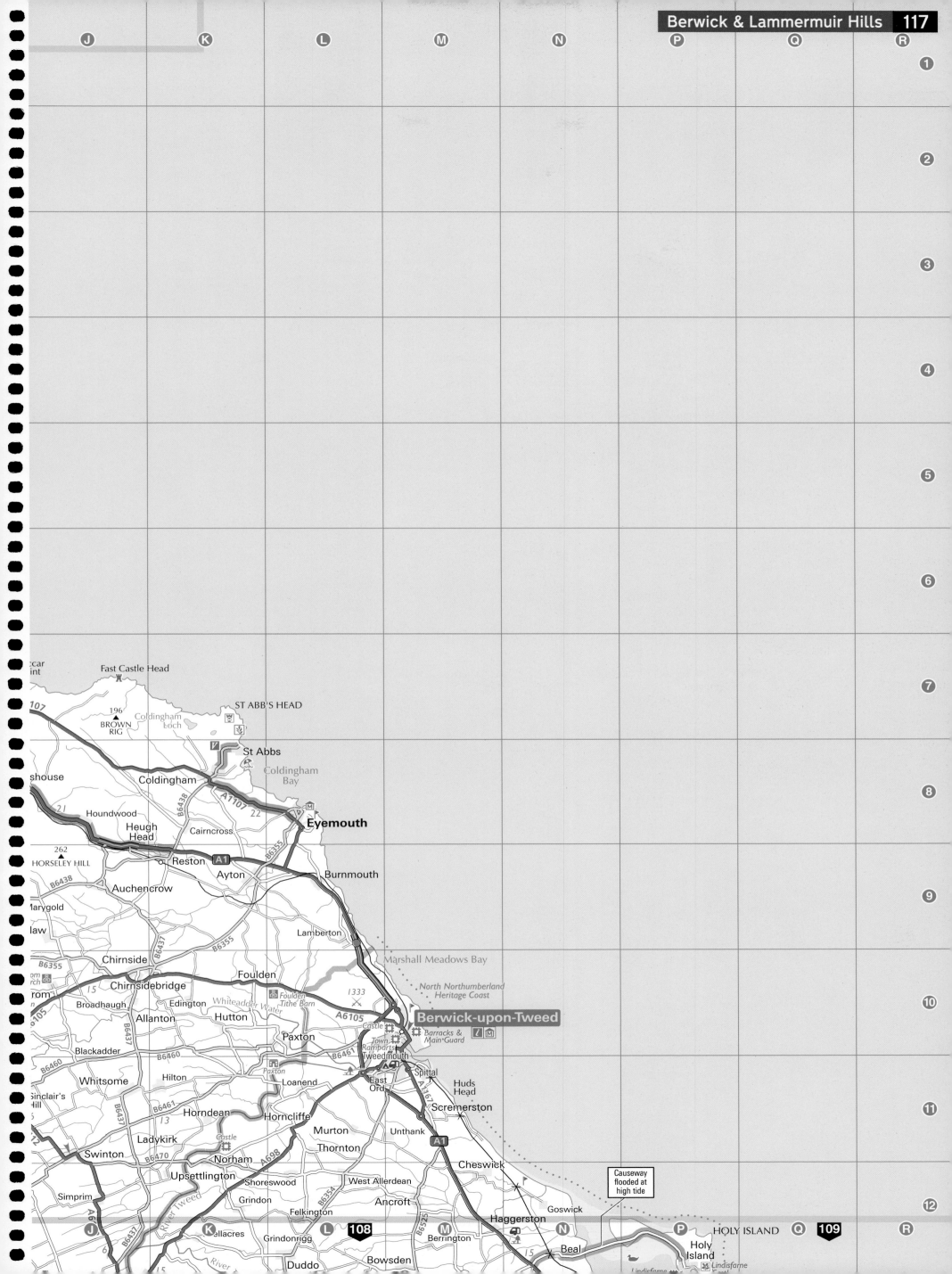

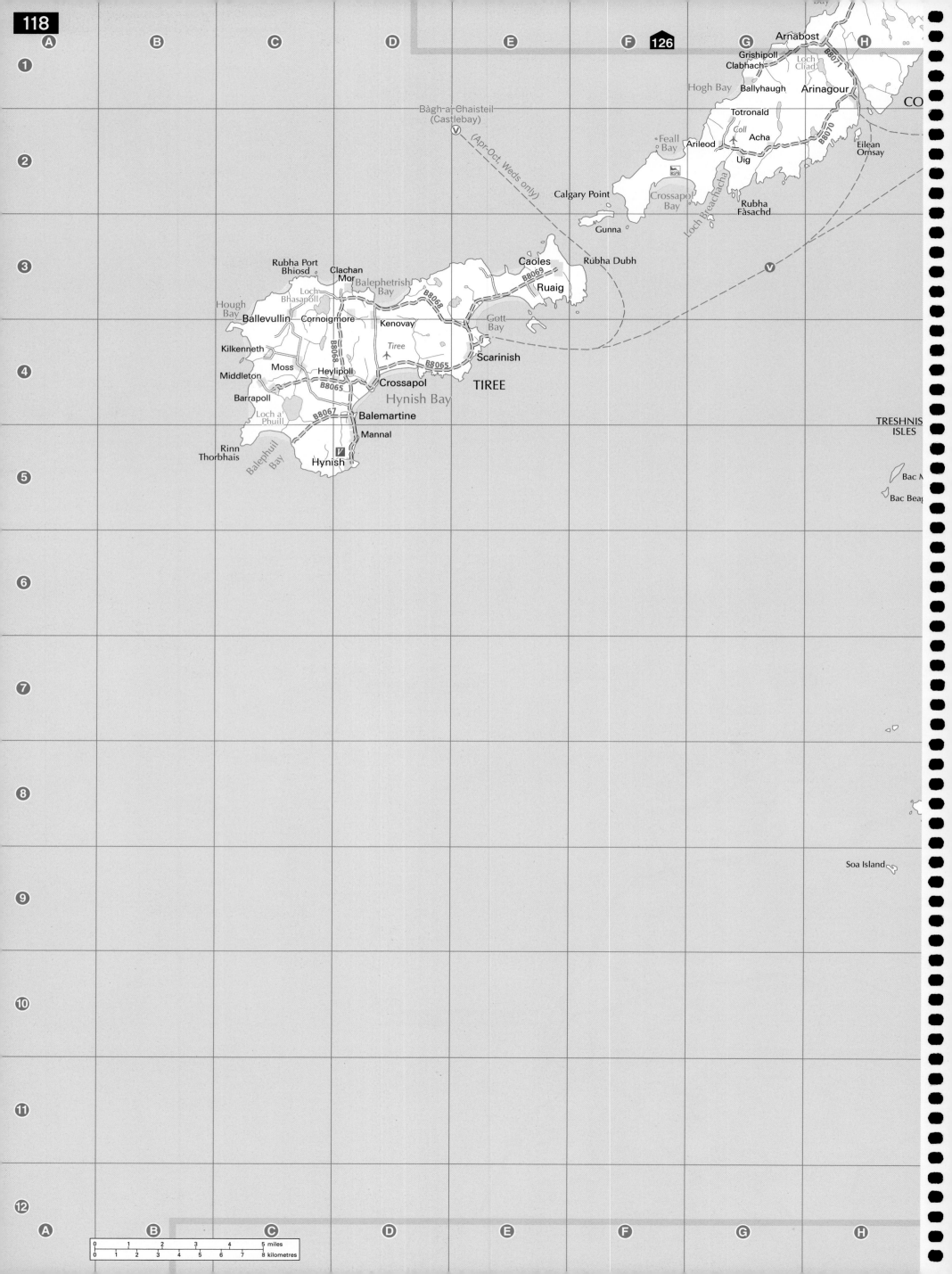

A B C D E F 126 G H

1

Bàgh-a-Chaisteil
(Castlebay)

2 (Apr-Oct, Weds only)

Arnabost
Grishipoll
Clabhach
Loch
Cliad
Hogh Bay Ballyhaugh Arinagour
CO

Totronald
Coll
Feall Arileod Acha
Bay Uig
Crossapol Eilean
Bay Ornsay
Calgary Point Rubha
Fàsachd
Gunna
Loch Breachacha
V

3
Rubha Port Caoles
Bhiosd Clachan Rubha Dubh
Mor Balephetrish B8069
Hough Bay Ruaig
Bay Loch Balevullin Cornoigmore Kenovay Gott
Bhasapoll Bay
Balevullin Cornoigmore B8068 Scarinish
Kilkenneth Tiree B8065

4
Moss Heylipoll
Middleton B8068
Barrapoll B8065 Crossapol TIREE TRESHNIS
Loch a' Hynish Bay ISLES
Phuill B8067 Balemartine
Rinn Mannal Bac M
Thorbhais Balephuil Bac Beag
Bay Hynish

5

6

7

8

Soa Island

9

10

11

12

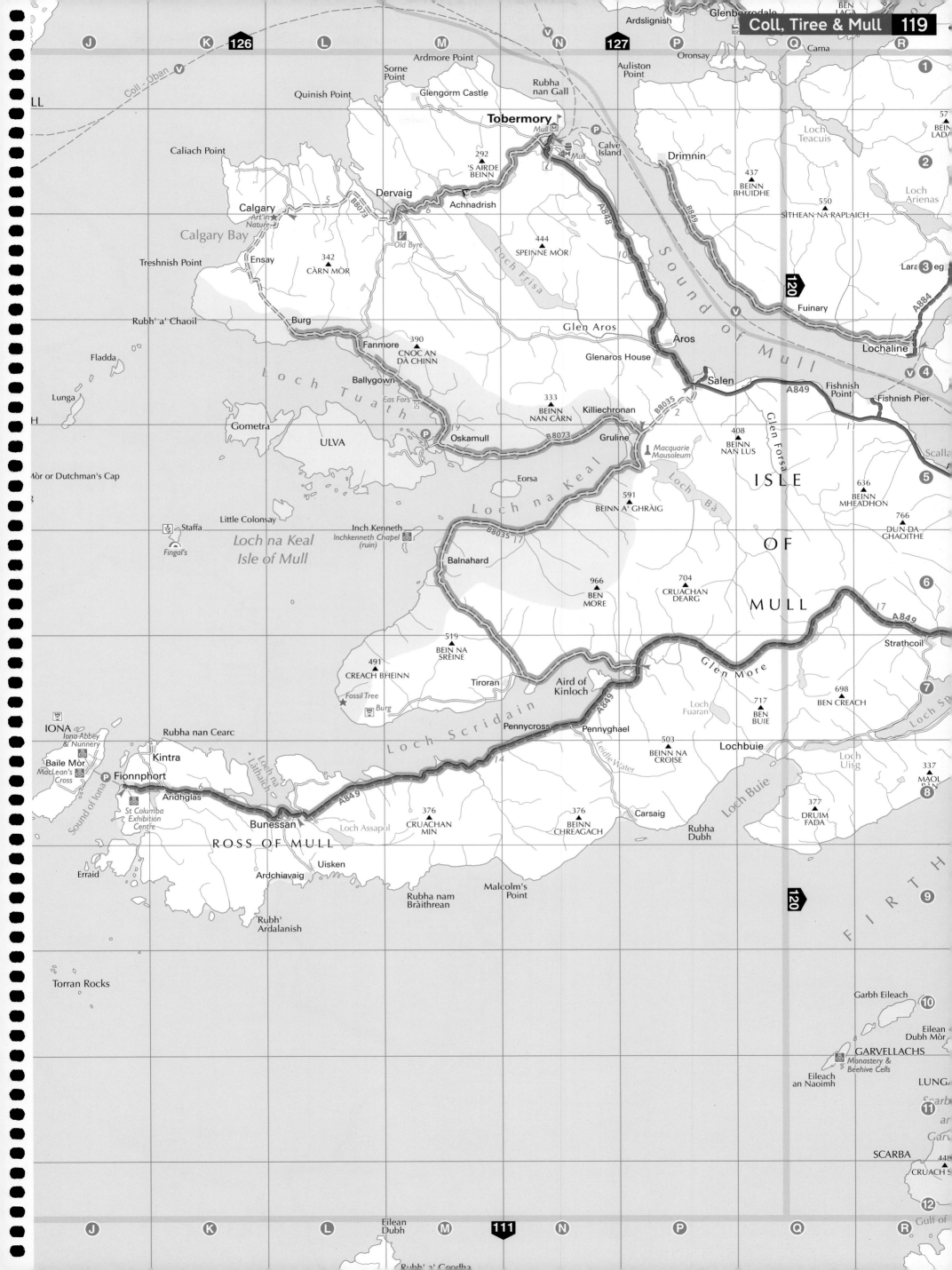

J K **126** L M **127** P Q R

1

Glenborrodale
BEN LAGA
Ardslignish
Carna
Loch Teacuis
BEN LAD
57

Ardmore Point
Sorne Point
Coll - Oban
Rubha nan Gall
Auliston Point
Oronsay

Quinish Point
Glengorm Castle
Tobermory
Mull
Calve Island
Drimnin
BEINN BHUIDHE
437
SÌTHEAN-NA-RAPLAICH
550
Loch Arienas

Caliach Point
292
'S AIRDE BEINN
P
Mull

2

Dervaig
Achnadrish
A848
Lara eg
A884

Calgary
Art in Nature
B8073
5
Loch Frisa
Fuinary
120

Calgary Bay
Old Byre
SPEINNE MÒR
444
Glen Aros
Aros
Lochaline

3

Ensay
CÀRN MÒR
342
10
Sound of Mull

Treshnish Point
Glenaros House

Rubh' a' Chaoil
Burg
Fanmore
CNOC AN DÀ CHINN
390
Salen
Fishnish Point
Fishnish Pier

4

Fladda
Ballygown
Eas Fors
BEINN NAN CÀRN
333
Killiechronan
B8035
2
A849
Glen Forsa
V

Lunga
Gometra
Loch Tuath
ULVA
Oskamull
P
19
B8073
Gruline
Macquarie Mausoleum
BEINN NAN LUS
408
ISLE
BEINN MHEADHON
636

5

Mòr or Dutchman's Cap
Little Colonsay
Eorsa
B8035
17
BEINN A' GHRÀIG
591
Loch Bà
OF
DUN DA GHAOITHE
766

Staffa
Loch na Keal
Isle of Mull
Inch Kenneth
Inchkenneth Chapel (ruin)
Balnahard
CRUACHAN DEARG
704
MULL

6

Fingal's
BEN MORE
966
17
A849
Strathcoil

BEIN NA SRÈINE
519
Glen More
BEN CREACH
698

7

CREACH BHEINN
491
Tiroran
Aird of Kinloch
A849
Loch Fuaran
BEN BUIE
717
Loch Sp

Fossil Tree
Burg
Pennycross
Pennyghael
BEINN NA CROISE
503
Lochbuie
MAOL
337

8

IONA
Iona Abbey & Nunnery
Rubha nan Cearc
Loch Scridain
14
Leidle Water
DRUIM FADA
377

Baile Mòr
MacLean's Cross
Kintra
Loch na Làthaich
Loch Buie

9

Fionnphort
P
Aridhglas
A849
CRUACHAN MIN
376
Carsaig
Rubha Dubh
120

St Columba Exhibition Centre
Bunessan
Loch Assapol
BEINN CHREAGACH
376
FIRTH

Erraid
ROSS OF MULL
Uisken
Ardchiavaig
Malcolm's Point

Rubh' Ardalanish
Rubha nam Bràithrean

Torran Rocks

Garbh Eileach

10

Eilean Dubh Mòr

GARVELLACHS
LUNG

Monastery & Beehive Cells
Eileach an Naoimh
Garv

11

SCARBA

12

J K L M **111** N P Q R Gulf of

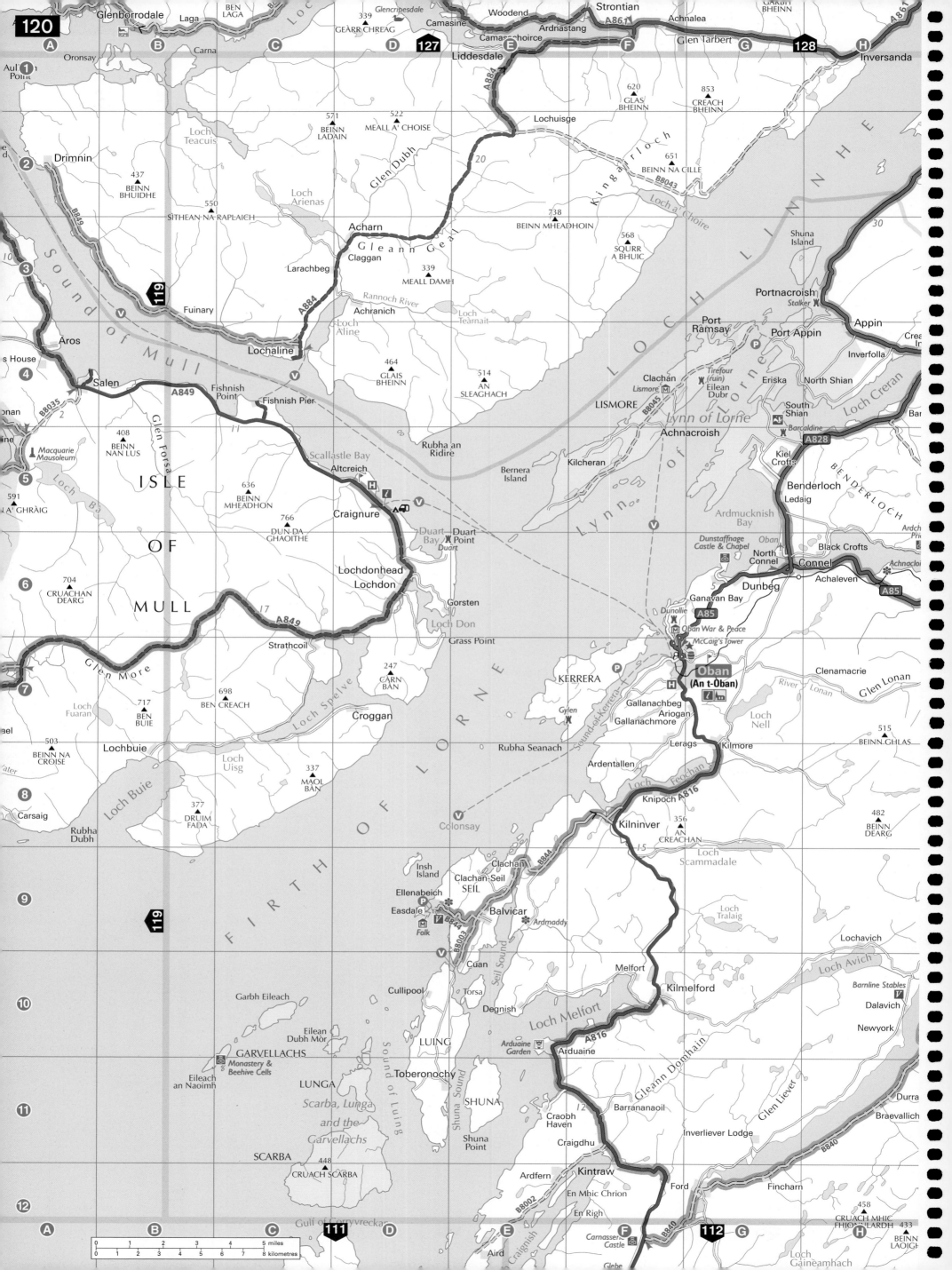

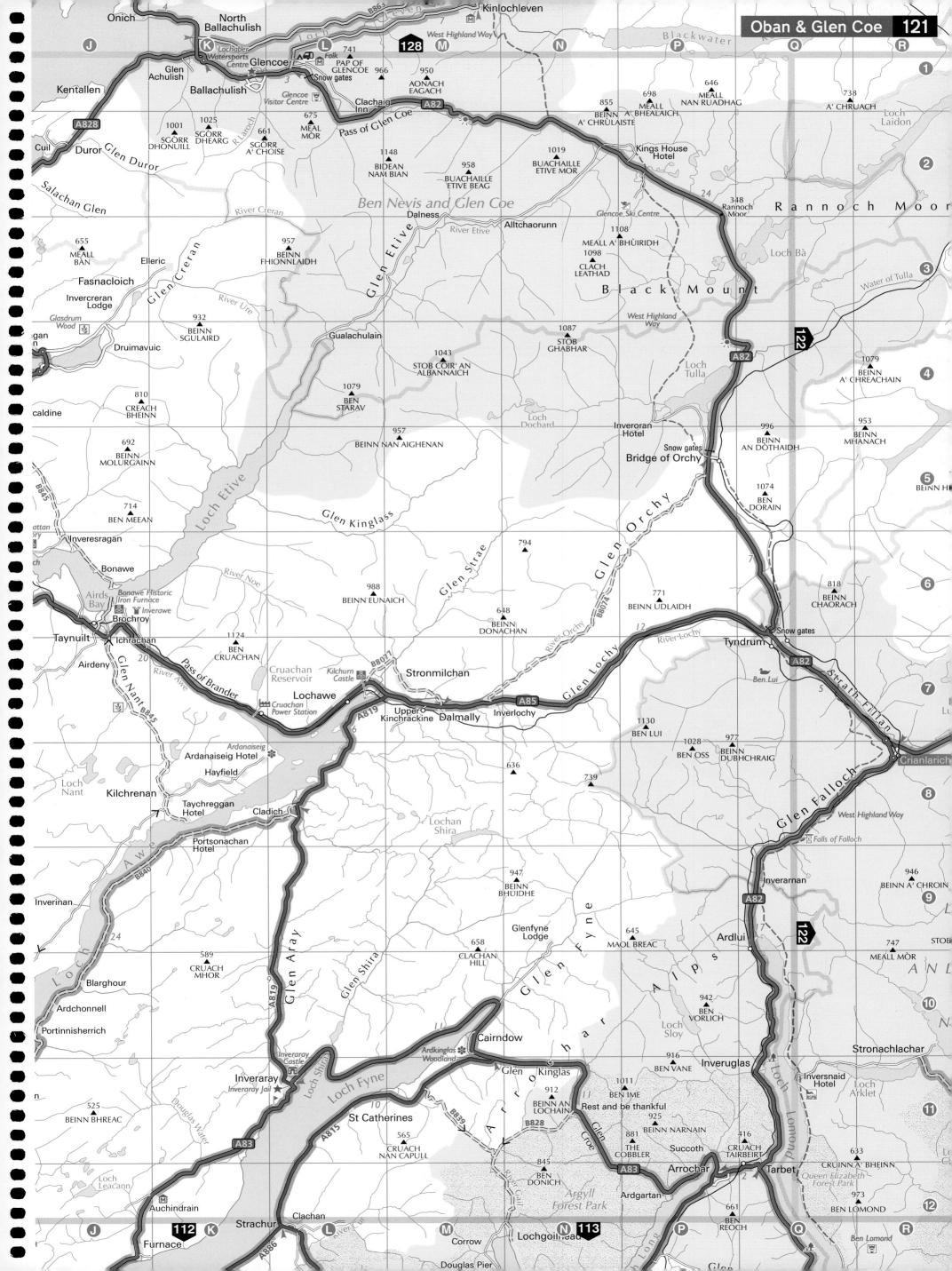

Onich
North Ballachulish
Kinlochleven
B863
Loch Leven
West Highland Way
Blackwater

J
K
Lochaber Watersports Centre
L
741
Folk
M
128
N
P
Q
R

1

Glen Achulish
Glencoe
PAP OF GLENCOE 966
Snow gates
950 AONACH EAGACH
MEALL NAN RUADHAG 646
738 A' CHRUACH
Loch Laidon

Kentallen
Ballachulish
Glencoe Visitor Centre
Clachaig Inn
675 MEAL MÒR
855 BEINN A' CHRÙLAISTE
698 MEALL A' BHEALAICH

A828
1001 SGORR DHONUILL
1025 SGORR DHEARG
Pass of Glen Coe
A82
1019 BUACHAILLE ETIVE MOR
Kings House Hotel

2

Cuil
Duror
Glen Duror
661 SGORR A' CHOISE
1148 BIDEAN NAM BIAN
958 BUACHAILLE ETIVE BEAG
Glencoe Ski Centre
24
348 Rannoch Moor
Rannoch Moor

Salachan Glen
Dalness
River Etive
Alltchaorunn
1108
1098 CLACH LEATHAD
MEALL A' BHÙIRIDH
Black Mount
Loch Bà
Water of Tulla

3

655 MEALL BÀN
Elleric
957 BEINN FHIONNLAIDH
Glen Creran
River Ure
West Highland Way

Fasnacloich
Invercreran Lodge
932 BEINN SGULAIRD
Gualachulain
1087 STOB GHABHAR
A82
122

4

Glasdrum Wood
Druimavuic
1043 STOB COIR' AN ALBANNAICH
Loch Tulla
1079 BEINN A' CHREACHAIN

810 CREACH BHEINN
1079 BEN STARAV
Loch Dochard
Inveroran Hotel
996 BEINN AN DÒTHAIDH
953 BEINN MHANACH

caldine
692 BEINN MOLURGAINN
957 BEINN NAN AIGHENAN
Snow gates
Bridge of Orchy
5
BEINN H...

714 BEN MEEAN
Glen Kinglass
1074 BEN DORAIN

Inveresragan
Bonawe
Bonawe Historic Iron Furnace
Inverawe
Glen Strae
794
Glen Orchy
818 BEINN CHAORACH
6

Airds Bay
Brochroy
Taynuilt
Ichrachan
988 BEINN EUNAICH
648 BEINN DONACHAN
River Orchy
B8074
771 BEINN UDLAIDH
12
River Lochy
Tyndrum
Snow gates
A82
7

Airdeny
Glen Nant B845
Pass of Brander
River Awe
20
1124 BEN CRUACHAN
Cruachan Reservoir
Kilchurn Castle
B8077
Stronmilchan
Glen Lochy
Ben Lui
5
Strath Fillan

Loch Nant
Kilchrenan
Cruachan Power Station
Lochawe
Upper Kinchrackine
Dalmally
A85
Inverlochy
1130 BEN LUI
1028 BEN OSS
977 BEINN DUBHCHRAIG
Crianlarich
8

Ardanaiseig
Ardanaiseig Hotel
Hayfield
A819
6
636
739
Glen Falloch
West Highland Way

Taychreggan Hotel
Cladich
Lochan Shira
946 BEINN A' CHROIN
9

Portsonachan Hotel
Loch Awe
B840
Falls of Falloch
Inverarnan
A82
122

Inverinan
24
947 BEINN BHUIDHE
645 MAOL BREAC
Ardlui
747 MEALL MÒR
AN...

589 CRUACH MHOR
Glen Aray
A819
9
Glen Shira
Glen Fyne
Glenfyne Lodge
10

Blarghour
658 CLACHAN HILL
942 BEN VORLICH
Loch Sloy
11

Ardchonnell
Portinnisherrich
Arrochar Alps
916 BEN VANE
Inveruglas
Inversnaid Hotel
Loch Arklet

Cairndow
Ardkinglas Woodland
1011 BEN IME
Rest and be thankful
Stronachlachar

525 BEINN BHREAC
Inveraray
Inveraray Castle
Inveraray Jail
Loch Fyne
11
Glen Kinglas
912 BEINN AN LOCHAIN
B828
925 BEINN NARNAIN
Glen Croe

A83
St Catharines
10
565 CRUACH NAN CAPULL
B839
881 THE COBBLER
Succoth
416 CRUACH TAIRBEIRT
633 CRÙINN A' BHEINN

112
J
K
Auchindrain
A815
Strachur
Clachan
L
River Cur
M
Corrow
N
Lochgoilhead
845 BEN DONICH
Ardgartan
A83
Arrochar
Tarbet
Loch Long
2
P
Q
661 BEN REOCH
Queen Elizabeth Forest Park
973 BEN LOMOND
R
12

Furnace
A886
Douglas Pier
Argyll Forest Park
River Goil
Ben Lomond
113
113

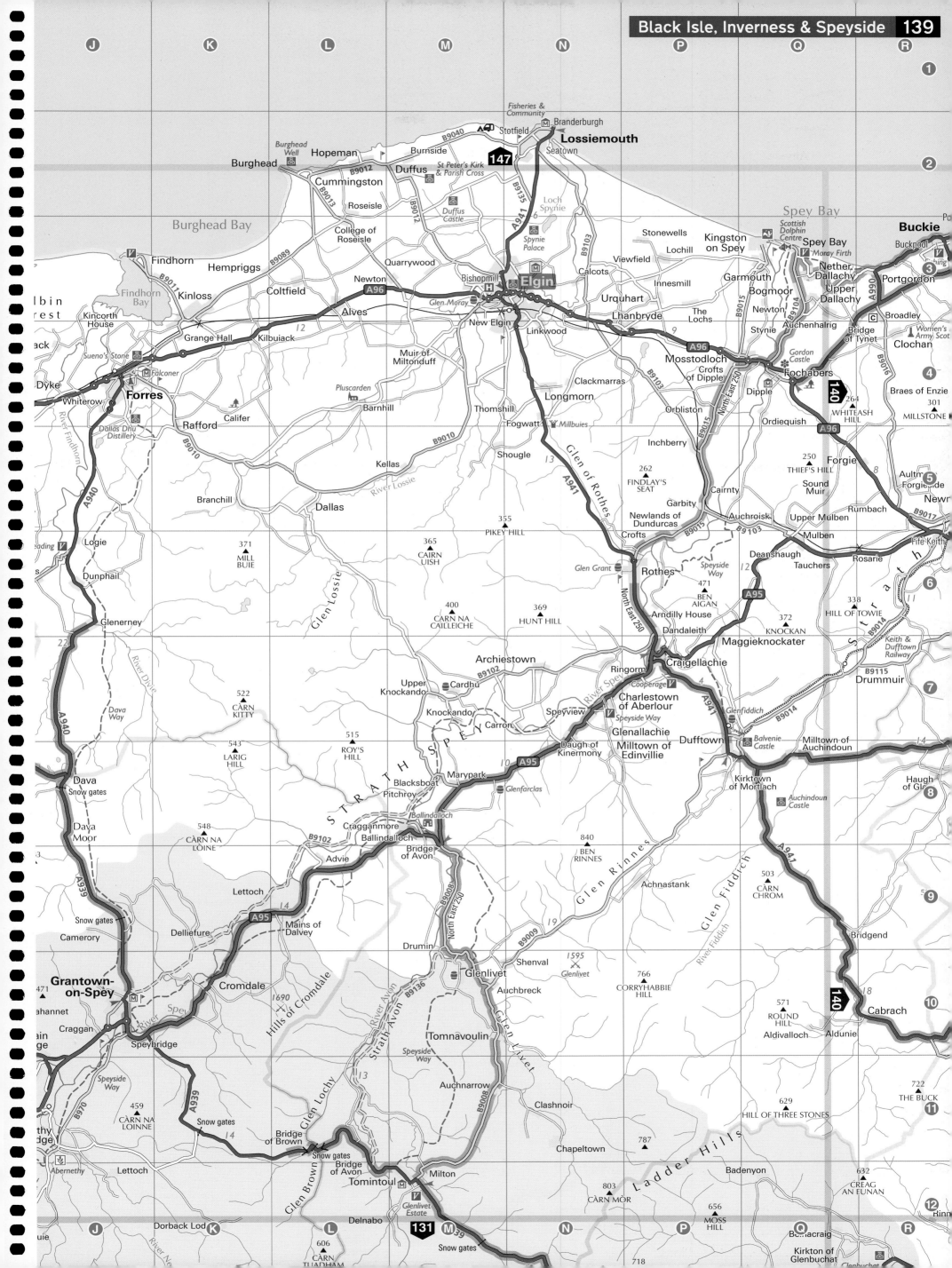

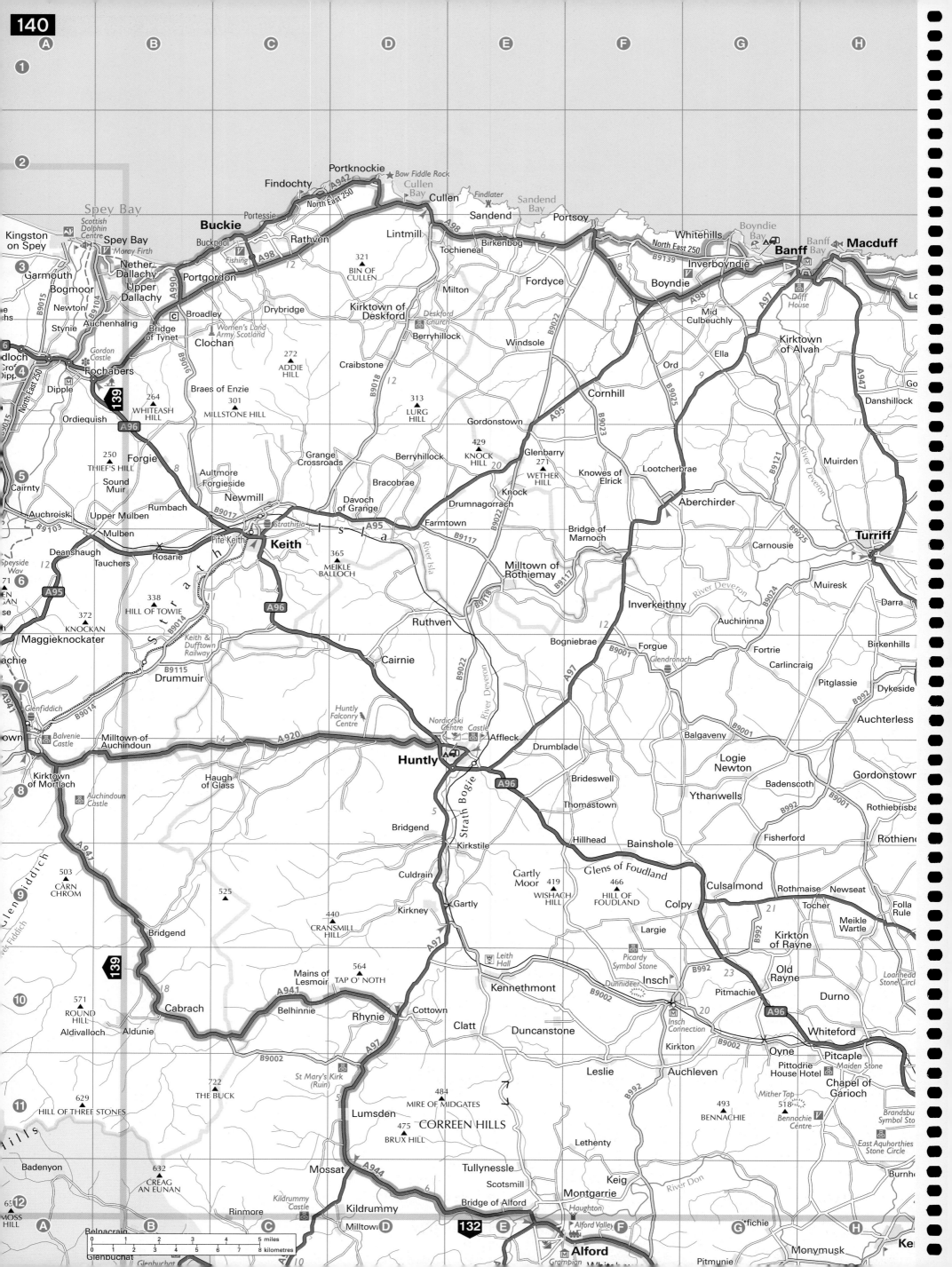

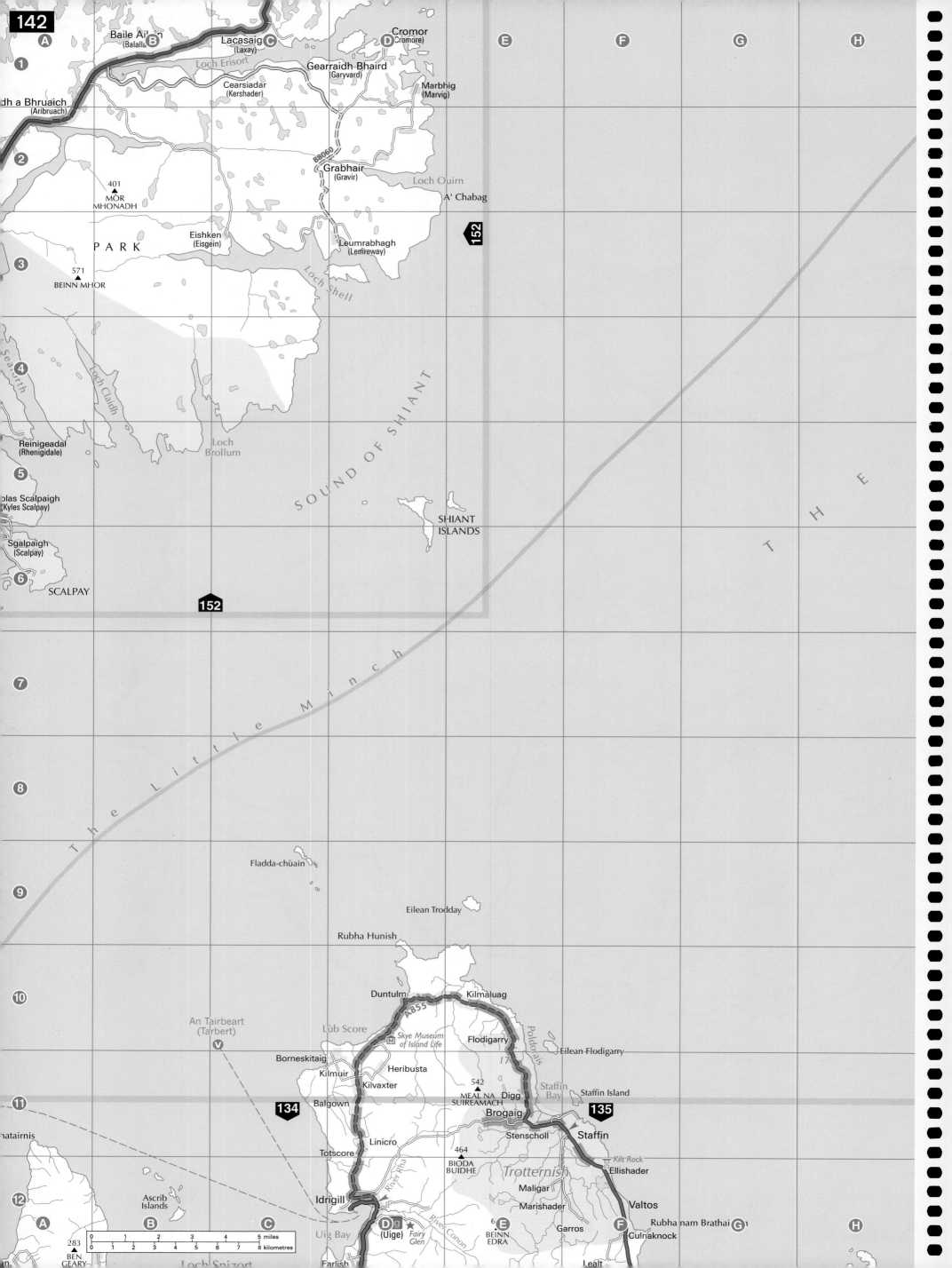

A   B   C   D   E   F   G   H

1

2

3

4

5

6

7

8

9

10

11

12

Baile Ailein
(Balallan)
Lacasaig
(Laxay)
Cromor
(Cromore)
Gearraidh Bhaird
(Garyvard)
Cearsiadar
(Kershader)
Marbhig
(Marvig)
dh a Bhruaich
(Aribruach)
Loch Erisort
B8060
Grabhair
(Gravir)
Loch Ouirn
401
MÒR
MHONADH
A' Chabag
152
Eishken
(Eisgein)
Leumrabhagh
(Lemreway)
PARK
571
BEINN MHOR
Loch Shell
Reinigeadal
(Rhenigidale)
Loch Claidh
Loch
Brollum
SOUND OF SHIANT
olas Scalpaigh
(Kyles Scalpay)
SHIANT
ISLANDS
T H E
Sgalpaigh
(Scalpay)
SCALPAY
152
The Little Minch
Fladda-chùain
Eilean Troddday
Rubha Hunish
Duntulm
Kilmaluag
A855
An Tairbeart
(Tarbert)
Lùb Score
Skye Museum
of Island Life
Flodigarry
Eilean-Flodigarry
Borneskitaig
Heribusta
Staffin
Bay
Staffin Island
Kilmuir
Kilvaxter
542
MEAL NA
SUIREAMACH
Digg
Balgown
Brogaig
135
134
Stenscholl
Staffin
Totscore
Linicro
464
BIODA
BUIDHE
Trotternish
Kilt Rock
Ellishader
atairnis
River Rha
Idrigill
Maligar
Marishader
Valtos
Ascrib
Islands
Uig Bay
(Uige)
Fairy
Glen
River Conon
BEINN
EDRA
Garros
Rubha nam Brathai
Culnaknock
283
BEN
GEARY
0   1   2   3   4   5 miles
0 1 2 3 4 5 6 7 8 kilometres
Loch Snizort
Farlish
Lealt

148

Q

Baddidarrach

Inverkirkaig 1

Rubha Còigeach

Eilean Mòr 2

Enard Bay

Rubha Mòr

Reiff

Achnahaird

Altandhu 144

Eilean Mullagrach

Isle Ristol

Polbain

Loch Osgaig

Loch Bad a' Ghaill 3

Badentarbet

Achiltibuie

Glas-leac Mòr

SUMMER ISLES

Tanera Beg

Badentarbat Bay

Polglass

Ben M Coigac

Steornabhagh (Stornoway)

Tanera Mòr

Horse Island

Horse Sound

Achduart 4

Glas-leac Beag

Culnacraig

BE CO

Eilean Dubh

Priest Island

Leac Dhonn

Isle Martin 5

Greenstone Point

Cailleach Head

Rubha Beag

Scoraig

Annat Bay

Mellon Udrigle

Stattic Point

Ruigh'riabhach 6

GRUINARD ISLAND

Badluarach

635 BEINN GHOBHLACH

Achgarve

Little Loch Broom

Foura

A832

Badrallach

Rubha Rèidh

Rubha nan Sasan

Laide

Gruinard Bay

Badcaul

North Coast 500

Cove

Mellon Charles

Ormiscaig

Gruinard

Ardessie

Camus 7

32

Aultbea

Loch a' Bhaid-luachraich

764 SAIL MHÒR

Dundonnell

Melvaig

AN CUAIDH 296

ISLE OF EWE

Loch a

Little Gruinard River

347 CREAG-MHEAL BEAG

Lochan Gaineamhaich

Aultgrishin

Loch Ewe

Loch Fada

Gruinard River

1062 AN TEALLACH 8

Inverasdale

293 CNOC BREAC

144

Strathnasheallag Forest

Naast

Inverewe Garden

250 MEALL NA MEINE

681 BEINN A' CHAISGEIN BEAG

Loch na Sealga

Fisherfield Forest

North Erradale

13

Londubh

Fionn Loch

Wester Ross

906 BEINN DEARG MHOR 9

Poolewe

Big Sand

Strath

Heritage

A832

Dubh Loch

Smithstown

Auchtercairn

791 BEINN AIRIDH CHARR

Longa Island

Lonemore

Gairloch & Loch Ewe

974 SGÙRRBÀN 10

Loch Gairloch

Gairloch

421 MEALL AN DOIREIN

1019 MULLACH COIRE MHIC FHEARCHAIR

Charlestown

Loch

859 BEINN LÀIR

Port Henderson

Eilean Horrisdale

B8056

Lochan Fada

Badachro

Loch Maree Islands

Letterewe Forest

Opinan

River Kerry

Letterewe

South Erradale

Loch Bad an Sgalaig

981 SLIOCH 11

Red Point 135

Victoria Falls 19

Talladale 136

A832

Maree

Red Point

Loch Ghaineamhach

680 BEINN A' MHÙINIDH

Kinlochewe Forest

Loch a' Ghodhainn

875 BAOSBHEINN

Loch na h-Oidhche

North Coast 500 12

619 BEINN BHREAC

855 BEINN AN EÒIN

724

Incheril

J

Loch Torridon

K

L

M

N

P

Q

Beinn Eighe

Kinlochewe

Rubha na Fearn

985

1009

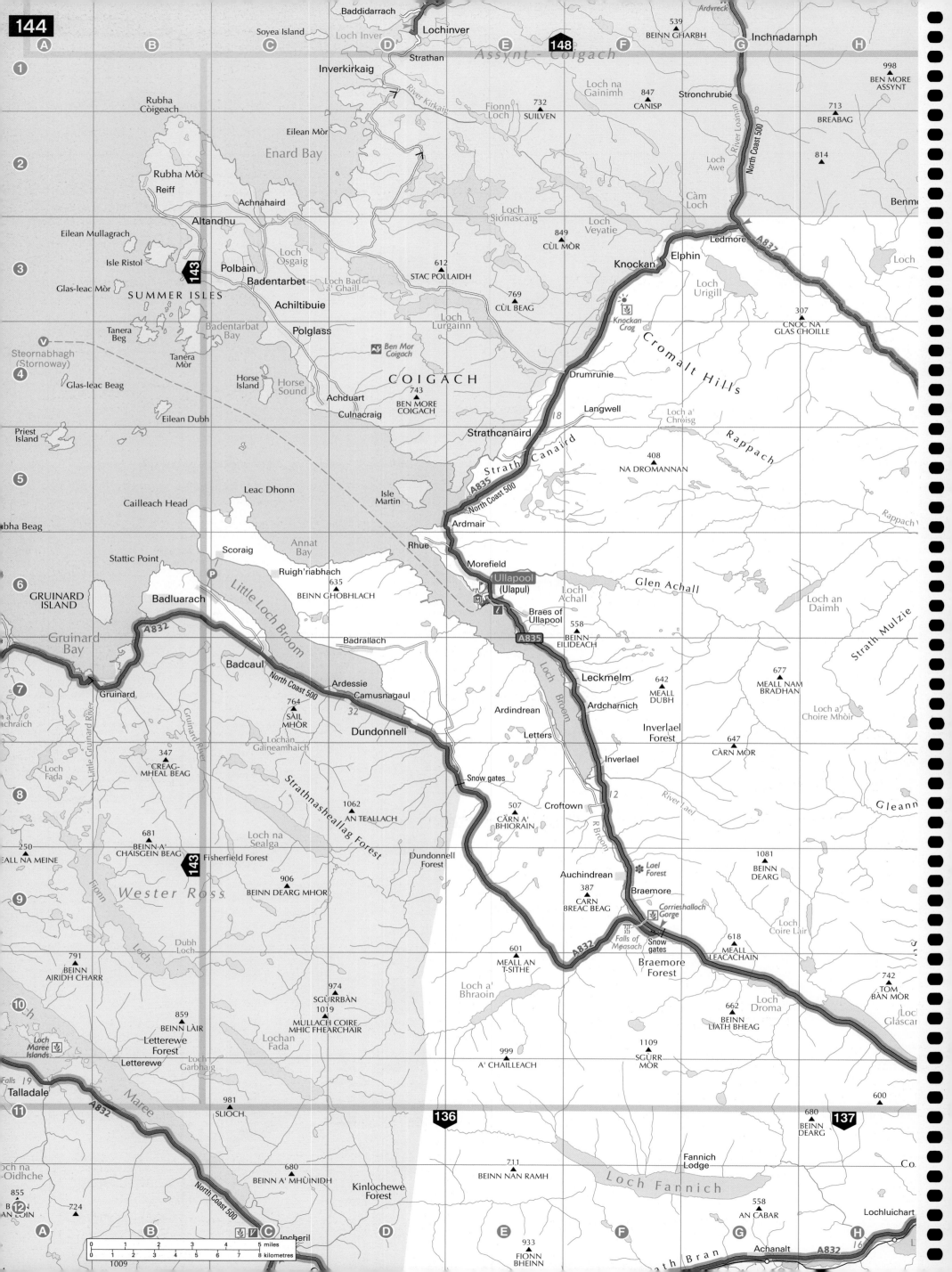

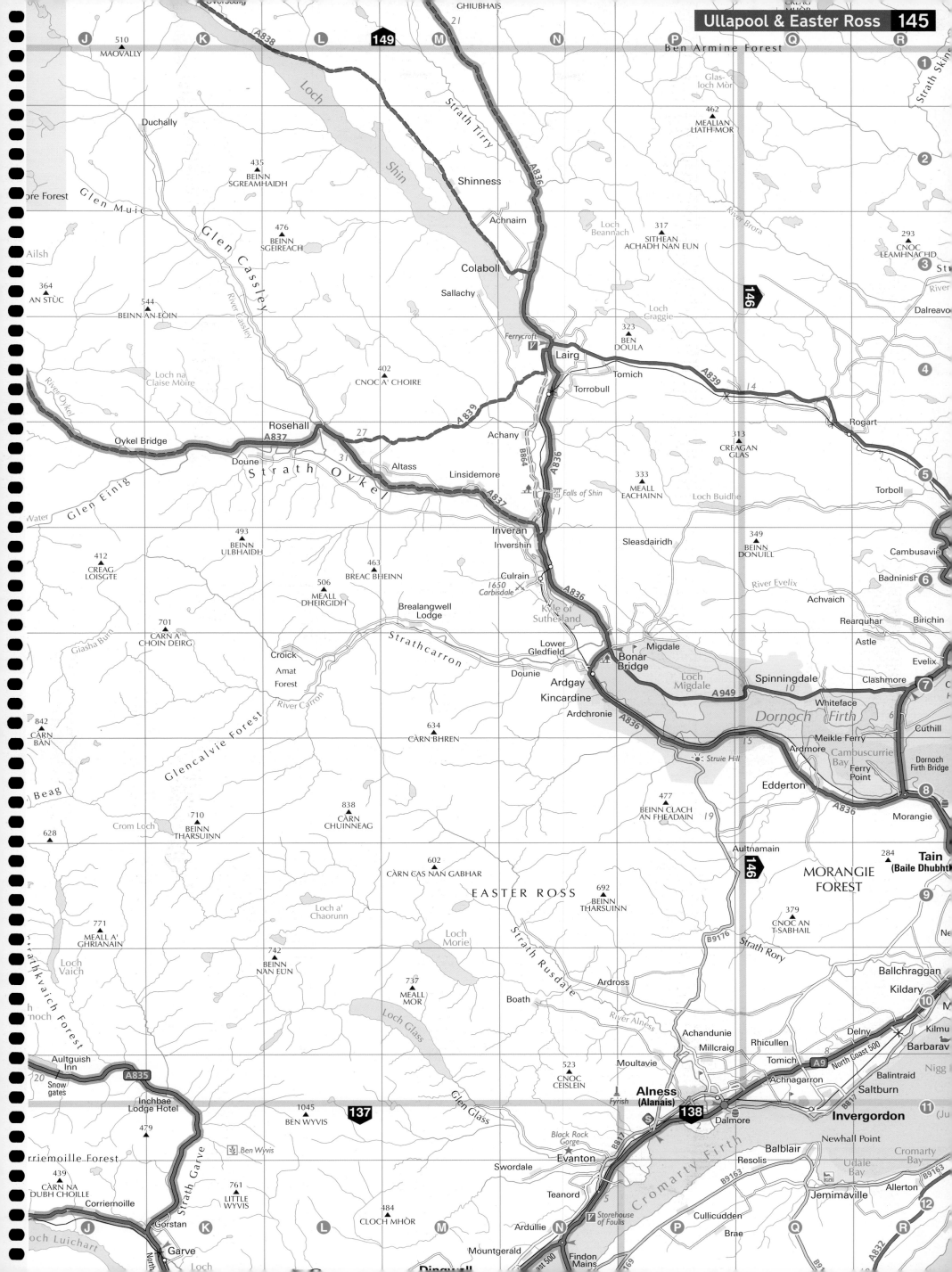

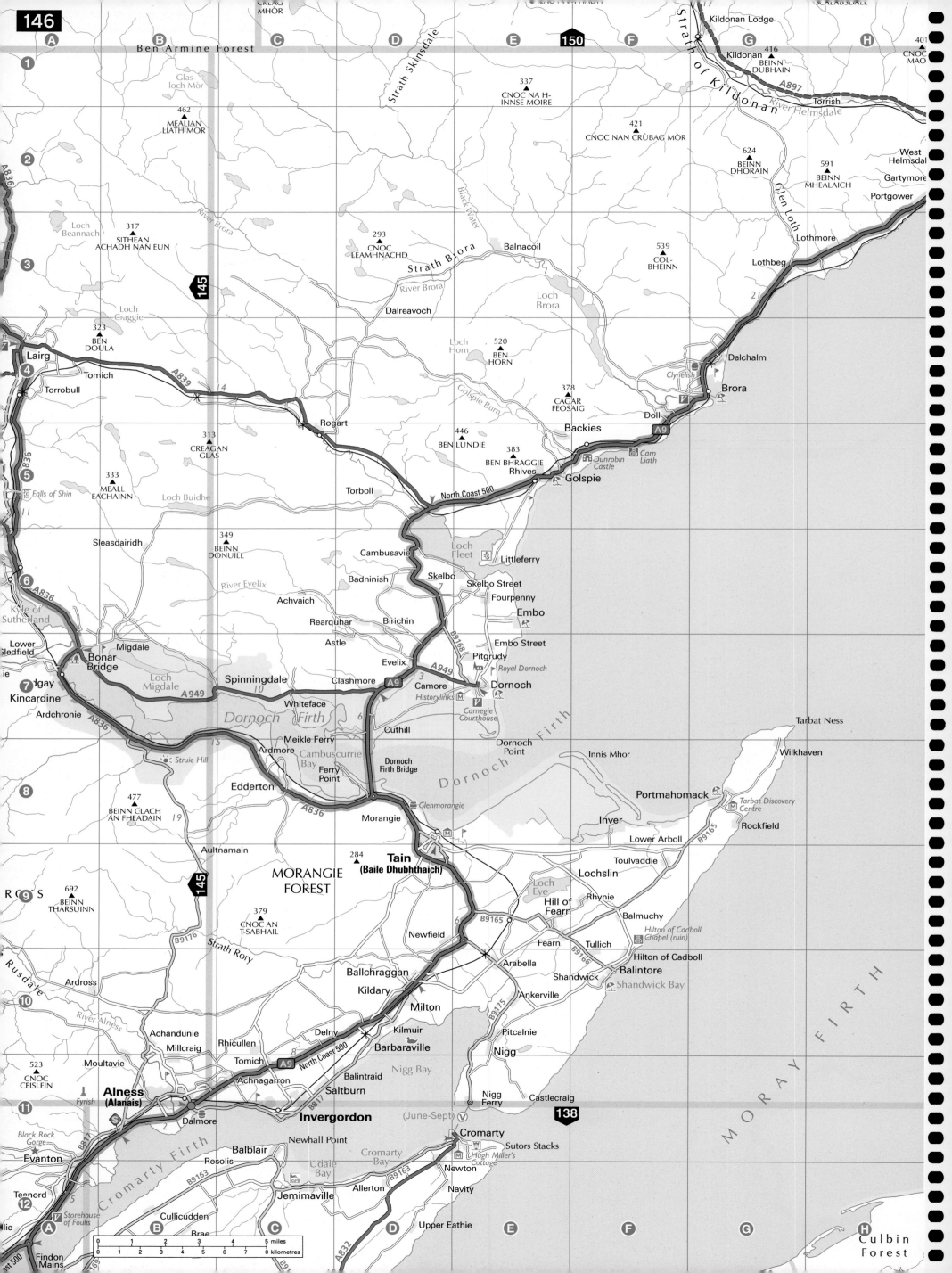

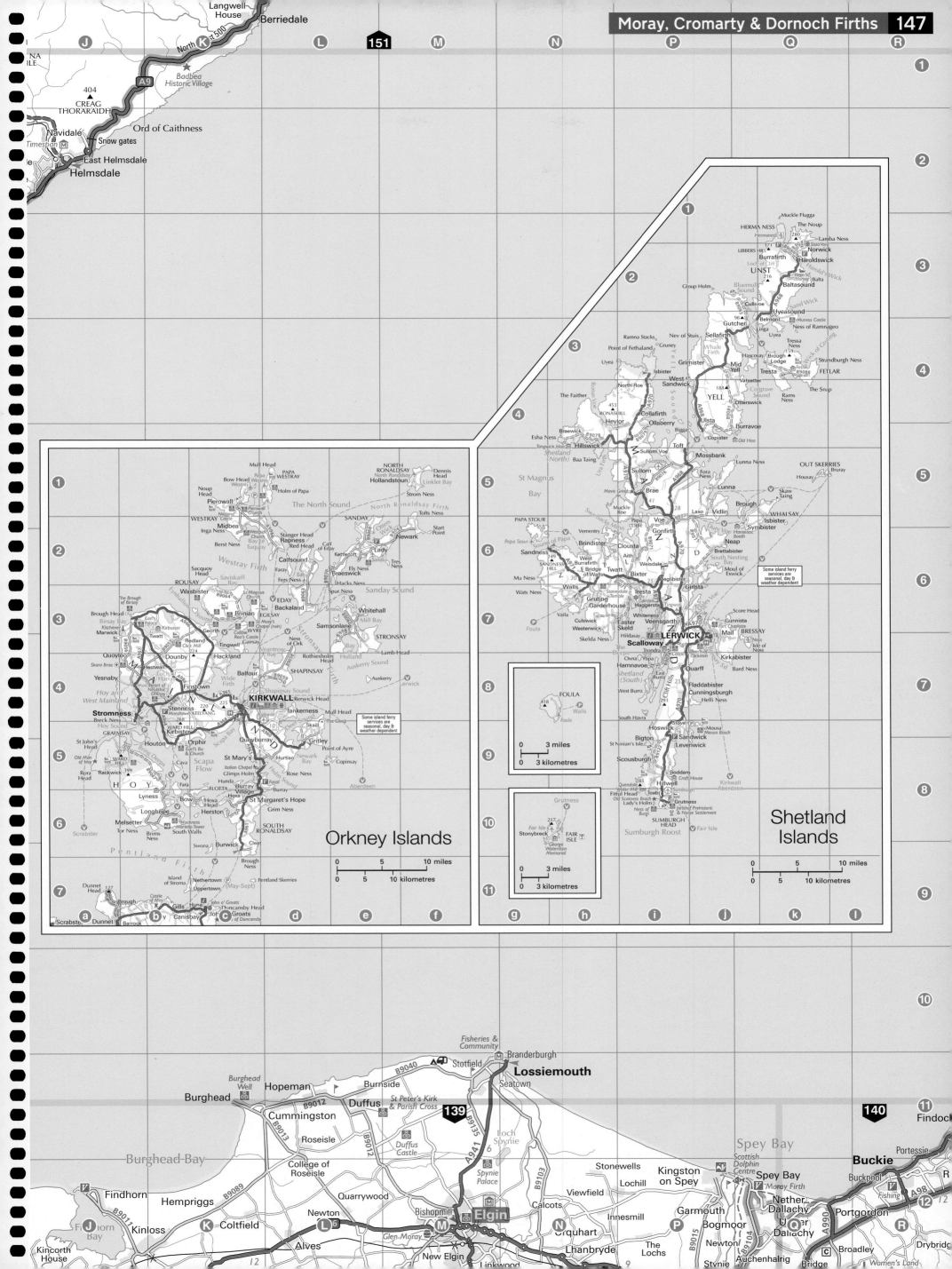

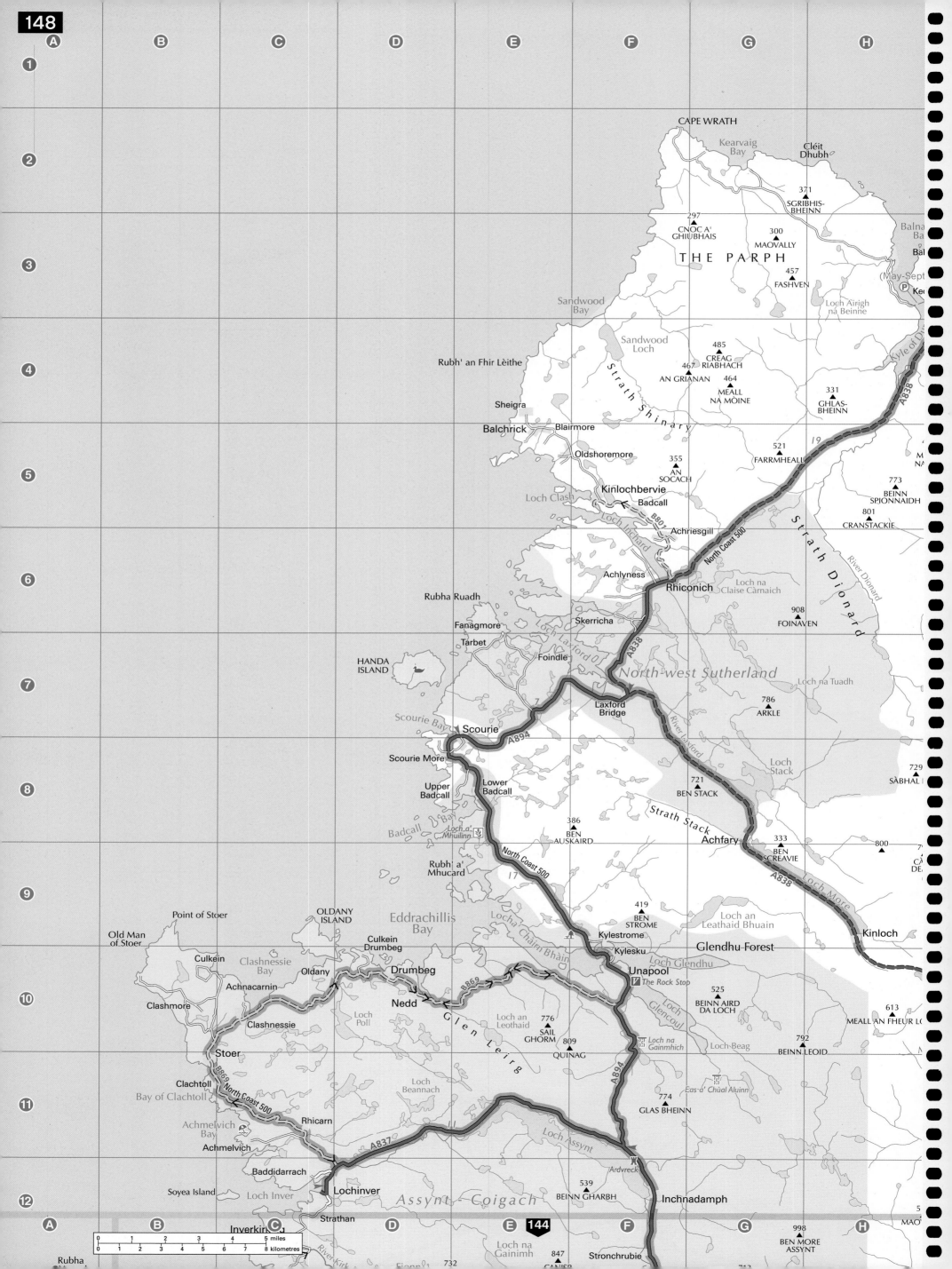

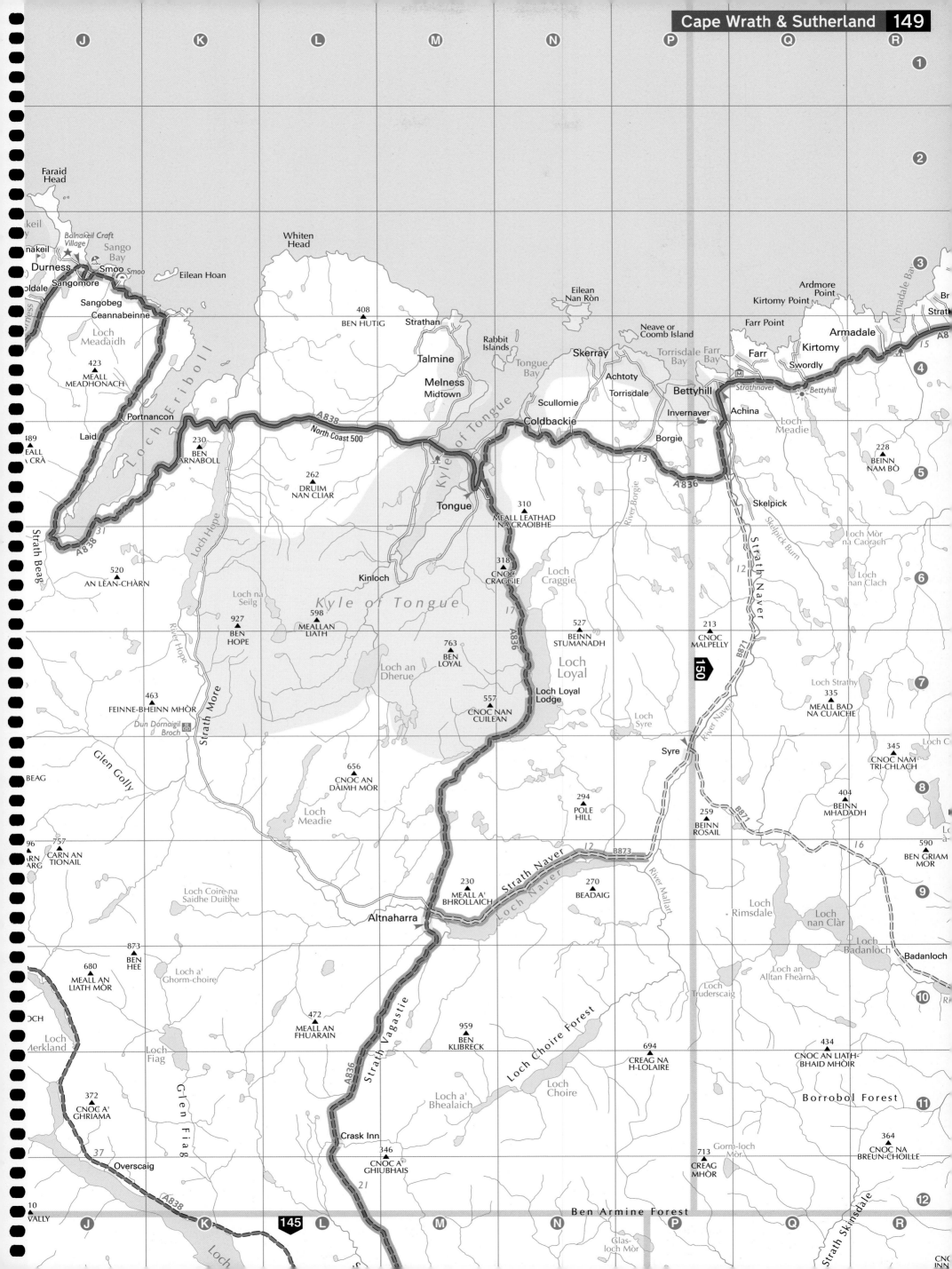

Faraid Head

Balnakeil Craft Village
Sango Bay
Durness
Smoo *Smoo*
Sangomore
Sangobeg
Ceannabeinne
Eilean Hoan

Whiten Head

408 ▲ BEN HUTIG
Strathan

Eilean Nan Ròn
Rabbit Islands

Neave or Coomb Island

Torrisdale Farr Bay
Farr Bay

Ardmore Point
Kirtomy Point
Farr Point
Armadale
Kirtomy
Farr
Swordly

Armadale Bay
Br
Strath
A8
15

Loch Meadaidh

423 ▲ MEALL MEADHONACH

Talmine
Skerray
Achtoty
Torrisdale

Melness
Midtown
Tongue Bay

Scullomie
Coldbackie

Bettyhill
Invernaver
Achina

Strathnaver
Bettyhill

489 ▲ EALL CRÀ

Portnancon
Laid

230 ▲ BEN ARNABOLL

A838
North Coast 500

Kyle of Tongue

Borgie
13
A836

River Borgie

Skelpick

228 ▲ BEINN NAM BÒ

Loch Meadie

Loch Mòr na Caorach

Loch nan Clach

Strath Beag
A838
31

520 ▲ AN LÈAN-CHÀRN

262 ▲ DRUIM NAN CLIAR

Tongue

310 ▲ MEALL LEATHAD NA CRAOIBHE

318 ▲ CNOC CRAGGIE

Loch Craggie

Strath Naver
B871
12

213 ▲ CNOC MALPELLY

Loch Strathy

335 ▲ MEALL BAD NA CUAICHE

Loch Hope

Kinloch

Loch na Seilg

927 ▲ BEN HOPE

598 ▲ MEALLAN LIATH

Kyle of Tongue

Loch an Dherue

763 ▲ BEN LOYAL

A836
17

Loch Loyal

Loch Loyal Lodge

527 ▲ BEINN STUMANADH

Loch Syre

150

345 ▲ CNOC NAM TRI-CHLACH
Loch C

Glen Golly

Strath More

463 ▲ FEINNE-BHEINN MHÒR

Dun Dornaigil Broch

557 ▲ CNOC NAN CUILEAN

Syre

River Naver

404 ▲ BEINN MHADADH

BEAG

96 ARN ARG

757 ▲ CARN AN TIONAIL

656 ▲ CNOC AN DÀIMH MÒR

Loch Meadie

294 ▲ POLE HILL

259 ▲ BEINN ROSAIL
B871

16

590 ▲ BEN GRIAM MOR
Lo

Loch Coire na Saidhe Duibhe

230 ▲ MEALL A' BHROLLAICH

Strath Naver

Loch Naver

270 ▲ BEADAIG

B873
12

River Mallart

Loch Rimsdale

Loch nan Clàr

Loch Badanloch

Badanloch
10

873 ▲ BEN HEE

680 ▲ MEALL AN LIATH MÒR

Loch a' Ghorm-choire

Altnaharra

472 ▲ MEALL AN FHUARAIN

A836
Strath Vagastie

959 ▲ BEN KLIBRECK

Loch Choire Forest

Loch a' Bhealaich

Loch Choire

Loch Truderscaig

Loch a' Alltan Fhearna

694 ▲ CREAG NA H-LOLAIRE

434 ▲ CNOC AN LIATH-BHAID MHÒIR

Loch Merkland

OCH

Loch Fiag

Glen Fiag

372 ▲ CNOC A' GHRIAMA

Crask Inn

346 ▲ CNOC A' GHIUBHAIS

713 ▲ CREAG MHÒR

Gorm-loch Mòr

364 ▲ CNOC NA BREUN-CHOILLE

Borrobol Forest
11

CNO INN

37
A838

Overscaig

21

Ben Armine Forest

Strath Skinsdale

10
VALLY

145

Glas-loch Mòr

12

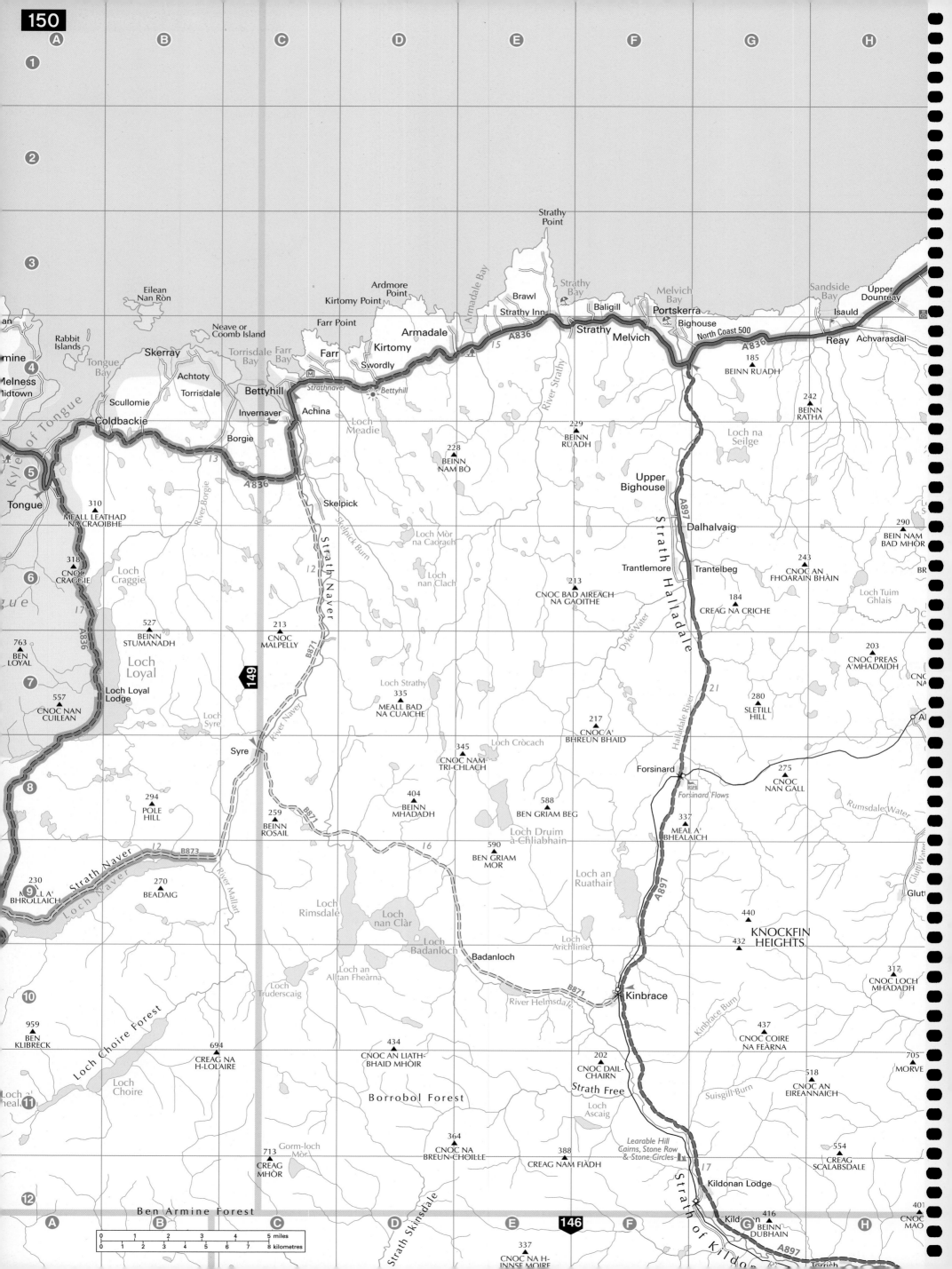

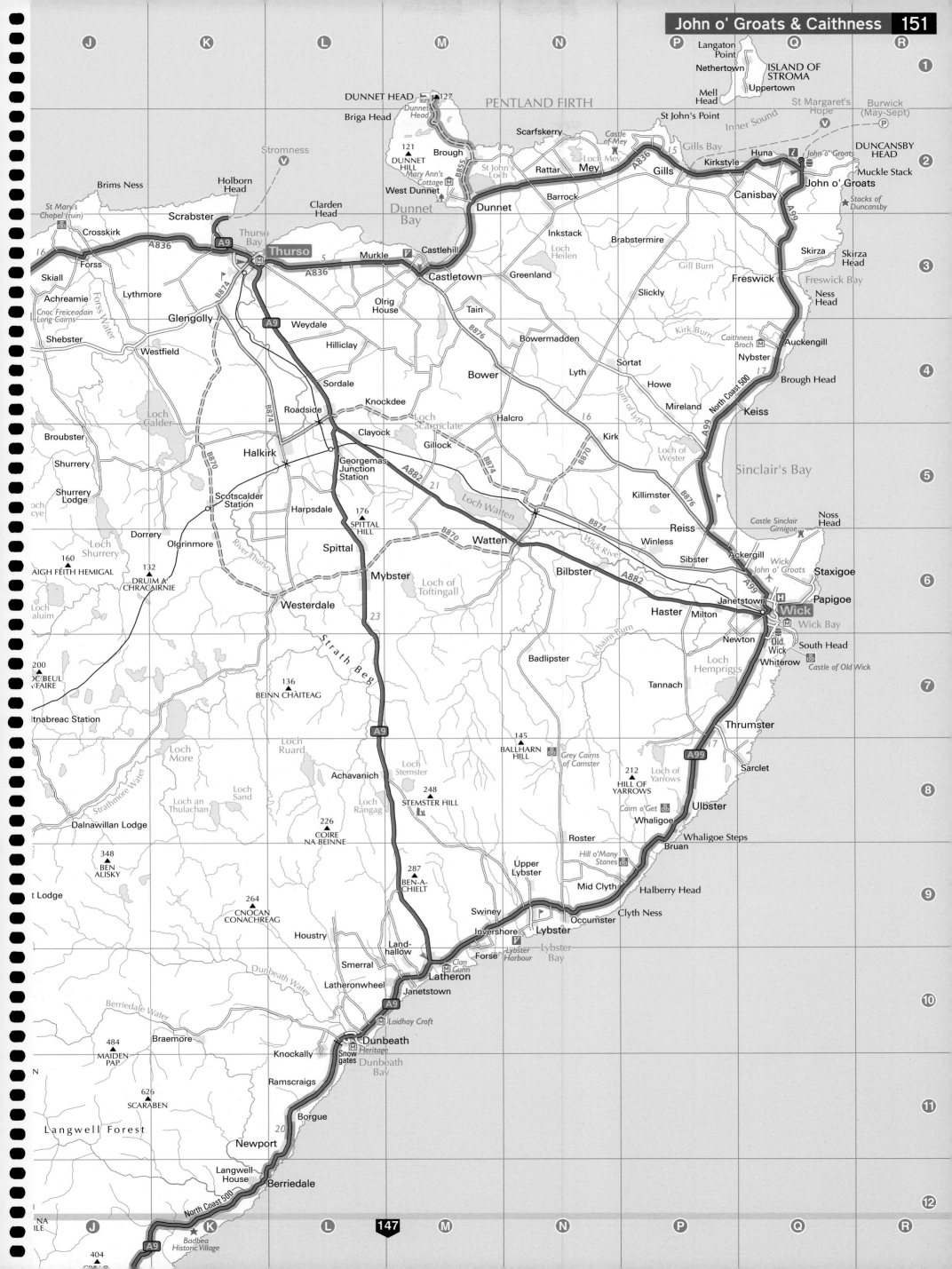

Burnt Hill – Charlcutt 167

Burnt Hill W Berk 31 M7
Burnthouse Cnwll 3 J7
Burnt Houses Dur 91 J2
Burntisland Fife 115 N4
Burnt Oak E Susx 15 P5
Burnton E Ayrs 105 J8
Burntwood Flints 75 J10
Burntwood Staffs 65 K10
Burntwood Green Staffs 65 K10
Burnt Yates N York 85 K3
Burnworthy Somset 21 K10
Burpham Surrey 32 E12
Burpham W Susx 14 E9
Burradon N Tyne 100 H4
Burradon Nthumb 108 F8
Burrafirth Shet 147 k2
Burras Cnwll 2 H7
Burraton Cnwll 4 F3
Burravoe Shet 147 j4
Burray Village Ork 147 c5
Burrells Cumb 89 R3
Burrelton P & K 124 D5
Burridge Devon 9 Q3
Burridge Devon 19 L6
Burridge Hants 13 J3
Burrill N York 91 L9
Burringham N Linc 79 L2
Burrington Devon 19 M10
Burrington Herefs 51 M6
Burrington N Som 28 G10
Burrough End Cambs 57 M9
Burrough Green Cambs 57 M9
Burrough on the Hill Leics 67 J10
Burrow Lancs 89 Q11
Burrow Somset 20 E5
Burrow Bridge Somset 21 M7
Burrowhill Surrey 32 D9
Burrows Cross Surrey 14 F2
Burry Swans 26 C4
Burry Green Swans 26 C4
Burry Port Carmth 26 C2
Burscough Lancs 75 M1
Burscough Bridge Lancs 75 M1
Bursea E R Yk 86 E8
Burshill E R Yk 87 K5
Bursledon Hants 12 H3
Burslem C Stke 64 F2
Burstall Suffk 47 K3
Burstock Dorset 10 C4
Burston Norfk 58 H4
Burston Staffs 64 H6
Burstow Surrey 15 K3
Burstwick E R Yk 87 N9
Burtersett N York 90 E9
Burtholme Cumb 98 G5
Burthorpe Green Suffk 57 P8
Burthwaite Cumb 98 E8
Burthy Cnwll 3 M3
Burtle Somset 21 N5
Burtle Hill Somset 21 N4
Burtoft Lincs 68 E5
Burton BCP 12 B6
Burton Ches W 75 K9
Burton Ches W 75 N11
Burton Dorset 10 G6
Burton Nthumb 109 K3
Burton Pembks 37 J9
Burton Somset 21 K4
Burton Somset 22 C10
Burton Wilts 22 H7
Burton Wilts 29 N6
Burton Agnes E R Yk 87 L3
Burton Bradstock Dorset 10 D7
Burton-by-Lincoln Lincs 79 N9
Burton Coggles Lincs 67 N7
Burton Dassett Warwks 54 C10
Burton End Essex 45 P7
Burton End Suffk 46 B3
Burton Fleming E R Yk 93 M12
Burton Green Warwks 53 P5
Burton Green Wrexhm 75 K12
Burton Hastings Warwks 54 C3
Burton Hill Wilts 29 Q5
Burton-in-Kendal Cumb 89 N11
Burton-in-Kendal Services Cumb 89 N11
Burton in Lonsdale N York 89 Q12
Burton Joyce Notts 66 G3
Burton Latimer Nhants 55 M6
Burton Lazars Leics 67 J9
Burton Leonard N York 85 L2
Burton on the Wolds Leics 66 F8
Burton Overy Leics 54 H1
Burton Pedwardine Lincs 68 C4
Burton Pidsea E R Yk 87 N9
Burton Salmon N York 85 P9
Burton's Green Essex 46 E6
Burton upon Stather N Linc 86 G11
Burton upon Trent Staffs 65 N7
Burton Waters Lincs 79 M9
Burtonwood Warrtn 75 P5
Burtonwood Services Warrtn 75 P5
Burwardsley Ches W 75 N12
Burwarton Shrops 52 B4
Burwash E Susx 16 B6
Burwash Common E Susx 16 B6
Burwash Weald E Susx 16 B6
Burwell Cambs 57 L7
Burwell Lincs 80 G8
Burwen IoA 72 G5
Burwick Ork 147 c6
Bury Bury 76 E1
Bury Cambs 56 F4
Bury Somset 20 E8
Bury W Susx 14 E8
Bury End C Beds 44 G5
Bury Green Herts 45 N7
Bury St Edmunds Suffk 58 C8
Burythorpe N York 86 E2
Busby E Rens 113 Q10
Busby Stoop N York 91 P10
Buscot Oxon 30 F3
Bush Abers 133 J11
Bush Cnwll 7 J3
Bush Bank Herefs 51 M10
Bushbury Wolves 64 G11
Bushby Leics 66 G11
Bushey Herts 32 G3
Bushey Heath Herts 32 G3
Bush Green Norfk 59 J3
Bush Green Suffk 58 D9
Bush Hill Park Gt Lon 33 L3
Bushley Worcs 41 P5
Bushley Green Worcs 41 P5
Bushmead Bed 56 C8
Bushmoor Shrops 51 M3
Bushton Wilts 30 C7
Busk Cumb 98 H10
Buslingthorpe Lincs 79 Q6
Bussage Gloucs 41 P11
Bussex Somset 21 M6
Butcher's Cross E Susx 15 Q6
Butcombe N Som 28 G10
Bute Ag & B 112 F7
Butleigh Somset 22 C6
Butleigh Wootton Somset 22 C6
Butler's Cross Bucks 44 B10
Butler's Hill Notts 66 E3
Butlers Marston Warwks 53 Q10
Butley Suffk 59 M10
Butley High Corner Suffk 59 M10
Buttercrambe N York 86 D4
Butterdean Border 116 H8
Butterknowle Dur 91 J2
Butterleigh Devon 9 J3
Butterley Derbys 66 C2
Buttermere Cumb 88 G3
Buttermere Wilts 30 H10
Butters Green Staffs 64 E2
Buttershaw C Brad 84 H9
Butterstone P & K 123 Q4
Butterton Staffs 64 F4
Butterton Staffs 77 K12
Butterwick Dur 101 K12
Butterwick Lincs 68 G4
Butterwick N York 87 J1
Butterwick N York 92 E11
Butt Green Ches E 64 C2
Buttington Powys 62 H10
Buttonbridge Shrops 52 D5
Buttonoak Shrops 52 D6
Buttsash Hants 12 G3
Buttsbear Cross Cnwll 7 K4
Butt's Green Essex 46 D11
Buxhall Suffk 58 E9
Buxhall Fen Street Suffk 58 E9
Buxted E Susx 15 P6
Buxton Derbys 77 K9
Buxton Norfk 71 J7
Buxton Heath Norfk 71 J8
Buxworth Derbys 77 J7
Bwlch Powys 39 Q7
Bwlchgwyn Wrexhm 63 J2
Bwlchllan Cerdgn 49 K9
Bwlchnewydd Carmth 38 A7
Bwlchtocyn Gwynd 60 E7
Bwlch-y-cibau Powys 62 G8
Bwlch-y-Ddar Powys 62 G8
Bwlchyfadfa Cerdgn 48 G10
Bwlch-y-ffridd Powys 50 E2
Bwlch-y-groes Pembks 37 P3
Bwlchymyrdd Swans 26 E3
Bwlch-y-sarnau Powys 50 E6
Byermoor Gatesd 100 F7
Byers Green Dur 100 G11
Byfield Nhants 54 E10
Byfleet Surrey 32 F10
Byford Herefs 40 E3
Bygrave Herts 45 K4
Byker N u Ty 100 H5
Byland Abbey N York 92 B11
Bylaugh Norfk 70 F8
Bylchau Conwy 74 D11
Byley Ches W 76 D10
Bynea Carmth 26 E3
Byram N York 85 P10
Byrness Nthumb 108 C9
Bystock Devon 9 J8
Bythorn Cambs 55 Q5
Byton Herefs 51 L8
Bywell Nthumb 100 D6
Byworth W Susx 14 E6

C

Cabbacott Devon 18 H9
Cabourne Lincs 80 C3
Cabrach Ag & B 111 L8
Cabrach Moray 140 B10
Cabus Lancs 83 L5
Cackle Street E Susx 15 N5
Cackle Street E Susx 16 C7
Cackle Street E Susx 16 E7
Cadbury Devon 8 G4
Cadbury Barton Devon 19 N10
Cadbury World Birm 53 K4
Cadder E Duns 114 B7
Caddington C Beds 44 F8
Caddonfoot Border 107 L3
Cadeby Donc 78 E4
Cadeby Leics 66 C11
Cadeleigh Devon 8 G3
Cade Street E Susx 15 R6
Cadgwith Cnwll 2 H11
Cadham Fife 124 F12
Cadishead Salfd 76 D5
Cadle Swans 26 F3
Cadley Lancs 83 M9
Cadley Wilts 24 D3
Cadley Wilts 30 E9
Cadmore End Bucks 31 R4
Cadnam Hants 24 E10
Cadney N Linc 79 P3
Cadole Flints 74 H11
Cadoxton V Glam 27 Q8
Cadoxton Juxta-Neath Neath 26 H3
Cadwst Denbgs 62 D4
Caeathro Gwynd 72 H11
Caehopkin Powys 39 K9
Caenby Lincs 79 P6
Caerau Brdgnd 27 K4
Caerau Cardif 27 Q7
Cae'r-bont Powys 39 J9
Cae'r bryn Carmth 38 F9
Caerdeon Gwynd 61 L8
Caer Farchell Pembks 36 F5
Caergeiliog IoA 72 E8
Caergwrle Flints 75 J12
Caerhun Conwy 73 N9
Caerlanrig Border 107 K9
Caerleon Newpt 28 D4
Caernarfon Gwynd 72 H11
Caernarfon Castle Gwynd 72 H11
Caerphilly Caerph 27 R5
Caersws Powys 50 E2
Caerwedros Cerdgn 48 F9
Caerwent Mons 28 F4
Caerwys Flints 74 F9
Caerynwch Gwynd 61 N8
Caggle Street Mons 40 E8
Caim IoA 73 K7
Caio Carmth 38 G4
Cairinis W Isls 152 c8
Cairnbaan Ag & B 112 B3
Cairnbulg Abers 141 P3
Cairncross Border 117 K8
Cairncurran Inver 113 L7
Cairndow Ag & B 121 M10
Cairneyhill Fife 115 J4
Cairngarroch D & G 94 F9
Cairngorms National Park 131 K4
Cairnie Abers 140 D7
Cairnorrie Abers 141 L7
Cairnryan D & G 94 F4
Cairnty Moray 139 P5
Caister-on-Sea Norfk 71 Q9
Caistor Lincs 80 C3
Caistor St Edmund Norfk 71 J11
Cakebole Worcs 52 G6
Cake Street Norfk 58 G3
Calais Street Suffk 46 H4
Calanais W Isls 152 f3
Calbourne IoW 12 G7
Calceby Lincs 80 G8
Calcoed Flints 74 G9
Calcot Gloucs 42 C9
Calcot W Berk 31 N8
Calcot Row W Berk 31 N8
Calcots Moray 139 N3
Calcott Kent 35 L9
Calcott Shrops 63 M9
Calcutt N York 85 M4
Calcutt Wilts 30 C4
Caldbeck Cumb 98 C10
Caldbergh N York 91 J9
Caldecote Cambs 56 C3
Caldecote Cambs 56 G9
Caldecote Herts 45 J4
Caldecote Nhants 54 H10
Caldecott Nhants 55 N7
Caldecott Oxon 31 K3
Caldecott Rutlnd 55 L2
Caldecotte M Keyn 44 C5
Calder Cumb 88 D6
Calderbank N Lans 114 D8
Calder Bridge Cumb 88 D5
Calderbrook Rochdl 84 E11
Caldercruix N Lans 114 E7
Calder Grove Wakefd 85 L11
Caldermill S Lans 105 M1
Caldermore Rochdl 84 D12
Calder Vale Lancs 83 M6
Calderwood S Lans 114 B10
Caldey Island Pembks 37 M11
Caldicot Mons 28 G5
Caldmore Wsall 53 J1
Caldwell N York 91 K4
Caldy Wirral 74 H6
Calenick Cnwll 3 K6
Calf of Man IoM 102 a7
Calford Green Suffk 46 C3
Calfsound Ork 147 d2
Calgary Ag & B 119 L2
Califer Moray 139 K4
California Falk 114 G6
California Norfk 71 P9
California Cross Devon 5 L6
Calke Derbys 66 B8
Calke Abbey Derbys 66 B8
Callakille Highld 135 M5
Callander Stirlg 122 G11
Callanish W Isls 152 f3
Callaughton Shrops 52 B1
Callerton N u Ty 100 F4
Callestick Cnwll 3 J4
Calligarry Highld 127 L4
Callington Cnwll 4 E3
Callingwood Staffs 65 M7
Callow Herefs 40 G5
Callow End Worcs 52 F10
Callow Hill Wilts 30 B5
Callow Hill Worcs 52 D6
Callow Hill Worcs 53 J7
Callows Grave Worcs 51 Q7
Calmore Hants 24 E10
Calmsden Gloucs 42 B10
Calne Wilts 30 A8
Calow Derbys 78 C9
Calshot Hants 12 H4
Calstock Cnwll 4 G3
Calstone Wellington Wilts 30 B8
Calthorpe Norfk 71 J6
Calthorpe Street Norfk 71 M7
Calthwaite Cumb 98 F10
Calton N York 84 D3
Calton Staffs 65 L2
Calveley Ches E 75 Q12
Calver Derbys 77 N9
Calverhall Shrops 63 Q5
Calver Hill Herefs 51 L11
Calverleigh Devon 20 E10
Calverley Leeds 85 J8
Calver Sough Derbys 77 N8
Calvert Bucks 43 P7
Calverton M Keyn 43 R4
Calverton Notts 66 G2
Calvine P & K 130 E11
Calvo Cumb 97 N7
Calzeat Border 106 E3
Cam Gloucs 29 M2
Camasachoirce Highld 127 P12
Camasine Highld 127 N12
Camas Luinie Highld 136 C10
Camastianavaig Highld 135 J8
Camault Muir Highld 137 N8
Camber E Susx 16 G7
Camberley Surrey 32 C10
Camberwell Gt Lon 33 L7
Camblesforth N York 86 C10
Cambo Nthumb 100 C1
Cambois Nthumb 100 H2
Camborne Cnwll 2 G6
Camborne & Redruth Mining District Cnwll 2 G6
Cambourne Cambs 56 F8
Cambridge Cambs 57 J9
Cambridge Gloucs 41 M11
Cambridge Airport Cambs 57 J9
Cambrose Cnwll 2 H5
Cambus Clacks 114 F2
Cambusavie Highld 146 D6
Cambusbarron Stirlg 114 E3
Cambuskenneth Stirlg 114 E2
Cambuslang S Lans 114 B9
Cambus o' May Abers 132 C5
Cambuswallace S Lans 106 D2
Camden Town Gt Lon 33 K5
Cameley BaNES 29 K11
Camelford Cnwll 6 G8
Camelon Falk 114 F5
Camerory Highld 139 J9
Camer's Green Worcs 41 M5
Camerton BaNES 29 K11
Camerton Cumb 97 L12
Camghouran P & K 122 F2
Camieston Border 107 P4
Cammachmore Abers 133 L5
Cammeringham Lincs 79 N7
Camore Highld 146 D7
Campbeltown Ag & B 103 K6
Campbeltown Airport Ag & B 103 J5
Camperdown N Tyne 100 H4
Cample D & G 106 B11
Campmuir P & K 124 E5
Camps W Loth 115 K7
Campsall Donc 78 E1
Campsea Ash Suffk 59 L9
Camps End Cambs 45 R3
Campton C Beds 44 G4
Camptown Border 107 R7
Camrose Pembks 36 H6
Camserney P & K 123 L3
Camusnagaul Highld 128 F9
Camusnagaul Highld 144 D7
Camusteel Highld 135 N7
Camusterrach Highld 135 N7
Canada Hants 24 D9
Canal Foot Cumb 89 J11
Canaston Bridge Pembks 37 L7
Candacraig Abers 131 Q4
Candlesby Lincs 81 J10
Candle Street Suffk 58 F6
Candover Green Shrops 63 N11
Candy Mill Border 106 E1
Cane End Oxon 31 P6
Canewdon Essex 34 F3
Canford Bottom Dorset 11 P5
Canford Cliffs BCP 11 P7
Canford Heath BCP 11 P6
Canford Magna BCP 11 P5
Canhams Green Suffk 58 F7
Canisbay Highld 151 Q2
Canklow Rothm 78 C5
Canley Covtry 53 P5
Cann Dorset 23 J9
Canna Highld 126 D3
Cann Common Dorset 23 K9
Cannich Highld 137 K9
Cannington Somset 21 L5
Canning Town Gt Lon 33 M6
Cannock Staffs 64 H10
Cannock Chase Staffs 65 J8
Cannock Wood Staffs 65 K9
Cannon Bridge Herefs 40 F3
Canonbie D & G 98 E3
Canon Frome Herefs 41 K3
Canon Pyon Herefs 51 M11
Canons Ashby Nhants 54 F10
Canonstown Cnwll 2 E7
Canterbury Kent 35 L10
Canterbury Cathedral Kent 35 L10
Cantley Norfk 71 M11
Cantlop Shrops 63 N11
Canton Cardif 27 R7
Cantraywood Highld 138 E6
Cantsfield Lancs 89 Q12
Canvey Island Essex 34 C6
Canwick Lincs 79 N10
Canworthy Water Cnwll 7 J6
Caol Highld 128 F9
Caolas Scalpaigh W Isls 152 f6
Caoles Ag & B 118 E3
Caonich Highld 128 E6
Capel Kent 16 B2
Capel Surrey 14 H3
Capel Bangor Cerdgn 49 L4
Capel Betws Lleucu Cerdgn 49 K9
Capel Coch IoA 72 G7
Capel Curig Conwy 73 M12
Capel Cynon Cerdgn 48 F10
Capel Dewi Carmth 38 C7
Capel Dewi Cerdgn 38 C3
Capel-Dewi Cerdgn 49 K4
Capel Garmon Conwy 61 P1
Capel Green Suffk 59 M10
Capel Gwyn Carmth 38 C7
Capel Gwyn IoA 72 E8
Capel Gwynfe Carmth 38 H7
Capel Hendre Carmth 38 F10
Capel Isaac Carmth 38 F7
Capel Iwan Carmth 37 Q3
Capel-le-Ferne Kent 17 N3
Capelles Guern 12 c2
Capel Llanilltern Cardif 27 P6
Capel Mawr IoA 72 G9
Capel Parc IoA 72 G6
Capel St Andrew Suffk 59 M11
Capel St Mary Suffk 47 K4
Capel Seion Cerdgn 49 L5
Capel Trisant Cerdgn 49 M5
Capeluchaf Gwynd 60 G2
Capelulo Conwy 73 N8
Capel-y-ffin Powys 40 C5
Capel-y-graig Gwynd 73 J10
Capenhurst Ches W 75 L9
Capernwray Lancs 89 N12
Cape Wrath Highld 148 F2
Capheaton Nthumb 100 D2
Caplaw E Rens 113 N9
Capon's Green Suffk 59 K7
Cappercleuch Border 106 H5
Capstone Medway 34 D9
Capton Devon 5 P6
Capton Somset 20 H5
Caputh P & K 124 B5
Caradon Mining District Cnwll 7 K10
Caradon Town Cnwll 7 K10
Carbeth Stirlg 113 Q5
Carbis Cnwll 3 N3
Carbis Bay Cnwll 2 E7
Carbost Highld 134 G6
Carbost Highld 134 G9
Carbrook Sheff 78 C6
Carbrooke Norfk 70 D12
Carburton Notts 78 G9
Carclaze Cnwll 3 P4
Car Colston Notts 67 J4
Carcroft Donc 78 E2
Cardenden Fife 115 M2
Cardeston Shrops 63 L9
Cardewlees Cumb 98 D8
Cardhu Moray 139 M7
Cardiff Cardif 28 A7
Cardiff Airport V Glam 27 P9
Cardiff Gate Services Cardif 28 B6
Cardiff West Services Cardif 27 P6
Cardigan Cerdgn 48 B11
Cardinal's Green Cambs 45 R2
Cardington Bed 56 B11
Cardington Shrops 51 N2
Cardinham Cnwll 6 G11
Cardrain D & G 94 G12
Cardrona Border 107 J2
Cardross Ag & B 113 L6
Cardryne D & G 94 G11
Cardurnock Cumb 97 N6
Careby Lincs 67 P9
Careston Angus 132 E12
Carew Pembks 37 K9
Carew Cheriton Pembks 37 K10
Carew Newton Pembks 37 K9
Carey Herefs 40 H5
Carfin N Lans 114 E9
Carfraemill Border 116 C10
Cargate Green Norfk 71 M9
Cargenbridge D & G 97 J3
Cargill P & K 124 C5
Cargo Cumb 98 D6
Cargreen Cnwll 4 F4
Cargurrel Cnwll 3 L7
Carham Nthumb 108 C2
Carhampton Somset 20 F5
Carharrack Cnwll 3 J6
Carie P & K 122 G1
Carinish W Isls 152 c8
Carisbrooke IoW 12 H7
Cark Cumb 89 K11
Carkeel Cnwll 4 F5
Càrlabhagh W Isls 152 e2
Carland Cross Cnwll 3 L4
Carlbury Darltn 91 L4
Carlby Lincs 67 P9
Carlcroft Nthumb 108 D7
Carlecotes Barns 77 M3
Carleen Cnwll 2 F8
Carlesmoor N York 91 L12
Carleton Cumb 88 D5
Carleton Cumb 98 E7
Carleton Cumb 98 G12
Carleton Lancs 82 H7
Carleton Wakefd 85 P11
Carleton Forehoe Norfk 70 G11
Carleton-in-Craven N York 84 E5
Carleton Rode Norfk 58 G2
Carleton St Peter Norfk 71 L11
Carlidnack Cnwll 3 J8
Carlincraig Abers 140 G7
Carlingcott BaNES 29 L10
Carlin How R & Cl 92 E3
Carlisle Cumb 98 E7
Carlisle Lake District Airport Cumb 98 F6
Carloggas Cnwll 6 C11
Carlops Border 115 L10
Carloway W Isls 152 e2
Carlton Barns 78 B2
Carlton Bed 55 N9
Carlton Cambs 57 M10
Carlton Leeds 85 M9
Carlton Leics 66 C11
Carlton N York 86 C10
Carlton N York 90 H10
Carlton N York 92 C9
Carlton Notts 66 G4
Carlton S on T 91 P2
Carlton Suffk 59 M8
Carlton Colville Suffk 59 P3
Carlton Curlieu Leics 54 H1
Carlton Green Cambs 57 M10
Carlton Husthwaite N York 92 A11
Carlton-in-Cleveland N York 92 A6
Carlton in Lindrick Notts 78 F7
Carlton-le-Moorland Lincs 79 M12
Carlton Miniott N York 91 P10
Carlton-on-Trent Notts 79 K11
Carlton Scroop Lincs 67 N3
Carluke S Lans 114 F11
Carlyon Bay Cnwll 3 P4
Carmacoup S Lans 105 P4
Carmarthen Carmth 38 B7
Carmel Carmth 38 E8
Carmel Flints 74 G8
Carmel Gwynd 60 H1
Carmichael S Lans 106 B2
Carmunnock C Glas 114 A9
Carmyle C Glas 114 B9
Carmyllie Angus 125 L4
Carnaby E R Yk 87 L2
Carnbee Fife 125 K11
Carnbo P & K 123 Q12
Carn Brea Cnwll 2 H6
Carnbrogie Abers 141 K10
Carndu Highld 136 B10
Carnduff S Lans 114 B12
Carne Cnwll 3 J9
Carne Cnwll 3 M7
Carne Cnwll 3 N3
Carnell E Ayrs 105 J3
Carnewas Cnwll 6 B11
Carnforth Lancs 83 L1
Carn-gorm Highld 136 C11
Carnhedryn Pembks 36 F5
Carnhell Green Cnwll 2 F7
Carnie Abers 133 K3
Carnkie Cnwll 2 H6
Carnkie Cnwll 2 H7
Carnkiet Cnwll 3 J4
Carno Powys 50 C1
Carnock Fife 115 J3
Carnon Downs Cnwll 3 K6
Carnousie Abers 140 G6
Carnoustie Angus 125 L6
Carnsmerry Cnwll 3 P3
Carnwath S Lans 114 H12
Carnyorth Cnwll 2 B8
Carol Green Solhll 53 N5
Carpalla Cnwll 3 N4
Carperby N York 90 G9
Carr Rothm 78 E6
Carradale Ag & B 103 L2
Carradale Village Ag & B 103 L2
Carrbridge Highld 138 G11
Carrbrook Tamesd 77 J3
Carrefour Jersey 13 b1
Carreglefn IoA 72 F6
Carr Gate Wakefd 85 L10
Carrhouse N Linc 79 K2
Carrick Ag & B 112 D4
Carrick Castle Ag & B 113 J2
Carriden Falk 115 J5
Carrington Lincs 68 F1
Carrington Mdloth 115 P9
Carrington Traffd 76 D5
Carrog Conwy 62 A3
Carrog Denbgs 62 F3
Carron Falk 114 F5
Carron Moray 139 N7
Carronbridge D & G 105 R10
Carron Bridge Stirlg 114 D4
Carronshore Falk 114 G5
Carr Shield Nthumb 99 M8
Carrutherstown D & G 97 M4
Carruth House Inver 113 M8
Carr Vale Derbys 78 D9
Carrville Dur 100 H9
Carsaig Ag & B 119 P8
Carseriggan D & G 95 K5
Carsethorn D & G 97 K6
Carshalton Gt Lon 33 K9
Carsington Derbys 65 N2
Carskey Ag & B 103 J8
Carsluith D & G 95 N7
Carsphairn D & G 105 K11
Carstairs S Lans 114 G12
Carstairs Junction S Lans 114 H12
Carswell Marsh Oxon 30 G3
Carter's Clay Hants 24 E8
Carters Green Essex 45 P9
Carterton Oxon 42 G10
Carterway Heads Nthumb 100 D8
Carthew Cnwll 3 N3
Carthorpe N York 91 N10
Cartington Nthumb 108 G9
Cartland S Lans 114 F12
Cartledge Derbys 77 Q8
Cartmel Cumb 89 K11
Cartmel Fell Cumb 89 L9
Carway Carmth 38 C10
Carwinley Cumb 98 E4
Cashe's Green Gloucs 41 N10
Cashmoor Dorset 23 L10
Cassington Oxon 43 K9
Cassop Dur 101 J10
Castallack Cnwll 2 D9
Castel Guern 12 b2
Castell Conwy 73 N10
Castell-y-bwch Torfn 28 C4
Casterton Cumb 89 Q11
Castle Cnwll 3 Q3
Castle Acre Norfk 70 B9
Castle Ashby Nhants 55 L9
Castlebay W Isls 152 b13
Castle Bolton N York 90 G8
Castle Bromwich Solhll 53 L3
Castle Bytham Lincs 67 N8
Castlebythe Pembks 37 K5
Castle Caereinion Powys 62 G11
Castle Camps Cambs 46 A3
Castle Carrock Cumb 98 G7
Castlecary N Lans 114 E5
Castle Cary Somset 22 E7
Castle Combe Wilts 29 P7
Castlecraig Highld 146 E11
Castle Donington Leics 66 D7
Castle Douglas D & G 96 F5
Castle Eaton Swindn 30 D3
Castle Eden Dur 101 L10
Castle End C Pete 68 C10
Castleford Wakefd 85 N10
Castle Frome Herefs 41 K3
Castle Gate Cnwll 2 D7
Castle Green Cumb 89 N8
Castle Green Surrey 32 D10
Castle Gresley Derbys 65 P8
Castle Hedingham Essex 46 D4
Castlehill Border 106 G3
Castlehill Highld 151 M3
Castle Hill Kent 16 C2
Castle Hill Suffk 47 L2
Castlehill W Duns 113 M6
Castle Howard N York 86 D1
Castle Kennedy D & G 94 G6
Castle Lachlan Ag & B 112 E2
Castlemartin Pembks 36 H11
Castlemilk C Glas 114 A9
Castle Morris Pembks 36 H4
Castlemorton Worcs 41 M4
Castlemorton Common Worcs 41 M4
Castle O'er D & G 106 H11
Castle Rising Norfk 69 M7
Castleside Dur 100 D8
Castle Stuart Highld 138 D6
Castlethorpe M Keyn 44 A3
Castlethorpe N Linc 79 N2
Castleton Ag & B 112 C4
Castleton Border 107 N11
Castleton Derbys 77 M7
Castleton N York 92 E5
Castleton Newpt 28 C6
Castleton Rochdl 76 G2
Castletown Ches W 63 M2
Castletown Dorset 10 G10
Castletown Highld 151 M3
Castletown IoM 102 c7
Castletown Sundld 101 J6
Castley N York 85 K6
Caston Norfk 58 E1
Castor C Pete 56 C1
Caswell Bay Swans 26 E5
Catacol N Ayrs 112 D11
Cat and Fiddle Derbys 77 J9
Catbrain S Glos 29 J6
Catbrook Mons 40 G11
Catch Flints 74 H9
Catchall Cnwll 2 C9
Catchem's Corner Solhll 53 N5
Catchgate Dur 100 F8
Catcliffe Rothm 78 C6
Catcomb Wilts 30 B7
Catcott Somset 21 N5
Caterham Surrey 33 L11
Catfield Norfk 71 M8
Catfield Common Norfk 71 M8
Catford Gt Lon 33 L8
Catforth Lancs 83 L8
Cathcart C Glas 113 R9
Cathedine Powys 39 Q6
Catherine-de-Barnes Solhll 53 M5
Catherine Slack C Brad 84 G9
Catherington Hants 25 M10
Catherston Leweston Dorset 10 B6
Catherton Shrops 52 C5
Catisfield Hants 13 J3
Catley Herefs 41 K3
Catley Lane Head Rochdl 84 C12
Catlodge Highld 130 B6
Catlow Lancs 84 C8
Catlowdy Cumb 98 F3
Catmere End Essex 45 P4
Catmore W Berk 31 K6
Caton Devon 8 E10
Caton Lancs 83 M2
Caton Green Lancs 83 M2
Cator Court Devon 8 C9
Catrine E Ayrs 105 K5
Cat's Ash Newpt 28 E4
Catsfield E Susx 16 C8
Catsfield Stream E Susx 16 C8
Catsgore Somset 22 C8
Catsham Somset 22 D6
Catshill Worcs 52 H6
Catstree Shrops 52 D1
Cattadale Ag & B 103 J7
Cattal N York 85 P4
Cattawade Suffk 47 K5
Catterall Lancs 83 L6
Catteralslane Shrops 63 P4
Catterick N York 91 L7
Catterick Bridge N York 91 L7
Catterick Garrison N York 91 K7
Catterlen Cumb 98 F11
Catterline Abers 133 L8
Catterton N York 85 Q6
Catteshall Surrey 14 D2
Catthorpe Leics 54 F5
Cattishall Suffk 58 C7
Cattistock Dorset 10 F5
Catton N York 91 N11
Catton Nthumb 99 M7
Catwick E R Yk 87 L6
Catworth Cambs 56 B6
Caudle Green Gloucs 41 Q9
Caulcott C Beds 44 E3
Caulcott Oxon 43 L7
Cauldcots Angus 125 N3
Cauldhame Stirlg 114 B2
Cauldmill Border 107 N6
Cauldon Staffs 65 K2
Cauldon Lowe Staffs 65 K3
Cauldwell Derbys 65 N9
Caulkerbush D & G 97 J7
Caulside D & G 98 F2
Caundle Marsh Dorset 22 F10
Caunsall Worcs 52 F5
Caunton Notts 79 J11
Causeway Hants 25 N9
Causeway End Cumb 89 M9
Causeway End D & G 95 M6
Causeway End Essex 46 B8
Causewayend S Lans 106 D2
Causewayhead Cumb 97 M7
Causewayhead Stirlg 114 E2
Causeyend Abers 141 M12
Causey Park Nthumb 109 K10
Causey Park Bridge Nthumb 109 K10
Cavendish Suffk 46 E2
Cavenham Suffk 57 P6
Caversfield Oxon 43 M6
Caversham Readg 31 P7
Caverswall Staffs 64 H4
Caverton Mill Border 108 B5
Cavil E R Yk 86 E9
Cawdor Highld 138 F6
Cawkwell Lincs 80 F7
Cawood N York 86 A8
Cawsand Cnwll 4 F6
Cawston Norfk 70 H7
Cawston Warwks 54 D6
Cawthorn N York 92 F9
Cawthorne Barns 77 P2
Cawton N York 92 D11
Caxton Cambs 56 F9
Caxton End Cambs 56 F9
Caxton Gibbet Cambs 56 F8
Caynham Shrops 51 P6
Caythorpe Lincs 67 M2
Caythorpe Notts 66 H3
Cayton N York 93 L10
Ceannabeinne Highld 149 K3
Ceann a Bhaigh W Isls 152 b8
Ceannacroc Lodge Highld 128 H2
Cearsiadar W Isls 152 f4
Ceciliford Mons 40 G11
Cefn Newpt 28 C5
Cefn Berain Conwy 74 D10
Cefn-brîth Conwy 62 C2
Cefn-bryn-brain Carmth 38 H9
Cefn Byrle Powys 39 K9
Cefn Canel Powys 62 H6
Cefn Coch Powys 62 F7
Cefn-coed-y-cymmer Myr Td 39 N10
Cefn Cribwr Brdgnd 27 K6
Cefn Cross Brdgnd 27 K6
Cefn-ddwysarn Gwynd 62 C4
Cefn-Einion Shrops 51 J3
Cefneithin Carmth 38 E9
Cefngorwydd Powys 39 L3
Cefn-mawr Wrexhm 63 J4
Cefnpennar Rhondd 27 N2
Cefn-y-bedd Flints 63 K1
Cefn-y-pant Carmth 37 N5
Ceint IoA 72 H8
Cellan Cerdgn 49 K10
Cellardyke Fife 125 L12
Cellarhead Staffs 64 H3
Celleron Cumb 89 M2
Celynen Caerph 28 B3
Cemaes IoA 72 F5
Cemmaes Powys 61 P11
Cemmaes Road Powys 61 P11
Cenarth Cerdgn 37 P2
Cerbyd Pembks 36 F5
Ceres Fife 124 H10
Cerne Abbas Dorset 10 G4
Cerney Wick Gloucs 30 C3
Cerrigceinwen IoA 72 G9
Cerrigydrudion Conwy 62 C2
Cess Norfk 71 N8
Ceunant Gwynd 73 J11
Chaceley Gloucs 41 P5
Chacewater Cnwll 3 J5
Chackmore Bucks 43 P4
Chacombe Nhants 43 K3
Chadbury Worcs 42 B2
Chadderton Oldham 76 G3
Chadderton Fold Oldham 76 G2
Chaddesden C Derb 66 C5
Chaddesley Corbett Worcs 52 G6
Chaddlehanger Devon 7 N9
Chaddleworth W Berk 31 J7
Chadlington Oxon 42 G7
Chadshunt Warwks 53 Q10
Chadwell Leics 67 K7
Chadwell Shrops 64 E9
Chadwell End Bed 55 Q7
Chadwell Heath Gt Lon 33 N5
Chadwell St Mary Thurr 34 B6
Chadwick Worcs 52 F7
Chadwick End Solhll 53 N6
Chadwick Green St Hel 75 N4
Chaffcombe Somset 9 Q3
Chafford Hundred Thurr 33 R6
Chagford Devon 8 D7
Chailey E Susx 15 M7
Chainbridge Cambs 68 H12
Chainhurst Kent 16 C1
Chalbury Dorset 11 N3
Chalbury Common Dorset 11 P3
Chaldon Surrey 33 K11
Chaldon Herring Dorset 11 J8
Chale IoW 12 H9
Chale Green IoW 12 H9
Chalfont Common Bucks 32 E4
Chalfont St Giles Bucks 32 E4
Chalfont St Peter Bucks 32 E4
Chalford Gloucs 41 P11
Chalford Oxon 31 P2
Chalford Wilts 23 J3
Chalgrave C Beds 44 E6
Chalgrove Oxon 31 N3
Chalk Kent 34 B8
Chalk End Essex 46 A9
Chalkhouse Green Oxon 31 P6
Chalkway Somset 10 B3
Chalkwell Kent 34 F9
Challaborough Devon 5 L8
Challacombe Devon 19 N5
Challoch D & G 95 M5
Challock Kent 34 H12
Chalmington Dorset 10 F4
Chalton C Beds 44 E6
Chalton C Beds 56 C10
Chalton Hants 25 M10
Chalvey Slough 32 D6
Chalvington E Susx 15 P9
Chambers Green Kent 16 G2
Chandler's Cross Herts 32 F3
Chandlers Cross Worcs 41 M4
Chandler's Ford Hants 24 G9
Channel's End Bed 56 B9
Channel Tunnel Terminal Kent 17 L3
Chantry Somset 22 G4
Chantry Suffk 47 L3
Chapel Cumb 97 P12
Chapel Fife 115 N3
Chapel Allerton Leeds 85 L8
Chapel Allerton Somset 21 N3
Chapel Amble Cnwll 6 E9
Chapel Brampton Nhants 55 J7
Chapelbridge Cambs 56 F2
Chapel Chorlton Staffs 64 E5
Chapel Cross E Susx 15 R7
Chapel End Bed 56 B9
Chapel End C Beds 44 F3
Chapel End Cambs 56 C4
Chapel End Warwks 53 Q2
Chapelend Way Essex 46 C4
Chapel-en-le-Frith Derbys 77 K7
Chapel Field Bury 76 E2
Chapelgate Lincs 68 H7
Chapel Green Warwks 53 P4
Chapel Green Warwks 54 D8
Chapel Haddlesey N York 86 A10
Chapelhall N Lans 114 E8
Chapel Hill Abers 141 P9
Chapel Hill Lincs 68 D1
Chapel Hill Mons 28 H2
Chapel Hill N York 85 M6
Chapelhope Border 106 G6
Chapelknowe D & G 98 C4
Chapel Lawn Shrops 51 K5
Chapel-le-Dale N York 90 B11
Chapel Leigh Somset 20 H7
Chapel Milton Derbys 77 K7
Chapel of Garioch Abers 140 H11
Chapel Rossan D & G 94 G9
Chapel Row E Susx 16 B8
Chapel Row Essex 34 D2
Chapel Row W Berk 31 M8
Chapels Cumb 88 H10
Chapel St Leonards Lincs 81 L9
Chapel Stile Cumb 89 J6
Chapelton Abers 133 L6
Chapelton Angus 125 M3
Chapelton Devon 19 L8
Chapelton S Lans 114 C11
Chapeltown Bl w D 83 Q12
Chapel Town Cnwll 3 L3
Chapeltown Moray 139 N11
Chapeltown Sheff 78 B4
Chapmanslade Wilts 23 J4
Chapmans Well Devon 7 L6
Chapmore End Herts 45 L8
Chappel Essex 46 F6
Charaton Cnwll 4 D3
Chard Somset 9 Q3
Chard Junction Somset 9 Q4
Chardleigh Green Somset 9 Q3
Chardstock Devon 9 Q4
Charfield S Glos 29 L4
Chargrove Gloucs 41 Q8
Charing Kent 16 G1
Charing Heath Kent 16 G1
Charing Hill Kent 34 G12
Charingworth Gloucs 42 E4
Charlbury Oxon 42 H7
Charlcombe BaNES 29 M9
Charlcutt Wilts 30 A7

168 Charlecote – Colney Heath

Charlecote Warwks 53 P9
Charlemont Sandw 53 J2
Charles Devon 19 N7
Charleshill Surrey 14 C2
Charleston Angus 124 H4
Charlestown C Aber 133 M4
Charlestown C Brad 84 H7
Charlestown Calder 84 E10
Charlestown Cnwll 3 P4
Charlestown Cnwll 3 P4
Charlestown Derbys 77 J5
Charlestown Dorset 10 G9
Charlestown Fife 115 K4
Charlestown Highld 138 B6
Charlestown Highld 143 L10
Charlestown Salfd 76 E4
Charlestown of Aberlour Moray 139 N7
Charles Tye Suffk 58 F10
Charlesworth Derbys 77 J5
Charlinch Somset 21 K6
Charlottetown Fife 124 F10
Charlton Gt Lon 33 M7
Charlton Hants 24 F4
Charlton Herts 44 H6
Charlton Nhants 43 L4
Charlton Nthumb 99 M1
Charlton Oxon 31 J5
Charlton Somset 21 L8
Charlton Somset 22 E5
Charlton Somset 22 F3
Charlton Surrey 32 F8
Charlton W Susx 14 C8
Charlton Wilts 23 K9
Charlton Wilts 29 Q4
Charlton Worcs 42 B3
Charlton Worcs 52 F6
Charlton Wrekin 63 Q10
Charlton Abbots Gloucs 42 B7
Charlton Adam Somset 22 C7
Charlton All Saints Wilts 24 B8
Charlton Down Dorset 10 G6
Charlton Hill Shrops 63 P10
Charlton Horethorne Somset 22 F8
Charlton Kings Gloucs 41 Q7
Charlton Mackrell Somset 22 C7
Charlton Marshall Dorset 11 L4
Charlton Musgrove Somset 22 G7
Charlton-on-Otmoor Oxon 43 M8
Charlton on the Hill Dorset 11 L4
Charlton St Peter Wilts 30 D11
Charlwood Hants 25 L7
Charlwood Surrey 15 J3
Charminster Dorset 10 G6
Charmouth Dorset 10 B6
Charndon Bucks 43 P7
Charney Bassett Oxon 30 H3
Charnock Green Lancs 83 M11
Charnock Richard Lancs 83 M12
Charnock Richard Services Lancs 83 M12
Charsfield Suffk 59 K9
Chart Corner Kent 34 D12
Charter Alley Hants 31 M10
Charterhall Border 116 H11
Charterhouse Somset 22 C2
Chartershall Stirlg 114 E3
Charterville Allotments Oxon 42 G9
Chartham Kent 35 K11
Chartham Hatch Kent 35 K11
Chart Hill Kent 16 D1
Chartridge Bucks 44 D11
Chart Sutton Kent 16 E1
Chartway Street Kent 34 E12
Charvil Wokham 31 Q7
Charwelton Nhants 54 E9
Chase Terrace Staffs 65 J10
Chasetown Staffs 65 K10
Chastleton Oxon 42 F6
Chasty Devon 7 L4
Chatburn Lancs 84 A6
Chatcull Staffs 64 E5
Chatham Caerph 28 B4
Chatham Medway 34 D9
Chatham Green Essex 46 C8
Chathill Nthumb 109 K4
Chatley Worcs 52 F8
Chatsworth House Derbys 77 N9
Chattenden Medway 34 D8
Chatter End Essex 45 N6
Chatteris Cambs 56 H3
Chatterton Lancs 84 B11
Chattisham Suffk 47 K3
Chatto Border 108 C6
Chatton Nthumb 108 H4
Chaul End C Beds 44 F7
Chawleigh Devon 19 N11
Chawley Oxon 43 K10
Chawston Bed 56 C9
Chawton Hants 25 M6
Chaxhill Gloucs 41 L9
Chazey Heath Oxon 31 P7
Cheadle Staffs 65 J3
Cheadle Stockp 76 F6
Cheadle Heath Stockp 76 G6
Cheadle Hulme Stockp 76 G6
Cheam Gt Lon 33 J9
Cheapside W & M 32 D8
Chearsley Bucks 43 P9
Chebsey Staffs 64 F6
Checkendon Oxon 31 N6
Checkley Ches E 64 D3
Checkley Herefs 41 J4
Checkley Staffs 65 J5
Checkley Green Ches E 64 D3
Chedburgh Suffk 57 Q9
Cheddar Somset 21 P3
Cheddington Bucks 44 C8
Cheddleton Staffs 64 H2
Cheddleton Heath Staffs 65 J2
Cheddon Fitzpaine Somset 21 K8
Chedglow Wilts 29 Q4
Chedgrave Norfk 71 M12
Chedington Dorset 10 D4
Chediston Suffk 59 M5
Chediston Green Suffk 59 M5
Chedworth Gloucs 42 B9
Chedzoy Somset 21 M6
Cheeseman's Green Kent 17 J3
Cheetham Hill Manch 76 F3
Cheldon Devon 19 P10
Chelford Ches E 76 F9
Chellaston C Derb 66 B6
Chellington Bed 55 N9
Chelmarsh Shrops 52 D3
Chelmer Village Essex 46 C10
Chelmick Shrops 51 M2
Chelmondiston Suffk 47 M4
Chelmorton Derbys 77 L9
Chelmsford Essex 46 C10
Chelmsley Wood Solhll 53 M3
Chelsea Gt Lon 33 K7
Chelsfield Gt Lon 33 N9
Chelsham Surrey 33 L10
Chelston Somset 21 J9
Chelsworth Suffk 58 E11
Cheltenham Gloucs 41 Q7
Chelveston Nhants 55 N7
Chelvey N Som 28 G8
Chelwood BaNES 29 K10
Chelwood Common E Susx 15 M5
Chelwood Gate E Susx 15 M5
Chelworth Wilts 29 R3
Chelworth Lower Green Wilts 30 C4
Chelworth Upper Green Wilts 30 C4
Cheney Longville Shrops 51 M4
Chenies Bucks 32 E3
Chepstow Mons 28 H4
Chequerbent Bolton 76 C2
Chequers Corner Norfk 69 J10
Cherhill Wilts 30 B8
Cherington Gloucs 29 P3
Cherington Warwks 42 G4
Cheriton Devon 19 P4
Cheriton Hants 25 K7
Cheriton Kent 17 M3
Cheriton Pembks 37 J11
Cheriton Swans 26 C4
Cheriton Bishop Devon 8 E6
Cheriton Fitzpaine Devon 8 G3
Cherrington Wrekin 64 C8
Cherry Burton E R Yk 87 J7
Cherry Hinton Cambs 57 J9
Cherry Orchard Worcs 52 F10
Cherry Willingham Lincs 79 P9
Chertsey Surrey 32 F9
Cherwell Valley Services Oxon 43 L6
Cheselbourne Dorset 11 J5
Chesham Bucks 44 D11
Chesham Bury 76 E1
Chesham Bois Bucks 32 D2
Cheshunt Herts 45 L11
Chesil Beach Dorset 10 F9
Chesley Kent 34 E9
Cheslyn Hay Staffs 64 H10
Chessetts Wood Warwks 53 M6
Chessington Gt Lon 32 H9
Chessington World of Adventures Gt Lon 32 H10
Chester Ches W 75 L10
Chesterblade Somset 22 F5
Chesterfield Derbys 78 C9
Chesterfield Staffs 65 L11
Chesterhill Mdloth 115 Q8
Chester-le-Street Dur 100 H8
Chester Moor Dur 100 H8
Chesters Border 107 P5
Chesters Border 107 Q7
Chester Services Ches W 75 M8
Chesterton Cambs 56 C2
Chesterton Cambs 57 J8
Chesterton Gloucs 30 B2
Chesterton Oxon 43 M7
Chesterton Shrops 52 E1
Chesterton Staffs 64 F2
Chesterton Green Warwks 54 B9
Chesterwood Nthumb 99 M5
Chester Zoo Ches W 75 L9
Chestfield Kent 35 K9
Chestnut Street Kent 34 F9
Cheston Devon 5 L5
Cheswardine Shrops 64 D6
Cheswick Nthumb 117 M12
Cheswick Green Solhll 53 L5
Chetnole Dorset 10 F3
Chettiscombe Devon 20 F10
Chettisham Cambs 57 K4
Chettle Dorset 23 L10
Chetton Shrops 52 C3
Chetwode Bucks 43 N6
Chetwynd Wrekin 64 D8
Chetwynd Aston Wrekin 64 D8
Cheveley Cambs 57 N8
Chevening Kent 33 N10
Cheverton IoW 12 G8
Chevington Suffk 57 Q8
Cheviot Hills 108 B8
Chevithorne Devon 20 F10
Chew Magna BaNES 29 J9
Chew Moor Bolton 76 C2
Chew Stoke BaNES 28 H10
Chewton Keynsham BaNES 29 K9
Chewton Mendip Somset 22 D3
Chichacott Devon 8 B5
Chicheley M Keyn 44 C2
Chichester W Susx 14 B10
Chickerell Dorset 10 G8
Chickering Suffk 59 J5
Chicklade Wilts 23 K6
Chicksands C Beds 44 G4
Chickward Herefs 51 J10
Chidden Hants 25 L10
Chiddingfold Surrey 14 D4
Chiddingly E Susx 15 Q8
Chiddingstone Kent 15 P2
Chiddingstone Causeway Kent 15 P1
Chiddingstone Hoath Kent 15 P2
Chideock Dorset 10 C6
Chidham W Susx 13 N4
Chidswell Kirk 85 K10
Chieveley W Berk 31 K7
Chieveley Services W Berk 31 K8
Chignall St James Essex 46 B9
Chignall Smealy Essex 46 B9
Chigwell Essex 33 N3
Chigwell Row Essex 33 N4
Chilbolton Hants 24 F5
Chilcomb Hants 24 H7
Chilcombe Dorset 10 E6
Chilcompton Somset 22 E3
Chilcote Leics 65 P10
Childer Thornton Ches W 75 L8
Child Okeford Dorset 23 J10
Childrey Oxon 30 H5
Child's Ercall Shrops 64 C7
Childswickham Worcs 42 C4
Childwall Lpool 75 L6
Childwick Bury Herts 44 G9
Childwick Green Herts 44 G9
Chilfrome Dorset 10 F5
Chilgrove W Susx 25 P10
Chilham Kent 35 J11
Chilla Devon 7 N4
Chillaton Devon 7 N8
Chillenden Kent 35 N11
Chillerton IoW 12 H8
Chillesford Suffk 59 M10
Chillingham Nthumb 108 H5
Chillington Devon 5 N8
Chillington Somset 10 B3
Chilmark Wilts 23 L7
Chilmington Green Kent 16 H3
Chilson Oxon 42 G8
Chilsworthy Cnwll 7 M10
Chilsworthy Devon 7 L3
Chiltern Green C Beds 44 G8
Chiltern Hills 31 Q3
Chilthorne Domer Somset 22 C9
Chilton Bucks 43 P9
Chilton Devon 8 G4
Chilton Dur 100 H12
Chilton Kent 17 N2
Chilton Oxon 31 K5
Chilton Suffk 46 F3
Chilton Candover Hants 25 K5
Chilton Cantelo Somset 22 D9
Chilton Foliat Wilts 30 G8
Chilton Polden Somset 21 N5
Chilton Street Suffk 46 D2
Chilton Trinity Somset 21 L5
Chilwell Notts 66 E5
Chilworth Hants 24 G9
Chilworth Surrey 14 E1
Chimney Oxon 30 H2
Chineham Hants 25 L2
Chingford Gt Lon 33 M3
Chinley Derbys 77 K7
Chinnor Oxon 31 Q2
Chipchase Castle Nthumb 99 N3
Chipnall Shrops 64 D6
Chippenham Cambs 57 M6
Chippenham Wilts 29 Q7
Chipperfield Herts 44 F11
Chipping Herts 45 L5
Chipping Lancs 83 N6
Chipping Campden Gloucs 42 D4
Chipping Hill Essex 46 E8
Chipping Norton Oxon 42 G6
Chipping Ongar Essex 45 Q11
Chipping Sodbury S Glos 29 L6
Chipping Warden Nhants 54 E11
Chipshop Devon 7 N9
Chipstable Somset 20 G8
Chipstead Kent 33 P11
Chipstead Surrey 33 K11
Chirbury Shrops 51 J1
Chirk Wrexhm 63 J5
Chirnside Border 117 J10
Chirnsidebridge Border 117 J10
Chirton Wilts 30 C11
Chisbury Wilts 30 F9
Chiselborough Somset 21 P10
Chiseldon Swindn 30 E6
Chiselhampton Oxon 31 M2
Chiserley Calder 84 F9
Chisholme Border 107 L7
Chislehurst Gt Lon 33 N8
Chislet Kent 35 M9
Chiswell Green Herts 44 G10
Chiswick Gt Lon 33 J7
Chiswick End Cambs 45 L3
Chisworth Derbys 77 J5
Chitcombe E Susx 16 E7
Chithurst W Susx 25 P8
Chittering Cambs 57 J7
Chitterne Wilts 23 L5
Chittlehamholt Devon 19 M9
Chittlehampton Devon 19 M8
Chittoe Wilts 29 Q9
Chivelstone Devon 5 N9
Chivenor Devon 19 K6
Chiverton Cross Cnwll 3 J5
Chlenry D & G 94 G6
Chobham Surrey 32 D10
Cholderton Wilts 24 C5
Cholesbury Bucks 44 D10
Chollerford Nthumb 99 P4
Chollerton Nthumb 99 P4
Cholmondeston Ches E 76 B11
Cholsey Oxon 31 M5
Cholstrey Herefs 51 M9
Chop Gate N York 92 B7
Choppington Nthumb 100 H2
Chopwell Gatesd 100 E6
Chorley Ches E 63 P2
Chorley Lancs 83 N11
Chorley Shrops 52 C4
Chorley Staffs 65 K10
Chorleywood Herts 32 E3
Chorleywood West Herts 32 E3
Chorlton Ches E 64 D2
Chorlton-cum-Hardy Manch 76 E5
Chorlton Lane Ches W 63 M3
Choulton Shrops 51 L3
Chowley Ches W 75 N12
Chrishall Essex 45 N4
Chrisswell Inver 113 J6
Christchurch BCP 12 B6
Christchurch Cambs 57 J1
Christchurch Gloucs 40 H9
Christchurch Newpt 28 D4
Christian Malford Wilts 29 Q6
Christleton Ches W 75 M10
Christmas Common Oxon 31 P4
Christmas Pie Surrey 32 C12
Christon N Som 28 E11
Christon Bank Nthumb 109 K5
Christow Devon 8 F8
Christ's Hospital W Susx 14 G5
Chuck Hatch E Susx 15 N4
Chudleigh Devon 8 G9
Chudleigh Knighton Devon 8 F9
Chulmleigh Devon 19 N10
Chunal Derbys 77 J5
Church Lancs 83 R9
Churcham Gloucs 41 M8
Church Aston Wrekin 64 D8
Church Brampton Nhants 55 J7
Church Brough Cumb 90 C4
Church Broughton Derbys 65 M5
Church Cove Cnwll 2 H12
Church Crookham Hants 25 P3
Churchdown Gloucs 41 P7
Church Eaton Staffs 64 F8
Church End Bed 55 P9
Church End Bed 56 B9
Church End Bucks 43 Q10
Church End C Beds 44 D5
Church End C Beds 44 E5
Church End C Beds 44 E7
Church End C Beds 44 E8
Church End C Beds 44 H4
Church End C Beds 56 C10
Church End Cambs 56 B6
Church End Cambs 56 D4
Church End Cambs 56 F5
Churchend Essex 34 H4
Church End Essex 46 A7
Church End Essex 46 C6
Church End Essex 46 C8
Church End Gloucs 41 P4
Church End Gt Lon 33 J4
Church End Herts 44 G9
Church End Herts 45 K6
Church End Herts 45 N7
Church End Lincs 68 E5
Church End Lincs 80 H4
Church End Suffk 47 M4
Church End Warwks 53 N2
Church End Warwks 53 P2
Church Enstone Oxon 42 H6
Church Fenton N York 85 Q8
Churchfield Sandw 53 J2
Churchgate Herts 45 L11
Churchgate Street Essex 45 N9
Church Green Devon 9 M5
Church Gresley Derbys 65 P8
Church Hanborough Oxon 43 J9
Church Hill Staffs 65 J10
Church Houses N York 92 D7
Churchill Devon 9 P4
Churchill Devon 19 L5
Churchill N Som 28 F10
Churchill Oxon 42 G7
Churchill Worcs 52 G10
Churchill Worcs 52 G5
Churchinford Somset 21 K11
Church Knowle Dorset 11 M8
Church Laneham Notts 79 K8
Church Langton Leics 55 J2
Church Lawford Warwks 54 D5
Church Lawton Ches E 64 F1
Church Leigh Staffs 65 J5
Church Lench Worcs 53 J10
Church Mayfield Staffs 65 M3
Church Minshull Ches E 76 C11
Church Norton W Susx 14 B11
Churchover Warwks 54 E4
Church Preen Shrops 51 P1
Church Pulverbatch Shrops 63 M11
Churchstanton Somset 21 K10
Churchstoke Powys 51 J2
Churchstow Devon 5 M7
Church Stowe Nhants 54 G9
Church Street Essex 46 D3
Church Street Kent 34 C7
Church Street Suffk 59 P4
Church Stretton Shrops 51 M2
Churchthorpe Lincs 80 F4
Churchtown Bpool 82 H7
Churchtown Cnwll 6 G9
Churchtown Derbys 77 P11
Churchtown Devon 19 N4
Churchtown IoM 102 f3
Churchtown Lancs 83 L6
Church Town N Linc 79 K2
Churchtown Sefton 83 J11
Church Village Rhondd 27 P5
Church Warsop Notts 78 F10
Church Wilne Derbys 66 D6
Churnsike Lodge Nthumb 99 K3
Churston Ferrers Torbay 5 Q5
Churt Surrey 25 Q6
Churton Ches W 75 M12
Churwell Leeds 85 K9
Chwilog Gwynd 60 G4
Chyandour Cnwll 2 D8
Chyanvounder Cnwll 2 G10
Chyeowling Cnwll 3 K6
Chyvarloe Cnwll 2 G10
Cîl Powys 62 G11
Cilcain Flints 74 G10
Cilcennin Cerdgn 49 J8
Cilcewydd Powys 62 H11
Cilfrew Neath 27 J2
Cilfynydd Rhondd 27 P4
Cilgerran Pembks 37 N2
Cilgwyn Carmth 38 H6
Cilgwyn Gwynd 60 H1
Ciliau-Aeron Cerdgn 48 H9
Cilmaengwyn Neath 38 H10
Cilmery Powys 50 D10
Cilrhedyn Pembks 37 Q3
Cilsan Carmth 38 F7
Ciltalgarth Gwynd 62 B4
Cilycwm Carmth 38 H4
Cimla Neath 27 J3
Cinderford Gloucs 41 K9
Cinder Hill Wolves 52 H2
Cippenham Slough 32 D6
Cirencester Gloucs 30 B2
Citadilla N York 91 L7
City Gt Lon 33 L6
City V Glam 27 N7
City Airport Gt Lon 33 M6
City Dulas IoA 72 H6
Clabhach Ag & B 118 G1
Clachaig Ag & B 112 G5
Clachaig Inn Highld 121 L1
Clachan Ag & B 111 Q10
Clachan Ag & B 112 G1
Clachan Ag & B 120 E9
Clachan Ag & B 120 F4
Clachan Highld 135 K8
Clachan-a-Luib W Isls 152 c8
Clachan Mor Ag & B 118 D3
Clachan na Luib W Isls 152 c8
Clachan of Campsie E Duns 114 A5
Clachan-Seil Ag & B 120 E9
Clachnaharry Highld 138 B6
Clachtoll Highld 148 C11
Clacket Lane Services Surrey 33 M11
Clackmannan Clacks 114 G3
Clackmannanshire Bridge Fife 114 G4
Clackmarras Moray 139 N4
Clacton-on-Sea Essex 47 L8
Cladich Ag & B 121 L8
Cladswell Worcs 53 K9
Claggan Highld 120 D3
Claigan Highld 134 D5
Clandown BaNES 22 F2
Clanfield Hants 25 M10
Clanfield Oxon 42 G11
Clannaborough Devon 8 D4
Clanville Hants 24 E4
Clanville Somset 22 E7
Claonaig Ag & B 112 C10
Clapgate Dorset 11 N4
Clapgate Herts 45 N7
Clapham Bed 55 P10
Clapham Devon 8 G7
Clapham Gt Lon 33 K7
Clapham N York 83 R1
Clapham W Susx 14 G9
Clapham Green Bed 55 P10
Clap Hill Kent 17 J3
Clappersgate Cumb 89 K6
Clapton Somset 10 C3
Clapton Somset 22 E3
Clapton-in-Gordano N Som 28 G7
Clapton-on-the-Hill Gloucs 42 D8
Clapworthy Devon 19 N8
Clarach Cerdgn 49 K4
Claravale Gatesd 100 E5
Clarbeston Pembks 37 K6
Clarbeston Road Pembks 37 K6
Clarborough Notts 79 J7
Clare Suffk 46 D3
Clarebrand D & G 96 F5
Clarencefield D & G 97 M4
Clarewood Nthumb 100 C4
Clarilaw Border 107 N6
Clark's Green Surrey 14 H3
Clarkston E Rens 113 Q9
Clashmore Highld 146 D7
Clashmore Highld 148 B10
Clashnessie Highld 148 C10
Clashnoir Moray 139 N11
Clathy P & K 123 P9
Clathymore P & K 123 P8
Clatt Abers 140 E10
Clatter Powys 50 D2
Clatterford End Essex 46 A9
Clatworthy Somset 20 G7
Claughton Lancs 83 M2
Claughton Lancs 83 M7
Claughton Wirral 75 J6
Clavelshay Somset 21 L7
Claverdon Warwks 53 M7
Claverham N Som 28 F9
Clavering Essex 45 N5
Claverley Shrops 52 E2
Claverton BaNES 29 M9
Claverton Down BaNES 29 M9
Clawdd-coch V Glam 27 P7
Clawdd-newydd Denbgs 62 E2
Clawthorpe Cumb 89 N11
Clawton Devon 7 L5
Claxby Lincs 80 C5
Claxby Lincs 81 J9
Claxton N York 86 C3
Claxton Norfk 71 L11
Claybrooke Magna Leics 54 E3
Clay Common Suffk 59 P4
Clay Coton Nhants 54 F5
Clay Cross Derbys 78 C11
Claydon Oxon 54 D10
Claydon Suffk 58 H10
Clay End Herts 45 K7
Claygate D & G 98 E2
Claygate Kent 16 C2
Claygate Surrey 32 H9
Claygate Cross Kent 33 R11
Clayhall Gt Lon 33 M4
Clayhanger Devon 20 G9
Clayhanger Wsall 65 K11
Clayhidon Devon 21 J10
Clayhill E Susx 16 E6
Clayhill Hants 12 E3
Clayhithe Cambs 57 J8
Clayock Highld 151 L5
Claypit Hill Cambs 56 G9
Claypits Gloucs 41 M10
Claypole Lincs 67 L2
Claythorpe Lincs 80 H8
Clayton C Brad 84 H9
Clayton Donc 78 D2
Clayton W Susx 15 K8
Clayton Green Lancs 83 N10
Clayton-le-Moors Lancs 83 R9
Clayton-le-Woods Lancs 83 M10
Clayton West Kirk 77 N2
Clayworth Notts 79 J6
Cleadale Highld 126 H6
Cleadon S Tyne 101 K6
Cleadon Park S Tyne 101 K5
Clearbrook Devon 4 H4
Clearwell Gloucs 40 H10
Cleasby N York 91 L4
Cleat Ork 147 c6
Cleatlam Dur 91 J3
Cleator Cumb 88 D4
Cleator Moor Cumb 88 D4
Cleckheaton Kirk 85 J10
Cleedownton Shrops 51 P4
Cleehill Shrops 51 Q5
Cleekhimin N Lans 114 D9
Clee St Margaret Shrops 51 P4
Cleestanton Shrops 51 P5
Cleethorpes NE Lin 80 F2
Cleeton St Mary Shrops 51 Q5
Cleeve N Som 28 F9
Cleeve Oxon 31 M6
Cleeve Hill Gloucs 41 R6
Cleeve Prior Worcs 53 K10
Cleghornie E Loth 116 D5
Clehonger Herefs 40 F4
Cleish P & K 115 K2
Cleland N Lans 114 E9
Clement's End C Beds 44 E8
Clement Street Kent 33 P8
Clenamacrie Ag & B 120 H7
Clench Common Wilts 30 E9
Clenchwarton Norfk 69 L8
Clenerty Abers 141 J4
Clent Worcs 52 H5
Cleobury Mortimer Shrops 52 C5
Cleobury North Shrops 52 B3
Cleongart Ag & B 103 J3
Clephanton Highld 138 E6
Clerkhill D & G 106 H10
Cleuch-head D & G 105 Q9
Clevancy Wilts 30 B7
Clevedon N Som 28 F8
Cleveley Oxon 42 H7
Cleveleys Lancs 82 H6
Cleverton Wilts 29 R5
Clewer Somset 21 P3
Cley next the Sea Norfk 70 F3
Cliburn Cumb 89 P2
Cliddesden Hants 25 L3
Cliff Warwks 53 N1
Cliffe Lancs 83 Q8
Cliffe Medway 34 C7
Cliffe N York 86 C9
Cliffe N York 91 L4
Cliff End E Susx 16 F8
Cliffe Woods Medway 34 C7
Clifford Herefs 40 C3
Clifford Leeds 85 N6
Clifford Chambers Warwks 53 M10
Clifford's Mesne Gloucs 41 L7
Cliffsend Kent 35 P9
Clifton Bristl 28 H7
Clifton C Beds 44 H4
Clifton C Nott 66 E5
Clifton C York 86 B5
Clifton Calder 84 H10
Clifton Cumb 89 N1
Clifton Derbys 65 M3
Clifton Devon 19 L5
Clifton Donc 78 E4
Clifton Lancs 83 L9
Clifton N York 85 J5
Clifton Nthumb 100 G2
Clifton Oxon 43 K5
Clifton Salfd 76 E3
Clifton Worcs 41 N2
Clifton Campville Staffs 65 N10
Clifton Hampden Oxon 31 L3
Clifton Reynes M Keyn 55 M10
Clifton upon Dunsmore Warwks 54 E5
Clifton upon Teme Worcs 52 D8
Cliftonville Kent 35 Q8
Climping W Susx 14 E10
Clink Somset 22 H4
Clint N York 85 K3
Clinterty C Aber 133 K2
Clint Green Norfk 70 F10
Clintmains Border 107 P3
Clipiau Gwynd 61 P10
Clippesby Norfk 71 N9
Clipsham Rutlnd 67 N9
Clipston Nhants 54 H4
Clipston Notts 66 G5
Clipstone C Beds 44 D6
Clipstone Notts 78 F11
Clitheroe Lancs 83 R7
Clive Shrops 63 N7
Cliveden Bucks 32 C5
Clixby Lincs 80 B3
Cloatley Wilts 29 R4
Clocaenog Denbgs 62 E1
Clochan Moray 140 B4
Clock Face St Hel 75 N5
Cloddiau Powys 62 H10
Clodock Herefs 40 D6
Cloford Somset 22 G4
Clola Abers 141 N7
Clophill C Beds 44 F4
Clopton Nhants 55 Q5
Clopton Suffk 59 J10
Clopton Corner Suffk 59 J9
Clopton Green Suffk 57 P9
Clopton Green Suffk 58 E8
Clos du Valle Guern 12 d1
Closeburn D & G 106 B11
Closeburnmill D & G 106 B10
Closeclark IoM 102 c6
Closworth Somset 10 E3
Clothall Herts 45 K5
Clotton Ches W 75 N11
Cloudesley Bush Warwks 54 D3
Clouds Herefs 41 J4
Clough Oldham 76 H2
Clough Foot Calder 84 D10
Clough Head Calder 84 G11
Cloughton N York 93 K8
Cloughton Newlands N York 93 K7
Clousta Shet 147 h6
Clova Angus 131 Q9
Clovelly Devon 18 F8
Clovenfords Border 107 L2
Clovulin Highld 128 D11
Clow Bridge Lancs 84 B9
Clowne Derbys 78 D8
Clows Top Worcs 52 D6
Cloy Wrexhm 63 L4
Cluanie Inn Highld 128 F2
Cluanie Lodge Highld 128 F2
Clubworthy Cnwll 7 K6
Clugston D & G 95 L7
Clun Shrops 51 J4
Clunas Highld 138 G6
Clunbury Shrops 51 L4
Clunderwen Carmth 37 M6
Clune Highld 138 E10
Clunes Highld 128 H6
Clungunford Shrops 51 L5
Clunie P & K 124 C4
Clunton Shrops 51 K4
Cluny Fife 115 N2
Clutton BaNES 29 J10
Clutton Ches W 63 M1
Clutton Hill BaNES 29 K10
Clwt Conwy 74 C11
Clwt-y-bont Gwynd 73 K11
Clydach Mons 40 B9
Clydach Swans 26 G2
Clydach Vale Rhondd 27 M4
Clydebank W Duns 113 P7
Clydey Pembks 37 P3
Clyffe Pypard Wilts 30 C7
Clynder Ag & B 113 K4
Clyne Neath 27 J2
Clynnog Fawr Gwynd 60 G2
Clyro Powys 40 B3
Clyst Honiton Devon 9 J6
Clyst Hydon Devon 9 K4
Clyst St George Devon 9 J7
Clyst St Lawrence Devon 9 K5
Clyst St Mary Devon 9 J6
Cnoc W Isls 152 g3
Cnwch Coch Cerdgn 49 L6
Coad's Green Cnwll 7 K9
Coal Aston Derbys 78 B8
Coalbrookvale Blae G 40 B10
Coalburn S Lans 105 Q3
Coalburns Gatesd 100 E6
Coaley Gloucs 41 M11
Coalhill Essex 34 D3
Coalmoor Wrekin 64 C10
Coalpit Heath S Glos 29 K6
Coal Pool Wsall 65 J12
Coalport Wrekin 64 C11
Coalsnaughton Clacks 114 G2
Coal Street Suffk 59 J6
Coaltown of Balgonie Fife 115 P1
Coaltown of Wemyss Fife 115 P2
Coalville Leics 66 C9
Coanwood Nthumb 99 K6
Coat Somset 21 P9
Coatbridge N Lans 114 D8
Coatdyke N Lans 114 D8
Coate Swindn 30 E6
Coate Wilts 30 B10
Coates Cambs 56 F1
Coates Gloucs 29 R2
Coates Lincs 79 M7
Coates Notts 79 K7
Coates W Susx 14 E7
Coatham R & Cl 92 C2
Coatham Mundeville Darltn 91 M3
Cobbaton Devon 19 M8
Coberley Gloucs 41 Q8
Cobhall Common Herefs 40 F5
Cobham Kent 34 B8
Cobham Surrey 32 G10
Cobham Services Surrey 32 G10
Coblers Green Essex 46 C8
Cobley Dorset 23 M9
Cobnash Herefs 51 M8
Cobo Guern 12 c2
Cobridge C Stke 64 G2
Coburby Abers 141 M3
Cock Alley Derbys 78 C9
Cockayne N York 92 C7
Cockayne Hatley C Beds 56 E10
Cock Bank Wrexhm 63 K3
Cock Bevington Warwks 53 K10
Cock Bridge Abers 131 N3
Cockburnspath Border 116 H7
Cock Clarks Essex 46 E11
Cock & End Suffk 57 N10
Cockenzie and Port Seton E Loth 115 R6
Cocker Bar Lancs 83 L10
Cocker Brook Lancs 83 R10
Cockerham Lancs 83 L5
Cockermouth Cumb 97 M12
Cockernhoe Herts 44 G7
Cockersdale Leeds 85 K9
Cockett Swans 26 F3
Cockfield Dur 91 J2
Cockfield Suffk 58 D9
Cockfosters Gt Lon 33 K3
Cock Green Essex 46 C7
Cocking W Susx 14 C7
Cocking Causeway W Susx 14 C7
Cockington Torbay 5 Q4
Cocklake Somset 21 P3
Cockley Beck Cumb 88 H6
Cockley Cley Norfk 69 Q11
Cock Marling E Susx 16 F7
Cockpole Green Wokham 31 R6
Cocks Cnwll 3 J4
Cockshutford Shrops 51 P3
Cockshutt Shrops 63 M6
Cock Street Kent 34 D12
Cockthorpe Norfk 70 E4
Cockwells Cnwll 2 E7
Cockwood Devon 9 J8
Cockwood Somset 21 K5
Cockyard Derbys 77 K7
Cockyard Herefs 40 F5
Coddenham Suffk 58 H9
Coddington Ches W 63 M1
Coddington Herefs 41 L3
Coddington Notts 67 L1
Codford St Mary Wilts 23 L5
Codford St Peter Wilts 23 L5
Codicote Herts 45 J8
Codmore Hill W Susx 14 F7
Codnor Derbys 66 C2
Codrington S Glos 29 L6
Codsall Staffs 64 F11
Codsall Wood Staffs 64 F11
Coed Darcy Neath 26 H3
Coedely Rhondd 27 N5
Coed Hirwaun Neath 27 K5
Coedkernew Newpt 28 C6
Coed Morgan Mons 40 E9
Coedpoeth Wrexhm 63 J2
Coed Talon Flints 75 J11
Coedway Powys 63 K9
Coed-y-Bryn Cerdgn 48 F11
Coed-y-caerau Newpt 28 E4
Coed-y-Cwm Rhondd 27 P4
Coed-y-paen Mons 28 D3
Coed-yr-ynys Powys 39 R7
Coed Ystumgwern Gwynd 61 K7
Coelbren Powys 39 K9
Coffinswell Devon 5 Q3
Coffle End Bed 55 P9
Cofton Devon 8 H8
Cofton Hackett Worcs 53 J5
Cogan V Glam 28 A8
Cogenhoe Nhants 55 L8
Cogges Oxon 42 H9
Coggeshall Essex 46 E7
Coggin's Mill E Susx 15 Q5
Coignafearn Highld 138 C12
Coilacriech Abers 131 P5
Coilantogle Stirlg 122 G11
Coillore Highld 134 F8
Coity Brdgnd 27 L6
Col W Isls 152 g3
Colaboll Highld 145 N3
Colan Cnwll 3 L2
Colaton Raleigh Devon 9 K7
Colbost Highld 134 D6
Colburn N York 91 K7
Colby Cumb 89 Q3
Colby IoM 102 c7
Colby Norfk 71 J6
Colchester Essex 46 H6
Colchester Zoo Essex 46 G7
Cold Ash W Berk 31 L8
Cold Ashby Nhants 54 G5
Cold Ashton S Glos 29 M8
Cold Aston Gloucs 42 D8
Coldbackie Highld 149 N5
Coldbeck Cumb 90 B6
Cold Blow Pembks 37 M8
Cold Brayfield M Keyn 55 M10
Cold Cotes N York 83 Q1
Coldean Br & H 15 L9
Coldeast Devon 8 F9
Colden Calder 84 E9
Colden Common Hants 24 H9
Coldfair Green Suffk 59 N8
Coldham Cambs 68 H11
Cold Hanworth Lincs 79 P7
Coldharbour Cnwll 3 J5
Coldharbour Devon 20 G11
Coldharbour Gloucs 40 H11
Cold Harbour Herts 44 G8
Cold Harbour Oxon 31 N6
Coldharbour Surrey 14 G2
Cold Hatton Wrekin 64 B8
Cold Hatton Heath Wrekin 64 B8
Cold Hesledon Dur 101 K9
Cold Hiendley Wakefd 78 B1
Cold Higham Nhants 54 H10
Coldingham Border 117 K8
Cold Kirby N York 92 B10
Coldmeece Staffs 64 F6
Cold Newton Leics 66 H11
Cold Northcott Cnwll 7 J7
Cold Norton Essex 34 E2
Cold Overton Leics 67 K10
Coldred Kent 17 N1
Coldridge Devon 8 D3
Coldstream Border 108 D2
Coldwaltham W Susx 14 E7
Coldwell Herefs 40 F4
Coldwells Abers 141 M8
Cold Weston Shrops 51 P4
Cole Somset 22 F6
Colebatch Shrops 51 K3
Colebrook C Plym 4 H5
Colebrook Devon 9 J3
Colebrooke Devon 8 E5
Coleby Lincs 79 N11
Coleby N Linc 86 G11
Cole End Warwks 53 M3
Coleford Devon 8 E4
Coleford Gloucs 41 J9
Coleford Somset 22 F4
Coleford Water Somset 20 H6
Colegate End Norfk 59 J3
Cole Green Herts 45 K9
Cole Green Herts 45 M5
Cole Henley Hants 24 H3
Colehill Dorset 11 P4
Coleman Green Herts 44 H9
Coleman's Hatch E Susx 15 N4
Colemere Shrops 63 M6
Colemore Hants 25 M7
Colemore Green Shrops 52 D1
Colenden P & K 124 C7
Coleorton Leics 66 C9
Colerne Wilts 29 N8
Colesbourne Gloucs 42 B9
Cole's Cross Devon 5 N7
Coles Cross Dorset 10 B4
Colesden Bed 56 C9
Coles Green Suffk 47 K3
Coleshill Bucks 32 D3
Coleshill Oxon 30 F4
Coleshill Warwks 53 M3
Colestocks Devon 9 L5
Coley BaNES 22 D2
Colgate W Susx 15 J4
Colinsburgh Fife 125 J12
Colinton C Edin 115 M7
Colintraive Ag & B 112 F6
Colkirk Norfk 70 D7
Coll Ag & B 118 H1
Coll W Isls 152 g3
Collace P & K 124 D6
Collafirth Shet 147 i4
Coll Airport Ag & B 118 G2
Collaton Devon 5 M9
Collaton St Mary Torbay 5 P5
College of Roseisle Moray 139 L3
College Town Br For 32 B10
Collessie Fife 124 F10
Colleton Mills Devon 19 N10
Collier Row Gt Lon 33 P4
Collier's End Herts 45 L7
Collier's Green E Susx 16 D6
Colliers Green Kent 16 D3
Collier Street Kent 16 C2
Colliery Row Sundld 101 J8
Collieston Abers 141 P10
Collin D & G 97 L3
Collingbourne Ducis Wilts 24 D3
Collingbourne Kingston Wilts 24 D2
Collingham Leeds 85 N6
Collingham Notts 79 L11
Collington Herefs 52 C8
Collingtree Nhants 55 J9
Collins Green Warrtn 75 P5
Collins Green Worcs 52 D9
Colliston Angus 125 M4
Colliton Devon 9 L4
Collyweston Nhants 67 N11
Colmonell S Ayrs 94 G1
Colmworth Bed 56 B9
Colnabaichin Abers 131 P3
Colnbrook Slough 32 E7
Colne Cambs 56 G5
Colne Lancs 84 D7
Colne Bridge Kirk 85 J11
Colne Edge Lancs 84 D7
Colne Engaine Essex 46 E5
Colney Norfk 70 H10
Colney Heath Herts 44 H10

Colney Street Herts 44 H11
Coln Rogers Gloucs 42 C9
Coln St Aldwyns Gloucs....42 D10
Coln St Dennis Gloucs 42 C9
Colonsay Ag & B 111 J2
Colonsay Airport Ag & B ..110 H3
Colpy Abers..................140 G9
Colquhar Border 107 J1
Colquite Cnwll 6 F10
Colscott Devon 18 G10
Colsterdale N York 91 J10
Colsterworth Lincs 67 M7
Colston Bassett Notts 66 F6
Coltfield Moray 139 L3
Colt Hill Hants 25 N3
Coltishall Norfk 71 K8
Colton Cumb 89 J9
Colton Leeds 85 M8
Colton N York 85 Q6
Colton Norfk 70 G10
Colton Staffs 65 K8
Colt's Hill Kent 16 B2
Columbjohn Devon 8 H5
Colva Powys 50 H10
Colvend D & G 96 H7
Colwall Herefs 41 M3
Colwell Nthumb 99 Q3
Colwich Staffs 65 J8
Colwick Notts 66 G4
Colwinston V Glam 27 M7
Colworth W Susx 14 C10
Colwyn Bay Conwy 73 P8
Colyford Devon 9 N6
Colyton Devon 9 N6
Combe Devon 5 M9
Combe Herefs 51 L8
Combe Oxon 43 J8
Combe W Berk 30 H10
Combe Almer Dorset 11 M5
Combe Common Surrey 14 C4
Combe Down BaNES 29 M10
Combe Fishacre Devon......5 P4
Combe Florey Somset 21 K7
Combe Hay BaNES 29 L10
Combeinteignhead
    Devon 8 G10
Combe Martin Devon 19 L4
Combe Raleigh Devon 9 M4
Comberbach Ches W 76 B8
Comberford Staffs 65 M10
Comberton Cambs 56 G9
Comberton Herefs 51 N7
Combe St Nicholas
    Somset 10 G3
Combpyne Devon 9 P6
Combridge Staffs 65 K5
Combrook Warwks 53 P10
Combs Derbys 77 K8
Combs Suffk 58 F9
Combwich Somset 21 L5
Comers Abers 132 G3
Comeytrowe Somset 21 M8
Comhampton Worcs 52 F7
Commercial End Cambs 57 L8
Commins Coch Powys 61 P11
Commondale N York 92 D5
Common Edge Bpool 82 M8
Common End Cumb 4 C2
Common Moor Cnwll 4 C3
Common Platt Wilts 30 C5
Commonside Ches W 75 P9
Commonside Derbys 65 N4
Common Side Derbys 77 Q8
Commonwood Shrops 63 N6
Commonwood Wrexhm......63 L1
Compass Somset 21 L6
Compstall Stockp 76 H4
Compstonend D & G 96 D8
Compton Devon 5 Q3
Compton Hants 24 F7
Compton Hants 24 H8
Compton Staffs 52 F4
Compton Surrey 14 D1
Compton Surrey 25 N10
Compton W Susx 25 N10
Compton Wilts 23 P3
Compton Abbas Dorset 23 J9
Compton Abdale Gloucs....42 C8
Compton Bassett Wilts 30 C8
Compton Beauchamp
    Oxon..........................30 F5
Compton Bishop Somset ..21 N2
Compton Chamberlayne
    Wilts..........................23 M7
Compton Dando BaNES 29 K6
Compton Dundon Somset..21 N7
Compton Durville Somset..21 P10
Compton Greenfield
    S Glos 28 H6
Compton Martin BaNES 28 H11
Compton Pauncefoot
    Somset 22 E8
Compton Valence Dorset ..10 F6
Comrie Fife 115 J3
Comrie P & K 123 K8
Conaglen House Highld ..128 E4
Conchra Highld 136 B10
Concraigie P & K 124 C4
Conder Green Lancs 83 K4
Conderton Worcs 41 Q4
Condicote Gloucs 42 D6
Condorrat N Lans 114 D6
Condover Shrops 63 N11
Coney Hill Gloucs 41 N8
Coneyhurst W Susx 14 F5
Coneysthorpe N York 86 D11
Coneythorpe N York 85 N3
Coney Weston Suffk 58 E5
Conford Hants 25 P7
Congdon's Shop Cnwll......4 G6
Congerstone Leics 66 B11
Congham Norfk 69 N7
Congl-y-wal Gwynd 61 M3
Congresbury N Som 28 H9
Congreve Staffs 64 G9
Conheath D & G 97 K4
Conicavel Moray 138 H5
Coningsby Lincs 80 D12
Conington Cambs 56 D3
Conington Cambs 56 F7
Conisbrough Donc 78 E4
Conisholme Lincs 80 H4
Coniston Cumb 89 J7
Coniston E R Yk 87 M8
Coniston Cold N York 84 D4
Conistone N York 84 E2
Connah's Quay Flints 75 J9
Connel Ag & B 120 H1
Connel Park E Ayrs 105 L7
Connor Downs Cnwll 2 F6
Conon Bridge Highld 137 P5
Cononley N York..............84 E6
Consall Staffs 64 H2
Consett Dur..................100 E6
Constable Burton N York ..91 K8
Constable Lee Lancs 84 B10
Constantine Cnwll 2 H8
Constantine Bay Cnwll 6 C10
Contin Highld 137 M4
Conwy Conwy 73 M8
Conwy Castle Conwy 73 M8
Conyer Kent 34 G9
Conyer's Green Suffk 58 C7
Cooden E Susx 16 C9
Cookbury Devon 7 M3

Cookbury Wick Devon 7 M4
Cookham W & M 32 C5
Cookham Dean W & M......32 B5
Cookham Rise W & M 32 C5
Cookhill Worcs 53 K9
Cookley Suffk 59 L5
Cookley Worcs................52 F5
Cookley Green Oxon 31 P4
Cookney Abers 133 L6
Cooksbridge E Susx 15 M8
Cooksey Green Worcs 52 G7
Cook's Green Essex 47 L8
Cooks Green Suffk 58 E10
Cookshill Staffs 64 H3
Cooksland Cnwll 6 F11
Cooksmill Green Essex 46 B10
Cookson Green Ches W 75 P9
Coolham W Susx 14 F6
Cooling Medway 34 D7
Cooling Street Medway 34 D7
Coombe Cnwll 2 G6
Coombe Cnwll 3 M4
Coombe Cnwll 8 B10
Coombe Cnwll 6 G4
Coombe Devon 8 G10
Coombe Devon 6 L6
Coombe Gloucs................29 M3
Coombe Hants 25 L9
Coombe Wilts 23 P3
Coombe Bissett Wilts 23 P8
Coombe Cellars Devon 8 L9
Coombe Cross Hants........25 L9
Coombe Hill Gloucs..........41 P6
Coombe Keynes Dorset 11 K8
Coombe Pafford Torbay 5 Q3
Coombes W Susx 14 H9
Coombes-Moor Herefs 51 L8
Coombe Street Somset 22 G7
Coombeswood Dudley 52 F11
Coopersale Common
    Essex........................45 N11
Coopersale Street Essex ..45 N11
Cooper's Corner Kent......33 P12
Coopers Green E Susx 15 N6
Coopers Green Herts 44 H9
Cooper Street Kent..........35 P10
Cooper Turning Bolton......76 B2
Cootham W Susx 14 F8
Copdock Suffk 47 K3
Copford Essex 46 G7
Copford Green Essex 46 G7
Copgrove N York 85 M3
Copister Shet 147 j4
Cople Bed 56 B11
Copley Calder..................84 G10
Copley Dur 90 H2
Copley Tamesd 76 H4
Coplow Dale Derbys 77 M8
Copmanthorpe C York......85 R6
Copmere End Staffs 64 E6
Copp Lancs 83 K7
Coppathorne Cnwll 7 J5
Coppenhall Staffs 64 G8
Coppenhall Moss Ches W ..76 D12
Copperhouse Cnwll 2 F6
Coppicegate Shrops 52 D5
Coppingford Cambs 56 C5
Coppins Corner Kent 16 G1
Copplestone Devon 8 L4
Coppull Lancs 83 M12
Coppull Moor Lancs 75 P1
Copsale W Susx 14 H6
Copster Green Lancs 83 P8
Copston Magna Warwks ..54 C3
Cop Street Kent..............35 N10
Copthall Green Essex 33 M2
Copt Heath Solhll 53 M5
Copt Hewick N York 85 M1
Copthorne Cnwll 7 K6
Copthorne W Susx 15 K3
Copt Oak Leics 66 D9
Copy's Green Norfk..........70 D4
Copythorne Hants 24 E10
Coram Street Suffk 46 H3
Corbets Tey Gt Lon 33 Q5
Corbière Jersey 13 a3
Corbridge Nthumb 100 C5
Corby Nhants 55 M3
Corby Glen Lincs 67 N7
Corby Hill Cumb 98 F7
Cordon N Ayrs 103 Q4
Cordwell Derbys 77 P8
Coreley Shrops 52 B6
Cores End Bucks..............32 C5
Corfe Somset 21 K9
Corfe Castle Dorset 11 M8
Corfe Mullen Dorset 11 N5
Corfton Shrops 51 N4
Corgarff Abers 131 P3
Corhampton Hants 25 K9
Corks Pond Kent 16 B3
Corlae D & G 105 M10
Corley Warwks 53 P4
Corley Ash Warwks 53 P4
Corley Moor Warwks 53 P4
Corley Services Warwks ..53 P4
Cormuir Angus 131 P11
Cornard Tye Suffk 46 F3
Corndon Devon 8 C7
Corner Row Lancs 83 K8
Corney Cumb 88 E8
Cornforth Dur 101 J11
Cornhill Abers 140 F4
Cornhill-on-Tweed
    Nthumb 108 D2
Cornholme Calder 84 D10
Cornish Hall End Essex 46 B4
Cornoigmore Ag & B 118 D3
Cornriggs Dur 99 N10
Cornsay Dur 100 F9
Cornsay Colliery Dur 100 F9
Corntown Highld 137 P5
Corntown V Glam 27 L7
Cornwall Airport
    Newquay Cnwll 3 L7
Cornwell Oxon 42 F6
Cornwood Devon 5 N5
Cornworthy Devon............5 P5
Corpach Highld 128 F9
Corpusty Norfk 70 G6
Corrachree Abers............132 D3
Corran Highld 127 Q2
Corran Ag & B................113 J1
Corrany IoM 102 f4
Corrie D & G..................97 P3
Corrie N Ayrs 103 Q1
Corriecravie N Ayrs 103 N5
Corriegills N Ayrs 103 Q3
Corriegour Lodge Hotel
    Highld 129 J2
Corriemoillie Highld 137 L3
Corrimony Highld 137 L10
Corringham Lincs 79 L5
Corringham Thurr 34 C5
Corris Gwynd 61 N10
Corris Uchaf Gwynd 61 N10
Corrow Ag & B................113 J1
Corry Highld 135 L11
Corscombe Devon 8 D5
Corscombe Dorset 10 D4
Corse Gloucs 41 N6
Corse Lawn Gloucs..........41 N5
Corsham Wilts 29 P8
Corsindae Abers 132 G3
Corsley Wilts 23 J4
Corsley Heath Wilts 22 H4
Corsock D & G................96 F3

Corston BaNES 29 L9
Corston Wilts 29 Q5
Corstorphine C Edin 115 M7
Cortachy Angus 132 B12
Corton Suffk....................59 Q1
Corton Wilts 23 K5
Corton Denham Somset ..22 E9
Coruanan Highld 128 E4
Corwen Denbgs 62 E3
Coryates Dorset 10 F7
Coryton Devon 7 N8
Coryton Thurr 34 C6
Cosby Leics 54 F2
Coscote Oxon 31 K10
Coseley Dudley 52 H2
Cosford Shrops 64 E11
Cosgrove Nhants 55 J4
Cosham C Port 13 L4
Cosheston Pembks 37 K10
Coshieville P & K 123 K5
Cossall Notts 66 D4
Cossall Marsh Notts 66 D4
Cossington Leics 66 G9
Cossington Somset..........21 M5
Costessey Norfk 70 H9
Costock Notts 66 F7
Coston Leics 67 L8
Coston Norfk 70 F11
Cote Oxon 42 H11
Cote Somset 21 M4
Cotebrook Ches W 75 P10
Cotehill Cumb 98 F8
Cotes Cumb 89 M9
Cotes Leics 66 F8
Cotes Staffs 64 F5
Cotesbach Leics 54 E4
Cotes Heath Staffs..........64 F5
Cotford St Luke Somset ..21 J8
Cotgrave Notts 66 G4
Cothal Abers 133 L1
Cotham Notts 67 K3
Cothelstone Somset 21 J7
Cotherstone Dur..............90 G3
Cothill Oxon 31 K2
Cotleigh Devon 9 N4
Coton Cambs 56 H9
Coton Nhants..................54 H6
Coton Shrops 63 P5
Coton Staffs 64 E8
Coton Staffs 64 H6
Coton Staffs 65 M11
Coton Clanford Staffs 64 F7
Coton Hayes Staffs 65 J5
Coton Hill Shrops 63 N9
Coton in the Clay Staffs ..65 M6
Coton in the Elms Derbys ..65 N9
Coton Park Derbys 65 P8
Cotswolds 42 A10
Cotswold Airport Wilts 29 Q3
Cotswold Wildlife Park
    & Gardens Oxon..........42 F10
Cott Devon 5 N4
Cottam E R Yk 87 J2
Cottam Lancs 83 L8
Cottam Notts 79 K8
Cottenham Cambs 57 J7
Cotterdale N York 90 D8
Cottered Herts 45 K6
Cotteridge Birm 53 K5
Cotterstock Nhants 55 P3
Cottesbrooke Nhants 54 H6
Cottesmore Rutlnd 67 M9
Cottingham E R Yk 87 K8
Cottingham Nhants 55 L2
Cottingley C Brad 84 H7
Cottisford Oxon 43 M5
Cotton Suffk 58 G7
Cotton End Bed 44 F3
Cotton Tree Lancs 84 D7
Cottown Abers................133 J4
Cottown Abers................140 D10
Cottown of Gight Abers ..141 K8
Cotts Devon 4 G4
Cotwall Wrekin 63 Q8
Cotwalton Staffs 64 H5
Couch's Mill Cnwll 4 A5
Coughton Herefs 41 J7
Coughton Warwks 53 K8
Coulaghailtro Ag & B 111 Q8
Coulags Highld 136 D7
Coulby Newham Middsb ..92 A4
Coulderton Cumb 88 C5
Coull Abers 132 D4
Coulport Ag & B 113 J4
Coulsdon Gt Lon 33 K10
Coulston Wilts 23 L3
Coulter S Lans 106 D3
Coultershaw Bridge
    W Susx 14 D7
Coultings Somset 21 K5
Coulton N York 92 D12
Coultra Fife 124 G8
Cound Shrops 63 P11
Coundlane Shrops 63 P11
Coundon Dur 91 N12
Coundon Grange Dur 91 M12
Countersett N York 90 E9
Countess Wilts................23 N4
Countess Cross Essex 46 F5
Countess Wear Devon 8 H7
Countesswells C Aber 133 L3
Countesthorpe Leics 54 F2
Countisbury Devon..........19 P3
Coupar Angus P & K 124 C5
Coupland Cumb 90 B3
Coupland Nthumb 108 F4
Cour Ag & B..................112 B11
Court-at-Street Kent 17 K4
Courteachan Highld 127 M5
Courteenhall Nhants........55 J10
Court Henry Carmth..........38 E7
Courtsend Essex 35 J4
Courtway Somset 21 K6
Cousland Mdloth 115 Q7
Cousley Wood E Susx 16 B4
Cove Border 116 H7
Cove Devon 20 C9
Cove Hants 25 Q2
Cove Highld 143 L6
Cove Bay C Aber 133 M4
Cove Bottom Suffk 59 P5
Coveithe Suffk 59 Q5
Coven Staffs 64 G11
Coveney Cambs 57 J4
Covenham St
    Bartholomew Lincs......80 G5
Covenham St Mary Lincs..80 G5
Coven Heath Staffs 64 G11
Coventry Covtry 53 Q5
Coverack Cnwll 3 J11
Coverack Bridges Cnwll 2 G8
Coverham N York 91 J9
Covington Cambs 55 P6
Covington S Lans 106 C2
Cowan Bridge Lancs........89 Q11
Cowbeech E Susx 16 A8
Cowbit Lincs 68 E9
Cowbridge V Glam 27 M7
Cowdale Derbys 77 M9
Cowden Kent 15 N2
Cowdenbeath Fife 115 L1
Cowden Pound Kent 15 N2
Cowden Station Kent 15 N2
Cowers Lane Derbys 65 P3

Cowes IoW 12 H5
Cowesby N York..............91 Q9
Cowesfield Green Wilts 24 D8
Cowfold W Susx 15 J6
Cowgill Cumb 90 C9
Cow Green Suffk 58 F7
Cowhill S Glos 29 J3
Cowie Abers 133 L7
Cowie Stirlg 114 F3
Cowlam E R Yk................86 H2
Cowley Devon 8 G5
Cowley Gloucs 42 A8
Cowley Gt Lon 32 F6
Cowley Oxon 43 L11
Cowling Lancs 83 N11
Cowling N York 84 E6
Cowling N York 91 L9
Cowlinge Suffk 57 N10
Cowmes Kirk 85 L10
Cowpe Lancs 84 C11
Cowpen Nthumb 100 H2
Cowpen Bewley S on T 91 Q2
Cowplain Hants 13 M3
Cowshill Dur 99 N10
Cowslip Green N Som 28 H9
Cowthorpe N York............85 N5
Coxall Herefs 51 L6
Coxbank Ches E 64 C4
Coxbench Derbys 66 A4
Coxbridge Somset 22 C6
Cox Common Suffk 59 M4
Coxford Cnwll 6 H5
Coxford Norfk 70 C6
Coxgreen Staffs 52 E3
Coxheath Kent 34 C12
Coxhoe Dur 101 J11
Coxley Somset 22 C5
Coxley Wakefd 85 K11
Coxpark Cnwll 7 M10
Coxtie Green Essex..........33 P4
Coxwold N York 92 B11
Coychurch Brdgnd 27 M7
Coylton S Ayrs 104 H6
Coylumbridge Highld 130 G2
Coytrahen Brdgnd 27 L7
Crabbs Cross Worcs 53 K7
Crab Orchard Dorset 11 N3
Crabtree W Susx 15 J6
Crabtree Green Wrexhm ..63 K3
Crackenthorpe Cumb 89 Q2
Crackington Haven Cnwll ..6 H5
Crackley Staffs 64 F2
Crackley Warwks 54 C6
Crackleybank Shrops 64 E10
Crackpot N York 90 H8
Cracoe N York 84 E3
Craddock Devon..............20 H11
Cradle End Herts 45 M6
Cradley Dudley 52 G4
Cradley Herefs................41 M3
Cradley Heath Sandw 52 H3
Cradoc Powys 39 N5
Crafthole Cnwll 4 F6
Crafton Bucks 44 B8
Crag Foot Lancs 89 M12
Craggan Highld 139 J10
Cragganmore Moray........139 M8
Craggan N York 84 F2
Cragg Hill Leeds..............85 K7
Cragg Vale Calder............84 F10
Craghead Dur................100 G8
Cragside House &
    Garden Nthumb 108 H9
Craibstone Moray 140 D4
Craichie Angus 125 K3
Craig Angus 125 N2
Craig Highld..................136 E6
Craigbank E Ayrs 105 L7
Craigburn Border............115 N9
Craig-cefn-parc Swans....38 G11
Craigcleuch D & G 107 M3
Craigdam Abers 141 K10
Craigdarroch E Ayrs 105 L9
Craigdhu Ag & B 120 F11
Craigearn Abers 132 H2
Craigellachie Moray........139 P7
Craigend P & K 124 C9
Craigend Rens................113 N7
Craigendoran Ag & B 113 M4
Craigends Rens..............113 N8
Craighat Stirlg................113 N3
Craighlaw D & G 95 K6
Craighouse Ag & B 111 J8
Craigie P & K..................124 A4
Craigie S Ayrs 104 H3
Craigiefold Abers 141 M3
Craigley D & G................96 F6
Craig Llangiwg Neath 38 H10
Craiglockhart C Edin......115 M7
Craigmaud Abers 141 L5
Craigmillar C Edin..........115 N7
Craigneston D & G 105 M9
Craigneuk N Lans 114 D8
Craigneuk N Lans 114 D8
Craignure Ag & B 120 B7
Craigo Angus 132 H11
Craigrothie Fife 124 H10
Craig Penllyn V Glam 27 M7
Craigrothie Fife 124 H10
Craigruie Stirlg 122 C8
Craig's End Essex 46 C4
Craigton Angus 125 K5
Craigton C Aber 133 L4
Craigton of Airlie Angus ..124 G3
Craig-y-Duke Neath 38 H10
Craig-y-nos Powys 39 K8
Craik Border 107 M8
Crail Fife 125 M11
Crailing Border 107 R5
Crakehall N York 91 L9
Crakehill N York 91 Q12
Crakemarsh Staffs 65 K5
Crambe N York................86 D2
Crambeck N York 86 D2
Cramlington Nthumb 100 H4
Cramond C Edin 115 M6
Cramond Bridge C Edin ..115 M6
Crampmoor Hants 24 F9
Cranage Ches E 76 D10
Cranberry Staffs 64 F5
Cranborne Dorset 11 N3
Cranbourne Br for............32 D6
Cranbrook Devon..............8 H6
Cranbrook Kent 16 D4
Cranbrook Common Kent ..16 D3
Crane Moor Barns............77 N5
Crane's Corner Norfk 70 D9
Cranfield C Beds 44 D3
Cranford Devon 18 G8
Cranford Gt Lon 32 G7
Cranford St Andrew
    Nhants......................55 M5
Cranford St John Nhants ..55 M5
Cranham Gloucs 41 P9
Cranham Gt Lon 33 Q5
Crank St Hel 75 N4
Cranleigh Surrey 14 F3
Cranmer Green Suffk 58 F6
Cranmore IoW................12 F7
Cranmore Somset 22 E4
Cranoe Leics 55 J2
Cransford Suffk 59 M8
Cranshaws Border 116 F10
Cranstal IoM 102 f1
Cranswick E R Yk 87 J5
Crantock Cnwll 3 K2

Cranwell Lincs 67 P2
Cranwich Norfk 57 P2
Cranworth Norfk 70 E11
Craobh Haven Ag & B 120 E11
Crapstone Devon 4 H3
Crarae Ag & B 112 E2
Crask Inn Highld 149 L11
Crask of Aigas Highld 137 N7
Craster Nthumb 109 L6
Craswall Herefs 40 C4
Crateford Staffs 64 G10
Cratfield Suffk 59 L5
Crathes Abers 133 J5
Crathie Abers 131 N5
Crathie Highld 129 Q5
Crathorne N York 91 Q5
Craven Arms Shrops 51 N4
Crawcrook Gatesd..........100 E5
Crawford Lancs 75 N3
Crawford S Lans 106 C5
Crawfordjohn S Lans 106 A5
Crawick D & G 105 Q6
Crawley Hants 25 J8
Crawley Oxon 42 H9
Crawley W Susx..............15 K3
Crawley Down W Susx......15 L3
Crawleyside Dur 100 C10
Crawshawbooth Lancs 84 B10
Crawton Abers 133 L8
Craxe's Green Essex 46 G8
Cray N York 90 F11
Cray P & K 131 L11
Crayford Gt Lon 33 P7
Crayke N York 92 B11
Craymere Beck Norfk 70 F6
Crays Hill Essex 34 C4
Cray's Pond Oxon............31 N6
Craythorne Staffs 65 N7
Craze Lowman Devon 20 F10
Crazies Hill Wokham........31 N6
Creacombe Devon 20 C9
Creagan Ag & B 121 J4
Creag Ghoraidh W Isls ..152 c9
Creagorry W Isls 152 c9
Creaguaineach Lodge
    Highld 129 K10
Creamore Bank Shrops 63 N6
Creaton Nhants 54 H6
Creca D & G 97 N3
Credenhill Herefs 40 F3
Crediton Devon 8 L4
Creebank D & G..............95 L3
Creebridge D & G............95 M6
Creech Dorset 11 M8
Creech Heathfield
    Somset 21 L8
Creech St Michael
    Somset 21 L8
Creed Cnwll 3 M5
Creekmoor BCP 11 N6
Creekmouth Gt Lon 33 N6
Creeksea Essex 34 G4
Creeting St Mary Suffk 58 G9
Creeton Lincs 67 P8
Creetown D & G..............95 N6
Cregneash IoM 102 b7
Cregny Ba IoM 102 e5
Cregrina Powys 50 F10
Creich Fife 124 G8
Creigiau Cardif 27 P6
Cremyll Cnwll 4 G6
Cressage Shrops 63 Q11
Cressbrook Derbys 77 M9
Cresselly Pembks 37 L9
Cressex Bucks 32 C4
Cressing Essex 46 D7
Cresswell Nthumb 109 M11
Cresswell Pembks 37 L9
Cresswell Staffs 64 H4
Creswell Derbys 78 E9
Creswell Green Staffs 65 K10
Cretingham Suffk 59 J8
Cretshengan Ag & B 111 Q8
Crewe Ches E..................64 D1
Crewe-by-Farndon
    Ches W 63 M2
Crewe Green Ches E 64 D1
Crew Green Powys 63 K9
Crews Hill Gt Lon 33 L3
Crewton C Derb................66 B5
Crianlarich Stirlg 122 C6
Cribyn Cerdgn 49 J10
Criccieth Gwynd 60 H4
Crich Derbys 65 Q1
Crich Carr Derbys 65 Q1
Crichton Mdloth 115 Q9
Crick Mons 28 G4
Crick Nhants 54 F6
Crickadarn Powys............39 P3
Cricket St Thomas
    Somset 10 B3
Crickheath Shrops............63 J7
Crickhowell Powys 40 B8
Cricklade Wilts 30 C4
Cricklewood Gt Lon 33 J5
Cridling Stubbs N York 85 Q11
Crieff P & K 123 L8
Criggan Cnwll 3 P2
Criggion Powys 63 J9
Crigglestone Wakefd 85 L12
Crimble Rochdl 76 F1
Crimond Abers 141 P4
Crimplesham Norfk..........69 M11
Crimscote Warwks 42 H3
Crinaglack Highld 137 M8
Crinan Ag & B................112 A2
Crindledyke N Lans 114 E10
Cringleford Norfk 71 J11
Cringles C Brad 84 F5
Crinow Pembks 37 M7
Cripplesease Cnwll 2 E7
Cripplestyle Dorset..........23 N11
Cripp's Corner E Susx 16 D6
Croachy Highld 138 B10
Croanford Cnwll 6 E10
Crockenhill Kent 33 P9
Crocker End Oxon............31 N5
Crockerhill W Susx 14 C9
Crockernwell Devon 8 C6
Crocker's Ash Herefs 40 H8
Crockerton Wilts 22 H5
Crocketford D & G 96 G3
Crockey Hill N York 86 B6
Crockham Hill Kent 15 N1
Crockhurst Street Kent 16 A2
Crockleford Heath Essex ..47 J6
Crockleford Heath Essex ..47 J6
Crock Street Somset 21 M10
Croeserw Neath 39 J6
Croes-goch Pembks 36 F4
Croes-lan Cerdgn 48 B3
Croesor Gwynd 61 J3
Croesyceiliog Carmth 38 B8
Croesyceiliog Torfn 28 D3
Croes-y-mwyalch Torfn 28 D3
Croes-y-pant Mons 40 D11
Croft Leics 54 E11
Croft Lincs 81 K10
Crofton Warrtn 76 B5
Croftamie Stirlg 113 N3
Croft Mitchell Cnwll 2 G7
Crofton Cumb 98 D8
Crofton Wakefd 85 M11
Crofton Wilts 30 E9
Croft-on-Tees N York 91 M5
Croft's Bank Traffd 76 E4

Crofts of Dipple Moray ..139 P4
Crofts of Haddo Abers....141 K8
Crofts of Savoch Abers ..141 P4
Crofty Swans 26 D3
Crogen Gwynd 62 D5
Croggan Ag & B 120 D7
Croglin Cumb 98 H9
Croick Highld 145 L7
Cromarty Highld 138 E2
Crombie Fife 115 J4
Cromdale Highld 139 K10
Cromer Herts 45 K6
Cromer Norfk 71 J4
Cromford Derbys 77 P12
Cromhall Gloucs 29 L4
Cromhall Common
    S Glos 29 L4
Cromor W Isls 152 g4
Cromore W Isls 152 g4
Crompton Fold Oldham 76 H2
Cromwell Notts 79 K11
Cronberry E Ayrs 105 L5
Crondall Hants 25 N4
Cronkbourne IoM 102 e6
Cronk-y-Voddy IoM 102 d4
Cronton Knows 75 N6
Crook Cumb 89 M7
Crook Dur 100 F11
Crookdake Cumb 97 P9
Crooke Wigan 75 P2
Crooked End Gloucs 41 J8
Crookedholm E Ayrs 104 H2
Crooke N York 84 B6
Crooked Soley Wilts 31 J8
Crookes Sheff 77 Q6
Crookhall Dur 100 E8
Crookham Nthumb 108 E2
Crookham W Berk 31 M8
Crookham Village Hants ..25 N3
Crook Inn Border............106 E4
Crooklands Cumb 89 N10
Crook of Devon P & K 115 J2
Cropper Derbys 65 N5
Cropredy Oxon 43 K2
Cropston Leics 66 F10
Cropthorne Worcs 42 A3
Cropton N York................92 F9
Cropwell Bishop Notts......66 H4
Cropwell Butler Notts 66 H5
Cros W Isls 152 h1
Crosbost W Isls 152 g4
Crosby Cumb 97 N10
Crosby IoM 102 d5
Crosby N Linc 79 N1
Crosby Sefton 75 K4
Crosby Garret Cumb 90 B5
Crosby Ravensworth
    Cumb 89 Q4
Crosby Villa Cumb 97 N10
Croscombe Somset 22 D4
Crosland Edge Kirk 77 L1
Crosland Hill Kirk............84 H12
Cross Somset 21 N2
Crossaig Ag & B 112 B11
Crossapol Ag & B 118 C4
Cross Ash Mons 40 F8
Cross-at-Hand Kent..........16 D2
Crossbost W Isls 152 g4
Crosscanonby Cumb 97 L10
Cross Coombe Cnwll 2 H4
Crossdale Street Norfk 71 J5
Cross End Bed 55 Q9
Cross End Essex 46 F5
Crossens Sefton 83 J11
Cross Flatts C Brad..........84 G7
Crossford Fife 115 K4
Crossford S Lans 114 E12
Crossgate Cnwll 7 L7
Crossgate Lincs 68 E7
Crossgate Staffs 64 H5
Crossgatehall E Loth 115 Q7
Crossgates E Ayrs 113 M12
Crossgates Fife 115 L3
Cross Gates Leeds 85 M8
Crossgates N York 93 L10
Crossgates Powys 50 F7
Crossgill Lancs 83 M3
Cross Green Devon 7 M7
Cross Green Leeds 85 L9
Cross Green Staffs 64 G11
Cross Green Suffk 58 B10
Cross Green Suffk 58 C9
Cross Green Suffk 58 D9
Crosshands Carmth 38 N6
Cross Hands Carmth 38 D8
Crosshands E Ayrs 105 J3
Cross Hands Pembks 37 L7
Cross Hill Derbys 66 C2
Crosshill Fife 115 M2
Cross Hills N York 84 F6
Crosshouse E Ayrs 104 G2
Cross Houses Shrops 63 P11
Cross in Hand E Susx 15 Q6
Cross Inn Cerdgn 48 H4
Cross Inn Cerdgn 49 J8
Cross Inn Pembks 37 L7
Cross Keys Ag & B 113 L4
Crosskeys Caerph 28 B4
Cross Keys Wilts 29 P8
Crosskirk Highld 151 J3
Crosslands Cumb 89 K9
Cross Lane IoW 12 A2
Cross Lane Head Shrops ..52 D2
Cross Lanes Cnwll 3 J9
Cross Lanes N York 85 Q2
Cross Lanes Wrexhm 63 L3
Crosslanes Shrops............63 K8
Crosslee Rens 113 N6
Crossley Kirk 85 J11
Crossmichael D & G 96 E5
Cross Oak Powys 39 Q7
Cross o' th' hands Derbys ..65 P4
Cross of Jackston Abers ..141 J9
Crosspost W Susx 15 L3
Crossroads Abers 132 G5
Crossroads Abers 133 J5
Cross Roads C Brad..........84 F7
Cross Street Suffk............59 J5
Crosston Angus 125 K2
Cross Town Ches E..........76 D7
Crossway Mons 40 F7
Crossway Powys 50 E9
Crossway Street Worcs 52 F7
Crossways Dorset 11 J7
Crosswell Pembks 37 M3
Crosthwaite Cumb............89 M8
Croston Lancs 83 L11
Crostwick Norfk 71 K9
Crostwight Norfk..............71 L6
Crouch Kent 34 H5
Crouch End Gt Lon..........33 K5
Croucheston Wilts 23 N8
Crouch Hill Dorset 10 H2
Crough House Green
    Kent 15 N2
Croughton Nhants 43 M5
Crovie Abers 141 K4
Crow Hants....................12 A4
Crowan Cnwll 2 G7
Crowborough E Susx 15 P4

Crowborough Warren
    E Susx 15 P5
Crowcombe Somset 21 J6
Crowdecote Derbys 77 L10
Crowden Derbys 77 K4
Crowden Devon 7 P5
Crowdhill Hants 24 H9
Crowdleham Kent 33 Q10
Crow Edge Barns 77 M3
Crowell Oxon 31 Q2
Crow End Cambs..............56 F9
Crowfield Nhants 43 N3
Crowfield Suffk 58 H9
Crowfield Green Suffk......58 H9
Crowgate Street Norfk 71 K7
Crow Green Essex............33 Q3
Crowhill E Loth 116 G6
Crow Hill Herefs 41 K6
Crowhole Derbys 77 Q8
Crowhurst E Susx 16 D8
Crowhurst Surrey 15 M1
Crowhurst Lane End
    Surrey 15 M1
Crowland Lincs 68 E10
Crowland Suffk................58 F6
Crowlas Cnwll 2 D7
Crowle N Linc 79 K1
Crowle Worcs 52 G9
Crowle Green Worcs 52 G9
Crowmarsh Gifford Oxon ..31 N4
Crown Corner Suffk 59 K6
Crownhill C Plym..............4 G5
Crownhill Surrey 14 D3
Crownthorpe Norfk 70 G11
Crowntown Cnwll 2 G8
Crows-an-Wra Cnwll 2 C9
Crow's Green Essex 46 C6
Crowshill Norfk 70 D11
Crow's Nest Cnwll 4 C3
Crowsnest Shrops............63 L11
Crowthorne Wokham........32 B9
Crowton Ches W 75 P9
Croxby Lincs 80 D4
Croxdale Dur 100 H11
Croxden Staffs 65 K4
Croxley Green Herts 32 F3
Croxteth Lpool 75 L5
Croxton Cambs 56 E8
Croxton N Linc 80 B1
Croxton Norfk 58 C3
Croxton Staffs 64 E6
Croxtonbank Staffs 64 E6
Croxton Green Ches E 63 P2
Croxton Kerrial Leics 67 L6
Croy Highld 138 C6
Croy N Lans 114 D6
Croyde Devon 19 J5
Croyde Bay Devon............18 H5
Croydon Cambs 56 F10
Croydon Gt Lon 33 L9
Crubenmore Highld 130 C6
Cruckmeole Shrops 63 M10
Cruckton Shrops 63 M9
Cruden Bay Abers 141 Q8
Crudgington Wrekin 64 B8
Crudie Abers 141 J4
Crudwell Wilts 29 R4
Cruft Devon 7 P5
Crûg Powys 50 G6
Crugmeer Cnwll 6 C9
Crug-y-bar Carmth 38 H4
Crumlin Caerph 28 B3
Crumplehorn Cnwll 4 B6
Crumpsall Manch 76 F3
Crundale Kent..................17 J1
Crundale Pembks 37 J7
Crunwere Pembks 37 N8
Cruwys Morchard Devon ..20 D11
Crux Easton Hants 31 J4
Cruxton Dorset 10 F5
Cryers Hill Bucks 32 C3
Crymant Neath 39 J10
Crymych Pembks 37 N4
Crystal Palace Gt Lon 33 L7
Cuaig Highld..................135 N3
Cuan Ag & B 120 E10
Cubbington Warwks 53 Q7
Cubert Cnwll....................3 J3
Cubley Barns 77 N4
Cublington Bucks 44 B7
Cublington Herefs............40 E5
Cuckfield W Susx 15 K6
Cucklington Somset 22 G8
Cuckney Notts 78 G10
Cuckoo Bridge Lincs 68 E8
Cuckoo's Corner Hants 25 N5
Cuckoo's Nest Ches W 75 J11
Cuddesdon Oxon 43 M11
Cuddington Bucks 43 Q9
Cuddington Ches W 75 Q9
Cuddington Heath
    Ches W 63 M3
Cuddy Hill Lancs 83 L8
Cudham Gt Lon 33 N10
Cudliptown Devon 7 P9
Cudnell BCP 11 P5
Cudworth Barns 78 C2
Cudworth Somset 10 B2
Cuerdley Cross Warrtn 75 P6
Cufaude Hants 31 N11
Cuffley Herts 45 K11
Cuiltburn Stirlg 121 J2
Culbokie Highld 138 A4
Culbone Somset 20 B4
Culburnie Highld 137 N7
Culcabock Highld 138 C7
Culcharry Highld 138 E6
Culcheth Warrtn 76 C5
Culdrain Abers 140 E9
Culduie Highld................135 N8
Culford Suffk 58 B6
Culgaith Cumb 99 J12
Culham Oxon 43 L12
Culkein Highld 148 B10
Culkein Drumbeg Highld ..148 D10
Culkerton Gloucs 29 Q3
Cullen Moray 140 D2
Cullercoats N Tyne 101 J4
Cullerlie Abers 133 J4
Cullicudden Highld 138 B3
Cullingworth C Brad 84 G8
Cuillin Hills Highld 134 H11
Cullipool Ag & B 120 D10
Cullivoe Shet 147 j2
Culloden Highld 138 D6
Cullompton Devon 9 J3
Cullompton Services
    Devon 9 J3
Culm Davy Devon 20 H10
Culmington Shrops 51 N4
Culmstock Devon............20 H10
Culnacraig Highld 148 C4
Culnaightrie D & G 96 H8
Culnaknock Highld 135 J5
Culpho Suffk 59 J11
Culrain Highld 145 M4
Culross Fife 115 H4
Culroy S Ayrs 104 F7
Culsalmond Abers 140 G9
Culscadden D & G............95 N8
Culshabbin D & G 95 L7
Culswick Shet 147 h7
Cultercullen Abers 141 M11

Cults C Aber 133 L4
Culverstone Green Kent 34 B9
Culverthorpe Lincs 67 P4
Culworth Nhants 43 L2
Culzean Castle & Country Park S Ayrs 104 D8
Cumbernauld N Lans 114 D6
Cumbernauld Village N Lans 114 D6
Cumberworth Lincs 81 K9
Cumdivock Cumb 98 D8
Cuminestown Abers 141 K6
Cumledge Border 116 H10
Cummersdale Cumb 98 E7
Cummertrees D & G 97 N5
Cumming Moray 139 L2
Cumnock E Ayrs 105 K6
Cumnor Oxon 43 K11
Cumrew Cumb 98 G8
Cumrue D & G 97 L1
Cumwhinton Cumb 98 F7
Cumwhitton Cumb 98 F7
Cundall N York 91 P12
Cunninghamhead N Ayrs 104 G1
Cunningsburgh Shet 147 i8
Cupar Fife 124 G10
Cupar Muir Fife 124 G10
Curbar Derbys 77 N9
Curbridge Hants 13 J2
Curbridge Oxon 42 G10
Curdridge Hants 25 J10
Curdworth Warwks 53 M2
Curland Somset 21 L10
Curridge W Berk 31 K8
Currie C Edin 115 M8
Curry Mallet Somset 21 M9
Curry Rivel Somset 21 N8
Curteis Corner Kent 16 E3
Curtisden Green Kent 16 C3
Curtisknowle Devon 5 M6
Cury Cnwll 2 H10
Cushnie Abers 132 D2
Cushuish Somset 21 K7
Cusop Herefs 40 C3
Cusworth Donc 78 F3
Cutcloy D & G 95 N11
Cutcombe Somset 20 E5
Cutgate Rochdl 84 C12
Cuthill Highld 146 D7
Cutiau Gwynd 61 L8
Cutler's Green Essex 45 Q5
Cutmadoc Cnwll 3 Q2
Cutmere Cnwll 4 E4
Cutnall Green Worcs 52 G7
Cutsdean Gloucs 42 C6
Cutthorpe Derbys 77 Q9
Cuttivett Cnwll 4 E4
Cuxham Oxon 31 N3
Cuxton Medway 34 C9
Cuxwold Lincs 80 D3
Cwm Blae G 40 B10
Cwm Denbgs 74 E8
Cwmafan Neath 27 N2
Cwmaman Rhondd 27 N2
Cwmann Carmth 38 E2
Cwmavon Torfn 40 C10
Cwmbach Carmth 37 P5
Cwmbach Carmth 38 D11
Cwmbach Powys 40 A4
Cwmbâch Rhondd 39 N11
Cwmbach Llechrhyd Powys 50 E10
Cwmbelan Powys 50 C4
Cwmbran Torfn 28 C3
Cwmbrwyno Cerdgn 49 M4
Cwm Capel Carmth 38 C11
Cwmcarn Caerph 28 B3
Cwmcarvan Mons 40 G10
Cwm-celyn Blae G 40 B10
Cwm-Cewydd Gwynd 61 Q9
Cwm-cou Cerdgn 37 Q2
Cwm Crawnon Powys 39 Q7
Cwmdare Rhondd 39 N11
Cwmdu Carmth 38 F6
Cwmdu Powys 40 A7
Cwmdu Swans 26 F3
Cwmduad Carmth 38 B5
Cwm Dulais Swans 38 F11
Cwmdwr Carmth 38 H5
Cwmfelin Brdgnd 27 M4
Cwmfelin Myr Td 27 M7
Cwmfelin Boeth Carmth 37 N7
Cwmfelinfach Caerph 28 B4
Cwmfelin Mynach Carmth 37 P5
Cwmffrwd Carmth 38 B8
Cwmgiedd Powys 38 J9
Cwmgorse Carmth 38 Q9
Cwm Gwaun Pembks 37 K4
Cwmgwili Carmth 38 E9
Cwmgwrach Neath 38 K10
Cwmhiraeth Carmth 37 R3
Cwmifor Carmth 38 G6
Cwm Irfon Powys 49 Q10
Cwmisfael Carmth 38 D8
Cwm Llinau Powys 61 P10
Cwmllynfell Neath 38 H9
Cwmmawr Carmth 38 D9
Cwm Morgan Carmth 37 Q3
Cwmpengraig Carmth 37 R3
Cwmparc Rhondd 27 M3
Cwm Penmachno Conwy 61 N9
Cwmpennar Rhondd 27 N2
Cwmrhos Powys 40 B7
Cwmrhydyceirw Swans 26 G2
Cwmsychant Cerdgn 38 C2
Cwmtillery Blae G 40 B10
Cwm-twrch Isaf Powys 39 J9
Cwm-twrch Uchaf Powys 38 H9
Cwm-y-glo Carmth 38 E9
Cwm-y-glo Gwynd 73 J11
Cwmyoy Mons 40 D7
Cwmystwyth Cerdgn 49 N6
Cwrt Gwynd 61 M2
Cwrtnewydd Cerdgn 48 H11
Cwrt-y-gollen Powys 40 B8
Cyfarthfa Castle Museum Myr Td 39 P10
Cyffylliog Denbgs 74 E12
Cyfronydd Powys 62 G10
Cylibebyll Neath 38 H11
Cymau Flints 63 J1
Cymmer Neath 27 K3
Cymmer Rhondd 27 K3
Cyncoed Cardif 28 B6
Cynghordy Carmth 39 J4
Cynheidre Carmth 38 D10
Cynonville Neath 27 K3
Cynwyd Denbgs 62 E4
Cynwyl Elfed Carmth 38 B6

D

Daccombe Devon 5 Q3
Dacre Cumb 89 M1
Dacre N York 85 J3
Dacre Banks N York 85 J3
Daddry Shield Dur 90 P10
Dadford Bucks 43 N4
Dadlington Leics 54 C1
Daffy Green Norfk 70 E10
Dagenham Gt Lon 33 P5
Daglingworth Gloucs 42 H10
Dagnall Bucks 44 E8
Dagworth Suffk 58 F8

Dail bho Dheas W Isls 152 g1
Dailly S Ayrs 104 E9
Dainton Devon 5 J3
Dairsie Fife 124 H9
Daisy Hill Bolton 76 C3
Daisy Hill Leeds 85 K9
Dalabrog W Isls 152 b11
Dalavich Ag & B 120 H10
Dalballoch Highld 130 C6
Dalbeattie D & G 96 G6
Dalbury Derbys 65 N5
Dalby IoM 102 b6
Dalby Lincs 80 H9
Dalby N York 86 B1
Dalcapon P & K 123 M2
Dalchalm Highld 146 G4
Dalchreichart Highld 129 J2
Dalchruin P & K 123 J9
Dalcrue P & K 123 Q7
Dalderby Lincs 80 E10
Daldownie Ag & B 129 N8
Dale Derbys 66 C3
Dale Pembks 36 F9
Dale Abbey Derbys 66 C4
Dale Bottom Cumb 89 J2
Dale End Derbys 77 N11
Dale End N York 84 E6
Dale Hill E Susx 16 C5
Dalehouse N York 92 F3
Dalelia Highld 127 N10
Dalgarven N Ayrs 104 F1
Dalgety Bay Fife 115 L4
Dalgig E Ayrs 105 K7
Dalginross P & K 123 K8
Dalguise P & K 123 P3
Dalhalvaig Highld 150 F4
Dalham Suffk 57 N8
Dalhenzean P & K 123 P2
Daligan Ag & B 113 M7
Dalinlongart Ag & B 113 K12
Dalkeith Mdloth 115 Q8
Dallas Moray 139 L5
Dallinghoo Suffk 59 K9
Dallington E Susx 16 B7
Dallington Nhants 55 J8
Dallow N York 91 K12
Dalmally Ag & B 121 M7
Dalmary Stirlg 113 P2
Dalmellington E Ayrs 105 J9
Dalmeny C Edin 115 L6
Dalmore Highld 138 C3
Dalmuir W Duns 113 P7
Dalnabreck Highld 127 M8
Dalnacardoch P & K 130 D10
Dalnahaitnach Highld 138 F11
Dalnaspidal P & K 130 B9
Dalnawillan Lodge Highld 151 L8
Dalness Highld 121 M3
Dalqueich P & K 124 B12
Dalquhairn S Ayrs 104 F10
Dalreavoch Highld 146 D3
Dalry N Ayrs 104 F1
Dalrymple E Ayrs 104 F7
Dalserf S Lans 114 E11
Dalsmeran Ag & B 102 H7
Dalston Cumb 98 D8
Dalston Gt Lon 33 L5
Dalswinton D & G 97 K3
Dalton Cumb 89 N11
Dalton D & G 97 M3
Dalton Lancs 75 N2
Dalton N York 85 K4
Dalton N York 91 Q11
Dalton Nthumb 100 E4
Dalton Rothm 78 D5
Dalton-in-Furness Cumb 88 H12
Dalton-le-Dale Dur 101 K8
Dalton Magna Rothm 78 D5
Dalton-on-Tees N York 91 M5
Dalton Parva Rothm 78 D5
Dalton Piercy Hartpl 101 L12
Dalveich Stirlg 122 G8
Dalwhinnie Highld 130 B7
Dalwood Devon 9 N5
Damask Green Herts 45 J7
Damerham Hants 23 N10
Damgate Norfk 71 M10
Damnaglaur D & G 94 G11
Danaway Kent 34 F9
Danbury Essex 46 D10
Danby N York 92 E5
Danby Bottom N York 92 E6
Danby Wiske N York 91 N6
Dandaleith Moray 139 P6
Danderhall Mdloth 115 P7
Danebridge Ches E 76 H10
Dane End Herts 45 K7
Danegate E Susx 15 Q4
Danehill E Susx 15 M5
Danemoor Green Norfk 70 F11
Danesford Shrops 52 D2
Danesmoor Derbys 78 C9
Dane Street Kent 35 J11
Daniel's Water Kent 16 G3
Danshillock Abers 141 J4
Danskine E Loth 116 D8
Dantrope E R Yk 87 N8
Danzey Green Warwks 53 L7
Dapple Heath Staffs 65 K6
Darby Green Hants 32 B10
Darcy Lever Bolton 76 D2
Dardy Powys 40 B8
Darenth Kent 33 Q8
Daresbury Halton 75 P7
Darfield Barns 78 C4
Darfoulds Notts 78 F8
Dargate Kent 35 K10
Dargavel Rens 113 N7
Darite Cnwll 4 C3
Darland Medway 34 C9
Darland Wrexhm 75 L12
Darlaston Wsall 52 H1
Darlaston Green Wsall 52 H1
Darley Abbey C Derb 66 B4
Darley Dale Derbys 77 P11
Darley Bridge Derbys 77 P11
Darley Green Solhll 53 M6
Darleyhall Herts 44 F7
Darley Head N York 85 J3
Darlingscott Warwks 42 F3
Darlington Darltn 91 M4
Darliston Shrops 63 P5
Darnford Staffs 65 L11
Darnick Border 107 N3
Darowen Powys 61 P11
Darra Abers 140 H6
Darracott Devon 18 G9
Darracott Devon 19 J5
Darras Hall Nthumb 100 F4
Darrington Wakefd 85 P11
Darsham Suffk 59 N6
Darshill Somset 22 D5
Dartford Kent 33 Q7
Dartford Crossing Kent 33 Q7
Dartington Devon 5 M4
Dartmeet Devon 8 C10
Dartmoor National Park Devon 8 D9
Dartmouth Devon 5 N6
Darton Barns 77 P4
Darvel E Ayrs 105 K2
Darwell Hole E Susx 16 B7
Darwen Bl w D 83 Q10
Datchet W & M 32 E6
Datchworth Herts 45 K8
Datchworth Green Herts 45 K8

Daubhill Bolton 76 C2
Daugh of Kinnermony Moray 139 N7
Dauntsey Wilts 30 A6
Dava Highld 139 J8
Davenham Ches W 76 C9
Davenport Stockp 76 F8
Davenport Green Ches E 76 F8
Davenport Green Traffd 76 E6
Daventry Nhants 54 F8
Davidson's Mains C Edin 115 M6
Davidstow Cnwll 6 H7
David Street Kent 34 B9
Davington D & G 106 H9
Davington Hill Kent 34 H10
Daviot Abers 141 J10
Daviot Highld 138 D8
Daviot House Highld 138 D7
Davis's Town E Susx 15 N7
Davoch of Grange Moray 140 D5
Davyhulme Traffd 76 D4
Daw End Wsall 53 J12
Dawesgreen Surrey 15 J1
Dawley Wrekin 64 C10
Dawlish Devon 8 H9
Dawlish Warren Devon 9 J9
Dawn Conwy 73 Q9
Daws Green Somset 21 K9
Daws Heath Essex 34 E5
Daw's House Cnwll 7 L8
Dawsmere Lincs 68 H6
Daybrook Notts 66 F3
Day Green Ches E 76 E12
Dayhills Staffs 64 H5
Dayhouse Bank Worcs 52 H6
Daylesford Gloucs 42 F6
Ddol Cnwll 74 D9
Ddol-Cownwy Powys 62 D8
Deal Kent 35 Q12
Dean Cumb 88 E2
Dean Cumb 5 M4
Dean Devon 19 M4
Dean Devon 19 N4
Dean Dorset 23 L10
Dean Hants 24 G7
Dean Hants 25 J9
Dean Lancs 84 C10
Dean Oxon 42 H7
Dean Somset 22 D5
Dean Bottom Kent 33 Q8
Deanburnhaugh Border 107 K7
Deancombe Devon 5 L5
Dean Court Oxon 43 K10
Deane Bolton 76 C2
Deane Hants 25 J3
Dean End Devon 23 L10
Dean Head Barns 77 P4
Deanhead Kirk 84 F12
Deanland Dorset 23 M9
Deanlane End W Susx 25 N11
Dean Prior Devon 5 M4
Deanraw Nthumb 99 M6
Dean Row Ches E 76 G7
Deans W Loth 115 J7
Deanscales Cumb 88 E1
Deanshanger Nhants 43 Q4
Deanshaugh Moray 139 Q6
Deanston Stirlg 114 C1
Dean Street Kent 34 D11
Dearham Cumb 97 L11
Dearnley Rochdl 84 D12
Debach Suffk 59 K10
Debden Essex 33 N3
Debden Essex 45 Q5
Debden Green Essex 45 Q5
Debenham Suffk 58 H8
Deblin's Green Worcs 52 E11
Dechmont W Loth 115 J7
Dechmont Road W Loth 115 J7
Deddington Oxon 43 K5
Dedham Essex 47 J5
Dedham Heath Essex 47 J5
Dedworth W & M 32 D7
Deene Nhants 55 N2
Deenethorpe Nhants 55 N2
Deepcar Sheff 77 P4
Deepcut Surrey 32 C11
Deepdale Cumb 90 B9
Deepdale N York 90 E10
Deeping Gate C Pete 68 C10
Deeping St James Lincs 68 C10
Deeping St Nicholas Lincs 68 D9
Deerhurst Gloucs 41 P6
Deerhurst Walton Gloucs 41 P6
Deerton Street Kent 34 H9
Defford Worcs 41 Q3
Defynnog Powys 39 L6
Deganwy Conwy 73 N8
Degnish Ag & B 120 G8
Deighton C York 86 B6
Deighton N York 91 P6
Deiniolen Gwynd 73 K11
Delabole Cnwll 6 F6
Delamere Ches W 75 P10
Delamere Park Ches W 75 Q9
Delfrigs Abers 141 M11
Delley Devon 19 L8
Delliefure Highld 139 K9
Dell Quay W Susx 13 P4
Delly End Oxon 42 H9
Delnabo Moray 139 L12
Delny Highld 146 D10
Delph Oldham 77 J2
Delves Dur 100 E8
Delvin End Essex 46 E6
Dembleby Lincs 67 P5
Demelza Cnwll 3 N3
Denaby Donc 78 D4
Denaby Main Donc 78 E4
Denbies Surrey 32 G12
Denbigh Denbgs 74 E10
Denbrae Fife 124 H9
Denbury Devon 5 M4
Denby Derbys 66 B3
Denby Bottles Derbys 66 C3
Denby Dale Kirk 77 N4
Denchworth Oxon 30 H4
Dendron Cumb 82 G1
Denel End C Beds 44 E4
Denfield P & K 123 N9
Denford Nhants 55 N5
Dengie Essex 46 H11
Denham Bucks 32 F5
Denham Suffk 57 P8
Denham Suffk 58 H6
Denham End Suffk 57 P8
Denham Green Bucks 32 E5
Denham Green Suffk 59 J6
Denhead Abers 141 N6
Denhead of Gray C Dund 124 G6
Denholm Border 107 P6
Denholme C Brad 84 G8
Denholme Clough C Brad 84 G8
Denio Gwynd 60 F5
Denmead Hants 25 L11
Denmore C Aber 133 M4
Denne Park W Susx 14 F5
Dennington Suffk 59 K7
Denny Falk 114 E6
Dennyloanhead Falk 114 E5
Denshaw Oldham 76 H2
Denside of Durris Abers 133 M5
Densole Kent 17 M2
Denston Suffk 57 P10

Denstone Staffs 65 L4
Denstroude Kent 35 L9
Dent Cumb 90 B9
Denton Cambs 56 C3
Denton Darltn 91 L3
Denton E Susx 15 N10
Denton Kent 17 M1
Denton Kent 34 A6
Denton Lincs 67 N5
Denton N York 84 H5
Denton Nhants 55 L9
Denton Norfk 59 K3
Denton Oxon 43 M10
Denton Tamesd 76 G5
Denver Norfk 69 L11
Denwick Nthumb 109 K7
Deopham Norfk 70 F12
Deopham Green Norfk 70 F12
Depden Suffk 57 P9
Depden Green Suffk 57 P9
Deptford Gt Lon 33 L7
Deptford Wilts 23 M7
Derby C Derb 66 B5
Derby Devon 19 L6
Derbyhaven IoM 102 c7
Derculich P & K 123 M2
Dereham Norfk 70 E9
Deri Caerph 27 Q2
Derril Devon 7 K4
Derringstone Kent 35 M12
Derrington Staffs 64 G7
Derriton Devon 7 L4
Derry Hill Wilts 29 Q8
Derrythorpe N Linc 79 K2
Dersingham Norfk 69 N6
Dervaig Ag & B 119 M2
Derwen Denbgs 62 E2
Derwenlas Powys 61 M12
Derwent Valley Mills Derbys 65 P1
Derwent Water Cumb 88 H3
Derwydd Carmth 38 F9
Desborough Nhants 55 K4
Desford Leics 66 D11
Detchant Nthumb 108 H2
Detling Kent 34 D10
Deuxhill Shrops 52 C3
Devauden Mons 28 G3
Devil's Bridge Cerdgn 49 M5
Devitts Green Warwks 53 P3
Devizes Wilts 30 B10
Devonport C Plym 4 E5
Devonside Clacks 114 G2
Devoran Cnwll 3 K6
Devoran & Perran Cnwll 3 K7
Dewarton Mdloth 115 Q8
Dewlish Dorset 11 J5
Dewsbury Kirk 85 K11
Dewsbury Moor Kirk 85 K10
Deytheur Powys 62 H8
Dial N Som 28 H9
Dial Green W Susx 14 C5
Dial Post W Susx 14 H7
Dibberford Dorset 10 C4
Dibden Hants 12 G3
Dibden Purlieu Hants 12 G3
Dickens Heath Solhll 53 L5
Dickleburgh Norfk 58 H4
Didbrook Gloucs 42 B5
Didcot Oxon 31 L4
Diddington Cambs 56 D7
Diddlebury Shrops 51 N3
Didley Herefs 40 F5
Didling W Susx 25 N9
Didmarton Gloucs 29 N5
Didsbury Manch 76 F5
Didworthy Devon 5 L4
Digby Lincs 67 Q1
Digg Highld 134 H2
Diggle Oldham 77 J2
Digmoor Lancs 75 N3
Digswell Herts 45 J8
Digswell Water Herts 45 J8
Dihewyd Cerdgn 48 H9
Dilham Norfk 71 L7
Dilhorne Staffs 64 H3
Dillarburn S Lans 114 E11
Dillington Cambs 56 C7
Dilston Nthumb 100 C5
Dilton Wilts 23 J4
Dilton Marsh Wilts 23 J3
Dilwyn Herefs 51 L10
Dimple Bolton 83 Q12
Dimple Derbys 77 P11
Dinas Cnwll 3 M7
Dinas Cnwll 6 C10
Dinas Gwynd 60 D5
Dinas Gwynd 72 H6
Dinas Cross Pembks 37 J4
Dinas Dinlle Gwynd 72 G12
Dinas-Mawddwy Gwynd 61 Q9
Dinas Powys V Glam 27 R8
Dinder Somset 22 C5
Dinedor Herefs 40 H4
Dingestow Mons 40 F9
Dingle Lpool 75 L6
Dingleden Kent 16 E5
Dingley Nhants 55 K3
Dingwall Highld 137 P4
Dinham Mons 28 F4
Dinnet Abers 132 C5
Dinnington N u Ty 100 H4
Dinnington Rothm 78 E6
Dinnington Somset 21 N10
Dinorwig Gwynd 73 K11
Dinorwic Slate Landscape Gwynd 73 K11
Dinton Bucks 43 Q9
Dinton Wilts 23 M7
Dinwoodie D & G 106 E11
Dinworthy Devon 18 F10
Dipford Devon 21 K9
Dipley Hants 31 Q11
Dippen Ag & B 103 L2
Dippenhall Surrey 25 N4
Dippermill Devon 7 N8
Dippertown Devon 7 N8
Dippin Ayrs 103 Q5
Dipple Moray 139 Q4
Dipple S Ayrs 104 D9
Diptford Devon 5 M5
Dipton Dur 100 F7
Dirctonmill Nthumb 100 P4
Dirleton E Loth 116 C4
Dirt Pot Nthumb 99 N9
Discoed Powys 51 J8
Diseworth Leics 66 C7
Disforth N York 91 P12
Dishig Ches E 76 H7
Diss Norfk 58 H5
Disserth Powys 50 E9
Distington Cumb 88 D2
Ditcham Hants 25 N7
Ditcheat Somset 22 D6
Ditchingham Norfk 59 M2
Ditchling E Susx 15 L8
Ditherington Shrops 51 N1
Ditteridge Wilts 29 N8
Dittisham Devon 5 N6
Ditton Halton 75 M5
Ditton Kent 34 C10
Ditton Green Cambs 57 M9
Ditton Priors Shrops 51 Q3
Dixton Gloucs 41 Q5
Dixton Mons 40 G9
Dizzard Cnwll 6 G4
Dobcross Oldham 77 J2

Dobwalls Cnwll 4 C4
Doccombe Devon 8 E7
Dochgarroch Highld 138 B7
Dockenfield Surrey 25 N5
Docker Lancs 89 P11
Docking Norfk 69 P5
Docklow Herefs 51 P9
Dockray Cumb 89 L2
Dockray Cumb 98 D8
Dodbrooke Devon 5 M8
Doddinghurst Essex 33 Q2
Doddington Cambs 56 H2
Doddington Kent 34 G11
Doddington Lincs 79 M9
Doddington Nthumb 108 G2
Doddington Shrops 52 B5
Doddiscombsleigh Devon 8 F7
Dodd's Green Ches E 63 Q3
Doddshill Norfk 69 M6
Doddy Cross Cnwll 4 D4
Dodford Nhants 54 G8
Dodford Worcs 52 H6
Dodington S Glos 29 M6
Dodington Somset 21 J5
Dodleston Ches W 75 K11
Dodscott Devon 19 K9
Dodworth Barns 77 P4
Dodworth Bottom Barns 77 P4
Dodworth Green Barns 77 P4
Doe Bank Birm 53 L1
Doe Lea Derbys 78 D10
Dogdyke Lincs 68 D1
Dogley Lane Kirk 77 N3
Dogmersfield Hants 25 N3
Dogridge Wilts 30 C5
Dogsthorpe C Pete 68 D12
Dog Village Devon 9 N5
Dolanog Powys 62 E9
Dolau Powys 50 F8
Dolaucothi Carmth 38 G3
Dolbenmaen Gwynd 60 H4
Doley Staffs 64 D6
Dolfach Powys 50 F3
Dolfor Powys 50 F3
Dol-ffanog Gwynd 61 M9
Dolgarrog Conwy 73 N10
Dolgellau Gwynd 61 N8
Dolgoch Gwynd 61 L11
Dol-gran Carmth 38 C5
Doll Highld 146 F4
Dollar Clacks 114 H2
Dollarfield Clacks 114 H2
Dolley Green Powys 51 J7
Dollwen Cerdgn 49 M4
Dolphin Flints 74 H9
Dolphinholme Lancs 83 M4
Dolphinton S Lans 115 K12
Dolton Devon 19 L11
Dolwen Conwy 73 Q9
Dolwyddelan Conwy 61 M2
Dolybont Cerdgn 49 K3
Dolyhir Powys 50 H9
Domgay Powys 63 J8
Donald's Lodge Nthumb 108 D1
Doncaster Donc 78 F3
Doncaster Carr Donc 78 F3
Doncaster North Services Donc 78 H1
Doncaster Sheffield Airport Donc 78 G4
Donhead St Andrew Wilts 23 K8
Donhead St Mary Wilts 23 K8
Donibristle Fife 115 L3
Doniford Somset 20 H5
Donington Lincs 68 D4
Donington on Bain Lincs 80 E7
Donington Park Services Leics 66 D7
Donington Southing Lincs 68 C8
Donisthorpe Leics 65 P9
Donkey Street Kent 17 K4
Donkey Town Surrey 32 D10
Donnington Gloucs 42 E6
Donnington Herefs 41 L5
Donnington Shrops 51 N2
Donnington W Berk 31 K8
Donnington W Susx 13 N4
Donnington Wood Wrekin 64 D9
Donyatt Somset 21 L10
Doomsday Green W Susx 14 H5
Doonfoot S Ayrs 104 F6
Dora's Green Hants 25 P4
Dorback Lodge Highld 131 K5
Dorchester Dorset 10 H6
Dorchester-on-Thames Oxon 31 M3
Dordon Warwks 53 P2
Dore Sheff 77 P7
Dores Highld 137 Q9
Dorking Surrey 32 H12
Dorking Tye Suffk 46 G4
Dormansland Surrey 15 M2
Dormans Park Surrey 15 M3
Dormington Herefs 41 J3
Dormston Worcs 53 J9
Dorn Gloucs 42 E5
Dorney Bucks 32 D6
Dorney Reach Bucks 32 D6
Dornie Highld 136 B10
Dornoch Highld 146 E7
Dornock D & G 97 P5
Dorrery Highld 151 K6
Dorridge Solhll 53 M6
Dorrington Lincs 67 Q1
Dorrington Shrops 63 N11
Dorrington Shrops 64 D3
Dorsington Warwks 42 D3
Dorstone Herefs 40 D3
Dorton Bucks 43 N9
Dosthill Staffs 65 N12
Dottery Dorset 10 C6
Doughton Gloucs 29 Q4
Douglas IoM 102 e6
Douglas S Lans 105 Q4
Douglas and Angus C Dund 124 H6
Douglas Pier Ag & B 113 L5
Douglastown Angus 125 K3
Douglas Water S Lans 105 R3
Douglas West S Lans 105 R3
Doulting Somset 22 E5
Dounby Ork 147 b4
Doune Highld 145 L3
Doune Stirlg 114 D1
Dounepark S Ayrs 104 C10
Dounie Highld 145 N4
Dousland Devon 4 H4
Dovaston Shrops 63 K8
Dove Dale Derbys 65 L2
Dove Green Notts 66 D1
Dove Holes Derbys 77 K8
Dovenby Cumb 97 L11
Dover Kent 17 P2
Dover Wigan 75 P3
Dovercourt Essex 47 N5
Doverdale Worcs 52 G7
Doveridge Derbys 65 L5
Doversgreen Surrey 15 J1

Dowally P & K 123 P3
Dowbridge Lancs 83 K9
Dowdeswell Gloucs 42 B7
Dowlais Myr Td 39 P10
Dowland Devon 7 Q3
Dowlish Ford Somset 21 M10
Dowlish Wake Somset 21 N10
Downe Gt Lon 33 N10
Downend Gloucs 29 N1
Downend IoW 13 J7
Downend S Glos 29 K7
Downend W Berk 31 K7
Downfield C Dund 124 H6
Downgate Cnwll 7 K10
Downgate Cnwll 7 L8
Downham Essex 34 C3
Downham Gt Lon 33 M8
Downham Lancs 84 B6
Downham Market Norfk 69 L11
Down Hatherley Gloucs 41 P7
Downhead Somset 22 D8
Downhead Somset 22 E4
Downhill Cnwll 6 B11
Down St Mary Devon 8 E3
Downside Somset 22 E3
Downside Surrey 32 G10
Down Thomas Devon 4 H7
Downton Hants 12 D6
Downton Wilts 24 C9
Dowsby Lincs 68 C6
Dowsdale Lincs 68 F10
Doxey Staffs 64 G7
Doxford Nthumb 109 K5
Draethen Caerph 28 B5
Draffan S Lans 114 E12
Dragonby N Linc 79 M1
Dragons Green W Susx 14 G6
Drakeholes Notts 78 H5
Drakelow Worcs 52 F4
Drakemyre N Ayrs 113 K11
Drakes Broughton Worcs 52 H11
Drakewalls Cnwll 7 N10
Draughton N York 84 F5
Draughton Nhants 55 K5
Drax N York 86 C10
Drax Hales N York 86 C10
Draycote Warwks 54 D6
Draycot Foliat Swindn 30 D7
Draycott Derbys 66 D5
Draycott Gloucs 42 E4
Draycott Shrops 52 E2
Draycott Somset 21 Q4
Draycott Worcs 52 G9
Draycott Worcs 52 F11
Draycott in the Clay Staffs 65 M6
Draycott in the Moors Staffs 64 H4
Drayford Devon 19 Q10
Drayton C Port 13 L4
Drayton Leics 55 L2
Drayton Lincs 68 E4
Drayton Norfk 71 J9
Drayton Oxon 31 K3
Drayton Oxon 43 J3
Drayton Somset 21 N8
Drayton Worcs 52 H6
Drayton Worcs 52 G5
Drayton Bassett Staffs 65 M12
Drayton Beauchamp Bucks 44 C9
Drayton Manor Park Staffs 65 M12
Drayton Parslow Bucks 44 B6
Drayton St Leonard Oxon 31 M3
Drebley N York 84 F3
Dreemskerry IoM 102 f4
Dreen Hill Pembks 36 H7
Drefach Carmth 38 A4
Drefach Carmth 38 D9
Drefach Cerdgn 38 D3
Drefelin Carmth 38 A4
Dreghorn N Ayrs 104 F2
Drellingore Kent 17 M3
Drem E Loth 116 C5
Dresden C Stke 64 G4
Drewsteignton Devon 8 D6
Driby Lincs 80 G9
Driffield E R Yk 87 J4
Driffield Gloucs 30 C2
Driffield Cross Roads Gloucs 30 C3
Drift Cnwll 2 C8
Drigg Cumb 88 D7
Drighlington Leeds 85 K9
Drimnin Highld 119 P2
Drimpton Dorset 10 C4
Drimsallie Highld 128 D8
Dringhouses C York 86 B5
Drinkstone Suffk 58 D8
Drinkstone Green Suffk 58 D8
Drive End Dorset 10 F3
Driver's End Herts 45 J7
Droitwich Spa Worcs 52 G8
Droman Highld 148 C5
Dron P & K 124 C9
Dronfield Derbys 78 B8
Dronfield Woodhouse Derbys 77 Q8
Drongan E Ayrs 104 H6
Dronley Angus 124 G6
Droop Dorset 11 J3
Dropping Well Rothm 78 C5
Droxford Hants 25 K9
Droylsden Tamesd 76 G4
Druid Denbgs 62 D3
Druidston Pembks 36 G7
Druimarbin Highld 128 F10
Druimavuic Ag & B 121 J4
Druimdrishaig Ag & B 111 Q9
Druimindarroch Highld 127 M7
Drum Ag & B 112 D6
Drum P & K 115 J1
Drumalbin S Lans 106 B2
Drumbeg Highld 148 D10
Drumblade Abers 140 F8
Drumbreddon D & G 94 F9
Drumbuie Highld 135 Q9
Drumburgh Cumb 98 B6
Drumburn D & G 97 K6
Drumchapel C Glas 113 Q7
Drumchastle P & K 122 H1
Drumclog S Lans 105 M2
Drumeldrie Fife 125 J12
Drumelzier Border 106 F2
Drumfearn Highld 127 K4
Drumfrennie Abers 132 H5
Drumgley Angus 124 G3
Drumguish Highld 130 D7
Drumin Moray 139 L10
Drumjohn D & G 105 J10
Drumlamford S Ayrs 95 K3
Drumlasie Abers 132 G3
Drumleaning Cumb 98 B8

Drumlemble Ag & B 103 J6
Drumlithie Abers 133 J8
Drummoddie D & G 95 M9
Drummore D & G 94 G11
Drummuir Moray 140 B7
Drumnadrochit Highld 137 N10
Drumnagorrach Moray 140 E5
Drumoak Abers 133 J5
Drumpark D & G 96 H12
Drumrunie Highld 144 F4
Drumshang S Ayrs 104 E7
Drumuie Highld 134 H6
Drumuillie Highld 138 H5
Drumvaich Stirlg 122 H12
Drunzie P & K 124 C11
Druridge Nthumb 109 M10
Drury Flints 75 J10
Drws-y-coed Gwynd 61 J1
Drybeck Cumb 89 Q4
Drybridge Moray 140 C3
Drybridge N Ayrs 104 G2
Drybrook Gloucs 41 K8
Dryburgh Border 107 P3
Dry Doddington Lincs 67 L3
Dry Drayton Cambs 56 G8
Dryhill Kent 33 P11
Drymen Stirlg 113 P3
Drymuir Abers 141 L6
Drynoch Highld 134 G9
Dryslwyn Carmth 38 E7
Dry Street Essex 34 C5
Dryton Shrops 63 P11
Dubford Abers 141 J3
Dublin Suffk 58 H7
Duck End Bed 56 B8
Duck End Cambs 56 F7
Duck End Essex 46 B6
Duck End Essex 46 B6
Duckend Green Essex 46 C7
Duckington Ches W 63 N2
Ducklington Oxon 42 H10
Duck's Cross Bed 56 B9
Duddenhoe End Essex 45 M4
Duddingston C Edin 115 P7
Duddington Nhants 67 M12
Duddlestone Somset 21 K9
Duddleswell E Susx 15 N5
Duddlewick Shrops 52 C4
Duddo Nthumb 108 F1
Duddon Ches W 75 N11
Duddon Bridge Cumb 88 G9
Duddon Common Ches W 75 N10
Dudleston Shrops 63 K4
Dudleston Heath Shrops 63 L5
Dudley Dudley 52 H3
Dudley N Tyne 100 H4
Dudley Hill C Brad 85 J9
Dudley Port Sandw 52 H2
Dudnill Shrops 51 Q6
Dudsbury Dorset 11 P5
Dudswell Herts 44 D9
Duffield Derbys 65 Q3
Duffryn Neath 27 L3
Dufftown Moray 139 P8
Duffus Moray 139 M2
Dufton Cumb 90 A2
Duggleby N York 86 G2
Duirinish Highld 135 P9
Duisdalemore Highld 127 K4
Duisky Highld 128 F9
Dukestown Blae G 39 Q9
Dukinfield Tamesd 76 H4
Dulas IoA 72 H6
Dulcote Somset 22 D4
Dulford Devon 9 K3
Dull P & K 123 K4
Dullatur N Lans 114 C6
Dullingham Cambs 57 M9
Dullingham Ley Cambs 57 M9
Dulnain Bridge Highld 139 J11
Duloe Bed 56 C8
Duloe Cnwll 4 C5
Dulsie Bridge Highld 138 G7
Dulverton Somset 20 E8
Dulwich Gt Lon 33 L7
Dumbarton W Duns 113 M6
Dumbleton Gloucs 42 B4
Dumfries D & G 97 K3
Dumgoyne Stirlg 113 Q5
Dummer Hants 25 K4
Dun Angus 125 L2
Dunalastair P & K 123 J1
Dunan Ag & B 112 H7
Dunan Highld 135 K10
Dunan P & K 122 D1
Dunball Somset 21 M5
Dunbar E Loth 116 F5
Dunbeath Highld 151 L10
Dunbeg Ag & B 120 G6
Dunblane Stirlg 114 E1
Dunbog Fife 124 F9
Dunbridge Hants 24 E8
Duncanston Highld 137 P5
Duncanstone Abers 140 F10
Dunchideock Devon 8 G7
Dunchurch Warwks 54 D6
Duncote Nhants 54 H10
Duncow D & G 97 K2
Duncrievie P & K 124 C11
Duncton W Susx 14 D7
Dundee C Dund 124 H6
Dundee Airport C Dund 124 G7
Dundon Somset 21 P7
Dundonald S Ayrs 104 G3
Dundonnell Highld 144 D8
Dundraw Cumb 97 P8
Dundreggan Highld 129 K1
Dundrennan D & G 96 E8
Dundry N Som 28 H9
Dunecht Abers 133 J3
Dunfermline Fife 115 K4
Dunfield Gloucs 30 D3
Dunford Bridge Barns 77 M3
Dungate Kent 34 G10
Dungavel S Lans 105 M2
Dunge Wilts 23 J2
Dungeness Kent 17 K7
Dungworth Sheff 77 P6
Dunham Massey Traffd 76 D6
Dunham-on-the-Hill Ches W 75 M9
Dunham-on-Trent Notts 79 K9
Dunhampton Worcs 52 G7
Dunham Town Traffd 76 D6
Dunham Woodhouses Traffd 76 D6
Dunino Fife 125 K10
Dunipace Falk 114 F5
Dunkeld P & K 123 P4
Dunkeswell Devon 9 M3
Dunkeswick N York 85 L5
Dunkirk Ches W 75 L10
Dunkirk Kent 35 J10
Dunkirk S Glos 29 M5
Dunk's Green Kent 33 R11
Dunlappie Angus 132 F10
Dunley Hants 31 J10
Dunley Worcs 52 E7
Dunlop E Ayrs 113 M11

Dunmaglass Highld 137 Q11
Dunmere Cnwll 6 F11
Dunmore Falk 114 G3
Dunnet Highld 151 M2
Dunnichen Angus 125 K3
Dunning P & K 123 P10
Dunnington C York 86 C5
Dunnington E R Yk 87 M5
Dunnockshaw Lancs 53 N10
Dunnockshaw Lancs 84 B9
Dunn Street Kent 34 D10
Dunoon Ag & B 112 H6
Dunphail Moray 139 J6
Dunragit D & G 94 H7
Duns Border 116 H10
Dunsa Derbys 26 F4
Dunsby Lincs 68 B7
Dunscar Bolton 76 D1
Dunscore D & G 96 H1
Dunscroft Donc 78 G2
Dunsdale R & Cl 92 C3
Dunsden Green Oxon 31 Q7
Dunsdon Devon 7 K3
Dunsfold Surrey 14 E4
Dunsford Devon 8 F7
Dunshalt Fife 124 E10
Dunshillock Abers 141 N6
Dunsill Notts 78 D11
Dunsley N York 92 H4
Dunsley Staffs 64 F4
Dunsmore Bucks 44 B10
Dunsop Bridge Lancs 83 P5
Dunstable C Beds 44 E7
Dunstall Staffs 65 M8
Dunstall Common Worcs 41 P3
Dunstall Green Suffk 57 P8
Dunstan Nthumb 109 L6
Dunstan Steads Nthumb 109 L5
Dunster Somset 20 F5
Duns Tew Oxon 43 K6
Dunston Gatesd 100 G6
Dunston Lincs 79 Q11
Dunston Norfk 71 J11
Dunston Staffs 64 H8
Dunstone Devon 5 J6
Dunstone Devon 8 D9
Dunston Heath Staffs 64 G8
Dunsville Donc 78 G2
Dunswell E R Yk 87 K8
Dunsyre S Lans 115 K11
Dunterton Devon 7 M9
Dunthrop Oxon 43 R10
Duntisbourne Abbots Gloucs 41 R10
Duntisbourne Leer Gloucs 41 R10
Duntisbourne Rouse Gloucs 42 A10
Duntish Dorset 10 H3
Duntocher W Duns 113 P7
Dunton Bucks 44 B7
Dunton C Beds 45 J3
Dunton Norfk 70 C6
Dunton Bassett Leics 54 E3
Dunton Green Kent 33 P11
Dunton Wayletts Essex 34 B4
Duntulm Highld 142 D10
Dunure S Ayrs 104 E7
Dunvant Swans 26 D4
Dunvegan Highld 134 D6
Dunwich Suffk 59 P6
Dunwood Staffs 64 H1
Durdar Cumb 98 E8
Durgan Cnwll 3 J9
Durgates E Susx 16 B4
Durham Dur 100 H9
Durham Cathedral Dur 100 H10
Durham Services Dur 100 H11
Durham Tees Valley Airport S on T 91 P4
Durisdeer D & G 106 A9
Durisdeermill D & G 106 A9
Durkar Wakefd 85 L11
Durleigh Somset 21 L6
Durley Hants 24 G10
Durley Wilts 30 F9
Durley Street Hants 25 J10
Durlock Kent 35 N10
Durlock Kent 35 P9
Durlow Common Herefs 41 K4
Durn Rochdl 84 E12
Durness Highld 149 J3
Durno Abers 140 H10
Duror Highld 121 J2
Durran Ag & B 120 H11
Durrington W Susx 14 G9
Durrington Wilts 23 P4
Dursley Gloucs 29 M3
Dursley Cross Gloucs 41 L7
Durston Somset 21 L7
Durweston Dorset 11 L3
Duston Nhants 55 J8
Duthil Highld 138 H11
Dutlas Powys 50 H5
Duton Hill Essex 45 R6
Dutson Cnwll 7 L7
Dutton Ches W 75 P8
Duxford Cambs 45 N2
Duxford Oxon 30 H2
Duxford IWM Cambs 45 N2
Dwygyfylchi Conwy 73 M8
Dwyran IoA 72 G10
Dyce C Aber 133 L2
Dyer's End Essex 46 C4
Dyfatty Carmth 26 C2
Dyffrydan Gwynd 61 M9
Dyffryn Brdgnd 27 K3
Dyffryn Myr Td 39 P11
Dyffryn V Glam 27 P8
Dyffryn Ardudwy Gwynd 61 K7
Dyffryn Castell Cerdgn 49 N4
Dyffryn Cellwen Neath 39 K9
Dyke Lincs 68 B7
Dyke Moray 138 H4
Dykehead Angus 124 E2
Dykehead N Lans 132 B12
Dykehead Stirlg 114 A2
Dykelands Abers 132 H10
Dykends Angus 124 E1
Dykeside Abers 140 H7
Dykes of Gray C Dund 124 G6
Dylife Powys 49 Q2
Dymchurch Kent 17 K5
Dymock Gloucs 41 L5
Dyrham S Glos 29 L7
Dysart Fife 115 P3
Dyserth Denbgs 74 E8

E

Eachway Worcs 53 J5
Eachwick Nthumb 100 E4
Eagland Hill Lancs 83 K6
Eagle Lincs 79 L10
Eagle Barnsdale Lincs 79 L10
Eagle Moor Lincs 79 M10
Eaglescliffe S on T 91 P4
Eaglesfield Cumb 88 E1
Eaglesfield D & G 97 P3
Eaglesham E Rens 113 Q10
Eagley Bolton 76 D1
Eairy IoM 102 d6
Eakring Notts 78 E11
Ealand N Linc 79 L1
Ealing Gt Lon 32 H6
Eals Nthumb 99 K7
Eamont Bridge Cumb 89 N1
Earby Lancs 84 D6
Earcroft Bl w D 83 P10
Eardington Shrops 52 D2
Eardisland Herefs 51 L9
Eardisley Herefs 51 K11
Eardiston Shrops 63 L7
Eardiston Worcs 52 C7
Earith Cambs 56 G6
Earle Nthumb 108 F4
Earlestown St Hel 75 P5
Earley Wokham 31 Q8
Earlham Norfk 71 J10
Earlish Highld 134 G4
Earls Barton Nhants 55 L8
Earls Colne Essex 46 F6
Earls Common Worcs 52 H9
Earl's Croome Worcs 41 P3
Earlsditton Shrops 52 B5
Earlsdon Covtry 53 Q5
Earlsferry Fife 116 C1
Earlsfield Gt Lon 33 J8
Earlsford Abers 141 K9
Earl's Green Suffk 58 F7
Earlsheaton Kirk 85 K11
Earl Shilton Leics 54 D1
Earl Soham Suffk 59 J8
Earl Sterndale Derbys 77 K10
Earlston Border 107 P2
Earlston E Ayrs 104 G3
Earl Stonham Suffk 58 G9
Earlswood Surrey 15 L6
Earlswood Warwks 53 L6
Earlswood Common Mons 28 F3
Earnley W Susx 13 M6
Earnshaw Bridge Lancs 83 M10
Earsdon N Tyne 101 J4
Earsdon Nthumb 109 K11
Earsham Norfk 59 L3
Earswick C York 86 B4
Eartham W Susx 14 D9
Earthcott S Glos 29 J5
Easby N York 92 C5
Easdale Ag & B 120 C9
Easebourne W Susx 14 C6
Easenhall Warwks 54 B6
Eashing Surrey 14 D2
Easington Bucks 43 P9
Easington Dur 101 K9
Easington E R Yk 87 R11
Easington Nthumb 109 J3
Easington Oxon 31 N3
Easington R & Cl 92 F3
Easington Colliery Dur 101 L9
Easington Lane Sundld 101 J7
Easingwold N York 85 Q1
Easole Street Kent 35 N12
Eassie and Nevay Angus 124 D3
East Aberthaw V Glam 27 N7
East Allington Devon 5 N7
East Anstey Devon 20 D8
East Anton Hants 24 F4
East Appleton N York 91 J1
East Ashey IoW 13 K7
East Ashling W Susx 13 P3
East Aston Hants 24 G4
East Ayton N York 93 K9
East Balsdon Cnwll 7 K5
East Bank Blae G 40 B10
East Barkwith Lincs 80 D7
East Barming Kent 34 C11
East Barnby N York 92 H4
East Barnet Gt Lon 33 K3
East Barns E Loth 116 H6
East Barsham Norfk 70 D5
East Beckham Norfk 70 H4
East Bedfont Gt Lon 32 F6
East Bergholt Suffk 47 J5
East Bierley Kirk 85 J9
East Bilney Norfk 70 D8
East Blatchington E Susx 15 N10
East Bloxworth Dorset 11 L6
Eastbrook V Glam 27 R8
East Buckland Devon 19 N7
East Budleigh Devon 9 K8
Eastburn C Brad 84 F6
Eastburn E R Yk 87 J4
East Burnham Bucks 32 D6
East Burton Dorset 11 K7
East Butsfield Dur 100 E9
East Butterwick N Linc 79 L2
Eastby N York 84 F4
East Calder W Loth 115 K7
East Carleton Norfk 70 H11
East Carlton Leeds 85 J6
East Carlton Nhants 55 L3
East Chaldon Dorset 11 J8
East Challow Oxon 30 H5
East Charleton Devon 5 M8
East Chelborough Dorset 10 E4
East Chiltington E Susx 15 L8
East Chinnock Somset 22 C10
East Chisenbury Wilts 23 P3
East Cholderton Hants 24 C4
Eastchurch Kent 34 H8
East Clandon Surrey 32 F12
East Claydon Bucks 43 Q6
East Clevedon N Som 28 E8
East Coker Somset 22 C10
Eastcombe Gloucs 41 P10
Eastcombe Somset 21 J7
East Compton Somset 22 E5
East Cornworthy Devon 5 P6
Eastcote Gt Lon 32 F5
Eastcote Nhants 54 H10
Eastcote Solhll 53 N6
Eastcott Cnwll 18 E10
Eastcott Wilts 23 M2
East Cottingwith E R Yk 86 D7
Eastcourt Wilts 30 F10
Eastcourt Wilts 30 H5
East Cowes IoW 13 J7
East Cowick E R Yk 86 C11
East Cowton N York 91 M6
East Cramlington Nthumb 100 H4
East Cranmore Somset 22 F5
East Creech Dorset 11 M8
East Curthwaite Cumb 98 D8
East Dean E Susx 15 Q11
East Dean Gloucs 41 K7
East Dean Hants 24 C8
East Dean W Susx 14 C8
Eastdown Devon 6 S7
East Down Devon 19 L5
East Drayton Notts 79 K9
East Dulwich Gt Lon 33 L7
East Dundry N Som 28 H8
East Ella C KuH 87 K9
East End Bed 56 B9
East End C Beds 44 D3
East End E R Yk 87 M9
East End E R Yk 87 P9
Eastend Essex 34 G4
East End Essex 45 M9
East End Hants 12 F5
East End Hants 31 J10
East End Herts 45 N6
East End Kent 16 E4
East End Kent 34 H7
East End M Keyn 44 D3
East End Oxon 43 J8
East End Somset 22 F4
East End Suffk 47 K5
Easter Balmoral Abers 131 N5
Easter Compton S Glos 28 G5
Easter Dalziel Highld 138 D6
Eastergate W Susx 14 D9
Easter Howgate Mdloth 115 N8
Easter Kinkell Highld 137 Q5
Easter Moniack Highld 137 P7
Eastern Green Covtry 53 P5
Easter Ord Abers 133 K3
Easter Pitkierie Fife 125 L11
Easter Skeld Shet 147 h7
Easter Softlaw Border 108 B3
Easterton Wilts 23 M2
Eastertown Somset 21 N3
Easter Wenfield Wilts 24 C3
East Farleigh Kent 34 C11
East Farndon Nhants 55 J4
East Ferry Lincs 79 K4
Eastfield N Lans 114 G8
Eastfield N York 93 L9
East Firsby Lincs 79 P6
East Fortune E Loth 116 D5
East Garforth Leeds 85 N8
East Garston W Berk 30 H7
Eastgate Dur 99 Q10
Eastgate Lincs 68 B8
Eastgate Norfk 70 H7
East Ginge Oxon 31 J5
East Goscote Leics 66 H9
East Grafton Wilts 30 F10
East Green Suffk 59 M7
East Grimstead Wilts 24 C8
East Grinstead W Susx 15 M3
East Guldeford E Susx 16 G6
East Haddon Nhants 54 H7
East Hagbourne Oxon 31 L5
East Halton N Linc 87 L11
East Ham Gt Lon 33 M5
Eastham Wirral 75 K7
Eastham Ferry Wirral 75 L7
Easthampstead Herefs 51 L8
East Hanney Oxon 31 J4
East Hanningfield Essex 34 D2
East Hardwick Wakefd 85 P11
East Harling Norfk 58 E3
East Harlsey N York 91 P7
East Harnham Wilts 23 P7
East Harptree BaNES 28 H11
East Hartford Nthumb 100 H4
East Harting W Susx 25 N9
East Hatch Wilts 23 K7
East Hatley Cambs 56 F10
East Hauxwell N York 91 K8
East Haven Angus 125 L5
Eastheath Wokham 31 P9
East Heckington Lincs 68 D3
East Hedleyhope Dur 100 F9
East Helmsdale Highld 147 J2
East Hendred Oxon 31 K5
East Hesterton N York 93 J11
East Hewish N Som 28 F9
East Hoathly E Susx 15 P7
East Holme Dorset 11 L7
East Hope Dorset 90 H5
Easthope Shrops 51 P2
Easthorpe Essex 46 G7
Easthorpe Notts 66 H1
East Horrington Somset 22 D4
East Horsley Surrey 32 F12
East Horton Nthumb 108 G4
East Howe BCP 11 P6
East Huntspill Somset 21 M4
East Hyde C Beds 44 G8
East Ilkerton Devon 19 N4
East Ilsley W Berk 31 K6
Eastington Devon 8 B9
Eastington Gloucs 41 M10
Eastington Gloucs 42 D9
East Keal Lincs 80 G11
East Kennett Wilts 30 D9
East Keswick Leeds 85 M6
East Kilbride S Lans 114 B10
East Kimber Devon 7 N4
East Kirkby Lincs 80 F11
East Knighton Dorset 11 K7
East Knowstone Devon 20 C8
East Knoyle Wilts 23 K7
East Lambrook Somset 21 P9
Eastlands D & G 96 G4
East Langdon Kent 17 P2
East Langton Leics 55 J2
East Lavant W Susx 13 Q3
East Lavington W Susx 14 D7
East Layton N York 91 K5
Eastleach Martin Gloucs 42 E10
Eastleach Turville Gloucs 42 E10
East Leake Notts 66 F7
East Learmouth Nthumb 108 D2
East Leigh Devon 5 L6
East Leigh Devon 8 B5
East Leigh Devon 8 D4
Eastleigh Devon 19 J8
Eastleigh Hants 24 G9
East Lexham Norfk 70 C8
Eastling Kent 34 G11
East Linton E Loth 116 D6
East Liss Hants 25 N8
East Lockinge Oxon 31 J5
East Lound N Linc 79 K4
East Lulworth Dorset 11 L8
East Lutton N York 86 H1
East Lydeford Somset 21 J7
East Lydford Somset 22 D7
East Malling Kent 34 C11
East Malling Heath Kent 34 C11
East Marden W Susx 25 P10
East Markham Notts 79 J9
East Martin Hants 23 N9
East Marton N York 84 D5
East Meon Hants 25 L9
East Mere Devon 20 H8
East Mersea Essex 47 J9
East Midlands Airport Leics 66 D7
East Molesey Surrey 32 G9
Eastmoor Norfk 69 Q11
East Morden Dorset 11 M6
East Morton D & G 84 G7
East Morton D & G 106 A9
East Ness N York 92 E11
East Newton E R Yk 87 N9
Eastney C Port 13 L5
Eastnor Herefs 41 L4
East Norton Leics 67 J1
East Oakley Hants 24 H4
Eastoft N Linc 86 E12
East Ogwell Devon 5 P4
Easton Cambs 56 C6
Easton Cumb 98 D7
Easton Cumb 98 G2
Easton Devon 8 D7
Easton Dorset 10 H9
Easton Hants 24 H7
Easton Lincs 67 M7
Easton Norfk 70 H10
Easton Somset 22 C4
Easton Suffk 59 K9
Easton W Berk 31 J8
Easton Wilts 29 P5
Easton Grey Wilts 29 P5
Easton-in-Gordano N Som 28 G7
Easton Maudit Nhants 55 M9
Easton-on-the-Hill Nhants 67 P11
Easton Royal Wilts 30 E10
East Orchard Dorset 23 J10
East Ord Nthumb 117 L11
East Panson Devon 7 L6
East Parley BCP 11 Q5
East Peckham Kent 16 B1
East Pennard Somset 22 D6
East Portlemouth Devon 5 M9
East Prawle Devon 5 N9
East Preston W Susx 14 F10
East Pulham Dorset 10 H3
East Putford Devon 18 G10
East Quantoxhead Somset 21 J5
East Rainham Medway 34 E9
East Rainton Sundld 101 J8
East Ravendale NE Lin 80 E4
East Raynham Norfk 70 C7
Eastrea Cambs 56 F1
Eastriggs D & G 97 P4
East Rigton Leeds 85 M6
Eastrington E R Yk 86 E9
East Rolstone N Som 28 E10
Eastrop Swindn 30 E4
East Rounton N York 91 P6
East Rudham Norfk 70 B6
East Runton Norfk 71 J4
Eastry Kent 35 P11
East Saltoun E Loth 116 B8
Eastshaw W Susx 14 C6
East Sheen Gt Lon 32 H7
East Shefford W Berk 30 H7
East Sleekburn Nthumb 100 H2
East Somerton Norfk 71 P8
East Stockwith Lincs 79 K5
East Stoke Dorset 11 L7
East Stoke Notts 67 J2
East Stour Dorset 22 H9
East Stour Common Dorset 22 H9
East Stourmouth Kent 35 N10
East Stowford Devon 19 M8
East Stratton Hants 24 H5
East Studdal Kent 17 P1
East Sutton Kent 16 E1
East Taphouse Cnwll 4 B4
East-the-Water Devon 19 J8
East Thirston Nthumb 109 K9
East Tilbury Thurr 34 B7
East Tilbury Village Thurr 34 B7
East Tisted Hants 25 M7
East Torrington Lincs 80 C7
East Tuddenham Norfk 70 G10
East Tytherley Hants 24 D7
East Tytherton Wilts 29 Q7
East Village Devon 8 H4
Eastville Bristl 29 J7
Eastville Lincs 80 H12
East Wall Shrops 51 N2
East Walton Norfk 69 P9
East Water Somset 22 C3
East Week Devon 8 C6
Eastwell Leics 67 K6
East Wellow Hants 24 E9
East Wemyss Fife 115 Q2
East Whitburn W Loth 114 H8
Eastwick Herts 45 N9
East Wickham Gt Lon 33 N7
East Williamston Pembks 37 L9
East Winch Norfk 69 N9
East Winterslow Wilts 24 D6
East Wittering W Susx 13 M6
East Witton N York 91 K9
Eastwood Notts 66 D3
Eastwood Sthend 34 E5
East Woodburn Nthumb 99 P1
Eastwood End Cambs 56 H2
East Woodhay Hants 31 J10
East Woodlands Somset 22 H4
East Worldham Hants 25 N6
East Worthing W Susx 14 H10
East Wretham Norfk 58 D3
East Youlstone Devon 18 F10
Eathorpe Warwks 54 C7
Eaton Ches E 76 H3
Eaton Ches W 75 P11
Eaton Leics 67 K6
Eaton Norfk 71 J10
Eaton Notts 78 H9
Eaton Oxon 43 K11
Eaton Shrops 51 L4
Eaton Shrops 51 N3
Eaton Bishop Herefs 40 F4
Eaton Bray C Beds 44 D7
Eaton Constantine Shrops 63 Q11
Eaton Ford Cambs 56 D8
Eaton Green C Beds 44 D7
Eaton Hastings Oxon 30 F3
Eaton Mascott Shrops 63 P11
Eaton Socon Cambs 56 D9
Eaton upon Tern Shrops 64 C7
Eaves Brow Warrtn 76 B5
Eaves Green Solhll 53 N4
Ebberston N York 92 H10
Ebbesborne Wake Wilts 23 L8
Ebbw Vale Blae G 40 B9
Ebchester Dur 100 E7
Ebdon N Som 28 E9
Ebernoe W Susx 14 D5
Ebford Devon 9 J7
Ebley Gloucs 41 N10
Ebnal Ches W 63 N2
Ebnall Herefs 51 M8
Ebrington Gloucs 42 E4
Ebsworthy Devon 7 P6
Ecchinswell Hants 31 K10
Ecclaw Border 116 G6
Ecclefechan D & G 97 P3
Eccles Border 108 B2
Eccles Kent 34 C10
Eccles Salfd 76 E4
Ecclesall Sheff 77 E5
Eccles Green Herefs 51 L11
Eccleshall Staffs 64 F6
Eccleshill C Brad 85 J8
Ecclesmachan W Loth 115 K6
Eccles on Sea Norfk 71 N6
Eccles Road Norfk 58 F3
Eccleston Ches W 75 L11
Eccleston Lancs 83 M11
Eccleston St Hel 75 N4
Eccleston Green Lancs 83 M12
Echt Abers 132 H3
Eckford Border 108 B3
Eckington Derbys 78 C8
Eckington Worcs 41 Q4
Ecton Nhants 55 M8
Ecton Staffs 77 L12
Edale Derbys 77 L6
Eday Ork 147 d3
Eday Airport Ork 147 d2
Edburton W Susx 15 J8
Edderside Cumb 97 M8
Edderton Highld 146 D7
Edderton Cambs 56 H8
Eddleston Border 115 N11
Eddlewood S Lans 114 C10
Edenbridge Kent 15 N2
Edenfield Lancs 84 B11
Edenhall Cumb 98 H11
Edenham Lincs 67 Q8
Eden Mount Cumb 89 L11
Eden Park Gt Lon 33 L9
Edensor Derbys 77 N9
Edentaggart Ag & B 113 L3
Edenthorpe Donc 78 G2
Edern Gwynd 60 D5
Edgbaston Birm 53 J4
Edgcott Bucks 43 P7
Edgcott Somset 20 C6
Edgcumbe Cnwll 2 H8
Edge Gloucs 41 N9
Edge Shrops 63 L10
Edgebolton Shrops 63 P8
Edge End Gloucs 41 J9
Edgefield Norfk 70 G5
Edgefield Green Norfk 70 G5
Edge Bolton 76 C3
Edge Green Ches W 63 N3
Edgehill Warwks 42 H2
Edgeley Shrops 63 N4
Edgerton Kirk 84 H11
Edgeside Lancs 84 C10
Edgeworth Gloucs 41 Q10
Edginswell Torbay 5 Q3
Edgmond Wrekin 64 D8
Edgmond Marsh Wrekin 64 D8
Edgton Shrops 51 L3
Edgware Gt Lon 32 H4
Edgworth Bl w D 83 R11
Edinbane Highld 134 F6
Edinburgh C Edin 115 N7
Edinburgh Airport C Edin 115 L6
Edinburgh Castle C Edin 115 N6
Edinburgh Old & New Town C Edin 115 N6
Edinburgh Royal Botanic Gardens C Edin 115 N6
Edinburgh Zoo RZSS 115 M6
Edingale Staffs 65 N9
Edingham D & G 96 G6
Edingley Notts 78 E11
Edingthorpe Norfk 71 L6
Edingthorpe Green Norfk 71 L6
Edington Border 117 K10
Edington Nthumb 100 F2
Edington Somset 21 M5
Edington Wilts 23 J3
Edingworth Somset 21 N3
Edistone Devon 18 E9
Edithmead Somset 21 M3
Edith Weston Rutlnd 67 M11
Edlesborough Bucks 44 D8
Edlingham Nthumb 109 J8
Edlington Lincs 80 E9
Edmond Castle Cumb 98 G6
Edmondsham Dorset 11 P2
Edmondsley Dur 100 G8
Edmondstown Rhondd 27 N4
Edmondthorpe Leics 67 L8
Edmonton Cnwll 6 D10
Edmonton Gt Lon 33 L4
Edmundbyers Dur 100 C8
Ednam Border 108 B2
Ednaston Derbys 65 N4
Edney Common Essex 34 B2
Edradynate P & K 123 M2
Edrom Border 117 J10
Edstaston Shrops 63 N6
Edstone Warwks 53 M8
Edvin Loach Herefs 52 C9
Edwalton Notts 66 F5
Edwardstone Suffk 46 G3
Edwardsville Myr Td 27 P3
Edwinstowe Notts 78 G10
Edworth C Beds 45 J3
Edwyn Ralph Herefs 52 B9
Edzell Angus 132 F10
Edzell Woods Abers 132 F10
Efail-fach Neath 27 J3
Efail Isaf Rhondd 27 N5
Efailnewydd Gwynd 60 E5
Efail-Rhyd Powys 62 G7
Efailwenn Carmth 37 M5
Efenechtyd Denbgs 62 F2
Effgill D & G 107 J11
Effingham Surrey 32 G11
Effingham Junction Surrey 32 G11
Efflinch Staffs 65 M9
Efford Devon 8 H4
Egbury Hants 24 G3
Egdon Worcs 52 H9
Egerton Bolton 83 Q12
Egerton Kent 16 H2
Egerton Forstal Kent 16 F1
Eggborough N York 85 R10
Eggbuckland C Plym 4 H5
Eggesford Devon 8 B9
Eggington C Beds 44 D7
Egginton Derbys 65 P6
Egglescliffe S on T 91 P4
Eggleston Dur 90 G2
Egham Surrey 32 E8
Egham Wick Surrey 32 D8
Egleton Rutlnd 67 L11
Eglingham Nthumb 109 J6
Egloshayle Cnwll 6 E10
Egloskerry Cnwll 7 L5
Eglwys-Brewis V Glam 27 P8
Eglwys Cross Wrexhm 63 M4
Eglwys Fach Cerdgn 49 L3
Eglwyswrw Pembks 37 M3
Egmanton Notts 79 J10
Egremont Cumb 88 D9
Egremont Wirral 75 K5
Egton N York 92 G5
Egton Bridge N York 92 G5
Egypt Bucks 32 D5
Egypt Hants 24 H5
Eigg Highld 126 H7
Eilanreach Highld 135 P12
Eilean Donan Castle Highld 136 B10
Eisgein W Isls 152 f5
Eisteddfa Gurig Cerdgn 49 N4
Elan Valley Powys 50 D7
Elan Village Powys 50 C7
Elberton S Glos 29 J5
Elburton C Plym 4 H5
Elcombe Swindn 30 C4
Elcot W Berk 31 J9
Eldernell Cambs 68 F12
Eldersfield Worcs 41 N5
Elderslie Rens 113 N8
Elder Street Essex 45 Q5
Eldon Dur 91 L2
Eldwick C Brad 84 H7
Elerch Cerdgn 49 L3
Elfhill Abers 133 J7
Elford Nthumb 109 K3
Elford Staffs 65 M10
Elgin Moray 139 N3
Elgol Highld 127 J2
Elham Kent 17 L2
Elie Fife 116 C1
Elilaw Nthumb 108 F8
Elim IoA 72 F7
Eling Hants 24 F11
Elkesley Notts 78 H8
Elkstone Gloucs 41 Q9
Ella Abers 140 G4
Ellacombe Torbay 5 Q4
Elland Calder 84 H11
Elland Lower Edge Calder 84 H11
Ellary Ag & B 111 Q6
Ellastone Staffs 65 L3
Ellel Lancs 83 L4
Ellemford Border 116 G7
Ellenabeich Ag & B 120 D9
Ellenbrook Salfd 76 D3
Ellenborough Cumb 97 L11
Ellenhall Staffs 64 F7
Ellen's Green Surrey 14 G4
Ellerbeck N York 91 Q7
Ellerby N York 92 G4
Ellerdine Heath Wrekin 64 C7
Ellerhayes Devon 9 J4
Elleric Ag & B 121 K3
Ellerker E R Yk 86 G9
Ellers N York 84 F6
Ellerton E R Yk 86 D7
Ellerton N York 91 L7
Ellerton Shrops 64 D7
Ellesborough Bucks 44 B10
Ellesmere Shrops 63 L5
Ellesmere Port Ches W 75 L8
Ellingham Hants 12 B3
Ellingham Norfk 59 M2
Ellingham Nthumb 109 K5
Ellingstring N York 91 K10
Ellington Cambs 56 C6
Ellington Nthumb 109 M11
Ellington Thorpe Cambs 56 C6
Elliots Green Somset 22 H4
Ellisfield Hants 25 L4
Ellishader Highld 135 J3
Ellistown Leics 66 C10
Ellon Abers 141 M9
Ellonby Cumb 98 E11
Ellough Suffk 59 N3
Elloughton E R Yk 86 H9
Ellwood Gloucs 41 J9
Elm Cambs 69 J10
Elmbridge Worcs 52 G7
Elmdon Essex 45 N4
Elmdon Solhll 53 M4
Elmdon Heath Solhll 53 M4
Elmer W Susx 14 D10
Elmers End Gt Lon 33 L8
Elmer's Green Lancs 75 N2
Elmesthorpe Leics 54 D1
Elm Green Essex 46 D10
Elmhurst Staffs 65 L9
Elmington Nhants 55 Q3
Elmley Castle Worcs 41 R3
Elmley Lovett Worcs 52 G7
Elmore Gloucs 41 M8
Elmore Back Gloucs 41 M8
Elm Park Gt Lon 33 P5
Elmscott Devon 18 E9
Elmsett Suffk 47 J2
Elms Green Worcs 52 D7
Elmstead Heath Essex 47 J7
Elmstead Market Essex 47 J7
Elmstead Row Essex 47 J7
Elmsted Kent 17 J2
Elmstone Kent 35 N10
Elmstone Hardwicke Gloucs 41 Q7
Elmswell E R Yk 87 J4
Elmswell Suffk 58 E8
Elmton Derbys 78 E9
Elphin Highld 144 F3
Elphinstone E Loth 115 R7
Elrick Abers 133 K3
Elrig D & G 95 L8
Elrington Nthumb 99 N6
Elsdon Nthumb 108 E11
Elsecar Barns 78 C4
Elsenham Essex 45 P6
Elsfield Oxon 43 L9
Elsham N Linc 79 P1
Elsing Norfk 70 F9
Elslack N York 84 D5
Elson Hants 13 K4
Elson Shrops 63 L5
Elsrickle S Lans 106 D1
Elstead Surrey 14 C2
Elsted W Susx 25 N9
Elsted Marsh W Susx 25 N9
Elsthorpe Lincs 67 Q7
Elstob Dur 91 N2
Elston Lancs 83 N8
Elston Notts 67 J2
Elston Wilts 23 N4
Elstone Devon 19 N10
Elstow Bed 55 Q10
Elstree Herts 32 H3
Elstronwick E R Yk 87 N9
Elswick Lancs 83 K7
Elsworth Cambs 56 F8
Elterwater Cumb 89 J6
Eltham Gt Lon 33 M7
Eltisley Cambs 56 E9
Elton Bury 76 E1
Elton Cambs 55 Q2
Elton Ches W 75 M8
Elton Derbys 77 N11
Elton Gloucs 41 M7
Elton Herefs 51 M6
Elton Notts 67 J5
Elton S on T 91 P4
Elton Green Ches W 75 M8
Elton-on-the-Hill Notts 67 J4
Eltringham Nthumb 100 D6
Elvanfoot S Lans 106 C6
Elvaston Derbys 66 C5
Elveden Suffk 58 B5
Elvetham Heath Hants 25 N2
Elvingston E Loth 116 C6
Elvington C York 86 C6
Elvington Kent 35 N11
Elwell Devon 19 M7
Elwick Hartpl 101 L11
Elwick Nthumb 109 J2
Elworth Ches E 76 E10
Elworthy Somset 20 H6
Ely Cambs 57 K4
Ely Cardif 27 N7
Emberton M Keyn 55 M10
Embleton Cumb 97 N10
Embleton Dur 101 K12
Embleton Nthumb 109 L5
Embo Highld 146 E6
Emborough Somset 22 E3
Embo Street Highld 146 E6
Embsay N York 84 F4
Emery Down Hants 12 D4
Emersons Green S Glos 29 L7
Emery Green Reading 31 P7
Emmer Green Readg 31 P7
Emmington Oxon 43 Q11
Emneth Norfk 69 J10
Emneth Hungate Norfk 69 K10
Empingham Rutlnd 67 N10
Empshott Hants 25 M7
Empshott Green Hants 25 N7
Emsworth Hants 13 N5
Enborne W Berk 31 J9
Enborne Row W Berk 31 J10
Enchmarsh Shrops 51 N1
Enderby Leics 66 E12
Endmoor Cumb 89 N10
Endon Staffs 64 G1
Endon Bank Staffs 64 G1
Enfield Gt Lon 33 L3
Enfield Lock Gt Lon 33 L3
Enfield Wash Gt Lon 33 L3
Enford Wilts 23 N3
Engine Common S Glos 29 L5
England's Gate Herefs 51 P10
Englefield W Berk 31 N8
Englefield Green Surrey 32 E8
Engleseabrook Ches E 64 D2
English Bicknor Gloucs 41 J8
Englishcombe BaNES 29 J8
English Frankton Shrops 63 M6
Engollan Cnwll 6 B10
Enham Alamein Hants 24 F3
Enmore Somset 21 K6
Enmore Green Dorset 23 J8
Ennerdale Bridge Cumb 88 E12
Enniscaven Cnwll 3 N3
Enochdhu P & K 131 K11
Ensay Ag & B 119 K3
Ensbury BCP 11 Q5
Ensdon Shrops 63 L9
Ensis Devon 19 L8
Enson Staffs 64 H6
Enstone Oxon 43 J7
Enterkinfoot D & G 105 Q9
Enterpen N York 91 Q5
Enville Staffs 52 F3
Eochar W Isls 152 b10
Eòlaigearraidh W Isls 152 b12
Eolígarry W Isls 152 b12
Epney Gloucs 41 M9
Epperstone Notts 66 G2
Epping Essex 45 N11
Epping Green Essex 45 N11
Epping Green Herts 45 K10
Epping Upland Essex 45 N11
Eppleby N York 91 K4
Epsom Surrey 33 J10
Epwell Oxon 42 H4
Epworth N Linc 79 K3
Epworth Turbary N Linc 79 J3
Erbistock Wrexhm 63 K4
Erdington Birm 53 L2
Eridge Green E Susx 15 Q4
Eridge Station E Susx 15 P4
Erines Ag & B 112 C6
Eriska Ag & B 120 G4
Eriswell Suffk 57 N5
Erith Gt Lon 33 P7
Erlestoke Wilts 23 L3
Ermington Devon 5 K6
Erpingham Norfk 71 J6
Erriottwood Kent 34 G10
Errogie Highld 137 P11
Errol P & K 124 F8
Erskine Rens 113 P7
Erskine Bridge Rens 113 N7
Ervie D & G 94 E5
Erwarton Suffk 47 M5
Erwood Powys 39 Q3
Eryholme N York 91 N5
Eryrys Denbgs 74 H12
Escalls Cnwll 2 B9
Escomb Dur 100 F12
Escott Somset 21 H6
Escrick N York 86 B6
Esgair Carmth 38 B6
Esgair Carmth 38 G7
Esgairgeiliog Powys 61 N11
Esgerdawe Carmth 38 F3
Esgyryn Conwy 73 P8
Esh Dur 100 F9
Esher Surrey 32 G9
Esholt C Brad 85 J7
Eshott Nthumb 109 K10
Eshton N York 84 D4
Esh Winning Dur 100 G10
Eskadale Highld 137 M8
Eskbank Mdloth 115 P8
Eskdale Green Cumb 88 F6
Eskdalemuir D & G 106 H10
Eske E R Yk 87 K6
Eskham Lincs 80 G4
Eskholme Donc 86 B11
Esperley Lane Ends Dur 91 J2
Esprick Lancs 83 K8
Essendine Rutlnd 67 P9
Essendon Herts 45 K10
Essich Highld 138 B8
Essington Staffs 64 H11
Esslemont Abers 141 M9
Eston R & Cl 92 B3
Etal Nthumb 108 E2
Etchilhampton Wilts 30 B10
Etchingham E Susx 16 C5
Etchinghill Kent 17 L3
Etchinghill Staffs 65 J8
Etchingwood E Susx 15 P6
Etling Green Norfk 70 F9
Etloe Gloucs 41 M10
Eton W & M 32 D7
Eton Wick W & M 32 D6
Etruria C Stke 64 F3
Etteridge Highld 130 C6
Ettersgill Dur 99 H12
Ettiley Heath Ches E 76 D11
Ettingshall Wolves 52 H1
Ettington Warwks 53 P11
Etton C Pete 56 C11
Etton E R Yk 87 J6
Ettrick Border 106 H7
Ettrickbridge Border 107 K5
Ettrickhill Border 106 H7
Etwall Derbys 65 P6
Eudon George Shrops 52 C3
Euston Suffk 58 C5
Euximoor Drove Cambs 57 J2
Euxton Lancs 83 M11
Evancoyd Powys 51 J9
Evanton Highld 137 Q3
Evedon Lincs 68 B3
Evelith Shrops 64 D11
Evelix Highld 146 D7
Evenjobb Powys 51 J9
Evenley Oxon 43 M5
Evenlode Gloucs 42 F6
Evenwood Dur 91 J2
Evenwood Gate Dur 91 K2
Evercreech Somset 22 E6
Everingham E R Yk 86 F6
Everleigh Wilts 24 C3
Eversholt C Beds 44 D5
Evershot Dorset 10 E4
Eversley Hants 31 N10
Eversley Cross Hants 31 N10
Everthorpe E R Yk 86 G9
Everton C Beds 56 D10
Everton Hants 12 D6
Everton Lpool 75 K5
Everton Notts 78 H5

Evertown D & G 98 D3
Evesbatch Herefs 52 C11
Evesham Worcs 42 B8
Evington C Leic 66 G11
Ewden Village Sheff 77 P4
Ewell Surrey 33 J9
Ewell Minnis Kent 17 N2
Ewelme Oxon 31 N4
Ewen Gloucs 30 B3
Ewenny V Glam 27 L7
Ewerby Lincs 68 C3
Ewerby Thorpe Lincs 68 C3
Ewhurst Surrey 14 H2
Ewhurst Green E Susx 16 D6
Ewhurst Green Surrey 14 H2
Ewloe Flints 75 J10
Ewloe Green Flints 75 J10
Ewood Bl w D 83 P10
Ewood Bridge Lancs 84 B11
Eworthy Devon 7 N6
Ewshot Hants 25 P3
Ewyas Harold Herefs 40 E6
Exbourne Devon 8 B4
Exbury Hants 12 G5
Exceat E Susx 15 P11
Exebridge Somset 20 E8
Exelby N York 91 M9
Exeter Devon 9 M6
Exeter Airport Devon 9 M6
Exeter Services Devon 9 M6
Exford Somset 20 D6
Exfordsgreen Shrops 63 M11
Exhall Warwks 53 L9
Exhall Warwks 54 B3
Exlade Street Oxon 31 N6
Exley Head C Brad 84 F7
Exminster Devon 9 M7
Exmoor National Park 20 D5
Exmouth Devon 9 J8
Exning Suffk 57 M7
Exted Kent 17 L2
Exton Devon 9 M7
Exton Hants 25 K9
Exton Rutlnd 67 M10
Exton Somset 20 E6
Exwick Devon 8 G6
Eyam Derbys 77 N8
Eydon Nhants 54 E10
Eye C Pete 68 E11
Eye Herefs 51 M8
Eye Suffk 58 H6
Eye Green C Pete 68 E11
Eyemouth Border 117 L8
Eyeworth C Beds 45 J3
Eyhorne Street Kent 34 E11
Eyke Suffk 59 L10
Eynesbury Cambs 56 D9
Eynsford Kent 33 P9
Eynsham Oxon 43 J10
Eype Dorset 10 C6
Eyre Highld 134 G5
Eythorne Kent 17 N1
Eyton Herefs 51 L8
Eyton Shrops 51 L3
Eyton Shrops 63 L9
Eyton Shrops 63 M7
Eyton Wrexhm 63 K6
Eyton on Severn Shrops 63 P11
Eyton upon the Weald Moors Wrekin 64 C9

F

Faccombe Hants 30 H10
Faceby N York 91 R6
Fachwen Powys 62 E9
Facit Lancs 84 D11
Fackley Notts 78 D11
Faddiley Ches E 63 P2
Fadmoor N York 92 D9
Faerdre Swans 26 G8
Faifley W Duns 113 P6
Failand N Som 28 H8
Failford S Ayrs 104 H4
Failsworth Oldham 76 G3
Fairbourne Gwynd 61 K9
Fairburn N York 85 P9
Fairfield Derbys 77 K9
Fairfield Worcs 52 H5
Fairfield Park Herts 44 H5
Fairford Gloucs 30 D2
Fairford Park Gloucs 30 D2
Fairgirth D & G 96 H7
Fair Green Norfk 69 M8
Fairhaven Lancs 82 H9
Fair Isle Shet 147 h10
Fair Isle Airport Shet 147 h10
Fairlands Surrey 32 D11
Fairlie N Ayrs 113 J10
Fairlight E Susx 16 F8
Fairlight Cove E Susx 16 F8
Fairmile Devon 9 L5
Fairmile Surrey 32 G10
Fairmilehead C Edin 115 N7
Fairnilee Border 107 M3
Fair Oak Hants 24 H10
Fairoak Staffs 64 E5
Fair Oak Green Hants 31 N10
Fairseat Kent 34 A10
Fairstead Essex 46 D8
Fairstead Norfk 69 M8
Fairwarp E Susx 15 N5
Fairwater Cardif 27 Q7
Fairy Cross Devon 18 H8
Fakenham Norfk 70 C6
Fakenham Magna Suffk 58 D5
Fala Mdloth 116 B9
Fala Dam Mdloth 116 B9
Falcut Nhants 43 M3
Faldingworth Lincs 80 D7
Faldouët Jersey 13 d2
Falfield S Glos 29 K4
Falkenham Suffk 47 N4
Falkirk Falk 114 F6
Falkirk Wheel Falk 114 F5
Falkland Fife 124 E11
Fallburn S Lans 106 C2
Fallgate Derbys 78 B11
Fallin Stirlg 114 G12
Fallodon Nthumb 109 K5
Fallowfield Manch 76 F4
Fallowfield Nthumb 99 L6
Falmer E Susx 15 L9
Falmouth Cnwll 3 L6
Falnash Border 107 L7
Falsgrave N York 93 L9
Falstone Nthumb 108 B12
Fanagmore Highld 148 E6
Fancott C Beds 44 E6
Fanellan Highld 137 N7
Fangdale Beck N York 92 B8
Fangfoss E R Yk 86 E4
Fanmore Ag & B 119 L4
Fannich Lodge Highld 136 H3
Fans Border 107 P2
Far Bletchley M Keyn 44 B5
Farcet Cambs 56 D2
Far Cotton Nhants 55 J9
Farden Shrops 51 P5
Fareham Hants 13 J3
Farewell Staffs 65 K10
Far Forest Worcs 52 D6
Farforth Lincs 80 F7

Far Green Gloucs 29 M2
Faringdon Oxon 30 G3
Farington Lancs 83 N9
Farlam Cumb 98 H6
Farleigh N Som 28 G8
Farleigh Surrey 33 L10
Farleigh Hungerford Somset 29 N11
Farleigh Wallop Hants 25 K4
Farlesthorpe Lincs 81 J9
Farleton Cumb 89 N10
Farleton Lancs 83 N2
Farley Derbys 77 P11
Farley Staffs 65 K3
Farley Wilts 24 C7
Farley Green Suffk 57 P10
Farley Green Surrey 14 F2
Farley Hill Wokham 31 Q9
Farleys End Gloucs 41 M8
Farlington C Port 13 M4
Farlington N York 86 B2
Farlow Shrops 52 B4
Farmborough BaNES 29 K10
Farmbridge End Essex 46 A9
Farmcote Gloucs 42 C6
Farmcote Shrops 52 E2
Farmington Gloucs 42 D8
Farmoor Oxon 43 K10
Far Moor Wigan 75 N3
Farms Common Cnwll 2 H7
Farm Town Leics 66 C9
Farmtown Moray 140 D5
Farnah Green Derbys 65 Q3
Farnborough Gt Lon 33 N9
Farnborough Hants 32 C11
Farnborough W Berk 31 J6
Farnborough Warwks 54 C11
Farnborough Park Hants 32 C11
Farncombe Surrey 14 D2
Farndish Bed 55 M8
Farndon Ches W 63 L1
Farndon Notts 79 L2
Farne Islands Nthumb 109 L2
Farnell Angus 125 M2
Farnham Dorset 23 J10
Farnham Essex 45 N7
Farnham N York 85 M3
Farnham Suffk 59 M8
Farnham Surrey 25 P4
Farnham Common Bucks 32 E6
Farnham Green Essex 45 N6
Farnham Royal Bucks 32 D6
Farningham Kent 33 Q9
Farnley Leeds 85 K8
Farnley N York 85 J5
Farnley Tyas Kirk 77 M1
Farnsfield Notts 78 G12
Farnworth Bolton 76 D2
Farnworth Halton 75 N6
Far Oakridge Gloucs 41 Q11
Farr Highld 130 F4
Farr Highld 138 C9
Farr Highld 150 C4
Farraline Highld 137 P11
Farringdon Devon 9 M6
Farrington Gurney BaNES 22 E2
Far Sawrey Cumb 89 K7
Farsley Leeds 85 J8
Farther Howegreen Essex 34 E2
Farthing Green Kent 16 E2
Farthinghoe Nhants 43 L4
Farthingloe Kent 17 N3
Farthingstone Nhants 54 G9
Farthing Street Gt Lon 33 M9
Fartown Kirk 84 H11
Farway Devon 9 M6
Fasnacloich Ag & B 121 J3
Fasnakyle Highld 137 K10
Fassfern Highld 128 E8
Fatfield Sundld 100 H7
Faugh Cumb 98 G2
Fauld Staffs 65 L6
Fauldhouse W Loth 114 G9
Faulkbourne Essex 46 D8
Faulkland Somset 22 G2
Fauls Shrops 63 Q6
Faversham Kent 34 H10
Fawdington N York 91 Q12
Fawdon N u Ty 100 G4
Fawdon Nthumb 108 G6
Fawfieldhead Staffs 77 K11
Fawkham Green Kent 33 Q9
Fawler Oxon 42 H8
Fawley Bucks 31 Q5
Fawley Hants 12 G4
Fawley W Berk 30 H6
Fawley Chapel Herefs 41 J6
Fawnog Flints 74 H10
Fawsley Nhants 54 F9
Faxfleet E R Yk 86 F10
Faygate W Susx 15 J4
Fazeley Staffs 65 M11
Fearby N York 91 K10
Fearn Highld 146 E9
Fearnan P & K 123 J4
Fearnbeg Highld 135 N4
Fearnhead Warrtn 76 C4
Fearnmore Highld 135 M3
Fearnoch Ag & B 112 D5
Featherstone Staffs 64 H11
Featherstone Wakefd 85 N11
Feckenham Worcs 53 J8
Feering Essex 46 F7
Feetham N York 90 G7
Feizor N York 84 B2
Felbridge Surrey 15 L3
Felbrigg Norfk 71 J4
Felcourt Surrey 15 M3
Felden Herts 44 F10
Felindre Carmth 38 A4
Felindre Carmth 38 E7
Felindre Carmth 38 H6
Felindre Cerdgn 49 J9
Felindre Powys 40 A7
Felindre Powys 50 G5
Felindre Swans 38 F11
Felindre Farchog Pembks 37 L3
Felinfach Cerdgn 49 J9
Felinfach Powys 39 P5
Felinfoel Carmth 38 D11
Felingwmisaf Carmth 38 D7
Felingwmuchaf Carmth 38 D7
Felin-newydd Powys 39 Q4
Felixkirk N York 91 Q10
Felixstowe Suffk 47 N5
Felixstowe Ferry Suffk 47 N5
Felkington Nthumb 117 L2
Felkirk Wakefd 78 C1
Felling Gatesd 100 H6
Fell Lane C Brad 84 F7
Fell Side Cumb 98 C10
Felmersham Bed 55 M9
Felmingham Norfk 71 K6
Felpham W Susx 14 D11
Felsham Suffk 58 D9
Felsted Essex 46 B7
Feltham Gt Lon 32 G8
Felthamhill Surrey 32 G8
Felthorpe Norfk 70 H8
Felton Herefs 51 P11
Felton N Som 28 H9
Felton Nthumb 109 J9
Felton Butler Shrops 63 L8
Feltwell Norfk 57 N2
Fenay Bridge Kirk 85 J12

Fence Lancs 84 B8
Fence Rothm 78 D6
Fence Houses Sundld 101 J8
Fencott Oxon 43 M8
Fendike Corner Lincs 81 J11
Fen Ditton Cambs 57 J8
Fen Drayton Cambs 56 G7
Fen End Lincs 68 E8
Fen End Solhll 53 N6
Fenham Nthumb 108 H2
Feniscliffe Bl w D 83 P10
Feniscowles Bl w D 83 P10
Feniton Devon 9 L5
Feniton Court Devon 9 L5
Fenn Green Shrops 52 E4
Fenn Street Medway 34 D7
Fenny Bentley Derbys 65 M2
Fenny Bridges Devon 9 L5
Fenny Compton Warwks 54 C10
Fenny Drayton Leics 54 B1
Fenny Stratford M Keyn 44 C5
Fenrother Nthumb 109 K11
Fenstanton Cambs 56 F7
Fenstead End Suffk 57 Q10
Fen Street Norfk 58 E2
Fen Street Suffk 58 H8
Fenton C Stke 64 G3
Fenton Cambs 56 F5
Fenton Cumb 98 G2
Fenton Lincs 67 N4
Fenton Lincs 79 L8
Fenton Notts 79 K7
Fenton Nthumb 108 F3
Fenton Barns E Loth 116 C5
Fenwick Donc 86 B12
Fenwick E Ayrs 113 H1
Fenwick Nthumb 100 D4
Fenwick Nthumb 108 H1
Feock Cnwll 3 L5
Feolin Ferry Ag & B 111 K7
Fergushill N Ayrs 104 F1
Feriniquarrie Highld 134 C6
Fermain Bay Guern 12 b2
Fern Angus 132 D12
Ferndale Rhondd 27 N3
Ferndown Dorset 11 P4
Ferness Highld 138 H7
Fernham Oxon 30 G4
Fernhill Heath Worcs 52 F9
Fernhurst W Susx 14 C5
Fernie Fife 124 F9
Ferniegair S Lans 114 D10
Fernilea Highld 134 F9
Fernilee Derbys 77 J8
Fernwood Notts 67 K2
Ferrensby N York 85 M3
Ferrers Sluice N Linc 86 H11
Ferrindonald Highld 127 M3
Ferring W Susx 14 F10
Ferrybridge Wakefd 85 P10
Ferrybridge Services Wakefd 85 P10
Ferryden Angus 125 P2
Ferryhill Dur 100 H11
Ferryhill Station Dur 100 H12
Ferry Point Highld 146 D8
Ferryside Carmth 38 A9
Fersfield Norfk 58 F4
Fersit Highld 129 L8
Feshiebridge Highld 130 F3
Fetcham Surrey 32 G11
Fetterangus Abers 141 N6
Fettercairn Abers 132 G9
Fewcott Oxon 43 L6
Fewston N York 85 J4
Ffairfach Carmth 38 F7
Ffair Rhos Cerdgn 49 M7
Ffald-y-Brenin Carmth 38 G3
Ffarmers Carmth 38 G3
Ffawyddog Powys 40 B8
Ffestiniog Gwynd 61 K4
Ffestiniog Railway Gwynd 61 K4
Ffordd-las Denbgs 74 F10
Fforest Carmth 38 D10
Fforest Gôch Neath 26 H6
Ffostrasol Cerdgn 48 F11
Ffrith Flints 63 J1
Ffynnonddewi Cerdgn 48 F10
Ffynnongroyw Flints 74 F7
Ffynnon-oer Cerdgn 49 J10
Fickleshole Surrey 33 M10
Fiddington Gloucs 41 Q5
Fiddington Somset 21 K5
Fiddleford Dorset 22 H10
Fiddlers Green Cnwll 3 K3
Fiddlers Hamlet Essex 33 N2
Field Staffs 65 J5
Field Broughton Cumb 89 L10
Field Dalling Norfk 70 E4
Fieldhead Cumb 98 F10
Field Head Leics 66 E10

Finsbay W Isls 152 e6
Finstall Worcs 52 H6
Finsthwaite Cumb 89 K9
Finstock Oxon 42 H8
Finstown Ork 147 c4
Fintry Abers 141 J5
Fintry Stirlg 114 B4
Finzean Abers 132 F6
Fionnphort Ag & B 119 J8
Fionnsbhagh W Isls 152 e6
Firbank Cumb 90 B8
Firbeck Rothm 78 F6
Firby N York 86 D2
Firby N York 91 M9
Firgrove Rochdl 76 G1
Firle E Susx 15 N9
Firsby Lincs 81 J11
Firsdown Wilts 24 C7
Fir Tree Dur 100 F11
Fishbourne IoW 13 J6
Fishbourne W Susx 13 M4
Fishbourne Roman Palace W Susx 13 P4
Fishcross Clacks 114 G12
Fisher W Susx 14 B10
Fisherford Abers 140 G8
Fisherrow E Loth 115 Q6
Fisher's Pond Hants 24 H6
Fisher's Row Lancs 83 K5
Fisherstreet W Susx 14 D4
Fisherton Highld 138 D5
Fisherton S Ayrs 104 E6
Fisherton de la Mere Wilts 23 M6
Fisherwick Staffs 65 M10
Fishery W & M 32 C6
Fishguard Pembks 37 J3
Fishlake Donc 78 G1
Fishleigh Devon 7 Q4
Fishmere End Lincs 68 E4
Fishnish Pier Ag & B 120 C4
Fishpond Bottom Dorset 10 B5
Fishponds Bristl 29 J7
Fishtoft Lincs 68 G4
Fishtoft Drove Lincs 68 F3
Fishwick Lancs 83 M9
Fiskavaig Highld 134 F9
Fiskerton Lincs 79 P9
Fiskerton Notts 67 L1
Fitling E R Yk 87 N8
Fittleton Wilts 23 N6
Fittleworth W Susx 14 E7
Fitton End Cambs 68 H9
Fitz Shrops 63 M8
Fitzhead Somset 20 H7
Fitzroy Somset 21 J8
Fitzwilliam Wakefd 85 N12
Five Ash Down E Susx 15 N6
Five Ashes E Susx 15 Q5
Five Bells Somset 20 H4
Five Bridges Herefs 41 K2
Fivecrosses Ches W 75 N8
Fivehead Somset 21 M9
Five Lanes Mons 28 H4
Five Oak Green Kent 16 B2
Five Oaks Jersey 13 c2
Five Oaks W Susx 14 F5
Five Roads Carmth 38 D10
Five Wents Kent 34 E12
Flack's Green Essex 46 D8
Flackwell Heath Bucks 32 C4
Fladbury Worcs 42 A2
Fladdabister Shet 147 i8
Flagg Derbys 77 M10
Flamborough E R Yk 87 N1
Flamborough Head E R Yk 87 N1
Flamingo Land Theme Park N York 92 F10
Flamstead Herts 44 F8
Flamstead End Herts 45 L11
Flansham W Susx 14 D10
Flanshaw Wakefd 85 L11
Flappit Spring C Brad 84 F8
Flasby N York 84 F4
Flash Staffs 77 J10
Flashader Highld 134 E6
Flaunden Herts 32 E2
Flawborough Notts 67 K2
Flawith N York 85 P2
Flax Bourton N Som 28 H9
Flaxby N York 85 N4
Flaxley Gloucs 41 K9
Flaxmere Ches W 75 P9
Flaxpool Somset 20 H6
Flaxton N York 86 C3
Fleckney Leics 54 G2
Flecknoe Warwks 54 D8
Fledborough Notts 79 K9
Fleet Dorset 10 H8
Fleet Hants 13 M4
Fleet Hants 25 N3
Fleet Lincs 68 G7
Fleet Hargate Lincs 68 H7
Fleetend Hants 13 J4
Fleet Services Hants 25 P2
Fleetwood Lancs 82 H5
Fleggburgh Norfk 71 N8
Flemingston V Glam 27 K8
Flemington S Lans 114 B9
Flempton Suffk 57 Q7
Fletcherbridge Cnwll 6 G11
Fletcher's Green Kent 33 P12
Fletchertown Cumb 97 P9
Fletching E Susx 15 M5
Fleur-de-lis Caerph 27 R3
Flexbury Cnwll 7 K4
Flexford Surrey 32 D12
Flimby Cumb 97 M8
Flimwell E Susx 16 C4
Flint Flints 74 H9
Flint Mountain Flints 74 H9
Flinton E R Yk 87 N8
Flint's Green Solhll 53 P5
Flishinghurst Kent 16 D3
Flitcham Norfk 69 P6
Flitton C Beds 44 F4
Flitwick C Beds 44 F4
Flixborough N Linc 86 G12
Flixborough Stather N Linc 86 F12
Flixton N York 93 L11
Flixton Suffk 59 L3
Flixton Traffd 76 E4
Flockton Kirk 85 K12
Flockton Green Kirk 85 K12
Flodden Nthumb 108 F3
Flodigarry Highld 142 E10
Flood's Ferry Cambs 56 G2
Flookburgh Cumb 89 K11
Flordon Norfk 59 J1
Flore Nhants 54 G8
Flotterton Nthumb 108 G9
Flowers Green E Susx 15 Q8
Flowton Suffk 47 J3
Flushdyke Wakefd 85 L11
Flushing Cnwll 3 K8
Fluxton Devon 9 L5
Flyford Flavell Worcs 52 H9
Fobbing Thurr 34 C5
Fochabers Moray 139 Q4
Fochriw Caerph 27 M2
Fockerby N Linc 86 F11
Foddington Somset 22 D7

Foel Powys 62 D10
Foelgastell Carmth 38 E8
Foel y Dyffryn Brdgnd 27 K3
Foggathorpe E R Yk 86 D7
Fogo Border 116 H11
Fogwatt Moray 139 N4
Foindle Highld 148 E7
Folda Angus 131 M11
Fole Staffs 65 K5
Foleshill Covtry 54 B4
Folke Dorset 22 F10
Folkestone Kent 17 M4
Folkestone Services Kent 17 K3
Folkingham Lincs 67 Q5
Folkington E Susx 15 Q10
Folksworth Cambs 56 C3
Folkton N York 93 L10
Folla Rule Abers 140 H9
Follifoot N York 85 M5
Folly Gate Devon 8 B6
Folly Hill Surrey 25 P4
Fonmon V Glam 27 Q9
Fonthill Bishop Wilts 23 L7
Fonthill Gifford Wilts 23 J7
Fontmell Magna Dorset 23 J10
Fontmell Parva Dorset 23 J10
Fontwell W Susx 14 D9
Font-y-gary V Glam 27 Q9
Foolow Derbys 77 M8
Foots Cray Gt Lon 33 N8
Forbestown Abers 131 G2
Forcett N York 91 K4
Ford Ag & B 120 G12
Ford Bucks 43 Q10
Ford Derbys 78 C7
Ford Devon 5 K6
Ford Devon 18 H8
Ford Gloucs 42 C6
Ford Nthumb 108 F2
Ford Shrops 63 M9
Ford Somset 20 H7
Ford Staffs 77 J11
Ford W Susx 14 E10
Ford Wilts 23 P7
Ford Wilts 29 N7
Forda Devon 5 K6
Fordcombe Kent 15 P3
Fordell Fife 115 L4
Forden Powys 62 H12
Ford End Essex 46 B8
Forder Green Devon 5 N3
Fordham Cambs 57 M6
Fordham Essex 46 G6
Fordham Norfk 69 M12
Fordham Heath Essex 46 G6
Ford Heath Shrops 63 L10
Fordingbridge Hants 23 P10
Fordon E R Yk 93 L11
Fordoun Abers 133 J9
Ford's Green Suffk 58 F7
Fordstreet Essex 46 G6
Ford Street Somset 21 J9
Fordton Devon 8 F5
Fordwells Oxon 42 G9
Fordwich Kent 35 L10
Fordyce Abers 140 E3
Forebridge Staffs 64 H7
Foremark Derbys 65 Q7
Forest Guern 12 b2
Forest N York 91 M6
Forest Becks Lancs 84 B5
Forest Chapel Ches E 76 H9
Forest Gate Gt Lon 33 M5
Forest Green Surrey 14 G2
Forest Hall N Tyne 100 H4
Forest Hill Oxon 43 M10
Forest-in-Teesdale Dur 99 N12
Forest Lane Head N York 85 M4
Forest Mill Clacks 114 H2
Forest of Bowland Lancs 83 P4
Forest of Dean Gloucs 41 K9
Forest Row E Susx 15 M4
Forest Side IoW 12 H7
Forestside W Susx 25 N11
Forest Town Notts 78 F11
Forfar Angus 125 J3
Forgandenny P & K 124 B9
Forge Powys 61 N12
Forge Hammer Torfn 28 C3
Forge Side Torfn 40 C10
Forgie Moray 140 B5
Forgue Abers 140 F7
Forhill Worcs 53 J5
Formby Sefton 75 J2
Forncett End Norfk 58 H2
Forncett St Mary Norfk 58 H2
Forncett St Peter Norfk 58 H2
Fornham All Saints Suffk 57 Q7
Fornham St Martin Suffk 58 C7
Fornham St Genevieve Suffk 58 C7
Fornighty Highld 138 H6
Forres Moray 139 J4
Forsbrook Staffs 64 H4
Forse Highld 151 N9
Forshaw Heath Warwks 53 K6
Forsinard Highld 150 F8
Forss Highld 151 J3
Forston Dorset 10 G5
Fort Augustus Highld 129 L2
Forteviot P & K 123 Q9
Forth S Lans 114 G10
Forthampton Gloucs 41 P5
Fort Hommet Guern 12 b2
Forth Road Bridge C Edin 115 L5
Fortingall P & K 123 J4
Forton Hants 24 H3
Forton Lancs 83 L5
Forton Shrops 63 M9
Forton Somset 9 Q3
Forton Staffs 64 D8
Fort Richmond Guern 12 b2
Fortrie Abers 140 G6
Fortrose Highld 138 D5
Fortuneswell Dorset 10 G9
Fort William Highld 128 F9
Forty Green Bucks 32 C4
Forty Hill Gt Lon 33 L3
Forward Green Suffk 58 G8
Fosbury Wilts 30 G10
Foscot Oxon 42 F7
Foscote Nhants 43 N5
Fosdyke Lincs 68 F5
Fosdyke Bridge Lincs 68 F5
Foss P & K 123 K1
Fossebridge Gloucs 42 C9
Foss-y-ffin Cerdgn 48 G9
Fosterhouses Donc 86 D11
Foster Street Essex 45 N9
Foston Derbys 65 M6
Foston Leics 54 G2
Foston Lincs 67 N3
Foston N York 86 C2
Foston on the Wolds E R Yk 87 L4
Fotherby Lincs 80 H5
Fothergill Cumb 97 L8
Fotheringhay Nhants 55 Q2

Foula Shet 147 h8
Foula Airport Shet 147 h8
Foul Anchor Cambs 69 J8
Foulbridge Cumb 98 E10
Foulby Wakefd 85 L11
Foulden Border 117 L10
Foulden Norfk 69 P12
Foul End Warwks 53 N2
Foul Mile E Susx 16 A8
Foulness Island Essex 34 H4
Foulridge Lancs 84 D7
Foulsham Norfk 70 F7
Fountainhall Border 116 B11
Four Ashes Solhll 53 M6
Four Ashes Staffs 52 E3
Four Ashes Staffs 52 G10
Four Ashes Suffk 58 E6
Four Cabots Guern 12 c2
Four Crosses Powys 63 J8
Four Crosses Staffs 64 H10
Four Elms Kent 15 N1
Four Foot Somset 22 D7
Four Forks Somset 21 K6
Four Gates Bolton 76 D2
Four Gotes Cambs 69 J9
Four Lane End Barns 77 P2
Four Lane Ends Ches W 75 P11
Four Lanes Cnwll 2 H7
Fourlanes End Ches E 76 E11
Four Marks Hants 25 L6
Four Mile Bridge IoA 72 D8
Four Oaks Birm 53 L1
Four Oaks E Susx 16 F6
Four Oaks Gloucs 41 L6
Four Oaks Solhll 53 N4
Fourpenny Highld 146 E9
Four Points W Berk 31 L6
Four Roads Carmth 38 C10
Four Shire Stone Warwks 42 F5
Fourstones Nthumb 99 N5
Four Throws Kent 16 D5
Four Wents Kent 34 A12
Fovant Wilts 23 M7
Foveran Abers 141 N11
Fowey Cnwll 3 K3
Fowley Common Warrtn 76 C4
Fowlhall Kent 16 C2
Fowlis Angus 124 G6
Fowlis Wester P & K 123 N7
Fowlmere Cambs 45 M2
Fownhope Herefs 41 J5
Foxbar Rens 113 N9
Foxcombe Devon 7 P7
Fox Corner Surrey 32 D11
Foxcote Gloucs 42 B8
Foxcote Somset 22 G2
Foxdale IoM 102 c5
Foxearth Essex 46 E3
Foxendown Kent 34 B9
Foxfield Cumb 88 G3
Foxham Wilts 29 N7
Fox Hatch Essex 33 Q3
Foxhills Hants 12 E2
Foxhole Cnwll 3 N3
Foxholes N York 93 K12
Foxhunt Green E Susx 15 P7
Foxley Nhants 54 G10
Foxley Norfk 70 F7
Foxley Wilts 29 P5
Foxlydiate Worcs 53 J7
Fox Street Essex 47 J6
Foxt Staffs 65 J3
Foxton Cambs 56 H11
Foxton Dur 91 N2
Foxton Leics 54 H2
Foxup N York 90 E11
Foxwist Green Ches W 76 B10
Foxwood Shrops 52 B5
Foy Herefs 41 J6
Foyers Highld 137 N3
Foynesfield Highld 138 G5
Fraddam Cnwll 2 F7
Fraddon Cnwll 3 M3
Fradley Staffs 65 L9
Fradswell Staffs 65 J6
Fraisthorpe E R Yk 87 M3
Framfield E Susx 15 P7
Framingham Earl Norfk 71 L11
Framingham Pigot Norfk 71 L11
Framlingham Suffk 59 K8
Frampton Dorset 10 F6
Frampton Lincs 68 F4
Frampton Cotterell S Glos 29 K6
Frampton Mansell Gloucs 41 Q11
Frampton-on-Severn Gloucs 41 M10
Frampton West End Lincs 68 F4
Framsden Suffk 59 J8
Framwellgate Moor Dur 100 H9
Franche Worcs 52 F5
Frandley Ches W 76 B8
Frankaborough Devon 7 M6
Frankby Wirral 74 H6
Frankfort Norfk 71 L7
Franklands Gate Herefs 40 H2
Frankley Worcs 53 J4
Frankley Services Worcs 53 J4
Franksbridge Powys 50 F9
Frankton Warwks 54 C6
Frant E Susx 15 Q4
Fraserburgh Abers 141 N2
Frating Essex 47 J7
Frating Green Essex 47 K7
Fratton C Port 13 J5
Freathy Cnwll 4 F6
Freckenham Suffk 57 M6
Freckleton Lancs 83 K9
Freebirch Derbys 77 P9
Freeby Leics 67 K8
Freefolk Hants 24 H3
Freehay Staffs 65 J4
Freeland Oxon 43 J9
Freethorpe Norfk 71 N11
Freethorpe Common Norfk 71 N11
Freiston Lincs 68 G3
Fremington Devon 19 K7
Fremington N York 90 H7
Frenchay S Glos 29 J7
Frenchbeer Devon 8 E7
French Street Kent 33 N11
Frenich P & K 123 L3
Frensham Surrey 25 P5
Freshfield Sefton 74 H2
Freshford Wilts 29 M10
Freshwater IoW 12 E7
Freshwater Bay IoW 12 E7
Freshwater East Pembks 37 K11
Fressingfield Suffk 59 K5
Freston Suffk 47 K4
Freswick Highld 151 Q3
Fretherne Gloucs 41 L10
Frettenham Norfk 71 K8
Freuchie Fife 124 F11
Freystrop Pembks 37 J8
Friar Park Sandw 53 J2
Friar's Gate E Susx 15 N4
Friar's Hill N York 92 H9
Friar Waddon Dorset 10 G7
Friday Bridge Cambs 69 J11
Friday Street Suffk 59 L8
Friday Street Suffk 59 L10
Friday Street Surrey 14 G2
Fridaythorpe E R Yk 86 G3

Friden Derbys 77 M11
Friendly Calder 84 F10
Friern Barnet Gt Lon 33 K4
Friesthorpe Lincs 79 Q7
Frieston Lincs 67 M3
Frieth Bucks 31 R4
Friezeland Notts 78 D2
Frilford Oxon 31 J3
Frilsham W Berk 31 L8
Frimley Surrey 32 C10
Frimley Green Surrey 32 C10
Frindsbury Medway 34 C8
Fring Norfk 69 P5
Fringford Oxon 43 M6
Frinsted Kent 34 F11
Frinton-on-Sea Essex 47 M8
Friockheim Angus 125 L3
Friog Gwynd 61 K9
Frisby on the Wreake Leics 66 H8
Friskney Lincs 69 J1
Friskney Eaudike Lincs 69 J1
Friston E Susx 15 Q11
Friston Suffk 59 N8
Fritchley Derbys 66 B2
Frith Bank Lincs 68 F3
Frith Common Worcs 52 C7
Fritham Hants 24 C10
Frithelstock Devon 19 J9
Frithelstock Stone Devon 19 J9
Frithsden Herts 44 F9
Frithville Lincs 68 F2
Frittenden Kent 16 E3
Frittiscombe Devon 5 N8
Fritton Norfk 59 J2
Fritton Norfk 71 P12
Fritwell Oxon 43 L6
Frizinghall C Brad 84 H8
Frizington Cumb 88 D3
Frocester Gloucs 41 M11
Frodesley Shrops 63 N12
Frodsham Ches W 75 N8
Frogden Border 108 B4
Frog End Cambs 45 M2
Froggatt Derbys 77 N8
Froghall Staffs 65 J3
Frogham Hants 23 Q10
Frogham Kent 35 N11
Frogmore Devon 5 N8
Frognall Lincs 68 C10
Frogpool Cnwll 3 J6
Frog Pool Worcs 52 E7
Frogwell Cnwll 4 E3
Frolesworth Leics 54 E2
Frome Somset 22 G4
Frome St Quintin Dorset 10 F4
Fromes Hill Herefs 41 K2
Fron Gwynd 60 F5
Fron Gwynd 60 H4
Fron Powys 50 G1
Fron Powys 62 H11
Froncysyllte Wrexhm 63 J4
Fron-goch Gwynd 62 B5
Fron Isaf Wrexhm 63 J4
Frostenden Suffk 59 P4
Frosterley Dur 100 C11
Froxfield C Beds 44 D5
Froxfield Wilts 30 G8
Froxfield Green Hants 25 M8
Fryern Hill Hants 24 H8
Fryerning Essex 34 B2
Fryton N York 92 E11
Fuinary Highld 120 B3
Fulbeck Lincs 67 N2
Fulbourn Cambs 57 K9
Fulbrook Oxon 42 F8
Fulflood Hants 24 H7
Fulford C York 86 B5
Fulford Somset 21 K7
Fulford Staffs 64 H5
Fulham Gt Lon 33 J7
Fulking W Susx 15 J8
Fullaford Devon 19 N6
Fullarton N Ayrs 104 F2
Fuller's End Essex 45 P6
Fuller's Moor Ches W 63 M2
Fuller Street Essex 46 D8
Fuller Street Kent 33 Q11
Fullerton Hants 24 F5
Fulletby Lincs 80 F9
Fullready Warwks 42 G2
Full Sutton E R Yk 86 D4
Fullwood E Ayrs 113 N11
Fulmer Bucks 32 E5
Fulmodeston Norfk 70 E6
Fulnetby Lincs 80 B8
Fulney Lincs 68 E7
Fulstone Kirk 77 M2
Fulstow Lincs 80 G4
Fulwell Oxon 42 H7
Fulwell Sundld 101 K6
Fulwood Lancs 83 M9
Fulwood Notts 78 D12
Fulwood Sheff 77 P7
Fulwood Somset 21 K9
Fundenhall Norfk 58 H1
Funtington W Susx 13 M3
Funtley Hants 13 J3
Funtullich P & K 123 J7
Furley Devon 9 Q3
Furnace Ag & B 112 F1
Furnace Carmth 26 D2
Furnace Cerdgn 49 L12
Furnace End Warwks 53 N2
Furner's Green E Susx 15 M5
Furness Vale Derbys 77 J7
Furneux Pelham Herts 45 M6
Further Quarter Kent 16 F3
Furtho Nhants 43 Q3
Furzehill Devon 19 P4
Furzehill Dorset 11 P4
Furzehills Lincs 80 E9
Furzeley Corner Hants 13 L3
Furze Platt W & M 32 C6
Fyfett Somset 21 K10
Fyfield Essex 45 Q10
Fyfield Hants 24 D4
Fyfield Oxon 31 J3
Fyfield Wilts 30 C8
Fyfield Wilts 30 E10
Fyfield Bavant Wilts 23 M8
Fylingthorpe N York 93 J6
Fyning W Susx 25 P8
Fyvie Abers 141 J8

G

Gabroc Hill E Ayrs 113 N11
Gaddesby Leics 66 H9
Gaddesden Row Herts 44 F8
Gadfa IoA 72 G6
Gadgirth S Ayrs 104 G5
Gadlas Shrops 63 L5
Gaer Powys 40 A7
Gaerllwyd Mons 28 G3
Gaerwen IoA 72 H9
Gagingwell Oxon 43 J6
Gailes N Ayrs 104 F2
Gailey Staffs 64 G10
Gainford Dur 91 K3
Gainsborough Lincs 79 K6
Gainsborough Suffk 47 L3

Gainsford End Essex 46 C4
Gairloch Highld 143 L9
Gairlochy Highld 128 G7
Gairneybridge P & K 115 L2
Gaisgill Cumb 89 Q6
Gaitsgill Cumb 98 E9
Galashiels Border 107 M3
Galgate Lancs 83 L4
Galhampton Somset 22 E7
Gallanachbeg Ag & B 120 F7
Gallanachmore Ag & B 120 F7
Gallantry Bank Ches E 63 N1
Gallatown Fife 115 P2
Galley Common Warwks 53 P2
Galleywood Essex 46 C11
Gallovie Highld 129 P6
Galloway Forest Park 95 N1
Gallowfauld Angus 125 J4
Gallowhill P & K 124 D5
Gallows Green Essex 46 G6
Gallows Green Worcs 52 H8
Gallowstree Common Oxon 31 P6
Galltair Highld 135 P11
Gallt-y-foel Gwynd 73 K11
Gallypot Street E Susx 15 N4
Galmisdale Highld 127 J7
Galmpton Devon 5 L8
Galmpton Torbay 5 Q5
Galphay N York 91 L12
Galston E Ayrs 105 J2
Gamballs Green Staffs 77 J10
Gamblesby Cumb 99 J10
Gambles Green Essex 46 D8
Gamelsby Cumb 97 Q8
Gamesley Derbys 77 J5
Gamlingay Cambs 56 E10
Gamlingay Cinques Cambs 56 E10
Gamlingay Great Heath Cambs 56 D10
Gammersgill N York 90 H10
Gamrie Abers 141 J3
Gamston Notts 66 F5
Gamston Notts 78 H8
Ganarew Herefs 40 H8
Ganavan Bay Ag & B 120 F6
Gang Cnwll 4 D3
Ganllwyd Gwynd 61 M7
Gannachy Angus 132 F10
Ganstead E R Yk 87 L8
Ganthorpe N York 86 C1
Ganton N York 93 K11
Ganwick Corner Herts 33 J2
Gappah Devon 8 G9
Garbity Moray 139 P5
Garboldisham Norfk 58 E4
Garbole Highld 138 D11
Garchory Abers 131 P2
Garden City Flints 75 K10
Gardeners Green Wokham 32 B9
Gardenstown Abers 141 J3
Garden Village Sheff 77 N4
Garderhouse Shet 147 i7
Gardham E R Yk 86 H7
Gare Hill Somset 22 H5
Garelochhead Ag & B 113 J3
Garford Oxon 31 J3
Garforth Leeds 85 N8
Gargrave N York 84 D4
Gargunnock Stirlg 114 C2
Garlic Street Norfk 59 J4
Garlieston D & G 95 N9
Garlinge Kent 35 P8
Garlinge Green Kent 35 K11
Garlogie Abers 133 J3
Garmond Abers 141 K5
Garmouth Moray 139 Q3
Garmston Shrops 63 Q11
Garnant Carmth 38 G9
Garndolbenmaen Gwynd 60 H3
Garnett Bridge Cumb 89 N7
Garnfadryn Gwynd 60 D5
Garnlydan Blae G 39 R9
Garnswllt Swans 38 F9
Garn-yr-erw Torfn 40 B9
Garrabost W Isls 152 h3
Garrallan E Ayrs 105 K6
Garras Cnwll 2 H9
Garreg Gwynd 61 K4
Garrigill Cumb 99 L10
Garriston N York 91 K8
Garroch D & G 96 C2
Garrochtrie D & G 94 G10
Garrochty Ag & B 112 G10
Garros Highld 135 J3
Garsdale Cumb 90 B9
Garsdale Head Cumb 90 C8
Garsdon Wilts 29 Q5
Garshall Green Staffs 64 H5
Garsington Oxon 43 M11
Garstang Lancs 83 L6
Garston Herts 32 G2
Garston Lpool 75 L7
Garswood St Hel 75 P4
Gartachossan Ag & B 110 H9
Gartcosh N Lans 114 C7
Garth Brdgnd 27 K4
Garth Mons 28 D4
Garth Powys 50 C10
Garth Powys 51 J6
Garth Wrexhm 63 J4
Garthamlock C Glas 114 B8
Garthbrengy Powys 39 P5
Gartheli Cerdgn 49 K9
Garthmyl Powys 62 G12
Garthorpe Leics 67 L8
Garthorpe N Linc 86 F11
Garth Row Cumb 89 M7
Garths Cumb 89 N9
Gartly Abers 140 E9
Gartmore Stirlg 113 Q2
Gartness N Lans 114 E8
Gartness Stirlg 113 P4
Gartocharn W Duns 113 N4
Garton E R Yk 87 P8
Garton-on-the-Wolds E R Yk 86 H3
Gartymore Highld 147 J2
Garva Bridge Highld 129 P5
Garvald Border 115 K11
Garvald E Loth 116 D7
Garvan Highld 128 D9
Garvard Ag & B 111 J3
Garve Highld 137 L3
Garvellachs Ag & B 120 C10
Garvestone Norfk 70 F10
Garvock Inver 113 K7
Garway Herefs 40 F7
Garway Common Herefs 40 G7
Garway Hill Herefs 40 F6
Garynahine W Isls 152 f3
Garyvard W Isls 152 g4
Gasper Wilts 22 G7
Gastard Wilts 29 P8
Gasthorpe Norfk 58 E4
Gaston Green Essex 45 P8
Gatcombe IoW 12 H8
Gatebeck Cumb 89 N9
Gate Burton Lincs 79 L7
Gateford Notts 78 F7
Gateforth N York 85 R9
Gatehead E Ayrs 104 G2
Gate Helmsley N York 86 C4
Gatehouse Nthumb 108 C12
Gatehouse of Fleet D & G 96 C7
Gateley Norfk 70 E7
Gatenby N York 91 N9
Gatesgarth Cumb 88 G4
Gateshaw Border 108 C5
Gateshead Gatesd 100 G6
Gates Heath Ches W 75 M11
Gateside Angus 125 J4
Gateside E Rens 113 P9
Gateside Fife 124 D11
Gateside N Ayrs 113 M10
Gateslack D & G 106 A9
Gathurst Wigan 75 P2
Gatley Stockp 76 F6
Gatton Surrey 33 K11
Gattonside Border 107 N3
Gatwick Airport W Susx 15 K3
Gaufron Powys 50 D7
Gaulby Leics 66 H12
Gauldry Fife 124 H8
Gauldswell P & K 124 E3
Gaulkthorn Lancs 83 R10
Gaultree Norfk 69 J10
Gaunton's Bank Ches E 63 P3
Gaunt's Common Dorset 11 N4
Gaunt's End Essex 45 Q6
Gautby Lincs 80 D9
Gavinton Border 116 H11
Gawber Barns 77 Q2
Gawcott Bucks 43 P5
Gawsworth Ches E 76 G9
Gawthorpe Wakefd 85 K11
Gawthrop Cumb 90 A9
Gawthwaite Cumb 88 H9
Gay Bowers Essex 46 D10
Gaydon Warwks 54 B10
Gayhurst M Keyn 44 B2
Gayle N York 90 D9
Gayles N York 91 J5
Gay Street W Susx 14 F7
Gayton Nhants 54 H9
Gayton Norfk 69 N8
Gayton Staffs 64 H6
Gayton Wirral 75 J7
Gayton le Marsh Lincs 80 H7
Gayton Thorpe Norfk 69 P8
Gaywood Norfk 69 M8
Gazeley Suffk 57 N8
Gear Cnwll 2 H9
Gearraidh Bhaird W Isls 152 g4
Gearraidh na h-Aibhne W Isls 152 f3
Geary Highld 134 E3
Gedding Suffk 58 D9
Geddington Nhants 55 M4
Gedling Notts 66 G4
Gedney Lincs 68 H7
Gedney Broadgate Lincs 68 H7
Gedney Drove End Lincs 69 J6
Gedney Dyke Lincs 68 H7
Gedney Hill Lincs 68 F10
Gee Cross Tamesd 76 H5
Geeston Rutlnd 67 N11
Geirinis W Isls 152 c10
Geldeston Norfk 59 M2
Gelli Rhondd 27 M3
Gelli Torfn 28 C4
Gellideg Myr Td 39 N10
Gellifor Denbgs 74 F11
Gelligaer Caerph 27 Q3
Gelligroes Caerph 28 A3
Gelligron Neath 38 H11
Gellilydan Gwynd 61 L4
Gellinudd Neath 38 H11
Gelly Pembks 37 L6
Gellyburn P & K 124 C5
Gellywen Carmth 37 P6
Gelston D & G 96 F7
Gelston Lincs 67 M3
Gembling E R Yk 87 L4
Gentleshaw Staffs 65 K10
Georgefield D & G 107 J11
George Green Bucks 32 E6
Georgeham Devon 19 J5
Georgemas Junction Station Highld 151 L5
George Nympton Devon 19 N8
Georgetown Blae G 39 Q10
Georgia Cnwll 2 D7
Georth Ork 147 c3
Gerinish W Isls 152 c10
Gerlan Gwynd 73 L10
Germansweek Devon 7 N6
Germoe Cnwll 2 F8
Gerrans Cnwll 3 L7
Gerrards Cross Bucks 32 E5
Gerrick R & Cl 92 E4
Gestingthorpe Essex 46 E4
Gethsemane Pembks 37 L2
Geuffordd Powys 62 H9
Gib Hill Ches W 76 B8
Gibraltar Lincs 81 K12
Gibsmere Notts 67 J2
Giddeahall Wilts 29 P7
Giddy Green Dorset 11 K7
Gidea Park Gt Lon 33 P4
Gidleigh Devon 8 C7
Giffnock E Rens 113 Q9
Gifford E Loth 116 C7
Giffordtown Fife 124 F10
Giggleswick N York 84 B2
Gigha Ag & B 111 N11
Gilberdyke E R Yk 86 F9
Gilbert's End Worcs 41 N3
Gilbert Street Hants 25 L7
Gilchriston E Loth 116 C8
Gilcrux Cumb 97 M10
Gildersome Leeds 85 K9
Gildingwells Rothm 78 F6
Gilesgate Moor Dur 100 H9
Gileston V Glam 27 N9
Gilfach Caerph 27 R3
Gilfach Goch Brdgnd 27 M4
Gilfachrheda Cerdgn 48 G9
Gilgarran Cumb 88 D2
Gill Cumb 98 F12
Gillamoor N York 92 D8
Gillan Cnwll 3 J9
Gillen Highld 134 E4
Gillesbie D & G 106 F11
Gilling East N York 92 C11
Gillingham Dorset 22 H8
Gillingham Medway 34 D8
Gillingham Norfk 59 N2
Gilling West N York 91 K6
Gillock Highld 151 M5
Gillow Heath Staffs 76 G12
Gills Highld 151 P2
Gill's Green Kent 16 D4
Gilmanscleuch Border 107 J5
Gilmerton C Edin 115 P8
Gilmerton P & K 123 M8
Gilmonby Dur 90 G4
Gilmorton Leics 54 F3
Gilsland Nthumb 99 J5
Gilson Warwks 53 M3
Gilstead C Brad 84 H7
Gilston Border 116 B10
Gilston Herts 45 N9
Gilston Park Herts 45 M9
Giltbrook Notts 66 D3
Gilwern Mons 40 B9
Gimingham Norfk 71 K5
Ginclough Ches E 76 H8
Gingers Green E Susx 16 A8
Gipping Suffk 58 G8
Gipsey Bridge Lincs 68 F2
Girdle Toll N Ayrs 104 F2
Girlington C Brad 84 H8
Girlsta Shet 147 i7
Girsby N York 91 N5
Girtford C Beds 56 C10
Girthon D & G 96 C7
Girton Cambs 56 H8
Girton Notts 79 K10
Girvan S Ayrs 104 C10
Gisburn Lancs 84 B5
Gisleham Suffk 59 P3
Gislingham Suffk 58 G6
Gissing Norfk 58 H3
Gittisham Devon 9 L5
Givons Grove Surrey 32 H11
Gladestry Powys 50 H9
Gladsmuir E Loth 116 B6
Glais Swans 26 G2
Glaisdale N York 92 F5
Glamis Angus 124 H3
Glanaber Gwynd 61 L2
Glanaman Carmth 38 G9
Glandford Norfk 70 F3
Glan-Duar Carmth 38 D3
Glandwr Pembks 37 N5
Glan-Dwyfach Gwynd 60 H3
Glandy Cross Carmth 37 M5
Glandyfi Cerdgn 49 M1
Glangrwyney Powys 40 C8
Glanllynfi Brdgnd 27 K4
Glanmule Powys 50 G3
Glanrhyd Pembks 37 M2
Glan-rhyd Powys 39 J10
Glanton Nthumb 108 H7
Glanton Pike Nthumb 108 H7
Glanvilles Wootton Dorset 10 G3
Glan-y-don Flints 74 G8
Glan-y-llyn Rhondd 27 Q5
Glan-y-nant Powys 50 C4
Glan-yr-afon Gwynd 62 B4
Glan-yr-afon Gwynd 62 D4
Glan-yr-afon IoA 73 K7
Glan-yr-afon Swans 38 F10
Glan-y-wern Gwynd 61 K5
Glapthorn Nhants 55 P3
Glapwell Derbys 78 D10
Glasbury Powys 40 A4
Glascoed Denbgs 74 D9
Glascoed Mons 40 D11
Glascote Staffs 65 N11
Glascwm Powys 50 G10
Glasfryn Conwy 62 C2
Glasgow C Glas 113 R8
Glasgow Airport Rens 113 P8
Glasgow Prestwick Airport S Ayrs 104 G4
Glasgow Science Centre C Glas 113 Q8
Glasinfryn Gwynd 73 K10
Glasnacardoch Bay Highld 127 M5
Glasnakille Highld 127 K2
Glasphein Highld 134 C6
Glaspwll Powys 49 M1
Glassenbury Kent 16 D3
Glassford S Lans 114 D12
Glasshoughton Wakefd 85 N10
Glasshouse Gloucs 41 L7
Glasshouse Hill Gloucs 41 L7
Glasshouses N York 85 J2
Glasslaw Abers 141 K4
Glasson Cumb 97 Q6
Glassonby Cumb 98 H10
Glasson Dock Lancs 83 K4
Glasterlaw Angus 125 L3
Glaston Rutlnd 67 M12
Glastonbury Somset 22 C6
Glatton Cambs 56 C3
Glazebrook Warrtn 76 C5
Glazebury Warrtn 76 C4
Glazeley Shrops 52 D3
Gleadless Sheff 78 B7
Gleadsmoss Ches E 76 F10
Gleaston Cumb 82 G1
Glebe Highld 137 N12
Gledhow Leeds 85 L8
Gledpark D & G 96 C8
Gledrid Shrops 63 J5
Glemsford Suffk 58 B11
Glen Achulish Highld 121 K1
Glenallachie Moray 139 N7
Glenancross Highld 127 M6
Glenaros House Ag & B 119 P4
Glen Auldyn IoM 102 f3
Glenbarr Ag & B 103 J2
Glenbarry Abers 140 E5
Glenbeg Highld 127 K11
Glenbervie Abers 133 J8
Glenboig N Lans 114 C7
Glenborrodale Highld 127 L12
Glenbranter Ag & B 112 G2
Glenbreck Border 106 D5
Glenbrittle Highld 134 G11
Glenbuck E Ayrs 105 P3
Glencally Angus 131 Q11
Glencaple D & G 97 K4
Glencarse P & K 124 D8
Glencoe Highld 121 L1
Glencothe Border 106 E4
Glencraig Fife 115 M2
Glencrosh D & G 105 P12
Glendale Highld 134 C6
Glendaruel Ag & B 112 E4
Glendevon P & K 123 P12
Glendoe Lodge Highld 129 L2
Glendoick P & K 124 E8
Glenduckie Fife 124 F9
Glenegedale Ag & B 110 H11
Glenelg Highld 135 P12
Glenerney Moray 139 J6
Glenfarg P & K 124 C10
Glenfield Leics 66 E11
Glenfinnan Highld 128 B8
Glenfintaig Lodge Highld 128 H7
Glenfoot P & K 124 D9
Glenfyne Lodge Ag & B 121 N9
Glengarnock N Ayrs 113 L10
Glengolly Highld 151 K3
Glengorm Castle Ag & B 119 M1
Glengrasco Highld 134 H7
Glenholm Border 106 E3
Glenhoul D & G 105 L12
Glenkin Ag & B 112 H5
Glenkindie Abers 132 C2
Glenlivet Moray 139 M10
Glenlochar D & G 96 E5
Glenlomond P & K 124 D12
Glenluce D & G 94 H7
Glenmassen Ag & B 112 G4
Glenmavis N Lans 114 D8
Glen Maye IoM 102 c5
Glen Mona IoM 102 f4
Glenmore Highld 134 H8
Glenmore Lodge Highld 130 H2
Glen Nevis House Highld 128 G10
Glenochil Clacks 114 F2
Glen Parva Leics 66 F12
Glenquiech Angus 132 C12
Glenralloch Ag & B 112 C7
Glenridding Cumb 89 K3
Glenrothes Fife 115 N1
Glenshero Lodge Highld 129 P6
Glenstriven Ag & B 112 G5
Glentham Lincs 79 P6
Glentrool D & G 95 L3
Glen Trool Lodge D & G 95 M2
Glentruim Highld 130 C5
Glentworth Lincs 79 N6
Glenuig Highld 127 M9
Glenvarragill Highld 134 H8
Glen Vine IoM 102 d5
Glenwhilly D & G 94 H4
Glespin S Lans 105 Q4
Glewstone Herefs 40 H7
Glinton C Pete 68 C11
Glooston Leics 55 J2
Glossop Derbys 77 J5
Gloster Hill Nthumb 109 L9
Gloucester Gloucs 41 N8
Gloucester Services Gloucs 41 N9
Gloucestershire Airport Gloucs 41 P7
Glusburn N York 84 F6
Glutt Lodge Highld 150 H9
Gluvian Cnwll 3 M2
Glympton Oxon 43 J7
Glynarthen Cerdgn 48 E11
Glyn Ceiriog Wrexhm 62 H4
Glyncoch Rhondd 27 P4
Glyncorrwg Neath 27 L3
Glynde E Susx 15 N9
Glyndebourne E Susx 15 N8
Glyndyfrdwy Denbgs 62 G4
Glynneath Neath 39 L10
Glynogwr Brdgnd 27 M5
Glyntaff Rhondd 27 P5
Glyntawe Powys 39 K8
Glynteg Carmth 38 A4
Gnosall Staffs 64 F8
Gnosall Heath Staffs 64 F8
Goadby Leics 67 J12
Goadby Marwood Leics 67 K7
Goatacre Wilts 30 B7
Goatham Green E Susx 16 E7
Goathill Dorset 22 F10
Goathland N York 92 G6
Goathurst Somset 21 L6
Goathurst Common Kent 33 P12
Goat Lees Kent 17 J1
Gobowen Shrops 63 J5
Godalming Surrey 14 D2
Goddard's Corner Suffk 59 K7
Goddard's Green Kent 16 E4
Goddards Green W Susx 15 K7
Godden Green Kent 33 Q11
Godford Cross Devon 9 L4
Godington Oxon 43 N6
Godley Tamesd 76 H5
Godmanchester Cambs 56 E6
Godmanstone Dorset 10 G5
Godmersham Kent 35 J12
Godney Somset 22 B5
Godolphin Cross Cnwll 2 F8
Godre'r-graig Neath 38 H10
Godshill Hants 24 B10
Godshill IoW 13 J8
Godstone Staffs 65 J5
Godstone Surrey 33 L12
Godsworthy Devon 7 P9
Godwinscroft Hants 12 C5
Goetre Mons 40 D10
Goff's Oak Herts 45 L11
Gogar C Edin 115 L7
Goginan Cerdgn 49 M4
Golan Gwynd 61 J4
Golant Cnwll 3 R4
Golberdon Cnwll 7 L10
Golborne Wigan 75 Q4
Golcar Kirk 84 G12
Goldcliff Newpt 28 E6
Golden Cross E Susx 15 P8
Golden Green Kent 16 B1
Golden Grove Carmth 38 E8
Goldenhill C Stke 64 F2
Golden Hill Pembks 37 J10
Golden Pot Hants 25 M5
Golden Valley Derbys 66 C2
Golders Green Gt Lon 33 J5
Goldfinch Bottom W Berk 31 L9
Goldhanger Essex 46 F10
Gold Hill Cambs 57 K2
Gold Hill Dorset 23 J10
Golding Shrops 63 P11
Goldington Bed 55 Q10
Goldsborough N York 85 M4
Goldsborough N York 92 G4
Golds Green Sandw 53 J2
Goldsithney Cnwll 2 E8
Goldstone Kent 35 N10
Goldstone Shrops 64 D6
Goldthorpe Barns 78 D3
Goldworthy Devon 18 G9
Golford Kent 16 D3
Golford Green Kent 16 D3
Gollanfield Highld 138 E5
Gollinglith Foot N York 91 K10
Golly Wrexhm 75 K12
Golsoncott Somset 20 G5
Golspie Highld 146 E5
Gomeldon Wilts 24 C6
Gomersal Kirk 85 J10
Gomshall Surrey 14 F1
Gonalston Notts 66 H3
Gonerby Hill Foot Lincs 67 M5
Gonerby Moor Lincs 67 M4
Gonfirth Shet 147 i6
Goodameavy Devon 4 H4
Good Easter Essex 46 A9
Gooderstone Norfk 69 P11
Goodleigh Devon 19 L6
Goodmanham E R Yk 86 G6
Goodmayes Gt Lon 33 N5
Goodnestone Kent 35 J10
Goodnestone Kent 35 N11
Goodrich Herefs 40 H8
Goodrington Torbay 5 Q5
Goodshaw Lancs 84 B10
Goodshaw Fold Lancs 84 B10
Goodstone Devon 8 E10
Goodwick Pembks 37 J3
Goodworth Clatford Hants 24 F5
Goodyers End Warwks 53 Q3
Goole E R Yk 86 D10
Goole Fields E R Yk 86 E11
Goom's Hill Worcs 53 J9
Goonbell Cnwll 2 H4
Goonhavern Cnwll 3 K4
Goonvrea Cnwll 2 H4
Goosecruives Abers 133 J7
Gooseford Devon 8 C6
Goose Green Essex 47 L6
Goose Green Kent 16 E3
Goose Green Kent 34 B12
Goose Green S Glos 29 K7
Goose Green W Susx 14 G7
Goose Green Wigan 75 P3
Gooseham Cnwll 18 E10
Gooseham Mill Cnwll 18 E10
Goosehill Green Worcs 52 H8
Goose Pool Herefs 40 G4
Goosey Oxon 31 J4
Goosnargh Lancs 83 M8
Goostrey Ches E 76 E9
Gordano Services N Som 28 G7
Gorddinog Conwy 73 L9
Gordon Border 107 Q1
Gordon Arms Hotel Border 107 J5
Gordonstown Abers 140 E5
Gordonstown Abers 140 H8
Gore Powys 51 J9
Gorebridge Mdloth 115 Q9
Gorefield Cambs 68 H9
Gore Pit Essex 46 F8
Gores Wilts 30 C10
Gore Street Kent 35 N9
Gorey Jersey 13 d2
Goring Oxon 31 M6
Goring-by-Sea W Susx 14 G10
Goring Heath Oxon 31 N6
Gorleston-on-Sea Norfk 71 Q11
Gorrachie Abers 140 H4
Gorran Churchtown Cnwll 3 N6
Gorran Haven Cnwll 3 P6
Gorran High Lanes Cnwll 3 N6
Gorrig Cerdgn 38 B3
Gors Cerdgn 49 K5
Gorsedd Flints 74 G8
Gorseddau Slate Landscape Gwynd 61 J3
Gorse Hill Swindn 30 D5
Gorseinon Swans 26 F3
Gorseybank Derbys 65 P2
Gorsgoch Cerdgn 48 H10
Gorslas Carmth 38 E9
Gorsley Gloucs 41 K6
Gorsley Common Herefs 41 K6
Gorstage Ches W 75 Q9
Gorstan Highld 137 L3
Gorstella Ches W 75 K11
Gorsten Ag & B 120 D6
Gorst Hill Worcs 52 D6
Gorsty Hill Staffs 65 L6
Gorthleck Highld 137 P11
Gorton Manch 76 G4
Gosbeck Suffk 58 H9
Gosberton Lincs 68 E6
Gosberton Clough Lincs 68 D6
Gosfield Essex 46 D6
Gosford Devon 9 L5
Gosford Oxon 43 K9
Gosforth Cumb 88 E6
Gosforth N u Ty 100 G4
Gosling Street Somset 22 C7
Gosmore Herts 44 H6
Gospel End Staffs 52 G2
Gospel Green W Susx 14 D4
Gosport Hants 13 K5
Gossard's Green C Beds 44 D3
Gossington Gloucs 41 L11
Goswick Nthumb 117 N12
Gotham Notts 66 E6
Gotherington Gloucs 41 Q6
Gotton Somset 21 L7
Goudhurst Kent 16 C3
Goulceby Lincs 80 E8
Gourdas Abers 141 J7
Gourdie C Dund 124 G6
Gourdon Abers 133 K10
Gourock Inver 113 K6
Govan C Glas 113 Q8
Goveton Devon 5 M7
Govilon Mons 40 C9
Gowdall E R Yk 86 B10
Gower Highld 137 N4
Gower Swans 26 D4
Gowerton Swans 26 E3
Gowkhall Fife 115 J3
Gowthorpe E R Yk 86 E4
Goxhill E R Yk 87 M6
Goxhill N Linc 87 L11
Goytre Neath 27 J4
Grabhair W Isls 152 g4
Graby Lincs 68 B6
Grade Cnwll 2 H11
Gradeley Green Ches E 63 Q2
Graffham W Susx 14 C7
Grafham Cambs 56 C7
Grafham Surrey 14 E2
Grafton Herefs 40 G4
Grafton N York 85 N3
Grafton Oxon 30 G2
Grafton Shrops 63 M8
Grafton Worcs 42 A4
Grafton Worcs 51 P8
Grafton Flyford Worcs 52 H9
Grafton Regis Nhants 43 Q2
Grafton Underwood Nhants 55 N5
Grafty Green Kent 16 F1
Graianrhyd Denbgs 74 H12
Graig Conwy 73 P9
Graig Denbgs 74 F9
Graigfechan Denbgs 62 G1
Grain Medway 34 F7
Grains Bar Oldham 76 H3
Grainsby Lincs 80 E4
Grainthorpe Lincs 80 G4
Grampound Cnwll 3 M5
Grampound Road Cnwll 3 M4
Gramsdal W Isls 152 c9
Gramsdale W Isls 152 c9
Granborough Bucks 43 Q6
Granby Notts 67 J5
Grandborough Warwks 54 E7
Grand Chemins Jersey 13 c2
Grandes Rocques Guern 12 c1
Grandtully P & K 123 M2
Grange Cumb 88 H3
Grange Medway 34 D8
Grange P & K 124 F8
Grange Wirral 74 H6
Grange Crossroads Moray 140 D5
Grange Hall Moray 139 K4
Grangehall S Lans 106 C1
Grange Hill Essex 33 N3
Grangemill Derbys 77 N12
Grange Moor Kirk 85 J12
Grangemouth Falk 114 G5
Grange of Lindores Fife 124 E9
Grange-over-Sands Cumb 89 L11
Grangepans Falk 115 J5
Grange Park Nhants 55 J9
Grangetown R & Cl 92 B3
Grangetown Sundld 101 K7
Grange Villa Dur 100 G8
Gransmoor E R Yk 87 L4
Gransmore Green Essex 46 C7
Granston Pembks 36 H4
Grantchester Cambs 56 H9
Grantham Lincs 67 M5
Granton C Edin 115 N6
Grantown-on-Spey Highld 139 J10
Grantsfield Herefs 51 N8
Grantshouse Border 116 H8
Grappenhall Warrtn 76 B6
Grasby Lincs 79 Q3
Grasmere Cumb 89 K5
Grasscroft Oldham 76 H3
Grassendale Lpool 75 L6
Grassgarth Cumb 98 D9
Grass Green Essex 46 C4
Grassington N York 84 F2
Grassmoor Derbys 78 C10
Grassthorpe Notts 79 K10
Grateley Hants 24 D4
Gratwich Staffs 65 J6
Graveley Cambs 56 E8
Graveley Herts 45 J6
Gravelly Hill Birm 53 L2
Gravelsbank Shrops 63 K12
Graveney Kent 35 J9
Gravesend Kent 34 B7
Gravir W Isls 152 g4
Grayingham Lincs 79 M4
Grayrigg Cumb 89 P7
Grays Thurr 34 A7
Grayshott Hants 14 C4
Grayson Green Cumb 88 D2
Grayswood Surrey 14 C4
Graythorpe Hartpl 92 B1
Grazeley Wokham 31 P9
Greasbrough Rothm 78 C4
Greasby Wirral 75 J6
Greasley Notts 66 D3
Great Abington Cambs 57 K11
Great Addington Nhants 55 N5
Great Alne Warwks 53 L8
Great Altcar Lancs 75 K2
Great Amwell Herts 45 L9
Great Asby Cumb 89 R4
Great Ashfield Suffk 58 E7
Great Ayton N York 92 B4
Great Baddow Essex 46 C10
Great Badminton S Glos 29 N6
Great Bardfield Essex 46 B5
Great Barford Bed 56 C10
Great Barr Sandw 53 K2
Great Barrington Gloucs 42 E9
Great Barrow Ches W 75 M10
Great Barton Suffk 58 C7
Great Barugh N York 92 F11
Great Bavington Nthumb 100 C2
Great Bealings Suffk 59 J11
Great Bedwyn Wilts 30 F9
Great Bentley Essex 47 K7
Great Billing Nhants 55 K8
Great Bircham Norfk 69 P6
Great Blakenham Suffk 58 G10
Great Blencow Cumb 98 F11
Great Bolas Wrekin 64 B8
Great Bookham Surrey 32 G11
Great Bosullow Cnwll 2 C8
Great Bourton Oxon 43 K3
Great Bowden Leics 55 J3
Great Bradley Suffk 57 N10
Great Braxted Essex 46 F9
Great Bricett Suffk 58 F10
Great Brickhill Bucks 44 C5
Great Bridgeford Staffs 64 G7
Great Brington Nhants 54 H7
Great Bromley Essex 47 K6
Great Broughton Cumb 97 L12
Great Broughton N York 92 B5
Great Budworth Ches W 76 C8
Great Burdon Darltn 91 N3
Great Burstead Essex 34 B4
Great Busby N York 92 B5
Great Canfield Essex 45 Q8
Great Carlton Lincs 80 H6
Great Casterton Rutlnd 67 P10
Great Chalfield Wilts 29 P9
Great Chart Kent 16 H2
Great Chatwell Staffs 64 E9
Great Chell C Stke 64 F2
Great Chesterford Essex 45 P3
Great Cheverell Wilts 23 L2
Great Chishill Cambs 45 M4
Great Clacton Essex 47 L8
Great Cliff Wakefd 85 L12
Great Clifton Cumb 97 L12
Great Coates NE Lin 80 E2
Great Comberton Worcs 41 Q3
Great Comp Kent 34 A11
Great Corby Cumb 98 F7
Great Cornard Suffk 46 F4
Great Cowden E R Yk 87 N7
Great Coxwell Oxon 30 F4
Great Cransley Nhants 55 L5
Great Cressingham Norfk 70 C11
Great Crosthwaite Cumb 88 H2
Great Cubley Derbys 65 M4
Great Cumbrae Island N Ayrs 112 H10
Great Dalby Leics 67 J9
Great Denham Bed 55 P11
Great Doddington Nhants 55 M7
Great Doward Herefs 40 H8
Great Dunham Norfk 70 C9
Great Dunmow Essex 46 A7
Great Durnford Wilts 23 P6
Great Easton Essex 45 R6
Great Easton Leics 55 L2
Great Eccleston Lancs 83 K7
Great Edstone N York 92 E10
Great Ellingham Norfk 58 F1
Great Elm Somset 22 G3
Great Everdon Nhants 54 F9
Great Eversden Cambs 56 G10
Great Fencote N York 91 M8
Greatfield Wilts 30 C5
Great Finborough Suffk 58 F9
Greatford Lincs 68 B10
Great Fransham Norfk 70 C9
Great Gaddesden Herts 44 E9
Greatgate Staffs 65 K4
Great Gidding Cambs 56 C4
Great Givendale E R Yk 86 E4
Great Glemham Suffk 59 L8
Great Glen Leics 54 G1
Great Gonerby Lincs 67 M4
Great Gransden Cambs 56 E9
Great Green Cambs 45 K3
Great Green Norfk 59 K3
Great Green Suffk 58 D7
Great Green Suffk 58 D9
Great Habton N York 92 F11
Great Hale Lincs 68 C4
Great Hallingbury Essex 45 P8
Greatham Hants 25 N7
Greatham Hartpl 91 R1
Greatham W Susx 14 F7
Great Hampden Bucks 32 B2
Great Harrowden Nhants 55 L6
Great Harwood Lancs 83 Q8
Great Haseley Oxon 43 N11
Great Hatfield E R Yk 87 M6
Great Haywood Staffs 65 J7
Great Heck N York 86 B11
Great Henny Essex 46 F4
Great Hinton Wilts 29 P10
Great Hockham Norfk 58 D2
Great Holland Essex 47 M8
Great Hollands Br For 32 B9
Great Horkesley Essex 46 H5
Great Hormead Herts 45 M6
Great Horton C Brad 84 H9
Great Horwood Bucks 43 Q5
Great Houghton Barns 78 C2
Great Houghton Nhants 55 K9
Great Hucklow Derbys 77 M8
Great Kelk E R Yk 87 L3
Great Kimble Bucks 44 B10
Great Kingshill Bucks 32 C3
Great Langdale Cumb 89 J5
Great Langton N York 91 M7
Great Leighs Essex 46 C8
Great Limber Lincs 80 C2
Great Linford M Keyn 44 B3
Great Livermere Suffk 58 C6
Great Longstone Derbys 77 M9
Great Lumley Dur 100 H8
Great Lyth Shrops 63 M10
Great Malvern Worcs 41 M3
Great Maplestead Essex 46 E5
Great Marton Bpool 82 H8
Great Massingham Norfk 69 Q7
Great Melton Norfk 70 H10
Great Meols Wirral 74 H5
Great Milton Oxon 43 N11
Great Missenden Bucks 32 C2
Great Mitton Lancs 83 Q7
Great Mongeham Kent 35 P12
Great Moulton Norfk 58 H3
Great Munden Herts 45 L7
Great Musgrave Cumb 90 C4
Great Ness Shrops 63 L8
Great Notley Essex 46 D7
Great Oak Mons 40 E9
Great Oakley Essex 47 L6
Great Oakley Nhants 55 L3
Great Offley Herts 44 G6
Great Ormside Cumb 90 B3
Great Orton Cumb 98 D7
Great Ouseburn N York 85 P3
Great Oxendon Nhants 55 J4
Great Oxney Green Essex 46 B10
Great Palgrave Norfk 70 B9
Great Park N u Ty 100 G4
Great Parndon Essex 45 N10
Great Pattenden Kent 16 C2
Great Paxton Cambs 56 D8
Great Plumpton Lancs 83 J8
Great Plumstead Norfk 71 L10
Great Ponton Lincs 67 M6
Great Potheridge Devon 19 K10
Great Preston Leeds 85 N9
Great Purston Nhants 43 L4
Great Raveley Cambs 56 E4
Great Rissington Gloucs 42 E8
Great Rollright Oxon 42 G5
Great Ryburgh Norfk 70 E7
Great Ryle Nthumb 108 G7
Great Ryton Shrops 63 N11
Great Saling Essex 46 C6
Great Salkeld Cumb 98 G11
Great Sampford Essex 46 B4
Great Saredon Staffs 64 H10
Great Saughall Ches W 75 K9
Great Saxham Suffk 57 Q8
Great Shefford W Berk 30 H7
Great Shelford Cambs 57 J10
Great Smeaton N York 91 N6
Great Snoring Norfk 70 D5
Great Somerford Wilts 29 Q6
Great Soudley Shrops 64 D6
Great Stainton Darltn 91 N2
Great Stambridge Essex 34 F4
Great Staughton Cambs 56 C7
Great Steeping Lincs 80 H10
Great Stonar Kent 35 P10
Greatstone-on-Sea Kent 17 K6
Great Strickland Cumb 89 P2
Great Stukeley Cambs 56 E6
Great Sturton Lincs 80 D8
Great Sutton Ches W 75 L8
Great Sutton Shrops 51 N4
Great Swinburne Nthumb 99 P3
Great Tew Oxon 43 J6
Great Tey Essex 46 F6
Great Thurlow Suffk 57 N10
Great Torrington Devon 19 J9
Great Tosson Nthumb 108 G9
Great Totham Essex 46 F9
Great Totham Essex 46 F9
Great Tows Lincs 80 E5
Great Urswick Cumb 88 H11
Great Wakering Essex 34 G5
Great Waldingfield Suffk 46 F3
Great Walsingham Norfk 70 D5
Great Waltham Essex 46 C9
Great Warford Ches E 76 E8
Great Warley Essex 33 Q4
Great Washbourne Gloucs 42 A5
Great Weeke Devon 8 D7
Great Welnetham Suffk 58 C9
Great Wenham Suffk 47 J4
Great Whittington Nthumb 100 C4
Great Wigborough Essex 46 G8
Great Wilbraham Cambs 57 K9
Great Wilne Derbys 66 D6
Great Wishford Wilts 23 N6
Great Witchingham Norfk 70 G8
Great Witcombe Gloucs 41 Q8
Great Witley Worcs 52 D7
Great Wolford Warwks 42 F5
Greatworth Nhants 43 L3
Great Wratting Suffk 57 N11
Great Wymondley Herts 45 J6
Great Wyrley Staffs 65 J10
Great Wytheford Shrops 63 P8
Great Yarmouth Norfk 71 Q10
Great Yeldham Essex 46 D4
Grebby Lincs 80 H10
Greeba IoM 102 d5
Green Denbgs 74 E10
Green Bank Cumb 89 K10
Greenbottom Cnwll 3 J5
Greenburn W Loth 114 G9
Greencroft Hall Dur 100 F8
Green Cross Surrey 14 B3
Green Down Somset 22 D3
Green End Bed 55 P11
Green End Bed 55 Q7
Green End Bed 56 B8
Green End Bed 56 C10
Green End Cambs 56 C4
Green End Cambs 56 E6
Green End Cambs 56 G9
Green End Cambs 57 J7
Green End Cambs 57 J8
Green End Herts 45 J5
Green End Herts 45 L5
Green End Herts 45 L7
Greenend Oxon 42 G7
Green End Warwks 53 N3
Greenfield Ag & B 113 K3
Greenfield C Beds 44 F5
Greenfield Flints 74 H8
Greenfield Highld 128 H4
Greenfield Oldham 77 J3
Greenfield Oxon 31 P4
Greenford Gt Lon 32 G6
Greengairs N Lans 114 E7
Greengates C Brad 85 J8
Greengill Cumb 97 M10
Greenhalgh Lancs 83 J8
Greenham Somset 20 H9
Greenham W Berk 31 K9
Green Hammerton N York 85 P4
Greenhaugh Nthumb 108 C12
Green Head Cumb 98 D8
Greenhead Nthumb 99 J5
Green Heath Staffs 65 J9
Greenheys Salfd 76 D3
Greenhill D & G 97 M2
Greenhill Falk 114 E5
Greenhill Herefs 52 D11
Greenhill Kent 35 L9
Greenhill Leics 66 D9
Greenhill S Lans 106 B3
Green Hill Wilts 30 C5
Greenhillocks Derbys 66 C2
Greenhills S Lans 114 B10
Greenhithe Kent 33 Q7
Greenholm E Ayrs 105 K2
Greenholme Cumb 89 P5
Greenhouse Border 107 N5
Greenhow Hill N York 84 H2
Greenland Highld 151 N3
Greenland Sheff 78 C6
Greenlands Bucks 31 Q5
Green Lane Devon 8 E9
Green Lane Worcs 53 K7
Greenlaw Border 116 G12
Greenlea D & G 97 L3

Thornhill – Twickenham 189

Thornhill D & G 105 R10
Thornhill Derbys 77 M7
Thornhill Kirk 85 K11
Thornhill Stirlg 114 B1
Thornhill Lees Kirk 85 K11
Thornhills Calder 84 H10
Thornholme E R Yk 87 L2
Thornicombe Dorset 11 L4
Thornington Nthumb 108 E3
Thornley Dur 100 E10
Thornley Dur 101 J10
Thornley Gate Nthumb 99 M7
Thornliebank E Rens 113 Q9
Thorns Suffk 57 P9
Thornsett Derbys 77 J6
Thorns Green Ches E 76 E7
Thornthwaite Cumb 88 H2
Thornthwaite N York 85 J3
Thornton Angus 124 H3
Thornton Bucks 43 Q4
Thornton C Brad 84 G8
Thornton E R Yk 86 E6
Thornton Fife 115 P2
Thornton Lancs 82 H7
Thornton Leics 66 D10
Thornton Lincs 80 E10
Thornton Middsb 91 Q4
Thornton Nthumb 117 L11
Thornton Pembks 36 H9
Thornton Sefton 75 K3
Thornton Curtis N Linc 87 K11
Thorntonhall S Lans 113 R10
Thornton Heath Gt Lon 33 K8
Thornton Hough Wirral 75 J7
Thornton-in-Craven N York 84 D5
Thornton in Lonsdale N York 89 R12
Thornton-le-Beans N York 91 P8
Thornton-le-Clay N York 86 C2
Thornton-le-Dale N York 92 G10
Thornton le Moor Lincs 79 P4
Thornton-le-Moor N York 91 P9
Thornton-le-Moors Ches W 75 M9
Thornton-le-Street N York 91 P9
Thorntonloch E Loth 116 G6
Thornton Rust N York 90 F9
Thornton Steward N York 91 K9
Thornton Watlass N York 91 L9
Thornwood Common Essex 45 N10
Thornydykes Border 116 E11
Thornythwaite Cumb 89 L2
Thoroton Notts 67 J4
Thorp Arch Leeds 85 N6
Thorpe Derbys 65 M2
Thorpe E R Yk 87 J6
Thorpe Lincs 81 J7
Thorpe N York 84 F3
Thorpe Norfk 59 N1
Thorpe Notts 67 J2
Thorpe Surrey 32 E8
Thorpe Abbotts Norfk 59 J5
Thorpe Acre Leics 66 E8
Thorpe Arnold Leics 67 K8
Thorpe Audlin Wakefd 85 P12
Thorpe Bassett N York 92 H12
Thorpe Bay Sthend 34 G5
Thorpe by Water Rutlnd 55 M1
Thorpe Common Rothm 78 C5
Thorpe Constantine Staffs 65 N10
Thorpe End Norfk 71 K10
Thorpe Green Essex 47 L7
Thorpe Green Lancs 83 N10
Thorpe Green Suffk 58 D9
Thorpe Hesley Rothm 78 B4
Thorpe in Balne Donc 78 F2
Thorpe Langton Leics 55 J2
Thorpe Larches Dur 91 P2
Thorpe Lea Surrey 32 E8
Thorpe le Fallows Lincs 79 M7
Thorpe-le-Soken Essex 47 L7
Thorpe le Street E R Yk 86 F6
Thorpe Malsor Nhants 55 L5
Thorpe Mandeville Nhants 43 L3
Thorpe Market Norfk 71 K5
Thorpe Marriot Norfk 70 H9
Thorpe Morieux Suffk 58 D10
Thorpeness Suffk 59 P8
Thorpe on the Hill Leeds 85 L10
Thorpe on the Hill Lincs 79 M10
Thorpe Park Surrey 32 E8
Thorpe St Andrew Norfk 71 K10
Thorpe St Peter Lincs 81 J11
Thorpe Salvin Rothm 78 E7
Thorpe Satchville Leics 67 J10
Thorpe Thewles S on T 91 P2
Thorpe Tilney Lincs 80 C12
Thorpe Underwood N York 85 P3
Thorpe Underwood Nhants 55 K4
Thorpe Waterville Nhants 55 P4
Thorpe Willoughby N York 86 A9
Thorpland Norfk 69 M10
Thorrington Essex 47 K7
Thorverton Devon 8 H4
Thrales End C Beds 44 G8
Thrandeston Suffk 58 G5
Thrapston Nhants 55 P5
Threapland Cumb 97 N10
Threapland N York 84 E3
Threapwood Ches W 63 M3
Threapwood Staffs 65 J4
Threapwood Head Staffs 65 J4
Threave S Ayrs 104 F8
Three Ashes Herefs 40 G7
Three Bridges W Susx 15 K3
Three Burrows Cnwll 3 J5
Three Chimneys Kent 16 E3
Three Cocks Powys 40 A4
Three Crosses Swans 26 E9
Three Cups Corner E Susx 16 B7
Three Gates Worcs 52 C8
Threehammer Common Norfk 71 L8
Three Hammers Cnwll 7 J7
Three Holes Norfk 69 K12
Threekingham Lincs 68 B5
Three Leg Cross E Susx 16 B4
Three Legged Cross Dorset 11 Q4
Three Mile Cross Wokham 31 P9
Threemilestone Cnwll 3 J5
Threemiletown W Loth 115 K6
Three Oaks E Susx 16 E8
Threlkeld Cumb 89 J2
Threshers Bush Essex 45 P10
Threshfield N York 84 E2
Thrigby Norfk 71 P9
Thringarth Dur 90 F2
Thringstone Leics 66 C8
Thrintoft N York 91 N8
Thriplow Cambs 45 N2
Throapham Rothm 78 E6
Throckenhalt Lincs 68 G10
Throcking Herts 45 L5
Throckley N u Ty 100 F5
Throckmorton Worcs 52 H10
Throop BCP 11 Q6
Throop Dorset 11 K6
Throphill Nthumb 100 E1
Thropton Nthumb 108 G9
Throsk Stirlg 114 F3
Througham Gloucs 41 Q10
Throughgate D & G 96 H1
Throwleigh Devon 8 C6
Throwley Kent 34 H11
Throwley Forstal Kent 34 H11
Thrumpton Notts 66 E6
Thrumpton Notts 78 H7
Thrumster Highld 151 P7
Thrunscoe NE Lin 80 F2
Thrunton Nthumb 108 H7
Thrup Oxon 30 G3
Thrupp Gloucs 41 P11
Thrupp Oxon 43 K8
Thrushelton Devon 7 N7
Thrussington Leics 66 G9
Thruxton Hants 24 D4
Thruxton Herefs 40 F5
Thrybergh Rothm 78 D5
Thulston Derbys 66 C6
Thundersley Essex 34 D5
Thurcaston Leics 66 F10
Thurcroft Rothm 78 E6
Thurdon Cnwll 7 K3
Thurgarton Norfk 71 J5
Thurgarton Notts 66 H2
Thurgoland Barns 77 P3
Thurlaston Leics 66 E12
Thurlaston Warwks 54 D6
Thurlbear Somset 21 L9
Thurlby Lincs 68 B9
Thurlby Lincs 79 M11
Thurlby Lincs 81 J8
Thurleigh Bed 55 Q9
Thurlestone Devon 5 L8
Thurloxton Somset 21 L7
Thurlstone Barns 77 N3
Thurlton Norfk 59 N1
Thurlwood Ches E 76 E12
Thurmaston Leics 66 G10
Thurnby Leics 66 G11
Thurne Norfk 71 M9
Thurnham Kent 34 E10
Thurning Nhants 56 B4
Thurning Norfk 70 G6
Thurnscoe Barns 78 D3
Thurrock Services Thurr 33 Q6
Thursby Cumb 98 C8
Thursden Lancs 84 D8
Thursford Norfk 70 E5
Thursley Surrey 14 C3
Thurso Highld 151 K3
Thurstaston Wirral 74 H7
Thurston Suffk 58 D7
Thurston Clough Oldham 76 H2
Thurstonfield Cumb 98 C7
Thurstonland Kirk 77 M2
Thurston Planche Suffk 58 D8
Thurton Norfk 71 L12
Thurvaston Derbys 65 N5
Thuxton Norfk 70 F10
Thwaite N York 90 E7
Thwaite Suffk 58 G7
Thwaite Head Cumb 89 K8
Thwaites C Brad 84 G7
Thwaite St Mary Norfk 59 L2
Thwaites Brow C Brad 84 G7
Thwing E R Yk 87 K1
Tibbermore P & K 123 Q8
Tibbers D & G 105 Q10
Tibberton Gloucs 41 M7
Tibberton Worcs 52 G9
Tibberton Wrekin 64 C8
Tibenham Norfk 58 H3
Tibshelf Derbys 78 D11
Tibshelf Services Derbys 78 D11
Tibthorpe E R Yk 86 H4
Ticehurst E Susx 16 C5
Tichborne Hants 25 J7
Tickencote Rutlnd 67 N10
Tickenham N Som 28 F8
Tickford End M Keyn 44 C3
Tickhill Donc 78 F5
Ticklerton Shrops 51 N2
Ticknall Derbys 66 B7
Tickton E R Yk 87 K7
Tidbury Green Solhll 53 L5
Tidcombe Wilts 30 G10
Tiddington Oxon 43 N10
Tiddington Warwks 53 N9
Tiddleywink Wilts 29 P7
Tidebrook E Susx 15 R5
Tideford Cnwll 4 E5
Tideford Cross Cnwll 4 E4
Tidenham Gloucs 28 H3
Tideswell Derbys 77 M8
Tidmarsh W Berk 31 N7
Tidmington Warwks 42 F4
Tidpit Hants 23 N9
Tidworth Wilts 24 D4
Tiers Cross Pembks 36 H8
Tiffield Nhants 54 H10
Tigerton Angus 132 E11
Tigh a' Ghearraidh W Isls 152 b8
Tigharry W Isls 152 b8
Tighnabruaich Ag & B 112 E7
Tigley Devon 5 M4
Tilbrook Cambs 55 Q7
Tilbury Thurr 34 B7
Tilbury Dock Thurr 34 B7
Tilbury Green Essex 46 D3
Tilbury Juxta Clare Essex 46 D4
Tile Cross Birm 53 M3
Tile Hill Covtry 53 P5
Tilehouse Green Solhll 53 M5
Tilehurst Readg 31 N7
Tilford Surrey 14 B2
Tilgate W Susx 15 K4
Tilgate Forest Row W Susx 15 J4
Tilham Street Somset 22 D6
Tillers Green Gloucs 41 L5
Tillicoultry Clacks 114 G2
Tillietudlem S Lans 114 E12
Tillingham Essex 46 H11
Tillington Herefs 40 G3
Tillington W Susx 14 D6
Tillington Common Herefs 40 F3
Tillybirloch Abers 132 G3
Tillyfourie Abers 132 G2
Tillygreig Abers 141 L11
Tillyrie P & K 124 C11
Tilmanstone Kent 35 N12
Tilney All Saints Norfk 69 L8
Tilney High End Norfk 69 L8
Tilney St Lawrence Norfk 69 K9
Tilshead Wilts 23 M4
Tilstock Shrops 63 P5
Tilston Ches W 63 M2
Tilstone Bank Ches W 75 P12
Tilstone Fearnall Ches W 75 P11
Tilsworth C Beds 44 D7
Tilton on the Hill Leics 67 J11
Tiltups End Gloucs 29 N3
Tilty Essex 45 Q6
Timberland Lincs 80 C12
Timbersbrook Ches E 76 G11
Timberscombe Somset 20 F5
Timble N York 85 J4
Timewell Devon 20 E8
Timpanheck D & G 98 C3
Timperley Traffd 76 E6
Timsbury BaNES 29 K10
Timsbury Hants 24 E8
Timsgarry W Isls 152 d3
Timsgearraidh W Isls 152 d3
Timworth Suffk 58 C7
Timworth Green Suffk 58 C7
Tincleton Dorset 11 J6
Tindale Cumb 99 J6
Tingewick Bucks 43 N5
Tingley Leeds 85 L10
Tingrith C Beds 44 E5
Tingwall Airport Shet 147 i7
Tingwell Ork 147 c3
Tinhay Devon 7 M7
Tinker's Hill Hants 24 F4
Tinkersley Derbys 77 P10
Tinsley Sheff 78 C5
Tinsley Green W Susx 15 K3
Tintagel Cnwll 6 F7
Tintern Mons 28 H2
Tintinhull Somset 22 C9
Tintwistle Derbys 77 J4
Tinwald D & G 97 K2
Tinwell Rutlnd 67 P11
Tippacott Devon 19 P4
Tipp's End Norfk 57 K2
Tiptoe Hants 12 D5
Tipton Sandw 52 H2
Tipton Green Sandw 52 H2
Tipton St John Devon 9 L6
Tiptree Essex 46 F8
Tiptree Heath Essex 46 F8
Tirabad Powys 39 L3
Tircoed Swans 26 F2
Tiree Ag & B 118 E4
Tiree Airport Ag & B 118 D4
Tiretigan Ag & B 111 Q9
Tirley Gloucs 41 N6
Tiroran Ag & B 119 N7
Tirphil Caerph 39 Q11
Tirril Cumb 89 N1
Tir-y-fron Flints 75 J11
Tisbury Wilts 23 L7
Tisman's Common W Susx 14 F4
Tissington Derbys 65 M2
Titchberry Devon 18 E8
Titchfield Hants 13 J4
Titchfield Common Hants 13 J3
Titchmarsh Nhants 55 P5
Titchwell Norfk 69 P3
Tithby Notts 66 H5
Titley Herefs 51 K8
Titmore Green Herts 45 J6
Titsey Surrey 33 M11
Titson Cnwll 7 J4
Tittensor Staffs 64 G4
Tittleshall Norfk 70 C8
Titton Worcs 52 F6
Tiverton Ches W 75 P11
Tiverton Devon 20 E10
Tivetshall St Margaret Norfk 58 H3
Tivetshall St Mary Norfk 58 H3
Tivington Somset 20 E4
Tivy Dale Barns 77 P2
Tixall Staffs 64 H7
Tixover Rutlnd 67 N12
Toab Shet 147 i10
Toadhole Derbys 78 C12
Toadmoor Derbys 65 Q1
Tobermory Ag & B 119 N2
Toberonochy Ag & B 120 D11
Tobha Mòr W Isls 152 b10
Tocher Abers 140 H9
Tochieneal Moray 140 D3
Tockenham Wilts 30 B6
Tockenham Wick Wilts 30 B6
Tocketts R & Cl 92 C3
Tockholes Bl w D 83 P10
Tockington S Glos 29 J5
Tockwith N York 85 P5
Todber Dorset 22 H9
Todburn Nthumb 109 J10
Toddington C Beds 44 E6
Toddington Gloucs 42 B5
Toddington Services C Beds 44 E6
Todds Green Herts 45 J6
Todenham Gloucs 42 F4
Todhills Angus 124 H5
Todhills Cumb 98 D6
Todhills Dur 100 G11
Todhills Rest Area Cumb 98 D6
Todmorden Calder 84 D10
Todwick Rothm 78 E7
Toft Cambs 56 G9
Toft Ches E 76 E8
Toft Lincs 67 Q9
Toft Shet 147 i5
Toft Warwks 54 D6
Toft Hill Dur 91 K1
Toft Hill Lincs 80 E11
Toft Monks Norfk 59 N2
Toft next Newton Lincs 79 P6
Toftrees Norfk 70 C6
Toftwood Norfk 70 E10
Togston Nthumb 109 L9
Tokavaig Highld 127 L2
Tokers Green Oxon 31 P7
Tolastadh bho Thuath W Isls 152 h2
Toldish Cnwll 3 M3
Tolland Somset 20 H7
Tollard Farnham Dorset 23 L10
Tollard Royal Wilts 23 L10
Toll Bar Donc 78 F2
Tollbar End Covtry 54 B5
Toller Fratrum Dorset 10 F5
Toller Porcorum Dorset 10 E5
Tollerton N York 85 Q2
Tollerton Notts 66 G5
Toller Whelme Dorset 10 D4
Tollesbury Essex 46 G9
Tolleshunt D'Arcy Essex 46 G9
Tolleshunt Knights Essex 46 G8
Tolleshunt Major Essex 46 F9
Tollingham E R Yk 86 F8
Toll of Birness Abers 141 N9
Tolpuddle Dorset 11 J6
Tolworth Gt Lon 32 H9
Tomatin Highld 138 E10
Tomchrasky Highld 129 J2
Tomdoun Highld 128 G4
Tomich Highld 137 K10
Tomich Highld 137 P6
Tomich Highld 145 N4
Tomich Highld 146 C11
Tomintoul Moray 139 M12
Tomlow Warwks 54 D8
Tomnacross Highld 137 N7
Tomnavoulin Moray 139 M10
Tompkin Staffs 64 H2
Ton Mons 28 E3
Ton Mons 28 D2
Tonbridge Kent 15 Q2
Tondu Brdgnd 27 L5
Tonedale Somset 20 H9
Tonfanau Gwynd 61 J11
Tong C Brad 85 J9
Tong Kent 34 G11
Tong Shrops 64 E10
Tong W Isls 152 g3
Tonge Leics 66 C7
Tong Green Kent 34 H11
Tongham Surrey 14 C1
Tongland D & G 96 E7
Tong Norton Shrops 64 E10
Tongue Highld 149 M5
Tongue End Lincs 68 C8
Tongwynlais Cardif 27 Q6
Tonmawr Neath 27 J3
Tonna Neath 27 J3
Ton-teg Rhondd 27 P5
Tonwell Herts 45 L8
Tonypandy Rhondd 27 N4
Tonyrefail Rhondd 27 N5
Toot Baldon Oxon 31 M2
Toot Hill Essex 45 P11
Toothill Hants 24 F9
Toothill Swindn 30 D6
Tooting Gt Lon 33 K8
Tooting Bec Gt Lon 33 K8
Topcliffe N York 91 P11
Topcroft Norfk 59 K2
Topcroft Street Norfk 59 K2
Top End Bed 55 P8
Topham Donc 86 B11
Top of Hebers Rochdl 76 F2
Toppesfield Essex 46 C4
Toprow Norfk 58 H1
Topsham Devon 8 H7
Top-y-rhos Flints 75 J12
Torbeg N Ayrs 103 N4
Torboll Highld 146 D5
Torbreck Highld 138 B7
Torbryan Devon 5 N3
Torcastle Highld 128 G8
Torcross Devon 5 N8
Tore Highld 137 Q5
Torfrey Cnwll 3 Q4
Torinturk Ag & B 112 B8
Torksey Lincs 79 L8
Torlundy Highld 128 G9
Tormarton S Glos 29 M6
Tormore N Ayrs 103 N3
Tornagrain Highld 138 E6
Tornaveen Abers 132 F3
Torness Highld 137 Q10
Toronto Dur 100 G12
Torpenhow Cumb 97 P10
Torphichen W Loth 114 H7
Torphins Abers 132 F4
Torpoint Cnwll 4 G6
Torquay Torbay 5 Q4
Torquhan Border 116 B11
Torr Devon 5 J6
Torran Highld 135 K6
Torrance E Duns 114 B6
Torranyard N Ayrs 104 F1
Torre Somset 20 G5
Torridon Highld 136 C5
Torridon House Highld 136 B4
Torin Highld 135 K11
Torrisdale Ag & B 103 L3
Torrisdale Highld 149 P4
Torrish Highld 146 H1
Torrisholme Lancs 83 K2
Torrobull Highld 145 N4
Torry C Aber 133 M3
Torryburn Fife 115 J4
Torteval Guern 12 b3
Torthorwald D & G 97 L3
Tortington W Susx 14 E10
Torton Worcs 52 F6
Tortworth S Glos 29 L4
Torvaig Highld 135 J7
Torver Cumb 89 J8
Torwood Falk 114 F4
Torwoodlee Border 107 M2
Torworth Notts 78 G6
Tosberry Devon 18 E9
Toscaig Highld 135 N8
Toseland Cambs 56 E8
Tosside Lancs 84 A4
Tostock Suffk 58 D8
Totaig Highld 134 C6
Tote Highld 134 G6
Tote Highld 135 J4
Tote Hill W Susx 14 B6
Totford Hants 25 J6
Tothill Lincs 80 H7
Totland IoW 12 E7
Totley Sheff 77 P8
Totley Brook Sheff 77 P7
Totnes Devon 5 N5
Toton Notts 66 E5
Totronald Ag & B 118 G2
Totscore Highld 134 G3
Tottenham Gt Lon 33 L4
Tottenhill Norfk 69 M10
Totteridge Gt Lon 33 J3
Totternhoe C Beds 44 D7
Tottington Bury 76 E1
Tottleworth Lancs 83 Q9
Totton Hants 24 F10
Touchen End W & M 32 C7
Toulston N York 85 P6
Toulton Somset 21 K7
Toulvaddie Highld 146 F9
Tovil Kent 34 D11
Towan Cnwll 3 P5
Towan Cnwll 6 C10
Toward Ag & B 112 H7
Toward Quay Ag & B 112 G7
Towcester Nhants 54 H11
Towednack Cnwll 2 D7
Tower of London Gt Lon 33 L6
Towersey Oxon 43 Q10
Towie Abers 132 C2
Tow Law Dur 100 E10
Town End Cambs 56 H2
Town End Cumb 89 K10
Town End Cumb 89 L10
Town End Cumb 89 Q2
Townend W Duns 113 M6
Towngate Cumb 98 G9
Towngate Lincs 68 C10
Town Green Lancs 75 L3
Town Green Norfk 71 M9
Townhead Barns 77 M3
Town Head Cumb 89 L6
Townhead Cumb 97 M11
Townhead Cumb 99 J11
Townhead D & G 106 C12
Town Head N York 84 B3
Townhead of Greenlaw D & G 96 F5
Townhill Fife 115 K3
Town Kelloe Dur 101 J11
Townlake Devon 7 M9
Town Lane Wigan 76 C4
Town Littleworth E Susx 15 M7
Town of Lowton Wigan 75 Q4
Town Row E Susx 15 Q5
Towns End Hants 31 M10
Townsend Somset 21 N10
Townshend Cnwll 2 F8
Town Street Suffk 57 P3
Townwell S Glos 29 L4
Town Yetholm Border 108 C4
Towthorpe C York 86 B3
Towthorpe E R Yk 86 G3
Towton N York 85 P7
Towyn Conwy 74 D8
Toxteth Lpool 75 L6
Toynton All Saints Lincs 80 H11
Toynton Fen Side Lincs 80 H11
Toynton St Peter Lincs 80 H11
Toy's Hill Kent 33 N12
Trabboch E Ayrs 104 H5
Trabbochburn E Ayrs 104 H5
Traboe Cnwll 3 J10
Tracebridge Somset 20 G9
Tradespark Highld 138 F5
Trafford Park Traffd 76 E4
Trallong Powys 39 M6
Tranent E Loth 115 R7
Tranmere Wirral 75 K6
Trantelbeg Highld 150 F6
Trantlemore Highld 150 F6
Tranwell Nthumb 100 F2
Trap Carmth 38 G8
Traprain E Loth 116 D6
Trap's Green Warwks 53 L7
Trapshill W Berk 30 H9
Traquair Border 107 J3
Trash Green W Berk 31 N8
Trawden Lancs 84 D7
Trawscoed Cerdgn 49 L6
Trawsfynydd Gwynd 61 M5
Trealaw Rhondd 27 N4
Treales Lancs 83 K8
Trearddur Bay IoA 72 D8
Treator Cnwll 6 C9
Tre Aubrey V Glam 27 N8
Trebanog Rhondd 27 N4
Trebanos Neath 38 H11
Trebartha Cnwll 7 K9
Trebarwith Cnwll 6 F7
Trebeath Cnwll 7 J7
Trebetherick Cnwll 6 D9
Treborough Somset 20 F6
Trebudannon Cnwll 3 L2
Trebullett Cnwll 7 L9
Treburgett Cnwll 6 F9
Treburley Cnwll 7 L9
Treburrick Cnwll 6 B10
Trebyan Cnwll 3 Q2
Trecastle Powys 39 L6
Trecogo Cnwll 7 K8
Trecott Devon 8 C5
Trecwn Pembks 37 J4
Trecynon Rhondd 39 N11
Tredaule Cnwll 7 J8
Tredavoe Cnwll 2 D9
Tredegar Blae G 39 Q10
Tredethy Cnwll 6 F10
Tredington Gloucs 41 P6
Tredington Warwks 42 F3
Tredinnick Cnwll 3 P3
Tredinnick Cnwll 4 B3
Tredinnick Cnwll 4 C5
Tredinnick Cnwll 4 D5
Tredinnick Cnwll 6 D10
Tredomen Powys 39 Q5
Tredrizzick Cnwll 6 D9
Tredunnock Mons 28 E3
Tredustan Powys 39 Q5
Treen Cnwll 2 B10
Treen Cnwll 2 C7
Treesmill Cnwll 3 Q3
Treeton Rothm 78 C6
Trefasser Pembks 36 H3
Trefdraeth IoA 72 G9
Trefecca Powys 39 Q5
Trefechan Myr Td 39 N10
Trefeglwys Powys 50 C3
Trefenter Cerdgn 49 K7
Treffgarne Pembks 37 J6
Treffgarne Owen Pembks 36 G5
Treffynnon Pembks 36 G5
Trefil Blae G 39 Q9
Trefilan Cerdgn 49 J9
Trefin Pembks 36 G4
Treflach Wood Shrops 63 J7
Trefnannau Powys 62 H9
Trefnant Denbgs 74 E9
Trefonen Shrops 63 J7
Trefor Gwynd 60 F3
Trefor IoA 72 F7
Treforest Rhondd 27 P4
Trefrew Cnwll 6 G8
Trefriw Conwy 73 N11
Tregadillett Cnwll 7 K8
Tre-gagle Mons 40 H10
Tregaian IoA 72 G7
Tregare Mons 40 F9
Tregarne Cnwll 3 K10
Tregaron Cerdgn 49 M9
Tregarth Gwynd 73 K10
Tregaswith Cnwll 3 L2
Tregatta Cnwll 6 F7
Tregawne Cnwll 6 E11
Tregeare Cnwll 7 J7
Tregeiriog Wrexhm 62 G5
Tregele IoA 72 F5
Tregellist Cnwll 6 E9
Tregenna Cnwll 3 L6
Tregeseal Cnwll 2 B8
Tregew Cnwll 3 K7
Tre-Gibbon Rhondd 39 N10
Tregidden Cnwll 3 J10
Tregiskey Cnwll 3 P5
Treglemais Pembks 36 F5
Tregole Cnwll 6 H5
Tregolls Cnwll 3 J7
Tregonce Cnwll 6 D10
Tregonetha Cnwll 3 N2
Tregonning & Gwinear Mining District Cnwll 2 F8
Tregony Cnwll 3 M5
Tregoodwell Cnwll 6 G8
Tregorrick Cnwll 3 P4
Tregoss Cnwll 3 N2
Tregoyd Powys 40 B4
Tregrehan Mills Cnwll 3 P4
Tre-groes Cerdgn 38 B3
Tregullon Cnwll 3 P2
Tregunna Cnwll 6 D10
Tregunnon Cnwll 7 J8
Tregurrian Cnwll 6 B11
Tregynon Powys 50 F1
Tre-gynwr Carmth 38 B8
Trehafod Rhondd 27 P4
Trehan Cnwll 4 F5
Treharris Myr Td 27 P3
Treharrock Cnwll 6 E9
Trehemborne Cnwll 6 C10
Treherbert Carmth 38 E2
Treherbert Rhondd 27 M3
Trehunist Cnwll 4 D4
Trekenner Cnwll 7 L9
Treknow Cnwll 6 F7
Trelan Cnwll 3 J10
Trelash Cnwll 6 H7
Trelassick Cnwll 3 M4
Trelawne Cnwll 4 C6
Trelawnyd Flints 74 F8
Treleague Cnwll 3 K10
Treleaver Cnwll 3 K11
Trelech Carmth 37 Q4
Trelech a'r Betws Carmth 37 Q5
Treleddyd-fawr Pembks 36 E5
Trelew Cnwll 3 K7
Trelewis Myr Td 27 Q3
Treligga Cnwll 6 E8
Trelights Cnwll 6 E9
Trelill Cnwll 6 F9
Trelinnoe Cnwll 7 L8
Trelion Cnwll 3 M4
Trelissick Cnwll 3 L7
Trellech Mons 40 G10
Trelleck Grange Mons 28 G2
Trelogan Flints 74 F7
Trelow Cnwll 6 D10
Trelowarren Cnwll 2 H9
Trelowia Cnwll 4 D5
Treluggan Cnwll 3 L7
Trelystan Powys 63 J11
Tremadog Gwynd 61 J4
Tremail Cnwll 6 H7
Tremain Cerdgn 48 C11
Tremaine Cnwll 7 J7
Tremar Cnwll 4 C3
Trematon Cnwll 4 F5
Trembraze Cnwll 4 C4
Tremeirchion Denbgs 74 F9
Tremethick Cross Cnwll 2 C8
Tremore Cnwll 6 E11
Tre-Mostyn Flints 74 G8
Trenance Cnwll 3 K10
Trenance Cnwll 6 B11
Trenance Cnwll 6 D10
Trenarren Cnwll 3 P5
Trench Wrekin 64 C9
Trench Green Oxon 31 P7
Trendeal Cnwll 3 L4
Trendrine Cnwll 2 D6
Treneague Cnwll 6 E10
Trenear Cnwll 2 H8
Treneglos Cnwll 7 J7
Trenerth Cnwll 2 F7
Trenewan Cnwll 4 B6
Trenewth Cnwll 6 F9
Trengune Cnwll 6 H6
Treninnick Cnwll 3 K2
Trenowah Cnwll 3 K3
Trenoweth Cnwll 3 J8
Trent Dorset 22 D9
Trentham C Stke 64 G4
Trentishoe Devon 19 M4
Trentlock Derbys 66 D6
Trent Port Lincs 79 L7
Trent Vale C Stke 64 F3
Trenwheal Cnwll 2 G8
Treoes V Glam 27 M7
Treorchy Rhondd 27 M3
Trequite Cnwll 6 E9
Tre'r-ddol Cerdgn 49 L2
Trerhyngyll V Glam 27 N7
Trerulefoot Cnwll 4 D5
Tresaith Cerdgn 48 D10
Tresawle Cnwll 3 L5
Tresco IoS 2 b1
Trescott Staffs 52 F1
Trescowe Cnwll 2 F8
Tresean Cnwll 3 J3
Tresham Gloucs 29 M4
Treshnish Isles Ag & B 118 H5
Tresillian Cnwll 3 L5
Tresinney Cnwll 6 G8
Treskinnick Cross Cnwll 7 J5
Tresmeer Cnwll 7 J7
Tresparrett Cnwll 6 G6
Tressait P & K 130 E12
Tresta Shet 147 i6
Tresta Shet 147 k3
Treswell Notts 79 K8
Treswithian Cnwll 2 G7
Tre Taliesin Cerdgn 49 L2
Trethevey Cnwll 6 F7
Trethewey Cnwll 2 B9
Trethomas Caerph 28 A4
Trethosa Cnwll 3 M4
Trethurgy Cnwll 3 P3
Tretio Pembks 36 F5
Tretire Herefs 40 G7
Tretower Powys 40 B7
Treuddyn Flints 75 J12
Trevadlock Cnwll 7 K9
Trevalga Cnwll 6 F7
Trevalyn Wrexhm 75 L12
Trevanger Cnwll 6 D9
Trevanson Cnwll 6 E10
Trevarrack Cnwll 2 D8
Trevarren Cnwll 3 M2
Trevarrian Cnwll 6 B11
Trevarrick Cnwll 3 N6
Trevarth Cnwll 2 H6
Trevaughan Carmth 37 N7
Tre-vaughan Carmth 38 B7
Treveal Cnwll 2 D6
Treveal Cnwll 3 J3
Treveighan Cnwll 6 F9
Trevellas Downs Cnwll 3 J4
Trevelmond Cnwll 4 B4
Trevemper Cnwll 3 K3
Treveor Cnwll 3 N6
Treverbyn Cnwll 3 L5
Treverbyn Cnwll 3 P3
Treverva Cnwll 3 J8
Trevescan Cnwll 2 B9
Trevethin Torfn 40 C11
Trevia Cnwll 6 G8
Trevigro Cnwll 4 E3
Trevilla Cnwll 3 K7
Trevilson Cnwll 3 L3
Treviscoe Cnwll 3 M3
Treviskey Cnwll 3 M6
Trevithick Cnwll 3 L2
Trevithick Cnwll 3 N5
Trevoll Cnwll 3 K3
Trevone Cnwll 6 C9
Trevor Wrexhm 63 J4
Trevorgans Cnwll 2 C9
Trevorrick Cnwll 6 D10
Trevose Cnwll 6 B9
Trew Cnwll 2 F8
Trewalder Cnwll 6 F8
Trewalkin Powys 39 R5
Trewarmett Cnwll 6 F7
Trewassa Cnwll 6 H7
Trewavas Cnwll 2 F9
Trewavas Mining District Cnwll 2 F9
Treween Cnwll 7 J8
Trewellard Cnwll 2 B8
Trewen Cnwll 7 J8
Trewennack Cnwll 2 H9
Trewent Pembks 37 K11
Trewern Powys 63 J10
Trewetha Cnwll 6 E8
Trewethern Cnwll 6 E9
Trewidland Cnwll 4 C5
Trewillis Cnwll 3 J11
Trewint Cnwll 4 D4
Trewint Cnwll 7 J8
Trewithian Cnwll 3 L7
Trewoodloe Cnwll 7 L10
Trewoon Cnwll 2 H10
Trewoon Cnwll 3 N4
Treworga Cnwll 3 L6
Treworgan Cnwll 3 K4
Treworlas Cnwll 3 L7
Treworld Cnwll 6 G6
Treworthal Cnwll 3 L7
Tre-wyn Mons 40 D7
Treyarnon Cnwll 6 B10
Treyford W Susx 25 P9
Trickett's Cross Dorset 11 Q4
Triermain Cumb 98 H5
Triffleton Pembks 37 J6
Trillacott Cnwll 7 K7
Trimdon Dur 101 K11
Trimdon Colliery Dur 101 K11
Trimdon Grange Dur 101 K11
Trimingham Norfk 71 K4
Trimley Lower Street Suffk 47 N4
Trimley St Martin Suffk 47 N4
Trimley St Mary Suffk 47 N4
Trimpley Worcs 52 E5
Trimsaran Carmth 38 C10
Trims Green Herts 45 N8
Trimstone Devon 19 K5
Trinafour P & K 130 D11
Trinant Caerph 28 B2
Tring Herts 44 C9
Tringford Herts 44 C9
Tring Wharf Herts 44 C9
Trinity Angus 132 F12
Trinity Jersey 13 c1
Trinity Gask P & K 123 N9
Triscombe Somset 21 J6
Trislaig Highld 128 F9
Trispen Cnwll 3 K4
Tritlington Nthumb 109 K11
Troan Cnwll 3 L3
Trochry P & K 123 P5
Troedrhiwfuwch Caerph 39 Q10
Troedyraur Cerdgn 48 E11
Troedyrhiw Myr Td 39 P11
Trofarth Conwy 73 Q9
Trois Bois Jersey 13 b2
Troon Cnwll 2 G7
Troon S Ayrs 104 F4
Tropical World Roundhay Park Leeds 85 L7
Trossachs Stirlg 122 E11
Trossachs Pier Stirlg 122 E11
Troston Suffk 58 C6
Troswell Cnwll 7 J6
Trotshill Worcs 52 G9
Trottiscliffe Kent 34 B10
Trotton W Susx 25 P9
Troughend Nthumb 108 D11
Trough Gate Lancs 84 D11
Troutbeck Cumb 89 L1
Troutbeck Cumb 89 L6
Troutbeck Bridge Cumb 89 L7
Troway Derbys 78 C8
Trowbridge Wilts 29 P10
Trowell Notts 66 D4
Trowell Services Notts 66 E4
Trowle Common Wilts 29 N10
Trowley Bottom Herts 44 F9
Trowse Newton Norfk 71 K10
Troy Leeds 85 K7
Trudoxhill Somset 22 G5
Trull Somset 21 K9
Trumfleet Donc 78 F1
Trumpan Highld 134 D4
Trumpet Herefs 41 K4
Trumpington Cambs 56 H9
Trumpsgreen Surrey 32 E9
Trunch Norfk 71 K5
Trunnah Lancs 82 H6
Truro Cnwll 3 K5
Truscott Cnwll 7 K7
Trusham Devon 8 F8
Trusley Derbys 65 N5
Trusthorpe Lincs 81 K7
Trysull Staffs 52 F2
Tubney Oxon 31 J3
Tuckenhay Devon 5 N5
Tuckhill Shrops 52 E3
Tuckingmill Cnwll 2 G6
Tuckingmill Wilts 23 L7
Tuckton BCP 12 B6
Tucoyse Cnwll 3 N5
Tuddenham Suffk 57 P6
Tuddenham Suffk 59 J11
Tudeley Kent 16 A2
Tudhoe Dur 100 H11
Tudorville Herefs 41 J7
Tudweiliog Gwynd 60 D5
Tuesley Surrey 14 D2
Tuffley Gloucs 41 N8
Tufton Hants 24 G4
Tufton Pembks 37 K5
Tugby Leics 67 J12
Tugford Shrops 51 P3
Tughall Nthumb 109 K4
Tullibody Clacks 114 F2
Tullich Abers 132 B5
Tullich Highld 138 B10
Tullich Highld 146 F10
Tulliemet P & K 123 P2
Tulloch Abers 141 J9
Tullochgorm Ag & B 112 E2
Tulloch Station Highld 129 L8
Tullymurdoch P & K 124 D2
Tullynessle Abers 140 E12
Tulse Hill Gt Lon 33 K8
Tumble Carmth 38 E9
Tumbler's Green Essex 46 E6
Tumby Lincs 80 E11
Tumby Woodside Lincs 80 E12
Tummel Bridge P & K 123 K1
Tunbridge Wells Kent 15 Q3
Tundergarth D & G 97 N2
Tunga W Isls 152 g3
Tungate Norfk 71 K6
Tunley BaNES 29 L10
Tunstall C Stke 64 F2
Tunstall E R Yk 87 P8
Tunstall Kent 34 F10
Tunstall Lancs 89 P12
Tunstall N York 91 L7
Tunstall Norfk 71 N10
Tunstall Staffs 64 E6
Tunstall Suffk 59 M9
Tunstall Sundld 101 K7
Tunstead Derbys 77 L8
Tunstead Norfk 71 L8
Tunstead Milton Derbys 77 J7
Tunworth Hants 25 L4
Tupsley Herefs 40 H4
Turgis Green Hants 31 P10
Turkdean Gloucs 42 C8
Tur Langton Leics 54 H2
Turleigh Wilts 29 N10
Turleygreen Shrops 52 E4
Turn Lancs 84 B11
Turnastone Herefs 40 E4
Turnberry S Ayrs 104 D8
Turnchapel C Plym 4 H6
Turnditch Derbys 65 P3
Turner Green Lancs 83 N9
Turner's Green E Susx 16 B7
Turner's Green Warwks 53 M7
Turners Hill W Susx 15 L4
Turners Puddle Dorset 11 K6
Turnford Herts 45 L10
Turnhouse C Edin 115 L6
Turnworth Dorset 11 K3
Turriff Abers 140 H6
Turton Bottoms Bl w D 83 Q12
Turves Cambs 56 G1
Turvey Bed 55 N10
Turville Bucks 31 Q4
Turville Heath Bucks 31 Q4
Turweston Bucks 43 M4
Tushielaw Inn Border 107 K7
Tutbury Staffs 65 N6
Tutnall Worcs 53 J6
Tutshill Gloucs 28 H3
Tuttington Norfk 71 J7
Tutts Clump W Berk 31 M8
Tutwell Cnwll 7 M9
Tuxford Notts 79 J9
Twatt Ork 147 b3
Twatt Shet 147 i6
Twechar E Duns 114 C6
Tweedbank Border 107 N3
Tweedmouth Nthumb 117 M10
Tweedsmuir Border 106 E5
Twelveheads Cnwll 3 J6
Twelve Oaks E Susx 16 C7
Twemlow Green Ches E 76 E10
Twenty Lincs 68 C8
Twerton BaNES 29 L9
Twickenham Gt Lon 32 H7

Twigworth Gloucs...41 N7
Twineham W Susx...15 J7
Twineham Green W Susx...15 J7
Twinhoe BaNES...29 M10
Twinstead Essex...46 F4
Twitchen Devon...20 B7
Twitchen Shrops...41 L6
Twitham Kent...35 N11
Two Bridges Devon...8 B9
Two Dales Derbys...77 P11
Two Gates Staffs...65 N12
Two Mile Ash W Susx...14 G5
Two Mile Oak Cross
  Devon...5 P3
Two Pots Devon...19 K4
Two Waters Herts...44 F10
Twycross Leics...65 Q11
Twycross Zoo Leics...65 P11
Twyford Bucks...43 N6
Twyford Hants...24 N8
Twyford Leics...67 J10
Twyford Lincs...67 M7
Twyford Norfk...70 F7
Twyford Wokham...31 R7
Twyford Common Herefs...40 G5
Twyn-carno Caerph...39 Q10
Twyning Gloucs...41 P4
Twyning Green Gloucs...41 K4
Twynllanan Carmth...38 H7
Twyn-yr-Odyn V Glam...27 Q7
Twyn-y-Sheriff Mons...40 F10
Twywell Nhants...55 N5
Tyberton Herefs...40 E4
Tyburn Birm...53 L2
Tycroes Carmth...38 F9
Ty Croes IoA...72 E9
Tycrwyn Powys...62 F8
Tydd Gote Lincs...69 J8
Tydd St Giles Cambs...68 H9
Tydd St Mary Lincs...68 H8
Tye Hants...13 M4
Tye Green Essex...45 P7
Tye Green Essex...45 Q4
Tye Green Essex...46 D7
Tyersal C Brad...85 J8
Tyldesley Wigan...76 C3
Tyler Hill Kent...35 L10
Tylers Green Bucks...32 C3
Tyler's Green Essex...45 P10
Tylers Green Surrey...33 L12
Tylorstown Rhondd...27 N3
Tylwch Powys...50 D5
Ty-nant Conwy...62 D3
Ty-nant Gwynd...62 B2
Tyncelyn Cerdgn...49 L8
Tyndrum Stirlg...121 Q6
Ty'n-dwr Denbgs...62 H4
Tyneham Dorset...11 L8
Tynemouth N Tyne...101 K4
Tyne Tunnel S Tyne...101 J5
Tynewydd Rhondd...27 M3
Tyninghame E Loth...116 E5
Tynron D & G...105 P11
Ty'n-y-bryn Rhondd...27 N3
Ty'n-y-coedcae Caerph...28 B5
Tynygongl IoA...72 H7
Tynygraig Cerdgn...49 M7
Ty'n-y-Groes Conwy...73 N9
Tyn-y-nant Rhondd...27 P5
Tyrie Abers...141 M3
Tyringham M Keyn...44 B2
Tyseley Birm...53 L4
Tythegston Brdgnd...27 K6
Tytherington Ches E...76 H9
Tytherington S Glos...29 K5
Tytherington Somset...22 H4
Tytherington Wilts...23 K5
Tytherleigh Devon...9 Q4
Tytherton Lucas Wilts...29 Q7
Tyttenhanger Herts...44 H10
Tywardreath Cnwll...3 Q4
Tywardreath Highway
  Cnwll...3 Q3
Tywyn Conwy...73 N8
Tywyn Gwynd...61 K12

U

Ubbeston Green Suffk...59 L6
Ubley BaNES...28 H10
Uckerby N York...91 L6
Uckfield E Susx...15 N6
Uckinghall Worcs...41 P4
Uckington Gloucs...41 Q7
Uckington Shrops...63 P10
Uddingston S Lans...114 C9
Uddington S Lans...105 Q3
Udimore E Susx...16 F7
Udny Green Abers...141 L10
Udny Station Abers...141 L11
Uffcott Wilts...30 D7
Uffculme Devon...20 G10
Uffington Lincs...67 Q10
Uffington Oxon...30 G4
Uffington Shrops...63 N9
Ufford C Pete...68 B11
Ufford Suffk...59 L10
Ufton Warwks...54 C8
Ufton Nervet W Berk...31 N9
Ugadale Ag & B...103 L4
Ugborough Devon...5 N5
Uggeshall Suffk...59 N5
Ugglebarnby N York...92 H5
Ughill Sheff...77 N5
Ugley Essex...45 P6
Ugley Green Essex...45 P6
Ugthorpe N York...92 G4
Uibhist A Deas W Isls...152 c10
Uibhist A Tuath W Isls...152 b8
Uig Ag & B...118 C3
Uig Highld...134 C5
Uig Highld...134 C7
Uig W Isls...152 d3
Uigshader Highld...134 H6
Uisken Ag & B...119 L9
Ulbster Highld...151 P8
Ulcat Row Cumb...89 L2
Ulceby Lincs...80 H9
Ulceby N Linc...87 L12
Ulceby Skitter N Linc...87 L12
Ulcombe Kent...16 E1
Uldale Cumb...97 Q10
Uley Gloucs...29 M3
Ulgham Nthumb...109 L11
Ullapool Highld...144 E6
Ullenhall Warwks...53 L7
Ullenwood Gloucs...41 Q8
Ulleskelf N York...85 Q7
Ullesthorpe Leics...54 E3
Ulley Rothm...78 D6
Ullingswick Herefs...51 Q10
Ullock Cumb...88 E2
Ullswater Cumb...89 L3
Ullswater Steamers
  Cumb...89 L3
Ulnes Walton Lancs...83 L11
Ulpha Cumb...88 G8
Ulpha Cumb...89 M10
Ulrome E R Yk...87 M4
Ulsta Shet...147 j4
Ulting Wick Essex...46 E10
Ulva Ag & B...119 L5
Ulverley Green Solhll...53 L4
Ulverston Cumb...89 J11
Ulwell Dorset...11 N8

Ulzieside D & G...105 P8
Umberleigh Devon...19 M8
Unapool Highld...148 F10
Underbarrow Cumb...89 M8
Under Burnmouth Border...98 F2
Undercliffe C Brad...85 J8
Underdale Shrops...63 N9
Underling Green Kent...16 D2
Underriver Kent...33 Q12
Underwood Newpt...28 C3
Underwood Notts...78 D2
Undley Suffk...57 N4
Undy Mons...28 F5
Union Mills IoM...102 d6
Union Street E Susx...16 C4
Unst Shet...147 k2
Unstone Derbys...78 B8
Unstone Green Derbys...78 B8
Unthank Cumb...98 E8
Unthank Cumb...98 F11
Unthank Cumb...98 H10
Unthank Derbys...77 P8
Unthank Nthumb...117 M11
Upavon Wilts...23 P2
Up Cerne Dorset...10 G4
Upchurch Kent...34 E9
Upcott Devon...19 N7
Upcott Herefs...51 K10
Upend Cambs...57 N9
Up Exe Devon...8 H4
Upgate Norfk...70 H8
Upgate Street Norfk...58 G2
Upgate Street Norfk...59 K2
Uphall Dorset...10 E4
Uphall W Loth...115 K7
Upham Devon...8 G3
Upham Hants...25 J9
Uphampton Herefs...51 L8
Uphampton Worcs...52 F7
Uphill N Som...28 D10
Up Holland Lancs...75 N3
Uplawmoor E Rens...113 N10
Upleadon Gloucs...41 M6
Upleatham R & Cl...92 D3
Uplees Kent...34 H9
Uploders Dorset...10 E6
Uplowman Devon...20 F10
Uplyme Devon...9 Q6
Up Marden W Susx...25 N10
Upminster Gt Lon...33 Q5
Up Mudford Somset...22 D9
Up Nately Hants...25 M3
Upottery Devon...9 N3
Upper Affcot Shrops...51 M3
Upper Arley Worcs...52 E4
Upper Arncott Oxon...43 M8
Upper Astrop Nhants...43 L4
Upper Badcall Highld...148 E8
Upper Basildon W Berk...31 M7
Upper Batley Kirk...85 K8
Upper Beeding W Susx...14 H8
Upper Benefield Nhants...55 N3
Upper Bentley Worcs...53 J7
Upper Bighouse Highld...150 E4
Upper Birchwood Derbys...66 D1
Upper Boat Rhondd...27 N3
Upper Boddington
  Nhants...54 D10
Upper Borth Cerdgn...49 K3
Upper Brailes Warwks...42 G4
Upper Breinton Herefs...40 G4
Upper Broadheath Worcs...52 E9
Upper Buckenhill Herefs...40 H3
Upper Bucklebury W Berk...31 L8
Upper Burgate Hants...23 P10
Upper Bush Medway...34 C9
Upperby Cumb...98 E2
Upper Caldecote C Beds...44 H2
Upper Canada N Som...28 E10
Upper Canterton Hants...24 D10
Upper Catesby Nhants...54 E9
Upper Catshill Worcs...52 H6
Upper Chapel Powys...39 N4
Upper Cheddon Somset...21 K7
Upper Chicksgrove Wilts...23 L7
Upper Chute Wilts...24 E3
Upper Clapton Gt Lon...33 L5
Upper Clatford Hants...24 F5
Upper Coberley Gloucs...41 R8
Upper Cotton Staffs...65 K3
Upper Cound Shrops...63 P11
Upper Cudworth Barns...78 C2
Upper Cumberworth
  Kirk...77 N2
Upper Dallachy Moray...139 Q3
Upper Deal Kent...35 Q12
Upper Dean Bed...55 P7
Upper Denby Kirk...77 N2
Upper Denton Cumb...99 K5
Upper Dicker E Susx...15 Q9
Upper Dinchope Shrops...51 M4
Upper Dounreay Highld...150 H3
Upper Dovercourt Essex...47 M5
Upper Drumbane Stirlg...122 H11
Upper Dunsforth N York...85 N3
Upper Eashing Surrey...14 E2
Upper Eathie Highld...138 E3
Upper Egleton Herefs...40 H3
Upper Elkstone Staffs...77 K12
Upper Ellastone Staffs...65 L4
Upper End Derbys...77 K8
Upper Enham Hants...24 F3
Upper Farmcote Shrops...52 E2
Upper Farringdon Hants...25 M6
Upper Framilode Gloucs...41 M9
Upper Froyle Hants...25 N5
Upperglen Highld...134 F5
Upper Godney Somset...22 B5
Upper Gravenhurst
  C Beds...44 G4
Upper Green Mons...40 D8
Upper Green Suffk...57 P7
Upper Green W Berk...31 J8
Upper Grove Common
  Herefs...40 H6
Upper Hackney Derbys...77 P11
Upper Hale Surrey...25 P3
Upper Halliford Surrey...32 F8
Upper Halling Medway...34 C9
Upper Hambleton Rutlnd...67 M10
Upper Harbledown Kent...35 K10
Upper Hardres Court
  Kent...35 L12
Upper Hardwick Herefs...51 L9
Upper Hartfield E Susx...15 N4
Upper Hartshay Derbys...66 C2
Upper Hatherley Gloucs...41 Q7
Upper Hatton Staffs...64 F4
Upper Haugh Rothm...78 C4
Upper Hayton Shrops...51 P3
Upper Heaton Kirk...85 J11
Upper Helmsley N York...86 D4
Upper Hergest Herefs...51 J9
Upper Heyford Nhants...54 H8
Upper Heyford Oxon...43 K6
Upper Hill Herefs...51 M10
Upper Hockenden Kent...33 P8
Upper Hopton Kirk...85 J11
Upper Howsell Worcs...52 E11
Upper Hulme Staffs...77 J12
Upper Ifold Surrey...14 E4
Upper Inglesham Swindn...30 E3
Upper Kilcott Gloucs...29 M5
Upper Killay Swans...26 E4
Upper Kinchrackine
  Ag & B...121 M7
Upper Knockando Moray...139 M7

Upper Lambourn W Berk...30 G6
Upper Landywood Staffs...64 H11
Upper Langford N Som...28 F10
Upper Langwith Derbys...78 E9
Upper Largo Fife...124 H12
Upper Leigh Staffs...65 J5
Upper Littleton N Som...28 H9
Upper Lochton Abers...132 H5
Upper Longdon Staffs...65 K9
Upper Lydbrook Gloucs...41 J8
Upper Lyde Herefs...40 G3
Upper Lye Herefs...51 L7
Upper Maes-coed Herefs...40 D5
Upper Marham Norfk...69 N10
Upper Midhope Sheff...77 N4
Upper Milton Worcs...52 E6
Upper Minety Wilts...30 B4
Upper Moor Worcs...52 H11
Upper Moor Side Leeds...85 K9
Upper Mulben Moray...139 Q5
Upper Netchwood Shrops...52 B2
Upper Nobut Staffs...65 K5
Upper Norwood W Susx...14 E7
Upper Oddington Gloucs...42 E6
Upper Padley Derbys...77 P8
Upper Pennington Hants...12 E5
Upper Pollicott Bucks...43 R9
Upper Poppleton C York...85 Q4
Upper Quinton Warwks...42 E2
Upper Ratley Hants...24 E8
Upper Rissington Gloucs...42 E7
Upper Rochford Worcs...52 B7
Upper Ruscoe D & G...96 B6
Upper Saxondale Notts...66 H4
Upper Seagry Wilts...29 Q6
Upper Shelton C Beds...44 E3
Upper Sheringham Norfk...70 H2
Upper Skelmorlie N Ayrs...113 J8
Upper Slaughter Gloucs...42 D7
Upper Soudley Gloucs...41 K9
Upper Spond Herefs...51 K10
Upper Standen Kent...17 M3
Upper Staploe Bed...56 C8
Upper Stoke Norfk...71 K11
Upper Stondon C Beds...44 G4
Upper Stowe Nhants...54 G9
Upper Street Hants...23 P9
Upper Street Norfk...58 H5
Upper Street Norfk...71 L8
Upper Street Norfk...71 M9
Upper Street Suffk...47 L5
Upper Street Suffk...57 P10
Upper Street Suffk...58 G10
Upper Strensham Worcs...41 N4
Upper Sundon C Beds...44 E6
Upper Swell Gloucs...42 E6
Upper Tankersley Barns...77 P4
Upper Tean Staffs...65 J4
Upperthong Kirk...77 L2
Upperthorpe Derbys...78 D7
Upperthorpe N Linc...79 J2
Upper Threapwood
  Ches W...63 M3
Upper Town Derbys...65 N2
Upper Town Derbys...77 Q10
Upper Town Dur...100 D10
Upper Town Herefs...51 P11
Upper Town N Som...28 G9
Upper Tumble Carmth...38 E9
Upper Tysoe Warwks...42 H3
Upper Ufford Suffk...59 K10
Upperup Gloucs...30 B3
Upper Upham Wilts...30 F7
Upper Upnor Medway...34 D8
Upper Victoria Angus...125 K5
Upper Vobster Somset...22 H4
Upper Wardington Oxon...43 K3
Upper Weald M Keyn...44 A4
Upper Weedon Nhants...54 G9
Upper Welland Worcs...41 M3
Upper Wellingham E Susx...15 N8
Upper Weston BaNES...29 J7
Upper Weybread Suffk...59 J5
Upper Wick Worcs...52 F10
Upper Wield Hants...25 K5
Upper Winchendon
  Bucks...43 Q9
Upperwood Derbys...77 P12
Upper Woodford Wilts...23 P6
Upper Woolhampton
  W Berk...31 M8
Upper Wootton Hants...25 K2
Upper Wraxall Wilts...29 M3
Uppincott Devon...8 G3
Uppingham Rutlnd...67 L12
Uppington Shrops...63 Q10
Upsall N York...91 Q10
Upsettlington Border...117 K12
Upshire Essex...33 N3
Upstreet Kent...35 M9
Up Sydling Dorset...10 F4
Upthorpe Suffk...58 E6
Upton Bucks...43 Q9
Upton C Pete...68 B12
Upton Cambs...56 D5
Upton Ches W...75 L10
Upton Cnwll...7 J4
Upton Cnwll...7 K10
Upton Cumb...98 C10
Upton Devon...5 L8
Upton Devon...9 J5
Upton Dorset...10 H7
Upton Dorset...11 L6
Upton E R Yk...87 L4
Upton Halton...75 N6
Upton Hants...24 F10
Upton Hants...24 G3
Upton Leics...54 C2
Upton Lincs...79 J6
Upton Norfk...71 M9
Upton Notts...79 J1
Upton Notts...79 L9
Upton Oxon...31 L4
Upton Oxon...42 F9
Upton Pembks...37 J9
Upton R & Cl...92 F3
Upton Slough...32 D6
Upton Somset...20 D7
Upton Somset...21 M8
Upton Wakefd...78 D1
Upton Wirral...75 J6
Upton Bishop Herefs...41 K6
Upton Cheyney S Glos...29 L8
Upton Cressett Shrops...52 C2
Upton Crews Herefs...41 K6
Upton Cross Cnwll...7 K10
Upton End C Beds...44 G4
Upton Grey Hants...25 M4
Upton Heath Ches W...75 L10
Upton Hellions Devon...8 H4
Upton Lovell Wilts...23 K5
Upton Magna Shrops...63 P9
Upton Noble Somset...22 G5
Upton Pyne Devon...8 H5

Upton St Leonards
  Gloucs...41 Q8
Upton Scudamore Wilts...23 J4
Upton Snodsbury Worcs...52 H9
Upton Towans Cnwll...2 F6
Upton-upon-Severn
  Worcs...41 N4
Upton Warren Worcs...52 H7
Upwaltham W Susx...14 D8
Upware Cambs...57 K6
Upwell Norfk...69 J11
Upwey Dorset...10 G7
Upwick Green Herts...45 N7
Upwood Cambs...56 E4
Urchfont Wilts...30 B11
Urdimarsh Herefs...51 N11
Ure Bank N York...91 N12
Urlay Nook S on T...91 P4
Urmston Traffd...76 E5
Urpeth Dur...100 G7
Urquhart Moray...139 P3
Urquhart Castle Highld...137 P10
Urra N York...92 B6
Urray Highld...137 N5
Ury Abers...133 L7
Uryside Abers...141 J11
Usan Angus...125 P2
Ushaw Moor Dur...100 G9
Usk Mons...28 D3
Usselby Lincs...80 B5
Usworth Sundld...100 H7
Utkinton Ches W...75 P10
Uton Devon...8 H5
Utterby Lincs...80 F5
Uttoxeter Staffs...65 K5
Uwchmynydd Gwynd...60 B7
Uxbridge Gt Lon...32 F5
Uyeasound Shet...147 k3
Uzmaston Pembks...37 J7

V

Vale Guern...12 c1
Valley IoA...72 D8
Valley End Surrey...32 D9
Valley Truckle Cnwll...6 G8
Valtos Highld...135 J3
Valtos W Isls...152 e3
Vange Essex...34 C5
Varteg Torfn...40 C10
Vatsetter Shet...147 j3
Vatten Highld...134 E7
Vaynor Myr Td...39 P9
Vazon Bay Guern...12 b2
Veensgarth Shet...147 i7
Velindre Powys...40 B4
Vellow Somset...20 H6
Velly Devon...18 F8
Venngreen Devon...7 M2
Vennington Shrops...63 K10
Venn Ottery Devon...9 K6
Venny Tedburn Devon...8 F5
Venterdon Cnwll...7 L10
Ventnor IoW...13 J9
Venton Devon...5 J5
Vernham Dean Hants...30 H11
Vernham Street Hants...30 H11
Vernolds Common
  Shrops...51 N4
Verwood Dorset...11 Q3
Veryan Cnwll...3 M6
Veryan Green Cnwll...3 N6
Vicarage Devon...9 N7
Vickerstown Cumb...82 F1
Victoria Blae G...40 A10
Victoria Cnwll...3 N2
Vidlin Shet...147 j5
Viewfield Moray...139 P3
Viewpark N Lans...114 C9
Vigo Kent...34 B10
Village de Putron Guern...12 c3
Ville la Bas Jersey...13 a1
Villiaze Guern...12 b3
Vinehall Street E Susx...16 D7
Vines Cross E Susx...15 Q7
Virginia Water Surrey...32 E9
Virginstow Devon...7 M6
Vobster Somset...22 H4
Voe Shet...147 i6
Vowchurch Herefs...40 E4
Vulcan Village St Hel...75 P5

W

Waberthwaite Cumb...88 E8
Wackerfield Dur...91 K2
Wacton Norfk...58 H2
Wadborough Worcs...52 G11
Waddesdon Bucks...43 Q8
Waddeton Devon...5 P5
Waddicar Sefton...75 L4
Waddingham Lincs...79 N4
Waddington Lancs...83 Q6
Waddington Lincs...79 N11
Waddon Dorset...10 F7
Waddon Gt Lon...33 K9
Wadebridge Cnwll...6 E10
Wadeford Somset...9 Q3
Wadenhoe Nhants...55 P4
Wadesmill Herts...45 L8
Wadhurst E Susx...16 B4
Wadshelf Derbys...77 P9
Wadswick Wilts...29 N9
Wadworth Donc...78 F4
Waen Denbgs...74 D11
Waen Denbgs...74 F10
Waen Powys...62 H8
Waen Fach Powys...62 G8
Waen-pentir Gwynd...73 K10
Waen-wen Gwynd...73 K10
Wagbeach Shrops...63 L11
Wainfelin Torfn...28 C2
Wainfleet All Saints Lincs...81 J12
Wainfleet Bank Lincs...81 J11
Wainfleet St Mary Lincs...81 K12
Wainford Norfk...59 L3
Wainhouse Corner Cnwll...6 H6
Wainscott Medway...34 D8
Wain's Hill N Som...28 F8
Wainstalls Calder...84 G9
Waitby Cumb...90 B5
Waithe Lincs...80 F3
Wakefield Wakefd...85 M11
Wake Green Birm...53 L4
Wakehurst Place W Susx...15 L5
Wakerley Nhants...67 M12
Wakes Colne Essex...46 F6
Walberswick Suffk...59 P6
Walberton W Susx...14 E9
Walbottle N u Ty...100 F5
Walbutt D & G...96 F4
Walby Cumb...98 F2
Walcombe Somset...22 D4
Walcot Lincs...67 Q5
Walcot Lincs...79 N2
Walcot N Linc...86 G11
Walcot Shrops...51 K4
Walcot Shrops...63 N9
Walcot Swindn...30 D6
Walcot Warwks...42 E2
Walcote Leics...54 F4

Walcote Warwks...53 L9
Walcot Green Norfk...58 H4
Walcott Lincs...80 C12
Walcott Norfk...71 M4
Walden N York...90 G10
Walden Head N York...90 G10
Walden Stubbs N York...85 Q11
Walderslade Medway...34 D9
Walderton W Susx...13 M3
Walditch Dorset...10 D6
Waldley Derbys...65 L4
Waldridge Dur...100 G8
Waldringfield Suffk...47 N3
Waldron E Susx...15 R7
Wales Rothm...78 D6
Wales Somset...22 D8
Walesby Lincs...80 C5
Walesby Notts...78 H9
Walford Herefs...41 J7
Walford Herefs...51 M6
Walford Shrops...63 M8
Walford Staffs...64 F5
Walford Heath Shrops...63 M8
Walgherton Ches E...64 C2
Walgrave Nhants...55 K6
Walhampton Hants...12 F5
Walkden Salfd...76 D3
Walker N u Ty...100 H5
Walkerburn Border...107 K2
Walker Fold Lancs...83 P7
Walkeringham Notts...79 J5
Walkerith Lincs...79 J5
Walkern Herts...45 J6
Walker's Green Herefs...51 N11
Walker's Heath Birm...53 K5
Walkerton Fife...115 J1
Walkford BCP...12 D5
Walkhampton Devon...4 H3
Walkington E R Yk...86 H8
Walkley Sheff...77 Q6
Walkwood Worcs...53 J8
Wall Nthumb...99 P4
Wall Staffs...65 L11
Wallacetown S Ayrs...104 E6
Wallacetown S Ayrs...104 F5
Wallands Park E Susx...15 N8
Wallasey Wirral...75 J5
Wallasey (Kingsway)
  Tunnel Wirral...75 K5
Wall End Cumb...88 H10
Wall End Herefs...51 M9
Wallend Medway...34 F7
Waller's Green Herefs...41 K4
Wallhead Cumb...98 F14
Wall Heath Dudley...52 G3
Wall Houses Nthumb...100 D4
Wallingford Oxon...31 M4
Wallington Gt Lon...33 K9
Wallington Hants...13 K3
Wallington Herts...45 J5
Wallington Heath Wsall...65 J11
Wallis Pembks...37 K5
Wallisdown BCP...11 P6
Walliswood Surrey...14 H3
Walls Shet...147 h7
Wallsend N Tyne...100 H5
Wallthwaite Cumb...89 K1
Wall under Haywood
  Shrops...51 N2
Wallyford E Loth...115 Q7
Walmer Kent...35 Q12
Walmer Bridge Lancs...83 L10
Walmersley Bury...76 E1
Walmestone Kent...35 N10
Walmley Birm...53 L2
Walmley Ash Birm...53 L2
Walney Cumb...82 E2
Walpole Suffk...59 M6
Walpole Cross Keys Norfk...69 K8
Walpole Highway Norfk...69 K9
Walpole St Andrew Norfk...69 K8
Walpole St Peter Norfk...69 J9
Walrow Somset...21 L3
Walsall Wsall...53 J1
Walsall Wood Wsall...65 K11
Walsden Calder...84 D11
Walsgrave on Sowe
  Covtry...54 C4
Walsham le Willows
  Suffk...58 E6
Walshaw Bury...76 E1
Walshford N York...85 N5
Walsoken Norfk...69 J10
Walston S Lans...115 K12
Walsworth Herts...44 H5
Walter's Ash Bucks...32 B3
Walters Green Kent...15 P3
Walterston V Glam...27 Q7
Walterstone Herefs...40 D6
Waltham Kent...17 K1
Waltham NE Lincs...80 E3
Waltham Abbey Essex...33 M2
Waltham Chase Hants...25 J9
Waltham Cross Herts...33 L2
Waltham on the Wolds
  Leics...67 K7
Waltham St Lawrence
  W & M...32 B7
Waltham's Cross Essex...46 C5
Walthamstow Gt Lon...33 L4
Walton Cumb...98 G1
Walton Derbys...78 B10
Walton Leeds...85 N6
Walton Leics...54 F3
Walton M Keyn...44 B3
Walton Powys...51 J8
Walton Shrops...51 M5
Walton Somset...21 N6
Walton Staffs...64 F5
Walton Staffs...64 G5
Walton Suffk...47 N4
Walton W Susx...13 M3
Walton Wakefd...85 N6
Walton Warwks...53 P10
Walton Wrekin...63 P9
Walton Cardiff Gloucs...41 P5
Walton East Pembks...37 K6
Walton Elm Dorset...22 F10
Walton Grounds Nhants...43 L5
Walton Highway Norfk...69 J9
Walton-in-Gordano
  N Som...28 F7
Walton-le-Dale Lancs...83 M9
Walton-on-Thames
  Surrey...32 G9
Walton-on-the-Hill
  Staffs...64 H8
Walton-on-the-Hill
  Surrey...33 J11
Walton-on-the-Naze
  Essex...47 N7
Walton on the Wolds
  Leics...66 F8
Walton-on-Trent Derbys...65 N8
Walton Park N Som...28 F7
Walton West Pembks...36 G8
Walwen Flints...74 G9
Walwen Flints...74 G9
Walwen Flints...74 H9
Walwick Nthumb...99 P4
Walworth Darltn...91 L3
Walworth Gate Darltn...91 L3

Walwyn's Castle Pembks...36 G8
Wambrook Somset...9 P3
Wampool Cumb...97 P7
Wanborough Surrey...14 D1
Wanborough Swindn...30 E6
Wandon End Herts...44 G7
Wandsworth Gt Lon...33 J7
Wangford Suffk...59 P5
Wangford Suffk...57 N3
Wanlip Leics...66 F10
Wanlockhead D & G...105 R7
Wannock E Susx...15 Q9
Wansford C Pete...67 Q12
Wansford E R Yk...87 K4
Wanshurst Green Kent...16 D2
Wanstead Gt Lon...33 M5
Wanstrow Somset...22 G5
Wanswell Gloucs...29 K2
Wantage Oxon...31 J5
Wants Green Worcs...52 E9
Wapley S Glos...29 L6
Wappenbury Warwks...54 B7
Wappenham Nhants...43 M3
Warbleton E Susx...15 R7
Warborough Oxon...31 M4
Warboys Cambs...56 F5
Warbreck Bpool...82 H7
Warbstow Cnwll...7 J6
Warburton Traffd...76 C6
Warcop Cumb...90 B4
Warden Kent...35 J8
Warden Nthumb...99 P5
Ward End Birm...53 L3
Warden Street C Beds...44 F3
Ward Green Suffk...58 F8
Ward Green Cross Lancs...83 P8
Wardhedges C Beds...44 F4
Wardington Oxon...43 K2
Wardle Ches E...75 Q12
Wardle Rochdl...84 D11
Wardley Gatesd...100 H6
Wardley Rutlnd...67 L12
Wardley Salfd...76 E3
Wardlow Derbys...77 M8
Wardsend Ches E...76 H7
Wardy Hill Cambs...57 J4
Ware Herts...45 L9
Ware Street Kent...34 D11
Wareham Dorset...11 M7
Warehorne Kent...16 H4
Warenford Nthumb...109 J3
Waren Mill Nthumb...109 J3
Warenton Nthumb...109 J4
Wareside Herts...45 M8
Waresley Cambs...56 E9
Waresley Worcs...52 F6
Ware Street Kent...34 D11
Waters Upton Wrekin...64 B8
Water Yeat Cumb...89 J9
Watford Herts...32 G3
Watford Nhants...54 G7
Watford Gap Services
  Nhants...54 F7
Wath N York...84 H1
Wath N York...91 N11
Wath upon Dearne
  Rothm...78 C3
Watlington Norfk...69 M10
Watlington Oxon...31 P3
Watnall Notts...66 E3
Watten Highld...151 N6
Wattisfield Suffk...58 E6
Wattisham Suffk...58 E10
Watton Dorset...10 C6
Watton E R Yk...87 J3
Watton Norfk...70 D11
Watton-at-Stone Herts...45 K8
Watton Green Norfk...70 D12
Wattons Green Essex...33 P3
Wattston N Lans...114 D7
Wattstown Rhondd...27 N4
Wattsville Caerph...28 B4
Wauldby E R Yk...86 H9
Waulkmill Abers...132 G6
Waunarlwydd Swans...26 F3
Waun Fach Powys...40 B6
Waunfawr Cerdgn...49 K4
Waunfawr Gwynd...73 J11
Waungron Swans...38 E11
Waunlwyd Blae G...40 A10
Wavendon M Keyn...44 C4
Waverbridge Cumb...97 P8
Waverton Ches W...75 M11
Waverton Cumb...97 P9
Wawne E R Yk...87 K8
Waxham Norfk...71 N7
Waxholme E R Yk...87 P9
Way Kent...35 P9
Waye Devon...8 E10
Wayford Somset...10 B3
Waytown Dorset...10 C5
Way Village Devon...8 G3
Way Wick N Som...28 E10
Weacombe Somset...20 H5
Weald Oxon...42 G11
Wealdstone Gt Lon...32 H4
Weardley Leeds...85 L6
Weare Somset...21 N3
Weare Giffard Devon...19 J9
Wearhead Dur...99 N10
Wearne Somset...21 P8
Weasdale Cumb...90 A6
Weasenham All Saints
  Norfk...70 C8
Weasenham St Peter
  Norfk...70 C7
Weaste Salfd...76 E4
Weatheroak Hill Worcs...53 K6
Weaverham Ches W...76 C11
Weaverslake Staffs...65 L8
Weaverthorpe N York...86 H1
Webbington Somset...21 M2
Webb's Heath S Glos...29 K7
Webheath Worcs...53 J7
Webton Herefs...40 F4
Wedderlairs Abers...141 L9
Wedding Hall Fold N York...84 D6
Weddington Kent...35 N10
Weddington Warwks...54 C3
Wedhampton Wilts...30 C11
Wedmore Somset...21 N4
Wednesbury Sandw...52 H2
Wednesfield Wolves...64 H12
Weecar Notts...79 K11
Weedon Bucks...43 R8
Weedon Bec Nhants...54 G9
Weedon Lois Nhants...43 M3
Weeford Staffs...65 L11
Week Devon...19 N4
Week Devon...19 N8
Week Somset...20 C8
Weeke Devon...8 E3
Weeke Hants...24 H7
Weekley Nhants...55 M4
Week St Mary Cnwll...7 J5
Weel E R Yk...87 K7
Weeley Essex...47 K6
Weeley Heath Essex...47 L7
Ween P & K...123 L8
Weeping Cross Staffs...64 H7
Weethley Warwks...53 K9
Weeting Norfk...57 N3
Weeton E R Yk...87 Q10
Weeton Lancs...83 J8
Weeton N York...85 L5
Weetwood Leeds...85 L8
Weir Lancs...84 C10
Weirbrook Shrops...63 K7
Weir Quay Devon...4 F4
Weisdale Shet...147 i6

Welborne Norfk 70 F10
Welbourn Lincs 67 N1
Welburn N York 86 D2
Welbury N York 91 P6
Welby Lincs 67 N4
Welches Dam Cambs 57 J3
Welcombe Devon 18 E9
Weldon Nhants 55 M3
Weldon Bridge Nthumb 109 J10
Welford Nhants 54 G5
Welford W Berk 31 J8
Welford-on-Avon Warwks 53 L10
Welham Leics 55 J2
Welham Notts 79 J7
Welham Bridge E R Yk 86 E8
Welham Green Herts 45 J9
Well Hants 25 N4
Well Lincs 80 H9
Well N York 91 M10
Wellbank Angus 125 J5
Well End Bucks 32 C5
Well End Herts 32 H3
Wellesbourne Warwks 53 P9
Wellesbourne Mountford Warwks 53 P9
Well Head Herts 44 H6
Well Hill Kent 33 P9
Wellhouse W Berk 31 L8
Welling Gt Lon 33 N7
Wellingborough Nhants 55 M7
Wellingham Norfk 70 C8
Wellingore Lincs 79 N12
Wellington Cumb 88 E6
Wellington Herefs 51 N11
Wellington Somset 21 J9
Wellington Wrekin 64 C10
Wellington Heath Herefs 41 L4
Wellington Marsh Herefs 40 G2
Wellow BaNES 29 L10
Wellow IoW 12 F7
Wellow Notts 78 H10
Wellpond Green Herts 45 M7
Wells Somset 22 D4
Wellsborough Leics 66 B11
Wells Green Ches E 76 C1
Wells Head C Brad 84 G8
Wells-next-the-Sea Norfk 70 D3
Wellstye Green Essex 46 C1
Well Town Devon 8 G3
Welltree P & K 123 N8
Wellwood Fife 115 K3
Welney Norfk 57 K2
Welshampton Shrops 63 M5
Welsh Bicknor Herefs 41 J3
Welsh End Shrops 63 N5
Welsh Frankton Shrops 63 K5
Welsh Hook Pembks 36 H5
Welsh Newton Herefs 40 G8
Welshpool Powys 62 H10
Welsh St Donats V Glam 27 N7
Welton Cumb 98 D9
Welton E R Yk 86 H9
Welton Lincs 79 P8
Welton Nhants 54 F7
Welton le Marsh Lincs 81 J10
Welton le Wold Lincs 80 E8
Welwick E R Yk 87 Q11
Welwyn Herts 45 J8
Welwyn Garden City Herts 45 J9
Wem Shrops 63 N6
Wembdon Somset 21 L6
Wembley Gt Lon 32 H5
Wembury Devon 4 H7
Wembworthy Devon 8 G3
Wemyss Bay Inver 113 J7
Wenallt Cerdgn 49 L6
Wendens Ambo Essex 45 P4
Wendlebury Oxon 43 M8
Wendling Norfk 70 D9
Wendover Bucks 44 B10
Wendron Cnwll 2 H8
Wendron Mining District Cnwll 2 H8
Wendy Cambs 56 F11
Wenfordbridge Cnwll 6 F9
Wenhaston Suffk 59 N5
Wennington Cambs 56 E5
Wennington Gt Lon 33 P6
Wennington Lancs 83 M7
Wensley Derbys 77 N11
Wensley N York 90 H9
Wentbridge Wakefd 85 P11
Wentnor Shrops 51 L2
Wentworth Cambs 57 J5
Wentworth Rothm 78 C4
Wentworth Castle Barns 77 P6
Wenvoe V Glam 27 Q8
Weobley Herefs 51 L10
Weobley Marsh Herefs 51 L10
Wepham W Susx 14 F9
Wepre Flints 69 N11
Wereham Norfk 69 R12
Wergs Wolves 64 F12
Wern Gwynd 61 J4
Wern Powys 39 Q8
Wern Powys 63 J8
Wern Shrops 63 J5
Werneth Low Tamesd 76 H5
Wernffrwd Swans 26 D3
Wern-Gifford Mons 40 D7
Wern-y-gaer Flints 74 H10
Werrington C Pete 68 C11
Werrington Cnwll 7 L7
Werrington Staffs 64 H3
Wervin Ches W 75 M9
Wesham Lancs 83 K8
Wessington Derbys 78 B12
West Aberthaw V Glam 27 N9
West Acre Norfk 69 P9
West Allerdean Nthumb 117 L12
West Alvington Devon 5 M8
West Amesbury Wilts 23 P5
West Anstey Devon 20 C8
West Appleton N York 91 L8
West Ashby Lincs 80 E9
West Ashling W Susx 13 P3
West Ashton Wilts 23 J2
West Auckland Dur 91 J2
West Ayton N York 93 K9
West Bagborough Somset 21 J6
West Bank Blae G 40 B10
West Bank Halton 75 N7
West Barkwith Lincs 80 C7
West Barnby N York 92 G4
West Barns E Loth 116 F6
West Barsham Norfk 70 D5
West Bay Dorset 10 C6
West Beckham Norfk 70 H4
West Bedfont Surrey 32 F7
Westbere Kent 35 M10
West Bergholt Essex 46 G6
West Bexington Dorset 10 C7
West Bilney Norfk 69 N10
West Blatchington Br & H 15 K9
West Boldon S Tyne 101 J6
Westborough Lincs 67 L3
Westbourne BCP 11 H6
Westbourne W Susx 13 N3
West Bourton Dorset 22 G7
West Bowling C Brad 85 J9
West Brabourne Kent 17 K2
West Bradenham Norfk 70 D10
West Bradford Lancs 83 R6
West Bradley Somset 22 D6

West Bretton Wakefd 77 P1
West Bridgford Notts 66 F5
West Briscoe Dur 90 F3
West Bromwich Sandw 53 J2
Westbrook Kent 35 P8
Westbrook W Berk 31 J8
Westbrook Wilts 29 Q9
West Buckland Devon 19 M7
West Buckland Somset 21 J8
West Burrafirth Shet 147 h6
West Burton N York 90 H8
West Burton W Susx 14 E8
Westbury Bucks 43 N4
Westbury Shrops 63 K10
Westbury Wilts 23 J3
Westbury Leigh Wilts 23 J3
Westbury-on-Severn Gloucs 41 L9
Westbury-on-Trym Bristl 28 H7
Westbury-sub-Mendip Somset 22 C3
West Butsfield Dur 100 E8
West Butterwick N Linc 79 L3
Westby Lancs 83 J9
West Byfleet Surrey 32 F10
West Cairngaan D & G 94 G12
West Caister Norfk 71 P10
West Calder W Loth 115 J8
West Camel Somset 22 D8
West Chaldon Dorset 11 J8
West Challow Oxon 30 H5
West Charleton Devon 5 M8
West Chelborough Dorset 10 E4
West Chevington Nthumb 109 L11
West Chiltington W Susx 14 F7
West Chinnock Somset 21 P10
West Chisenbury Wilts 23 P3
West Clandon Surrey 32 F11
West Cliffe Kent 17 Q2
West Coker Somset 22 C10
West Combe Devon 5 M4
Westcombe Somset 22 F5
Westcote Gloucs 42 E7
Westcote Barton Oxon 43 J6
Westcott Bucks 43 P8
Westcott Devon 9 J4
Westcott Surrey 32 H12
West Cottingwith N York 86 C7
Westcourt Wilts 30 E10
West Cowick E R Yk 86 C11
West Cross Swans 26 F4
West Curry Cnwll 7 K6
West Curthwaite Cumb 98 C10
Westdean E Susx 15 P11
West Dean W Susx 14 B8
West Dean Wilts 24 D8
West Deeping Lincs 68 B10
West Derby Lpool 75 L5
West Dereham Norfk 69 M12
West Ditchburn Nthumb 109 J5
West Down Devon 19 K5
Westdown Camp Wilts 23 M4
Westdowns Cnwll 6 F8
West Drayton Gt Lon 32 F6
West Drayton Notts 78 H8
West Dunnet Highld 151 N2
Wested Kent 33 P9
West Ella E R Yk 87 J9
West End Bed 55 N10
West End B For 32 B8
West End Caerph 28 B3
West End Cumb 98 C6
West End E R Yk 86 G9
West End E R Yk 87 M9
West End E R Yk 87 P9
Westend Gloucs 41 M10
West End Hants 24 H10
West End Herts 25 L6
West End Herts 45 J10
West End Herts 45 L10
West End Lancs 83 Q9
West End Leeds 85 K7
West End Lincs 80 G4
West End N Som 28 F8
West End N York 85 J2
West End Norfk 70 H10
West End Norfk 71 P10
West End Oxon 31 M5
West End S Glos 29 L5
West End Somset 22 F6
West End Surrey 32 D10
West End Surrey 32 G9
West End W & M 32 B7
West End W Susx 14 H7
West End Wilts 23 K8
West End Wilts 23 L8
West End Wilts 29 R7
West End Green Hants 31 N10
Westend Town Nthumb 99 M5
Wester Aberchalder Highld 137 P11
Wester Balblair Highld 137 N7
Westerdale Highld 151 L6
Westerdale N York 92 D5
Westerfield Suffk 58 H11
Westergate W Susx 14 D10
Westerham Kent 33 N11
Westerhope N u Ty 100 F5
Westerland Devon 5 P4
Westerleigh S Glos 29 L6
Western Isles W Isls 152 e6
Wester Ochiltree W Loth 115 J6
Wester Pitkierie Fife 125 L11
Wester Ross Highld 143 P9
Westerton W Susx 14 C9
Westerton of Rossie Angus 125 N2
Westerwick Shet 147 h7
West Ewell Surrey 32 H9
West Farleigh Kent 34 C11
West Farndon Nhants 54 F10
West Felton Shrops 63 K7
Westfield BaNES 22 F3
Westfield Cumb 88 C1
Westfield E Susx 16 E8
Westfield Highld 151 J4
Westfield N Lans 114 D7
Westfield Norfk 70 E10
Westfield Surrey 32 F11
Westfield W Loth 114 G7
Westfields Dorset 10 H3
Westfields of Rattray P & K 124 D3
Westfield Sole Kent 34 D10
West Flotmanby N York 93 M9
Westford Somset 20 H9
Westgate Dur 99 P10
Westgate N Linc 79 K2
Westgate Norfk 70 E2
Westgate Hill C Brad 85 J9
Westgate-on-Sea Kent 35 P8
Westgate Street Norfk 71 J8
West Ginge Oxon 31 J6
West Grafton Wilts 30 D10
West Green Hants 31 Q11
West Grimstead Wilts 24 D8
West Grinstead W Susx 14 H6
West Haddlesey N York 85 R10
West Haddon Nhants 54 G6
West Hagbourne Oxon 31 L5

West Hagley Worcs 52 G4
Westhall Suffk 59 N4
West Hallam Derbys 66 C4
West Hallam Common Derbys 66 C4
West Halton N Linc 86 G11
Westham Dorset 10 G9
West Ham Gt Lon 33 M5
Westham Somset 21 N4
Westhampnett W Susx 14 C9
West Handley Derbys 78 C8
West Hanney Oxon 31 J4
West Hanningfield Essex 34 C2
West Harnham Wilts 23 P7
West Harptree BaNES 28 H11
West Harting W Susx 25 N9
West Hatch Somset 21 L9
West Hatch Wilts 23 K8
West Haven Angus 125 L6
Westhay Somset 21 P5
Westhead Lancs 75 L11
West Head Norfk 69 L11
West Heath Birm 53 J5
West Heath Hants 31 M10
West Helmsdale Highld 147 J2
West Hendred Oxon 31 J5
West Heslerton N York 93 J11
West Hewish N Som 28 E9
Westhide Herefs 41 J3
Westhill Abers 133 K3
West Hill Devon 9 K6
Westhill Highld 138 D7
West Hoathly W Susx 15 L4
West Holme Dorset 11 L7
Westholme Somset 22 D5
Westhope Herefs 51 M3
Westhope Shrops 51 M3
West Horndon Essex 34 A5
Westhorpe Lincs 68 D6
Westhorpe Suffk 58 F7
West Horrington Somset 22 D4
West Horsley Surrey 32 F11
West Horton Nthumb 108 G4
West Hougham Kent 17 N3
Westhoughton Bolton 76 C2
Westhouse N York 89 R12
Westhouses Derbys 78 C12
West Howe BCP 11 L6
West Howetown Somset 20 E6
Westhumble Surrey 32 H12
West Huntingtower P & K 124 B8
West Huntspill Somset 21 M4
West Hyde C Beds 44 E6
West Hyde Herts 32 F4
West Hythe Kent 17 K4
West Ilkerton Devon 19 N4
West Ilsley W Berk 31 K6
West Itchenor W Susx 13 P4
West Keal Lincs 80 G11
West Kennett Wilts 30 C8
West Kilbride N Ayrs 113 J11
West Kingsdown Kent 33 Q9
West Kington Wilts 29 M6
West Kirby Wirral 74 H6
West Knapton N York 92 H11
West Knighton Dorset 10 H7
West Knoyle Wilts 23 J6
West Kyloe Nthumb 108 H2
Westlake Devon 5 M6
West Lambrook Somset 21 P9
Westland Green Herts 45 M7
West Langdon Kent 17 P1
West Lavington W Susx 14 C6
West Lavington Wilts 23 M3
West Layton N York 91 J5
West Leake Notts 66 E6
West Learmouth Nthumb 108 D2
West Lees N York 91 P6
West Leigh Devon 8 C4
Westleigh Devon 19 J7
Westleigh Devon 20 G10
Westleton Suffk 59 N7
West Lexham Norfk 70 B8
Westley Shrops 63 K10
Westley Suffk 58 B8
Westley Waterless Cambs 57 M9
West Lilling N York 86 C2
Westlington Bucks 43 Q9
West Linton Border 115 L11
Westlinton Cumb 98 C6
West Littleton S Glos 29 M7
West Lockinge Oxon 31 J5
West Lulworth Dorset 11 K8
West Lutton N York 86 H1
West Lydford Somset 22 D7
West Lyn Devon 19 P4
West Lyng Somset 21 M7
West Lynn Norfk 69 L8
West Malling Kent 34 B10
West Malvern Worcs 41 M2
West Marden W Susx 25 N10
West Markham Notts 79 J9
Westmarsh Kent 35 N10
West Marsh NE Lin 80 E2
West Marton N York 84 D5
West Melbury Dorset 23 J8
West Melton Rothm 78 C3
West Meon Hants 25 L8
West Meon Hut Hants 25 L8
West Meon Woodlands Hants 25 L8
West Mersea Essex 46 H9
Westmeston E Susx 15 L8
West Mickley Nthumb 100 D6
West Midland Safari Park Worcs 52 E5
Westmill Herts 45 L6
Westmill Herts 45 J8
West Milton Dorset 10 D5
Westminster Gt Lon 33 K6
Westminster Abbey & Palace Gt Lon 33 K6
West Molesey Surrey 32 G8
West Monkton Somset 21 L7
West Moors Dorset 11 M4
West Morden Dorset 11 L6
West Morriston Border 107 P2
West Morton C Brad 84 G6
West Mudford Somset 22 D9
Westmuir Angus 124 G2
West Ness N York 92 E11
West Newbiggin Darltn 91 N3
Westnewton Cumb 97 N9
West Newton E R Yk 87 M7
West Newton Norfk 69 M6
West Newton Somset 21 L7
West Norwood Gt Lon 33 L7
Westoe S Tyne 101 K5
Westoning C Beds 44 E5
Weston BaNES 29 L8
Weston Ches E 64 D2
Weston Devon 9 M7
Weston Devon 10 C7
Weston Dorset 10 G10
Weston Halton 75 N7
Weston Hants 25 M9
Weston Herefs 51 K10
Weston Herts 45 J6
Weston Lincs 68 E7
Weston N York 85 J6
Weston Nhants 54 D3
Weston Notts 79 K10

Weston Shrops 63 J6
Weston Staffs 64 H7
Weston Suffk 59 N3
Weston Beggard Herefs 41 J3
Westonbirt Gloucs 29 M5
Weston by Welland Nhants 55 K2
Weston Colley Hants 25 J6
Weston Colville Cambs 57 L10
Weston Corbett Hants 25 K4
Weston Coyney C Stke 64 H3
Weston Favell Nhants 55 J8
Weston Green Cambs 57 M10
Weston Heath Shrops 64 E9
Weston Hills Lincs 68 E8
Weston in Arden Warwks 54 C3
Westoning C Beds 44 E5
Weston-in-Gordano N Som 28 F7
Westoning Woodend C Beds 44 E5
Weston Jones Staffs 64 E7
Weston Longville Norfk 70 G9
Weston Lullingfields Shrops 63 L6
Weston-on-Avon Warwks 53 M10
Weston-on-the-Green Oxon 43 L8
Weston Park Staffs 64 E10
Weston Patrick Hants 25 M4
Weston Rhyn Shrops 63 J5
Weston-sub-Edge Gloucs 42 D3
Weston-super-Mare N Som 28 D10
Weston Turville Bucks 44 B9
Weston-under-Lizard Staffs 64 E10
Weston under Penyard Herefs 41 K7
Weston-under-Redcastle Shrops 63 P6
Weston under Wetherley Warwks 54 B7
Weston Underwood Derbys 65 P4
Weston Underwood M Keyn 55 L10
Weston-upon-Trent Derbys 66 C6
Westonzoyland Somset 21 M6
West Orchard Dorset 22 H10
West Overton Wilts 30 C8
Westow N York 86 D2
West Panson Devon 7 L6
West Park Abers 133 J5
West Parley Dorset 11 Q5
West Peckham Kent 34 B11
West Peeke Devon 7 L6
West Pelton Dur 100 G7
West Pennard Somset 22 D5
West Pentire Cnwll 3 J2
West Pinchbeck Lincs 68 D7
West Porlock Somset 20 D4
Westport Somset 21 N9
West Pulham Dorset 10 G4
West Putford Devon 18 G10
West Quantoxhead Somset 20 H5
Westquarter Falk 114 E6
Westra V Glam 27 Q8
West Raddon Devon 8 G4
West Rainton Dur 101 J9
West Rasen Lincs 79 Q6
West Ravendale NE Lin 80 E4
Westray Ork 147 c2
Westray Airport Ork 147 c1
West Raynham Norfk 70 C7
West Retford Notts 78 H7
Westridge Green W Berk 31 M6
Westrigg W Loth 114 G8
Westrop Swindn 30 D5
West Rounton N York 91 P6
West Row Suffk 57 N5
West Rudham Norfk 70 B6
West Runton Norfk 70 H3
Westruther Border 116 E11
Westry Cambs 56 H1
West Saltoun E Loth 116 B8
West Sandford Devon 8 H4
West Sandwick Shet 147 i4
West Scrafton N York 90 H10
West Sleekburn Nthumb 100 H1
West Somerton Norfk 71 P8
West Stafford Dorset 10 H7
West Stockwith Notts 79 K5
West Stoke W Susx 13 P3
West Stonesdale N York 90 D6
West Stoughton Somset 21 P4
West Stour Dorset 22 H9
West Stourmouth Kent 35 N9
West Stow Suffk 57 Q6
West Stowell Wilts 30 C9
West Stratton Hants 25 J4
West Street Kent 34 F11
West Street Kent 35 P11
West Street Medway 34 E9
West Street Suffk 47 J1
Westward Cumb 98 C10
Westward Ho! Devon 18 H7
Westwell Kent 34 H1
Westwell Oxon 42 F9
Westwell Leacon Kent 16 G1
West Wellow Hants 24 E9
West Wembury Devon 4 H7
West Wemyss Fife 115 P1
Westwick Cambs 56 H7
Westwick Dur 90 H4
West Wick N Som 28 E10
West Wickham Cambs 57 L10
West Wickham Gt Lon 33 M8
West Williamston Pembks 36 H9
West Winch Norfk 69 M9
West Winterslow Wilts 24 C7
West Wittering W Susx 13 N5
West Witton N York 90 H9
Westwood Devon 9 P5
Westwood Kent 35 P9
Westwood Herefs 51 L9
Westwood Nthumb 100 C6
Westwood Wilts 29 M10
Westwood Heath Covtry 53 P5
Westwoodside N Linc 79 J4

West Worldham Hants 25 M6
West Worthing W Susx 14 G10
West Wratting Cambs 57 L10
West Wycombe Bucks 32 B3
West Wylam Nthumb 100 E6
West Yatton Wilts 29 N7
West Yoke Kent 33 Q9
West Youlstone Cnwll 18 E9
Wetham Green Kent 34 E8
Wetheral Cumb 98 F7
Wetherby Leeds 85 N5
Wetherby Services N York 85 N5
Wetherden Suffk 58 E8
Wetheringsett Suffk 58 H7
Wethersfield Essex 46 C5
Wetherup Street Suffk 58 H8
Wetley Rocks Staffs 64 H2
Wettenhall Ches E 76 B11
Wetton Staffs 65 L1
Wetwang E R Yk 86 H3
Wetwood Staffs 64 E5
Wexcombe Wilts 30 F10
Wexham Slough 32 E6
Wexham Street Bucks 32 E6
Weybourne Norfk 70 G4
Weybourne Surrey 25 P3
Weybread Suffk 59 K4
Weybread Street Suffk 59 K4
Weybridge Surrey 32 F9
Weycroft Devon 9 P5
Weydale Highld 151 L4
Weyhill Hants 24 E4
Weymouth Dorset 10 G10
Whaddon Bucks 44 A5
Whaddon Cambs 45 L2
Whaddon Gloucs 41 M3
Whaddon Wilts 24 C8
Whaddon Wilts 29 P10
Whale Cumb 89 N2
Whaley Derbys 78 E9
Whaley Bridge Derbys 77 J7
Whaley Thorns Derbys 78 E9
Whaligoe Highld 151 P8
Whalley Lancs 83 Q8
Whalley Banks Lancs 83 Q8
Whalsay Shet 147 k5
Whalton Nthumb 100 E2
Whaplode Lincs 68 G7
Whaplode Drove Lincs 68 G9
Wharf Warwks 54 C10
Wharfe N York 84 B1
Wharles Lancs 83 K8
Wharley End C Beds 44 H2
Wharncliffe Side Sheff 77 P5
Wharram-le-Street N York 86 F2
Wharton Ches W 76 C10
Wharton Herefs 51 N9
Whashton N York 91 K5
Whasset Cumb 89 N10
Whatcote Warwks 42 G3
Whateley Warwks 65 N12
Whatfield Suffk 47 J2
Whatley Somset 22 G4
Whatley Somset 22 G4
Whatley's End S Glos 29 K6
Whatlington E Susx 16 D7
Whatsole Street Kent 17 K2
Whatstandwell Derbys 65 Q1
Whatton-in-the-Vale Notts 67 J4
Whauphill D & G 95 M8
Whaw N York 90 G6
Wheatacre Norfk 59 P2
Wheatcroft Derbys 66 D3
Wheathampstead Herts 44 H9
Wheathill Shrops 52 B4
Wheathill Somset 22 D7
Wheatley Hants 25 N5
Wheatley Oxon 43 M10
Wheatley Hill Dur 101 K10
Wheatley Hills Donc 78 F3
Wheatley Lane Lancs 84 C7
Wheaton Aston Staffs 64 F9
Wheddon Cross Somset 20 E6
Wheelbarrow Town Kent 17 L2
Wheeler End Bucks 32 B4
Wheeler's Green Wokham 31 Q8
Wheelerstreet Surrey 14 D3
Wheelock Ches E 76 D12
Wheelock Heath Ches E 76 D12
Wheelton Lancs 83 N11
Wheldrake C York 86 C6
Wheldale Wakefd 85 P10
Whelford Gloucs 30 D3
Whelpley Hill Bucks 44 E10
Whelpo Cumb 98 C10
Whelston Flints 74 H8
Whempstead Herts 45 K7
Whenby N York 86 C1
Whepstead Suffk 58 B9
Wherstead Suffk 47 L3
Wherwell Hants 24 G4
Wheston Derbys 77 L8
Whetsted Kent 16 B2
Whetstone Gt Lon 33 J4
Whetstone Leics 54 F1
Wheyrigg Cumb 97 P8
Whicham Cumb 88 F10
Whichford Warwks 42 H5
Whickham Gatesd 100 G6
Whiddon Devon 7 N5
Whiddon Down Devon 8 F6
Whigstreet Angus 125 J3
Whilton Nhants 54 F7
Whimble Devon 7 L3
Whimple Devon 9 K5
Whimpwell Green Norfk 71 M6
Whinburgh Norfk 70 F10
Whin Lane End Lancs 83 J7
Whinnieliggate D & G 96 E8
Whinnow Cumb 98 C8
Whinnyfold Abers 141 P9
Whinny Hill S on T 91 N3
Whippingham IoW 12 H6
Whipsnade C Beds 44 E8
Whipsnade Zoo ZSL C Beds 44 E8
Whipton Devon 8 H6
Whirlow Sheff 77 N5
Whisby Lincs 79 M10
Whissendine Rutlnd 67 K9
Whissonsett Norfk 70 D7
Whistlefield Ag & B 113 J3
Whistlefield Inn Ag & B 113 J2
Whistley Green Wokham 31 R7
Whiston Knows 75 M5
Whiston Nhants 55 L8
Whiston Rothm 78 C5
Whiston Staffs 64 G9
Whiston Staffs 65 J3
Whiston Cross Shrops 64 E11
Whiston Eaves Staffs 65 K3
Whitacre Fields Warwks 53 N3
Whitbeck Cumb 88 F10
Whitbourne Herefs 52 D9
Whitburn S Tyne 101 K6
Whitburn W Loth 114 H8
Whitby Ches W 75 L8
Whitby N York 92 H5
Whitbyheath Ches W 75 L8
Whitchester Border 116 G9
Whitchurch BaNES 29 J9
Whitchurch Bucks 44 A7

Whitchurch Cardif 27 R6
Whitchurch Devon 7 Q10
Whitchurch Hants 24 H4
Whitchurch Herefs 40 H7
Whitchurch Oxon 31 N7
Whitchurch Pembks 36 F5
Whitchurch Shrops 63 P4
Whitchurch Canonicorum Dorset 10 B6
Whitchurch Hill Oxon 31 N6
Whitcombe Dorset 10 H7
Whitcot Shrops 51 L2
Whitcott Keysett Shrops 51 J4
Whiteacre Kent 17 K1
Whiteacre Heath Warwks 53 N2
Whiteash Green Essex 46 D5
White Ball Somset 20 H9
Whitebridge Highld 129 N1
Whitebrook Mons 40 H10
Whitebushes Surrey 15 K1
Whitecairns Abers 141 M12
Whitechapel Gt Lon 33 L6
White Chapel Lancs 83 M7
Whitechurch Pembks 37 M3
Whitecliff Gloucs 40 H9
White Colne Essex 46 F6
White Coppice Lancs 83 N11
Whitecraig E Loth 115 Q7
Whitecroft Gloucs 41 J10
Whitecrook D & G 94 H7
Whitecross Cnwll 2 E7
White Cross Cnwll 2 H10
Whitecross Cnwll 6 D10
Whitecross Falk 114 H6
White End Worcs 41 M5
Whiteface Highld 146 C7
Whitefarland N Ayrs 103 M1
Whitefaulds S Ayrs 104 E8
Whitefield Bury 76 E2
Whitefield Devon 19 N6
Whitefield Somset 20 G7
Whitefield Lane End Knows 75 M6
Whiteford Abers 140 H10
Whitegate Ches W 76 B10
Whitehall Hants 25 N3
Whitehall Ork 147 e3
Whitehall W Susx 14 G6
Whitehaven Cumb 88 C3
Whitehill Hants 25 N6
Whitehill Kent 34 H10
Whitehill Leics 66 C10
Whitehills Abers 140 G3
Whitehouse Abers 132 F1
Whitehouse Ag & B 112 B9
Whitehouse Common Birm 53 L1
Whitekirk E Loth 116 E5
White Kirkley Dur 100 C11
White Lackington Dorset 10 H5
Whitelackington Somset 21 N10
White Ladies Aston Worcs 52 G10
Whiteleaf Bucks 44 B10
White-le-Head Dur 100 F7
Whiteley Hants 13 J3
Whiteley Bank IoW 13 J8
Whiteley Green Ches E 76 G8
Whiteley Village Surrey 32 F9
Whitemans Green W Susx 15 K6
White Mill Carmth 38 C7
Whitemire Moray 138 C5
Whitemoor C Nott 66 E4
Whitemoor Cnwll 3 M3
Whitemoor Derbys 66 B3
Whitemoor Staffs 76 G11
Whiteness Shet 147 i7
White Notley Essex 46 D8
Whiteoak Green Oxon 42 H9
White Ox Mead BaNES 29 L10
Whiteparish Wilts 24 D8
White Pit Lincs 80 G8
Whiterashes Abers 141 L11
White Roding Essex 45 Q9
Whiterow Highld 151 Q6
Whiterow Moray 139 J4
Whiteshill Gloucs 41 N10
Whitesmith E Susx 15 P8
White Stake Lancs 83 M10
Whitestaunton Somset 9 P2
Whitestone Herefs 40 H3
Whitestone Warwks 54 C3
White Stone Herefs 40 H3
Whitestone Cross Devon 8 H7
Whitestreet Green Suffk 46 H4
Whitewall Corner N York 86 E1
White Waltham W & M 32 B7
Whiteway BaNES 29 J9
Whitewell Lancs 83 P6
Whiteworks Devon 5 Q4
Whitfield C Dund 125 J4
Whitfield Kent 17 N2
Whitfield Nhants 43 N4
Whitfield Nthumb 99 M7
Whitfield S Glos 29 K4
Whitfield Hall Nthumb 99 M7
Whitford Devon 9 P5
Whitford Flints 74 H8
Whitgift E R Yk 86 E10
Whitgreave Staffs 64 G6
Whithorn D & G 95 M10
Whiting Bay N Ayrs 103 Q4
Whitkirk Leeds 85 M8
Whitland Carmth 37 N7
Whitlaw Border 107 M7
Whitletts S Ayrs 104 G5
Whitley N York 85 R11
Whitley Readg 31 P8
Whitley Sheff 77 Q5
Whitley Wilts 29 N9
Whitley Bay N Tyne 101 K4
Whitley Chapel Nthumb 99 P7
Whitley Heath Staffs 64 F7
Whitley Lower Kirk 85 J11
Whitley Row Kent 33 P11
Whitlock's End Solhll 53 L5
Whitminster Gloucs 41 M10
Whitmore Dorset 11 P3
Whitmore Staffs 64 E4
Whitnage Devon 20 G10
Whitnash Warwks 53 Q8
Whitney-on-Wye Herefs 40 C2
Whitrigg Cumb 97 P7
Whitrigg Cumb 98 C9
Whitsbury Hants 23 P9
Whitsome Border 117 J10
Whitson Newpt 28 D4
Whitstable Kent 35 J9
Whitstone Cnwll 7 K4
Whittingham Nthumb 108 H9
Whittingslow Shrops 51 M3
Whittington Derbys 78 C8
Whittington Gloucs 42 B7
Whittington Lancs 89 R12
Whittington Norfk 69 N12
Whittington Shrops 63 K5
Whittington Staffs 52 E2
Whittington Staffs 65 M11
Whittington Warwks 53 N2
Whittington Worcs 52 F9
Whittington Moor Derbys 78 C8
Whittlebury Nhants 43 P3
Whittle-le-Woods Lancs 83 N11
Whittlesey Cambs 56 E1
Whittlesford Cambs 57 J11

Whittlestone Head Bl w D 83 Q11
Whitton N Linc 86 G10
Whitton Nthumb 108 H9
Whitton Powys 51 J7
Whitton S on T 91 P2
Whitton Shrops 51 P6
Whitton Suffk 58 H11
Whittonditch Wilts 30 F8
Whittonstall Nthumb 100 D7
Whitway Hants 31 K10
Whitwell Derbys 78 E8
Whitwell Herts 44 H7
Whitwell IoW 13 J9
Whitwell N York 91 M7
Whitwell Rutlnd 67 M10
Whitwell-on-the-Hill N York 86 D2
Whitwell Street Norfk 70 G8
Whitwick Leics 66 D9
Whitwood Wakefd 85 N10
Whitworth Lancs 84 D11
Whixall Shrops 63 N5
Whixley N York 85 N4
Whorlton Dur 91 J4
Whorlton N York 91 Q6
Whyle Herefs 51 P8
Whyteleafe Surrey 33 L10
Wibdon Gloucs 28 H3
Wibsey C Brad 84 H9
Wibtoft Warwks 54 D3
Wichelstowe Swindn 30 D6
Wichenford Worcs 52 E8
Wichling Kent 34 G11
Wick BCP 12 B6
Wick Devon 9 M4
Wick Highld 151 Q6
Wick S Glos 29 L8
Wick Somset 21 L4
Wick Somset 21 N8
Wick V Glam 27 L8
Wick W Susx 14 E10
Wick Wilts 23 Q9
Wick Worcs 41 Q3
Wicken Cambs 57 L6
Wicken Nhants 43 Q4
Wicken Bonhunt Essex 45 P5
Wickenby Lincs 80 B7
Wick End Bed 55 N10
Wicken Green Village Norfk 70 B6
Wickersley Rothm 78 D5
Wicker Street Green Suffk 46 H3
Wickford Essex 34 D4
Wickham Hants 13 K2
Wickham W Berk 31 J8
Wickham Bishops Essex 46 E9
Wickhambreaux Kent 35 M10
Wickhambrook Suffk 57 P9
Wickhamford Worcs 42 C3
Wickham Green Suffk 58 G7
Wickham Heath W Berk 31 J8
Wickham Market Suffk 59 L9
Wickhampton Norfk 71 N11
Wickham St Paul Essex 46 E4
Wickham Skeith Suffk 58 G7
Wickham Street Suffk 57 P10
Wickham Street Suffk 58 G7
Wickhurst Green W Susx 14 G5
Wick John o' Groats Airport Highld 151 Q6
Wicklewood Norfk 70 G11
Wickmere Norfk 70 H5
Wick St Lawrence N Som 28 E9
Wicksteed Park Nhants 55 L5
Wickstreet E Susx 15 P9
Wickwar S Glos 29 L5
Widdington Essex 45 P5
Widdop Calder 84 D8
Widdrington Nthumb 109 L10
Widdrington Station Nthumb 109 L11
Widecombe in the Moor Devon 8 D9
Widegates Cnwll 4 D5
Widemouth Bay Cnwll 7 J4
Wide Open N Tyne 100 G4
Widford Essex 46 C10
Widford Herts 45 M8
Widham Wilts 30 C5
Widmer End Bucks 32 C3
Widmerpool Notts 66 G6
Widmore Gt Lon 33 M8
Widnes Halton 75 N6
Widworthy Devon 9 N5
Wigan Wigan 75 P3
Wigborough Somset 21 P10
Wiggaton Devon 9 L6
Wiggenhall St Germans Norfk 69 L9
Wiggenhall St Mary Magdalen Norfk 69 L10
Wiggenhall St Mary the Virgin Norfk 69 L9
Wiggenhall St Peter Norfk 69 L9
Wiggens Green Essex 46 B3
Wiggenstall Staffs 77 K11
Wiggington Shrops 63 K5
Wigginton C York 86 B3
Wigginton Herts 44 D9
Wigginton Oxon 42 H5
Wigginton Staffs 65 N11
Wigginton Bottom Herts 44 D10
Wigglesworth N York 84 B4
Wiggonby Cumb 98 C7
Wiggonholt W Susx 14 F7
Wighill N York 85 N5
Wighton Norfk 70 D4
Wightwick Wolves 52 F1
Wigley Derbys 77 P9
Wigley Hants 24 E10
Wigmore Herefs 51 L6
Wigmore Medway 34 D9
Wigsley Notts 79 K9
Wigsthorpe Nhants 55 P4
Wigston Leics 54 G1
Wigston Fields Leics 66 F12
Wigston Parva Leics 54 D3
Wigthorpe Notts 78 F7
Wigtoft Lincs 68 E5
Wigton Cumb 98 C9
Wigtown D & G 95 M7
Wigwizzie Sheff 77 N4
Wike Leeds 85 K5
Wilberfoss E R Yk 86 D5
Wilburton Cambs 57 J6
Wilby Nhants 55 L7
Wilby Norfk 58 G2
Wilby Suffk 59 K6
Wilcot Wilts 30 D10
Wilcott Shrops 63 L8
Wilcove Cnwll 4 F5
Wilcrick Newpt 28 F4
Wilday Green Derbys 77 P9
Wildboarclough Ches E 76 H10
Wilden Bed 55 P9
Wilden Worcs 52 F6
Wilde Street Suffk 57 N5
Wildhern Hants 24 F3
Wildhill Herts 45 J10
Wildmanbridge S Lans 114 E10
Wildmill Brdgnd 27 J5
Wildmoor Hants 25 L2

Wildmoor Worcs...52 H5
Wildsworth Lincs...79 K4
Wilford C Nott...66 F5
Wilkesley Ches E...64 B4
Wilkhaven Highld...146 G8
Wilkieston W Loth...115 L7
Wilkin's Green Herts...44 H10
Wilksby Lincs...80 F11
Willand Devon...9 K3
Willards Hill Lincs...16 C6
Willaston Ches E...64 C2
Willaston Ches E...75 K8
Willen M Keyn...44 C3
Willenhall Covtry...54 B5
Willenhall Wsall...52 H1
Willerby E R Yk...87 J9
Willerby N York...93 K11
Willersey Gloucs...42 C4
Willersley Herefs...40 D2
Willesborough Kent...17 J2
Willesborough Lees Kent...17 J2
Willesden Gt Lon...33 J5
Willesleigh Devon...19 L7
Willesley Wilts...29 N5
Willett Somset...20 H6
Willey Shrops...64 C12
Willey Warwks...54 E4
Willey Green Surrey...32 D12
Williamscot Oxon...43 K3
Williamstown Rhondd...27 N4
Willian Herts...45 J5
Willicote Warwks...53 M10
Willingale Essex...45 Q10
Willingdon E Susx...15 Q10
Willingham Cambs...56 H6
Willingham by Stow Lincs...79 L7
Willingham Green Cambs...57 M10
Willingham St Mary Suffk...59 N4
Willington Bed...56 C10
Willington Derbys...65 P6
Willington Dur...100 G11
Willington Kent...34 D11
Willington N Tyne...101 J5
Willington Warwks...42 F4
Willington Corner Ches W...75 N10
Willitoft E R Yk...86 D8
Williton Somset...20 G5
Willoughby Lincs...81 J9
Willoughby Warwks...54 E7
Willoughby Hills Lincs...68 G3
Willoughby-on-the-Wolds Notts...66 G7
Willoughby Waterleys Leics...54 F2
Willoughton Lincs...79 M5
Willow Green Ches W...75 Q8
Willows Green S Glos...46 C8
Willsbridge S Glos...29 K8
Willsworthy Devon...7 P8
Willtown Somset...21 N8
Wilmcote Warwks...53 M9
Wilmington BaNES...29 L10
Wilmington Devon...9 N5
Wilmington E Susx...15 Q10
Wilmington Kent...33 P8
Wilmslow Ches E...76 F7
Wilnecote Staffs...65 N12
Wilpshire Lancs...83 Q8
Wilsden C Brad...84 G8
Wilsford Lincs...67 P4
Wilsford Wilts...23 P5
Wilsford Wilts...30 C11
Wilsham Devon...19 P4
Wilshaw Kirk...L2
Wilsill N York...85 J2
Wilsley Green Kent...16 D3
Wilsley Pound Kent...16 D3
Wilson Herefs...40 H7
Wilson Leics...66 C7
Wilsontown S Lans...114 H10
Wilstead Bed...44 F3
Wilsthorpe Lincs...68 B9
Wilstone Herts...44 C9
Wilstone Green Herts...44 C9
Wilton Cumb...88 D4
Wilton Herefs...41 J7
Wilton N York...92 H10
Wilton R & Cl...92 C3
Wilton Wilts...23 N7
Wilton Wilts...30 F10
Wilton Dean Border...107 M7
Wimbish Essex...45 Q4
Wimbish Green Essex...45 R5
Wimbledon Gt Lon...33 J8
Wimblington Cambs...56 H2
Wimboldsley Ches W...76 C11
Wimborne Minster Dorset...11 N5
Wimborne St Giles Dorset...11 P2
Wimbotsham Norfk...69 M11
Wimpole Cambs...56 G10
Wimpstone Warwks...53 N11
Wincanton Somset...22 G7
Winceby Lincs...80 F10
Wincham Ches W...76 C8
Winchburgh W Loth...115 K6
Winchcombe Gloucs...42 B6
Winchelsea E Susx...16 F7
Winchelsea Beach E Susx...16 G7
Winchester Hants...24 H7
Winchester Services Hants...25 J6
Winchet Hill Kent...16 C3
Winchfield Hants...25 N2
Winchmore Hill Bucks...32 D3
Winchmore Hill Gt Lon...33 K3
Wincle Ches E...76 H10
Wincobank Sheff...78 C5
Winder Cumb...88 D3
Windermere Cumb...89 L7
Windermere Jetty Cumb...89 L7
Winderton Warwks...42 G3
Windhill Highld...137 P6
Windlehurst Stockp...76 H6
Windlesham Surrey...32 D9
Windmill Cnwll...6 C9
Windmill Derbys...77 M8
Windmill Hill E Susx...16 B8
Windmill Hill Somset...21 M10
Windrush Gloucs...42 F9
Windsole Abers...140 E4
Windsor W & M...32 D7
Windsor Castle W & M...32 D7
Windsoredge Gloucs...29 N2
Windsor Green Suffk...58 C9
Windygates Fife...115 Q1
Windyharbour Ches E...76 F9
Windy Hill Wrexhm...63 J1
Wineham W Susx...15 J7
Winestead E R Yk...87 P10
Winewall Lancs...84 D7
Winfarthing Norfk...58 G4
Winford IoW...13 J8
Winford N Som...28 H9
Winfrith Newburgh Dorset...11 K8
Wing Bucks...44 C9
Wing Rutlnd...67 M11
Wingate Dur...101 K11
Wingates Bolton...76 C2
Wingates Nthumb...108 H9
Wingerworth Derbys...78 C10
Wingfield C Beds...44 E6

Wingfield Suffk...59 J5
Wingfield Wilts...29 N11
Wingfield Green Suffk...59 J5
Wingham Kent...35 M11
Wingland Lincs...69 J7
Wingmore Kent...17 L2
Wingrave Bucks...44 B8
Winkburn Notts...78 H12
Winkfield Br For...32 C8
Winkfield Row Br For...32 C8
Winkhill Staffs...65 K2
Winkhurst Green Kent...15 P1
Winkleigh Devon...8 H3
Winksley N York...85 K1
Winkton BCP...12 B5
Winlaton Gatesd...100 F6
Winlaton Mill Gatesd...100 F6
Winless Highld...151 P6
Winllan Powys...62 H8
Winmarleigh Lancs...83 L6
Winnall Wokham...24 H7
Winnersh Wokham...31 Q8
Winnington Ches W...76 B9
Winscales Cumb...88 D2
Winscombe N Som...28 F11
Winsford Ches W...76 C10
Winsford Somset...20 D6
Winsham Devon...19 K5
Winsham Somset...10 B3
Winshill Staffs...65 N8
Winshwen Swans...26 G3
Winskill Cumb...98 H11
Winslade Hants...25 L4
Winsley Wilts...29 M10
Winslow Bucks...43 Q6
Winson Gloucs...42 C10
Winsor Hants...24 E10
Winstanley Wigan...75 P3
Winster Cumb...89 L8
Winster Derbys...77 N11
Winston Dur...91 J3
Winston Suffk...58 H8
Winstone Gloucs...41 Q9
Winston Green Suffk...58 H8
Winswell Devon...19 J10
Winterborne Came Dorset...10 H7
Winterborne Clenston Dorset...11 J4
Winterborne Herringston Dorset...10 H7
Winterborne Houghton Dorset...11 K4
Winterborne Kingston Dorset...11 L5
Winterborne Monkton Dorset...10 G7
Winterborne Stickland Dorset...11 K4
Winterborne Tomson Dorset...11 L5
Winterborne Whitechurch Dorset...11 K5
Winterborne Zelston Dorset...11 L5
Winterbourne S Glos...29 K6
Winterbourne W Berk...31 K8
Winterbourne Abbas Dorset...10 F6
Winterbourne Bassett Wilts...30 C7
Winterbourne Dauntsey Wilts...24 B6
Winterbourne Earls Wilts...24 B6
Winterbourne Gunner Wilts...24 B6
Winterbourne Monkton Wilts...30 C8
Winterbourne Steepleton Dorset...10 F7
Winterbourne Stoke Wilts...23 N5
Winterbrook Oxon...31 M5
Winterburn N York...84 D3
Winteringham N Linc...86 H10
Winterley Ches E...76 D12
Wintersett Wakefd...85 M12
Winterslow Wilts...24 B6
Winterton N Linc...86 H11
Winterton-on-Sea Norfk...71 P8
Winthorpe Lincs...81 L10
Winthorpe Notts...79 K12
Winton BCP...11 Q6
Winton Cumb...90 C5
Winton E Susx...15 P10
Winton N York...91 P7
Wintringham Cambs...56 D8
Wintringham N York...92 H12
Winwick Cambs...56 B4
Winwick Nhants...54 G6
Winwick Warrtn...75 Q5
Wirksworth Derbys...65 P1
Wirral...75 J6
Wirswall Ches E...63 P3
Wisbech Cambs...68 H10
Wisbech St Mary Cambs...68 H10
Wisborough Green W Susx...14 F5
Wiseman's Bridge Pembks...37 M9
Wiseton Notts...79 J6
Wishanger Gloucs...41 Q9
Wishaw N Lans...114 E10
Wishaw Warwks...53 M2
Wisley Surrey...32 F10
Wisley Garden RHS Surrey...32 F10
Wispington Lincs...80 D9
Wissenden Kent...16 H3
Wissett Suffk...59 M5
Wissington Norfk...57 M1
Wissington Suffk...46 G5
Wistanstow Shrops...51 M4
Wistanswick Shrops...64 C8
Wistaston Ches E...64 C1
Wistaston Green Ches E...64 C1
Wisterfield Ches E...76 F9
Wiston Pembks...37 K7
Wiston S Lans...106 C3
Wiston W Susx...14 G8
Wistow Cambs...56 E4
Wistow Leics...54 G2
Wistow N York...86 B8
Wiswell Lancs...83 R7
Witcham Cambs...57 J3
Witchampton Dorset...11 N3
Witchford Cambs...57 J4
Witcombe Somset...21 Q9
Witham Essex...46 E9
Witham Friary Somset...22 G5
Witham on the Hill Lincs...67 P9
Witham St Hughs Lincs...79 M11
Withcall Lincs...80 F7
Witherenden Hill E Susx...16 B5
Witheridge Devon...20 C10
Witherley Leics...53 Q1
Withern Lincs...81 H7
Withernsea E R Yk...87 Q9
Withernwick E R Yk...87 M7
Withersdale Street Suffk...59 M11
Withersfield Suffk...57 M11
Witherslack Cumb...89 L10
Withiel Cnwll...6 E11
Withiel Florey Somset...20 F7
Withielgoose Cnwll...6 E11
Withington Gloucs...42 B9

Withington Herefs...40 H3
Withington Manch...76 F5
Withington Shrops...63 P9
Withington Staffs...65 J5
Withington Green Ches E...76 E9
Withington Marsh Herefs...40 H3
Withleigh Devon...20 D10
Withnell Lancs...83 P10
Withnell Fold Lancs...83 N10
Withybed Green Worcs...53 J4
Withybrook Warwks...54 D4
Withycombe Somset...20 F5
Withyham E Susx...15 P4
Withy Mills BaNES...29 K11
Withypool Somset...20 C6
Withywood Bristl...28 H9
Witley Surrey...14 D3
Witnesham Suffk...58 H10
Witney Oxon...42 H9
Wittering C Pete...67 Q11
Wittersham Kent...16 F5
Witton Birm...53 K2
Witton Norfk...71 L10
Witton Norfk...71 M9
Witton Gilbert Dur...100 G9
Witton Green Norfk...71 N10
Witton le Wear Dur...100 F12
Witton Park Dur...100 F12
Wiveliscombe Somset...20 H8
Wivelrod Hants...25 L6
Wivelsfield E Susx...15 L7
Wivelsfield E Susx...15 L7
Wivelsfield Station W Susx...15 L7
Wivenhoe Essex...47 J7
Wivenhoe Cross Essex...47 J7
Wiveton Norfk...70 F4
Wix Essex...47 L6
Wixams Bed...44 F3
Wixford Warwks...53 K9
Wix Green Essex...47 L6
Wixhill Shrops...63 P6
Wixoe Suffk...46 C3
Woburn C Beds...44 D5
Woburn Safari Park C Beds...44 D5
Woburn Sands M Keyn...44 C4
Wokefield Park W Berk...31 N9
Woking Surrey...32 E10
Wokingham Wokham...32 A8
Wolborough Devon...8 B10
Woldingham Surrey...33 L11
Wold Newton E R Yk...93 L12
Wold Newton NE Lin...80 E4
Wolfclyde S Lans...106 D3
Wolferlow Herefs...52 C8
Wolferton Norfk...69 M6
Wolfhampcote Warwks...54 E7
Wolfhill P & K...124 D6
Wolf Hills Nthumb...99 L6
Wolf's Castle Pembks...37 J5
Wolfsdale Pembks...36 H6
Wollaston Dudley...52 G4
Wollaston Nhants...55 M8
Wollaston Shrops...63 K9
Wollaton C Nott...66 E4
Wollerton Shrops...64 B6
Wollescote Dudley...52 H4
Wolseley Bridge Staffs...65 J8
Wolsingham Dur...100 D10
Wolstanton Staffs...64 F3
Wolston Warwks...54 C5
Wolsty Cumb...97 M8
Wolvercote Oxon...43 K9
Wolverhampton Wolves...64 G12
Wolverhampton Halfpenny Green Airport Staffs...52 F2
Wolverley Shrops...63 M6
Wolverley Worcs...52 G6
Wolverton Hants...31 L10
Wolverton Kent...17 N2
Wolverton M Keyn...44 B3
Wolverton Warwks...53 N8
Wolverton Wilts...22 H7
Wolverton Common Hants...31 M10
Wolvesnewton Mons...28 F2
Wolvey Warwks...54 C3
Wolvey Heath Warwks...54 D3
Wolviston S on T...91 Q2
Wombleton N York...92 D10
Wombourne Staffs...52 G2
Wombwell Barns...78 C3
Womenswold Kent...35 M12
Womersley N York...85 Q11
Wonastow Mons...40 G9
Wonersh Surrey...14 E2
Wonford Devon...8 H6
Wonson Devon...8 C7
Wonston Dorset...10 H3
Wonston Hants...24 H5
Wooburn Bucks...32 C5
Wooburn Green Bucks...32 C5
Wooburn Moor Bucks...32 C4
Woodacott Devon...7 M3
Woodale N York...90 H11
Woodall Rothm...78 D7
Woodall Services Rothm...78 D7
Woodbank Ches W...75 K9
Woodbastwick Norfk...71 L9
Woodbeck Notts...79 K8
Wood Bevington Warwks...53 K10
Woodborough Notts...66 G3
Woodborough Wilts...30 C10
Woodbridge Devon...9 M6
Woodbridge Dorset...23 J9
Woodbridge Suffk...59 K10
Wood Burcote Nhants...43 P2
Woodbury Devon...9 J7
Woodbury Salterton Devon...9 J7
Woodchester Gloucs...41 N11
Woodchurch Kent...16 G4
Woodchurch Wirral...75 J6
Woodcombe Somset...20 E4
Woodcote Gt Lon...33 K10
Woodcote Oxon...31 N6
Woodcote Wrekin...64 E9
Woodcote Green Worcs...52 G6
Woodcott Hants...24 H3
Woodcroft Gloucs...28 H3
Woodcutts Dorset...23 L10
Wood Dalling Norfk...70 G7
Woodditton Cambs...57 M9
Woodeaton Oxon...43 L9
Wood Eaton Staffs...64 F8
Wooden Pembks...37 M9
Wood End Bed...44 E2
Wood End Bed...56 B6
Wood End C Beds...44 D3
Wood End Cambs...56 G5
Wood End Gt Lon...32 G6
Wood End Herts...45 K6
Woodend Highld...127 P12
Woodend Nhants...43 N3
Woodend Staffs...65 M8
Woodend W Loth...114 G7
Wood End Warwks...53 L6
Wood End Warwks...53 N1
Wood End Warwks...53 L4
Wood End Wolves...64 H12

Wood Enderby Lincs...80 E11
Woodend Green Essex...45 Q6
Woodfalls Wilts...24 C9
Woodford Cnwll...18 E10
Woodford Devon...5 N6
Woodford Gloucs...29 L3
Woodford Gt Lon...33 M4
Woodford Nhants...55 M5
Woodford Stockp...76 G7
Woodford Bridge Gt Lon...33 M4
Woodford Green Gt Lon...33 M4
Woodford Halse Nhants...54 E10
Woodford Wells Gt Lon...33 M4
Woodgate Birm...53 J4
Woodgate Devon...20 H10
Woodgate Norfk...70 F9
Woodgate W Susx...14 C10
Woodgate Worcs...52 H7
Wood Green Gt Lon...33 K4
Woodgreen Hants...24 B10
Woodgreen Oxon...42 H9
Wood Hall N York...90 F8
Woodhall Hill Leeds...85 J8
Woodhall Spa Lincs...80 D11
Woodham Bucks...43 P8
Woodham Dur...91 M1
Woodham Surrey...32 E10
Woodham Ferrers Essex...34 D2
Woodham Mortimer Essex...46 E10
Woodham Walter Essex...46 E10
Wood Hayes Wolves...64 H11
Woodhead Abers...141 J8
Woodhill Shrops...52 D4
Woodhill Somset...21 M8
Woodhorn Demesne Nthumb...109 M12
Woodhouse Leics...85 L8
Woodhouse Leeds...E9
Woodhouse Sheff...78 C7
Woodhouse Wakefd...85 M11
Woodhouse Eaves Leics...66 E9
Woodhouse Green Staffs...76 G11
Woodhouselee Mdloth...115 M6
Woodhouselees D & G...98 E3
Woodhouse Mill Sheff...78 C6
Woodhouses Cumb...98 C8
Woodhouses Oldham...76 G4
Woodhouses Staffs...65 K10
Woodhouses Staffs...65 M8
Woodhuish Devon...5 Q6
Woodhurst Cambs...56 F5
Woodingdean Br & H...15 L9
Woodkirk Leeds...85 K10
Woodland Abers...141 L11
Woodland Devon...5 K5
Woodland Devon...5 N3
Woodland Dur...90 H1
Woodland Kent...17 M2
Woodland N Linc...87 K12
Woodland Oxon...43 K11
Woodland Shrops...63 K6
Woodland Staffs...65 L3
Woodland S Ayrs...104 C10
Woodland Head Devon...8 E5
Woodlands Donc...78 E2
Woodlands Dorset...11 P3
Woodlands Hants...12 E2
Woodlands Kent...33 Q10
Woodlands N York...85 L4
Woodlands Somset...21 J5
Woodlands of Durris Abers...133 J4
Woodlands Park W & M...32 B6
Woodlands St Mary W Berk...30 H7
Woodland Street Somset...22 C6
Woodland View Sheff...77 Q6
Wood Lane Shrops...63 L5
Wood Lane Staffs...64 E2
Woodleigh Devon...5 M7
Woodlesford Leeds...85 M9
Woodley Stockp...76 H5
Woodley Wokham...31 Q7
Woodmancote Gloucs...29 M3
Woodmancote Gloucs...41 R6
Woodmancote Gloucs...42 B10
Woodmancote W Susx...13 N3
Woodmancote W Susx...15 J8
Woodmancote Worcs...41 P3
Woodmancott Hants...25 J5
Woodmansey E R Yk...87 K7
Woodmansgreen W Susx...14 C6
Woodmansterne Surrey...33 K10
Woodmanton Devon...9 J7
Woodmarsh Wilts...23 J2
Woodmill Staffs...65 L8
Woodminton Wilts...23 N8
Woodnesborough Kent...35 P11
Woodnewton Nhants...55 P2
Woodnook Notts...66 D2
Wood Norton Norfk...70 E6
Woodplumpton Lancs...83 L8
Woodrising Norfk...70 E11
Wood Row Leeds...85 M9
Wood's Corner E Susx...16 B7
Woods Eaves Herefs...51 J11
Woodseaves Shrops...64 C6
Woodseaves Staffs...64 E7
Woodsend Wilts...30 E7
Woodsetts Rothm...78 F7
Woodsford Dorset...11 J6
Wood's Green E Susx...16 B4
Woodside Br For...32 D8
Woodside Cumb...97 L11
Woodside Essex...45 N11
Woodside Fife...124 H11
Woodside Hants...12 E6
Woodside Herts...45 J10
Woodside P & K...124 D5
Woodside Green Kent...34 F11
Woodstock Oxon...43 K8
Woodstock Pembks...37 K5
Woodston C Pete...56 D1
Wood Street Norfk...71 M8
Wood Street Village Surrey...32 D12
Woodthorpe Derbys...78 D9
Woodthorpe Leics...66 E9
Woodthorpe Lincs...81 J7
Woodthorpe Notts...59 N2
Woodton Norfk...59 M2
Woodtown Devon...18 H8
Woodvale Sefton...75 K2
Woodville Derbys...65 Q9
Woodwall Green Staffs...64 E6
Woodyates Dorset...23 M9
Woody Bay Devon...19 N4
Woofferton Shrops...51 N7
Wookey Somset...22 C4
Wookey Hole Somset...22 C4
Wool Dorset...11 K7
Woolacombe Devon...18 H3
Woolage Green Kent...17 M1
Woolage Village Kent...35 M12
Woolaston Gloucs...29 J3
Woolaston Common Gloucs...29 J2

Woolfold Bury...76 E1
Woolfords S Lans...115 J10
Woolhampton W Berk...31 M9
Woolhope Herefs...41 J4
Woolland Dorset...11 J3
Woollensbrook Herts...45 L9
Woolley BaNES...29 M8
Woolley Cambs...56 C6
Woolley Cnwll...18 E10
Woolley Derbys...78 B11
Woolley Wakefd...85 M12
Woolley Bridge Derbys...77 J5
Woolley Edge Services Wakefd...85 L12
Woolmere Green Worcs...52 H8
Woolmer Green Herts...45 J8
Woolmerston Somset...21 L6
Woolminstone Somset...10 C3
Woolpack Herefs...16 E3
Woolpit Suffk...58 E8
Woolpit Green Suffk...58 E8
Woolscott Warwks...54 E7
Woolsington N u Ty...100 H4
Woolstaston Shrops...51 M1
Woolsthorpe by Belvoir Lincs...67 L5
Woolsthorpe-by-Colsterworth Lincs...67 M7
Woolston C Sotn...12 G3
Woolston Devon...5 M6
Woolston Devon...5 M8
Woolston Shrops...51 M3
Woolston Shrops...51 M3
Woolston Somset...20 H5
Woolston Somset...22 G8
Woolston Warrtn...76 B6
Woolstone Gloucs...41 Q5
Woolstone M Keyn...44 C4
Woolstone Oxon...30 G5
Woolston Green Devon...5 L6
Woolton Lpool...75 M6
Woolton Hill Hants...31 J10
Woolverstone Suffk...47 L4
Woolverton Somset...22 G3
Woolwich Gt Lon...33 N6
Woonton Herefs...51 K10
Woonton Herefs...51 P8
Wooperton Nthumb...108 G6
Woore Shrops...64 D4
Wootten Green Suffk...59 J6
Wootton Bed...44 F3
Wootton Hants...12 D5
Wootton Herefs...51 J9
Wootton IoW...13 J6
Wootton Kent...17 M2
Wootton N Linc...87 K12
Wootton Nhants...55 J9
Wootton Oxon...43 K11
Wootton Oxon...43 J7
Wootton Shrops...51 K6
Wootton Shrops...63 L7
Wootton Staffs...65 J3
Wootton Staffs...65 L3
Wootton Bassett Wilts...30 B6
Wootton Bridge IoW...13 J6
Wootton Broadmead Bed...44 E3
Wootton Common IoW...13 J6
Wootton Courtenay Somset...20 E4
Wootton Fitzpaine Dorset...10 B5
Wootton Rivers Wilts...30 D9
Wootton St Lawrence Hants...25 K3
Wootton Wawen Warwks...53 M8
Worcester Worcs...52 G9
Worcester Park Gt Lon...33 J9
Wordsley Dudley...52 G3
Worfield Shrops...52 E2
Worgret Dorset...11 L7
Workhouse End Bed...56 C12
Workhouse Green Suffk...46 F4
Workington Cumb...88 D1
Worksop Notts...78 F8
Worlaby Lincs...80 G8
Worlaby N Linc...79 P1
Worlds End Bucks...44 B10
Worlds End Hants...25 L11
World's End W Berk...31 K7
Worlds End W Susx...15 L7
Worle N Som...28 E9
Worleston Ches E...76 C12
Worlingham Suffk...59 N3
Worlington Suffk...57 M5
Worlingworth Suffk...59 J7
Wormald Green N York...85 L2
Wormbridge Herefs...40 F5
Wormegay Norfk...69 M10
Wormelow Tump Herefs...40 G5
Wormhill Derbys...77 L9
Wormhill Herefs...40 F4
Wormingford Essex...46 G5
Worminghall Bucks...43 N10
Wormington Gloucs...42 C5
Worminster Somset...22 D5
Wormit Fife...124 H1
Wormleighton Warwks...54 D10
Wormley Herts...45 L9
Wormley Surrey...14 D3
Wormleybury Herts...45 L9
Wormley Hill Donc...86 C12
Wormshill Kent...34 F11
Wormsley Herefs...51 M11
Worplesdon Surrey...32 D11
Worrall Sheff...77 P5
Worrall Hill Gloucs...41 J8
Worsbrough Barns...78 B3
Worsbrough Bridge Barns...78 B3
Worsbrough Dale Barns...78 B3
Worsley Salfd...76 E3
Worstead Norfk...71 L7
Worsthorne Lancs...84 C8
Worston Devon...5 J6
Worston Lancs...84 A6
Worth Kent...35 P11
Worth Somset...22 C4
Worth W Susx...15 K4
Wortham Suffk...58 G5
Worthen Shrops...63 K11
Worthenbury Wrexhm...63 N3
Worthing Norfk...70 E8
Worthing W Susx...14 G9
Worthington Leics...66 C8
Worth Matravers Dorset...11 N9
Worthybrook Mons...40 H9
Worting Hants...25 K3
Wortley Barns...77 Q4
Wortley Gloucs...29 M4
Wortley Leeds...85 K8
Wortwell Norfk...59 M4
Wotherton Shrops...63 J11
Wotter Devon...5 J4
Wotton Surrey...14 G1
Wotton-under-Edge Gloucs...29 M4
Wotton Underwood Bucks...43 P8
Woughton on the Green M Keyn...44 C4
Wouldham Kent...34 C9
Woundale Shrops...52 E2

Wrabness Essex...47 L5
Wrafton Devon...19 J6
Wragby Lincs...80 C8
Wragby Wakefd...85 M11
Wramplingham Norfk...70 G11
Wrangaton Devon...5 L5
Wrangbrook Wakefd...78 E1
Wrangle Lincs...68 H2
Wrangle Common Lincs...68 H1
Wrangle Lowgate Lincs...68 H2
Wrangway Somset...20 H9
Wrantage Somset...21 M9
Wrawby N Linc...79 N1
Wraxall Dorset...10 E4
Wraxall N Som...28 G8
Wraxall Somset...22 E6
Wray Lancs...83 P3
Wraysbury W & M...32 E7
Wrayton Lancs...83 P12
Wrea Green Lancs...83 J9
Wreaks End Cumb...88 H9
Wreay Cumb...89 M2
Wreay Cumb...98 E5
Wrecclesham Surrey...25 P4
Wrekenton Gatesd...100 H6
Wrelton N York...92 F9
Wrenbury Ches E...63 Q3
Wrench Green N York...93 K9
Wreningham Norfk...70 H12
Wrentham Suffk...59 P4
Wrenthorpe Wakefd...85 L10
Wrentnall Shrops...63 M11
Wressle E R Yk...86 D9
Wressle N Linc...79 N2
Wrestlingworth C Beds...56 F11
Wretton Norfk...69 N12
Wrexham Wrexhm...63 K2
Wrexham Industrial Estate Wrexhm...63 L2
Wribbenhall Worcs...52 E5
Wrickton Shrops...52 B3
Wrightington Bar Lancs...75 P1
Wright's Green Essex...45 P8
Wrinehill Staffs...64 D3
Wrington N Som...28 G9
Writhlington BaNES...22 F2
Writtle Essex...46 B10
Wrockwardine Wrekin...64 B9
Wroot N Linc...78 H3
Wrose C Brad...85 J8
Wrotham Kent...33 R10
Wrotham Heath Kent...34 B10
Wrottesley Staffs...64 F12
Wroughton Swindn...30 C6
Wroxall IoW...13 J9
Wroxall Warwks...53 N6
Wroxeter Shrops...63 P10
Wroxham Norfk...71 L8
Wroxton Oxon...43 J3
Wyaston Derbys...65 M4
Wyatt's Green Essex...33 Q2
Wyberton Lincs...68 F4
Wyboston Bed...56 C9
Wybunbury Ches E...64 C2
Wychbold Worcs...52 G7
Wych Cross E Susx...15 M4
Wychnor Staffs...65 L8
Wychwood Ches E...64 D2
Wyck Hants...25 N5
Wyck Rissington Gloucs...42 E7
Wycliffe Dur...91 J4
Wycoller Lancs...84 D7
Wycomb Leics...67 K7
Wycombe Marsh Bucks...32 C4
Wyddial Herts...45 L5
Wye Kent...17 J1
Wyesham Mons...40 G9
Wyfordby Leics...67 K8
Wyke C Brad...84 H10
Wyke Devon...8 F5
Wyke Shrops...9 P5
Wyke Surrey...32 C12
Wyke Champflower Somset...22 F6
Wykeham N York...93 K10
Wyken Covtry...54 B4
Wyken Shrops...52 E2
Wyke Regis Dorset...10 G9
Wykey Shrops...63 L7
Wykin Leics...54 C2
Wylam Nthumb...100 H5
Wylde Green Birm...53 L2
Wylye Wilts...23 M6
Wymeswold Leics...66 G7
Wymington Bed...55 N8
Wymondham Leics...67 L8
Wymondham Norfk...70 G12
Wynford Eagle Dorset...10 E5
Wynyard Park S on T...91 Q2
Wynyard Village S on T...91 P1
Wyre Piddle Worcs...52 H11
Wysall Notts...66 G6
Wyson Herefs...51 N7
Wythall Worcs...53 K5
Wythall Green Worcs...53 K6
Wytham Oxon...43 K10
Wythburn Cumb...89 J4
Wythenshawe Manch...76 F6
Wythop Mill Cumb...97 N12
Wyton Cambs...56 E6
Wyton E R Yk...87 M8
Wyton on the Hill Cambs...56 E6
Wyverstone Suffk...58 F7
Wyverstone Street Suffk...58 F7
Wyville Lincs...67 L6

Y

Yaddlethorpe N Linc...79 M2
Yafford IoW...12 G8
Yafforth N York...91 N8
Yalberton Torbay...5 P5
Yalding Kent...34 C12
Yanwath Cumb...89 N1
Yanworth Gloucs...42 C9
Yapham E R Yk...86 E5
Yapton W Susx...14 D10
Yarborough N Som...28 E10
Yarbridge IoW...13 K7
Yarburgh Lincs...81 J5
Yarcombe Devon...9 N3
Yard Devon...19 P9
Yardley Birm...53 L3
Yardley Gobion Nhants...43 P3
Yardley Hastings Nhants...55 K9
Yardley Wood Birm...53 L5
Yardro Powys...50 H9
Yarford Somset...21 K7
Yarkhill Herefs...41 J3
Yarley Somset...22 C4
Yarlington Somset...22 E7
Yarm S on T...91 P4
Yarmouth IoW...12 F7
Yarnacott Devon...19 M7
Yarnbrook Wilts...23 J2
Yarner Devon...8 F9
Yarnfield Staffs...64 F6
Yarnscombe Devon...19 L8
Yarnton Oxon...43 K9
Yarpole Herefs...51 M7
Yarrow Border...107 K6
Yarrow Somset...21 N4
Yarrow Feus Border...107 J5

Yarrowford Border...107 L4
Yarsop Herefs...40 F2
Yarwell Nhants...55 Q1
Yate S Glos...29 L6
Yateley Hants...32 B10
Yatesbury Wilts...30 B7
Yattendon W Berk...31 L7
Yatton Herefs...51 M7
Yatton N Som...28 F9
Yatton Keynell Wilts...29 P7
Yaverland IoW...13 K7
Yawl Devon...10 B6
Yawthorpe Lincs...79 M5
Yaxham Norfk...70 E10
Yaxley Cambs...56 D2
Yaxley Suffk...58 G6
Yazor Herefs...40 E2
Yeading Gt Lon...32 G6
Yeadon Leeds...85 J7
Yealand Conyers Lancs...89 N11
Yealand Redmayne Lancs...89 N11
Yealand Storrs Lancs...89 M11
Yealmbridge Devon...5 J6
Yealmpton Devon...5 J6
Yearby R & Cl...92 C3
Yearngill Cumb...97 M9
Yearsley N York...92 C11
Yeaton Shrops...63 M8
Yeaveley Derbys...65 M4
Yeavering Nthumb...108 E4
Yedingham N York...92 H11
Yelford Oxon...42 H10
Yell Shet...147 j4
Yelland Devon...19 J7
Yelling Cambs...56 E8
Yelvertoft Nhants...54 F5
Yelverton Devon...4 H3
Yelverton Norfk...71 K11
Yenston Somset...22 G9
Yeoford Devon...8 E5
Yeolmbridge Cnwll...7 L2
Yeo Mill Devon...20 C8
Yeo Vale Devon...18 H8
Yeovil Somset...22 D9
Yeovil Marsh Somset...22 C9
Yeovilton Somset...22 D8
Yerbeston Pembks...37 L8
Yesnaby Ork...147 b4
Yetlington Nthumb...108 G8
Yetminster Dorset...10 E3
Yetson Devon...5 N5
Yettington Devon...9 K7
Yetts o'Muckhart Clacks...115 P2
Yew Green Warwks...53 N8
Yew Tree Sandw...53 J2
Y Felinheli Gwynd...73 J10
Y Ferwig Cerdgn...48 C10
Y Ffôr Gwynd...60 F4
Yielden Bed...55 P7
Yieldingtree Worcs...52 G6
Yieldshields S Lans...114 F11
Yiewsley Gt Lon...32 F6
Y Nant Wrexhm...63 J2
Ynys Gwynd...61 K5
Ynysboeth Rhondd...27 P3
Ynysddu Caerph...28 A4
Ynysforgan Swans...26 G2
Ynyshir Rhondd...27 N4
Ynyslas Cerdgn...49 K2
Ynysmaerdy Rhondd...27 N5
Ynysmeudwy Neath...38 H10
Ynystawe Swans...26 G2
Ynyswen Rhondd...27 M3
Ynyswen Powys...39 J3
Ynysybwl Rhondd...27 P3
Ynysymaengwyn Gwynd...61 K11
Yockenthwaite N York...90 H11
Yockleton Shrops...63 L10
Yokefleet E R Yk...86 F10
Yoker C Glas...113 P2
Yorkletts Kent...35 K9
Yorkley Gloucs...41 K8
Yorkshire Dales National Park...90 E11
York Town Surrey...32 C9
Yorton Heath Shrops...63 N7
Youlgreave Derbys...77 N11
Youlthorpe E R Yk...86 E4
Youlton N York...85 N3
Youngsbury Herts...45 L8
Young's End Essex...46 C8
Yoxall Staffs...65 L8
Yoxford Suffk...59 M7
Y Rhiw Gwynd...60 C6
Ysbyty Cynfyn Cerdgn...49 M5
Ysbyty Ifan Conwy...61 P2
Ysbyty Ystwyth Cerdgn...49 M6
Ysceifiog Flints...74 G9
Ysgubor-y-Coed Cerdgn...49 L3
Ystalyfera Neath...39 J10
Ystrad Rhondd...27 N3
Ystrad Aeron Cerdgn...49 J3
Ystradfellte Powys...39 J2
Ystrad Ffin Carmth...39 J2
Ystradgynlais Powys...39 J9
Ystrad Meurig Cerdgn...49 M5
Ystrad Mynach Caerph...27 Q3
Ystradowen Carmth...38 H9
Ystradowen V Glam...27 N7
Ystumtuen Cerdgn...49 M5
Ythanbank Abers...141 M6
Ythanwells Abers...140 G8
Ythsie Abers...141 M7

Z

Zeal Monachorum Devon...8 D4
Zeals Wilts...22 H7
Zelah Cnwll...3 K4
Zennor Cnwll...2 D7
Zoar Cnwll...3 J10
Zouch Notts...66 G7
ZSL London Zoo Gt Lon...33 K6
ZSL Whipsnade Zoo C Beds...44 E8